Advance Praise

For two neighbouring giants which had relations for two thousand years, the contemporary knowledge of the peoples of China and India about each other is abysmal. The slender media coverage between the two is also alleged to have largely reproduced stereotypes about the other. A number of meetings between representatives of the media and media scholars in the two countries were held in the "neutral space" of Singapore. Jeffrey and Sen have captured the results of these frank and free exchanges to produce a comprehensive view of India–China "media work" and the way forward.

—**Prasenjit Duara**, Director, Asia Research Institute, National University of Singapore and author of *The Crisis of Global Modernity: Asian Traditions and a Sustainable Future*

Despite the much-touted neologism "Chindia," genuine comparisons between India and China's media and communication industries are rare and difficult to undertake. Till this day, we do not have much in-depth empirical material that draws on first-hand experience of media practitioners from these countries. Still less do we know how Chinese and Indian media organizations and journalists perceive each other. This book showcases novel approaches to the study of media in the world's two most populous countries and makes a welcome contribution towards filling these gaps.

—**Wanning Sun**, Professor of Media and Communication Studies, University of Technology, Sydney and author of *Subaltern China: Rural Migrants, Media and Cultural Practices*

Media revolutions ferment in Asia's two giants, as power-hungry business tycoons play media magnate in India, propagandists in China are told to chase audiences and advertisers, and a billion-plus netizens and mobile phone users are empowered. Behind Himalayan levels of mutual ignorance, spurious stories—a naval clash, a Chinese plot to "Balkanize" India—take off and stereotypes prevail. This book is a timely exploration of an explosive subject.

—**Hamish McDonald**, former correspondent in New Delhi and Beijing and author of *Ambani & Sons: The Making of the World's Richest Brothers and Their Feud*

As the media institutions in China and India gain greater reach and influence, Jeffrey and Sen offer unarguably the best comparative perspective so far. Looking beyond the binary of "Chinese state media versus the free Indian press," the chapters in this book delve deep into the similarities and differences between the two. In probing their incapacity to facilitate a better popular understanding of each other, the book reveals the structural weaknesses of the Chinese and Indian media.

—**C. Raja Mohan**, Distinguished Fellow, Observer Research Foundation, Delhi and author of *Samudra Manthan: Sino-Indian Rivalry in the Indo-Pacific*

MEDIA AT WORK IN CHINA AND INDIA

Bulk Sales

SAGE India offers special discounts
for purchase of books in bulk.
We also make available special imprints
and excerpts from our books on demand.

For orders and enquiries, write to us at

Marketing Department
SAGE Publications India Pvt Ltd
B1/I-1, Mohan Cooperative Industrial Area
Mathura Road, Post Bag 7
New Delhi 110044, India

E-mail us at **marketing@sagepub.in**

Get to know more about SAGE

Be invited to SAGE events, get on our mailing list.
Write today to **marketing@sagepub.in**

This book is also available as an e-book.

MEDIA AT WORK IN CHINA AND INDIA

Discovering and Dissecting

Edited by
Robin Jeffrey
and
Ronojoy Sen

 www.sagepublications.com
Los Angeles • London • New Delhi • Singapore • Washington DC

First published in 2015 by

 SAGE Publications India Pvt Ltd
B1/I-1 Mohan Cooperative Industrial Area
Mathura Road, New Delhi 110 044, India
www.sagepub.in

SAGE Publications Inc
2455 Teller Road
Thousand Oaks, California 91320, USA

SAGE Publications Ltd
1 Oliver's Yard, 55 City Road
London EC1Y 1SP, United Kingdom

SAGE Publications Asia-Pacific Pte Ltd
3 Church Street
#10-04 Samsung Hub
Singapore 049483

Published by Vivek Mehra for SAGE Publications India Pvt Ltd, typeset in 10.5/12.5pt Minon Pro Regular by Zaza Eunice, Hosur, India and printed at Chaman Enterprises, New Delhi.

Library of Congress Cataloging-in-Publication Data

Media at work in China and India : discovering and dissecting / edited by Robin Jeffrey and Ronojoy Sen.
    pages cm
Includes bibliographical references and index.
1. Mass media—China. 2. Mass media and culture—China. 3. Mass media—India. 4. Mass media and culture—India. I. Jeffrey, Robin, editor. II. Sen, Ronojoy, editor.
    P92.C5M435   302.230951—dc23   2015   2015024100

ISBN: 978-93-515-0300-2 (HB)

The SAGE Team: Shambhu Sahu, Sandhya Gola and Anju Saxena
Editors' photos: Muhammad Yusuf
Cover Design: Minnie Doron

Contents

List of Tables

List of Figures

List of Abbreviations

2G	Second (2)-Generation wireless telephone technology
ABC	Audit Bureau of Circulations
ABC	Australian Broadcasting Corporation
ADAG	Anil Dhirubhai Ambani Group
ANI	Asian News International
AP	Associated Press
ASEAN	Association of Southeast Asian Nations
BBC	British Broadcasting Corporation
BBSs	Bulletin Board Systems
BCCL	Bennett Coleman and Co. Ltd
BCINA	British Commonwealth International Newsfilm Agency
BJP	Bharatiya Janata Party
BOP	Bottom of the Pyramid
BRICS	Brazil, Russia, India, China and South Africa
CAG	Comptroller and Auditor General
CBC	Canadian Broadcasting Corporation
CCP	Chinese Communist Party
CCTV	China Central Television
CIISS	China Institute for International Strategic Studies
CNC	China Xinhua News Network Co.
CNN	Cable News Network
CNN-IBN	Cable News Network-Indian Broadcasting Network
CNNIC	China Internet Network Information Center
CPC	Chinese Communist Party
CPD	Central Propaganda Department
CPD	Central Publicity Department
CPI-M	Communist Party of India-Marxist
CRI	China Radio International
DD	Doordarshan
FDI	Foreign Direct Investment
FIR	First Information Report
GAPP	General Administration of Press and Publication

GATT	General Agreement for Tariffs and Trade
GDP	Gross Domestic Product
GMR Infra	Grandhi Mallikarjuna Rao
ICTD	Information and Communication Technology for Development
IFWJ	Indian Federation of Working Journalists
IIMC	Indian Institute of Mass Communications
IJU	Indian Journalists Union
IPC	Indian Penal Code
IPO	Initial Public Offering
JNU	Jawaharlal Nehru University
JSPL	Jindal Steel and Power Ltd
LAC	Line of Actual Control
MEA	Ministry of External Affairs (India)
MOU	Memorandum of understanding
NBC	National Broadcasting Company
NGO	Non-governmental Organization
NSC	National Security Council (India)
NSE	National Stock Exchange (India)
NTPC	National Thermal Power Corporation
NWICO	New World Information and Communication Order
PLA	People's Liberation Army
PMO	Prime Minister's Office
PRC	People's Republic of China
PTI	Press Trust of India
PVR	Priya Village Roadshow Cinemas
QQ	Tencent QQ instant messaging software
RIM	Research in Motion
RNI	Registrar of Newspapers for India
SAARC	South Asian Association for Regional Cooperation
SAPPRFT	State Administration of Press, Publication, Radio, Film and Television
SARFT	State Administration of Radio, Film and Television
SEZ	Special Economic Zones
SME	Small and Medium Enterprises
SMS	Short Messaging Service
SNSs	Social Networking Services
SPU	Sardar Patel University, Anand
SUV	Sport Utility Vehicle

TDSAT	Telecom Disputes Settlement and Appellate Tribunal
TINA	There Is No Alternative
TOI	*Times of India*
SARS	Severe Acute Respiratory Syndrome
TPP	Trans-Pacific Partnership
TRAI	Telecom Regulatory Authority of India
UK	United Kingdom
UNESCO	United Nations Educational, Scientific and Cultural Organization
USA	United States of America
WTO	World Trade Organization

Figure A:
China, 2014: Provinces and places mentioned in the text

Source: Drawn by Lee Li Kheng, Geography, National University of Singapore, for the Institute of South Asian Studies.
Note: This figure is not to scale. It does not represent any authentic national or international boundaries and is used for illustrative purposes only.

Figure B:
India, 2014: States and places mentioned in the text

Source: Drawn by Lee Li Kheng, Geography, National University of Singapore, for the Institute of South Asian Studies.

Note: This figure is not to scale. It does not represent any authentic national or international boundaries and is used for illustrative purposes only.

Preface

Since its creation in 2004, more than 40 books have originated from the Institute of South Asian Studies (ISAS) at the National University of Singapore (NUS). This is yet another. The book owes its existence to the support of the Institute and other units of NUS, including the Asia Research Institute, Institute of Southeast Asian Studies and the East Asia Institute.

The idea for the book grew out of workshops beginning in 2009 that brought together Chinese and Indian media analysts and practitioners. The questions that provoked these gatherings arose from simple curiosity. Media in China and India were changing rapidly, but how? Precisely, who controlled media, how did they do it and were methods of control changing? What effect were mobile phones and their offsprings having on the capacity of vast new audiences to become both consumers and producers of media? How did people become "journalists" in China and India, what did they see as their responsibilities and how did they and their organizations portray the other country? Though this book is far from providing conclusive answers to such questions, it may encourage greater exchange, curiosity and comparative analysis.

Of the book's 18 contributors, 5 bear Chinese names, 9 Indian and 4 "Western." But the names do not tell the story. In 2014, six of the contributors worked in China, five in India, three in Singapore, three in the US and one in Australia. Of the chapters themselves, five deal largely with China, four largely with India and the others, in varying degrees, focus on interaction between the two countries. Their themes range from the analysis of the structures of media in each country to biographies of journalists whose career movements from countryside to metropolis illustrate how media now reach every corner of China and India.

Implicit in much of the book are questions about the role that media play in a one-party state and in a capitalist state of competing private media owners. In China, members of the Communist Party are in all media organizations to safeguard the party line. In India, rival owners influence what is published and broadcast from their newspapers and TV channels.

Behind these chapters, too, are questions about fundamental differences between India, a country that writes and speaks in more than a dozen languages and scripts, and China, with a single script intelligible throughout an immense country. Politically, Chinese has presupposed some form of central government for more than 2,000 years, but in India, political unity has been infrequent, even though cultural unity in song and story runs long and deep. Media in the twenty-first century provide the vehicles that perpetuate and extend such powerful perceptions and ideas.

In putting this book together, we have incurred a number of debts. The contributors to the book have been patient, diligent and good-humoured, and we thank them. The office staff at ISAS and the deputy director, Johnson Davasagayam, have readily backed the project at every stage. We thank Gloria Spitell and Rahul Advani for their help in drawing the manuscript together. Mrs Lee Li Kheng, a remarkable NUS cartographer, has drawn splendid maps. Finally, we thank the chairman of ISAS, Mr Gopinath Pillai, and the director, Professor Tan Tai Yong, who have made working for ISAS a little like playing for a football team managed by Sir Alec Ferguson and captained by Pele.

Robin Jeffrey
Melbourne

Ronojoy Sen
Singapore

Introduction: Media at Work—Four Sames and Three Differents

Robin Jeffrey and Ronojoy Sen

People who work in media in China and India sooner or later ask the question: "What is the aim of journalism?" Chinese may answer: "To promote harmony and prosperity." Indians are more likely to say: "To generate debate and contestation." Perhaps one can visualize the Emperor Akbar inviting Portuguese Jesuits to debate religion with Brahmin scholars long ago and contrast such episodes with the "state orthodoxy" of classical China and its elaborate examination systems.[1] In China, writes Benjamin Elman, "[t]he orthodox classical curriculum for examination candidates after 1300 guaranteed the long-term prevalence of Sung moral philosophy in elite intellectual life until 1905."[2] Indian "identity," on the other hand, has been characterized as "the combination of internal pluralism and external receptivity" coupled with "a general refusal to privilege any one narrowly circumscribed perspective."[3]

In the twentieth century, future leaders had experiences in early life that reflected the conditions of their countries and shaped their views of the world and the political systems they founded. Jawaharlal Nehru (1889–1964) attended Harrow School in England from the age of 15 and read Fabian tracts on British socialism. Mao Zedong (1893–1976) attended a local primary school in central China and at the age of 16 was a member of a revolutionary army.[4] In contemporary terms, Amartya Sen's *The Argumentative Indian* meets Richard McGregor's *The Party*. Indeed, McGregor and Sen offer anecdotes that capture some of the contrasts between the media worlds of China and India. When an aide of President Hu Jintao was told that an international gathering was intended to be "informal and free-flowing," he replied,

"President Hu does not do free-flowing." Sen, on the other hand, finds Indian attitudes embodied in a nineteenth-century Bengali verse about death:

Just consider how terrible the day of your death will be.
Others will go on speaking,
And you will not be able to argue back.

Such contrasts, tensions and questions run through this book.[5]

Control and manipulation of media have been at the core of politics since the modern industrial states made mass media possible. Whether the blatant propaganda of Soviet and Nazi-style states, or the "manufacture of consent" through the techniques of capitalist democracy, mass media shape politics. Control of mass media is something to struggle over.[6] The Chinese Communist Party has always viewed propaganda as "a proactive tool to be used in educating and shaping society."[7] M. K. Gandhi, India's "father of the nation," had a gentler but similarly all-embracing view: "I have taken up journalism not for its sake but merely as an aid to ... my mission in life ... to teach by example."[8] For the mission, journalism was crucial.

Today, two structural differences starkly separate Chinese and Indian media. At one level, they are as simple as the fact that China is a *one*-party state and India is a *multi*-party state. In China, provincial governments and their party bosses "do" media, thereby ensuring that party leaders like President Hu do not need to *do* "free flowing". Chinese presidents get the media they demand. Every provincial government in China is a creation of the Communist Party and directs and monopolizes all forms of media.[9] In the Indian federation, on the other hand, no state government is allowed to run a radio station or television channel; some have canvassed the possibility but been prevented. The central government has a monopoly on broadcasting under a quaint law—the Indian Telegraph Act of 1885.[10] India has a national broadcaster financed by the state, and, in theory, modelled on the BBC. The government of the day tries to use it as a mouthpiece, and its ponderous offerings fare poorly with viewers in the face of the ratings-oriented programming of private TV operators.

The second obvious difference is that every media outlet in China has members of the Communist Party on its staff who report to higher authority and are responsible for seeing that central directives are followed. And every media outlet, though it may operate on commercial lines and depend on advertisers, exists under the authority of the Communist Party. Some Indian politicians look enviously at such conditions, but whenever greater regulation has been mooted in India, widespread protests have quickly killed the suggestion. India's media are increasingly controlled by a few great commercial interests, notably the Ambani family, Bennett Coleman and Company Ltd (BCCL), which owns the *Times of India* group, and Rupert Murdoch's Star India. They rival the state in having power to determine what does *not* get published or broadcast. But these three media giants face vigorous competition from more than 20 well-resourced, if smaller, media barons.

The pre-1950 history of media in China and India were notably different, and the regimes that came to power in 1947 and 1949 reinforced those differences. Indian newspapers, such as the English-language *Hindu* of Chennai, the Bengali *Ananda Bazar Patrika* of Kolkata and the Hindi *Aaj* of Varanasi, originated as far back as the 1870s to voice Indian indignation at aspects of British rule. The multiplicity of languages, and the competition between Indian-owned and British-owned newspapers, meant that throughout the twentieth century, India's media choir sang a variety of tunes in a number of languages. Discord was standard and unavoidable. In China, as early as the 1920s, both major political actors, the Nationalists and Communists, opted for Leninist-style, single-voice movements and parties. By the time of Sun Yat-sen's death in 1925, "no newspaper published in the customary format and founded on fundamentally commercial lines could 'represent the party' in the way the party now expected to be represented."[11] In India, the national movement spoke with many voices, and nothing like a dominant "party paper" ever existed.[12]

Today, the significance of media in China and India is clear. The world's two most populous countries, containing close to 40 per cent of global population, have disputed boundaries and the legacy of a war in 1962 that India lost. Mass media in both countries play a pivotal role in domestic politics, and as part of that role, they may tell provocative nationalist stories. An Indian television editor explained in 2013: "The assumption is that China-bashing will sell compared to, say, a sober show discussing intricacies of the bilateral relations."[13] A survey in 2013 conducted by the Global Poll Center of the

Global Times, one of China's daily newspapers in English noted for its hard line positions on international affairs, found that "16.2 percent of Chinese media's reports on India have a positive perspective"; but "positive reporting on China only accounts for 4.2 percent in the Indian media." Indian outlets frequently used words like "provoke" and "aggression" when reporting on China.[14] The *Global Times* implied that Chinese media were positive and constructive; Indian media were sensational and war-like. An Indian commentator responded that the Chinese were "unable to come to grips with the role of a free, market-driven press" and were hoping "the tactics used to gag their own Party-run media" might work in India: government should make media be nice.[15]

Unflattering portrayal of one country by the other's media has a history as long as newspapers. Ronojoy Sen's survey in this book of the *Times of India's* coverage of China from 1838, before the start of the first Opium War, to Nehru's death in 1964 provides evidence. Media take their lead from governments, and the British-owned *ToI* defended Britain's profitable force-feeding of opium into China until well into the twentieth century. After the paper passed into Indian hands in the middle of 1940s, it usually reflected positions of the post-independence Indian government on the disputed borders with China. The media of the PRC never deviated from the Party's and government's position on relations with India.

Informational ping-pong between media of the two countries is a theme running through this book. When Jawaharlal Nehru died in 1964, the *Times of India* informed Indian readers that a Chinese newspaper's obituary referred to Nehru as "a small clown on the international stage."[16] These media exchanges continue, and their audiences have grown. Hundreds of millions of citizens in both countries not only read the products of their still-expanding newspaper industries but acquire mobile phones capable of connecting them to boundless sources of information. The potential for generating emotion throughout wide sections of both countries has never been greater.

When media organizations in the world's two largest countries swagger up to each other, recall past humiliations and amplify boundary confrontations to attract readers and viewers, one can see fleeting visions of crowds waving their newspapers in European squares in 1914 and shouting, "On to Berlin!" or "On to Paris!" Mass media can drive mass emotion and put pressure on governments and leaders.

Chinese leaders, Susan Shirk writes, fear popular feeling welling up against "a government perceived as too weak in the face of foreign pressure."[17] Indian governments are prone to the same anxiety.

Rudimentary factual information and understanding are scarce. Soon after his appointment as general secretary of the Communist Party in 2012, Xi Jinping told Chinese journalists, in effect, to get out more:

> Friends from the press, China needs to learn more about the world, and the world also needs to learn more about China. I hope you will continue to make more efforts and contributions to deepening the mutual understanding between China and the countries of the world.[18]

Contributors to this book point out that knowledge of each other's country would be improved by more on-the-ground correspondents covering social and technical issues and getting their stories into print and on air.[19] The knowledge problem was highlighted at the time of President Xi's visit to India in 2014. A newsreader on India's government TV network Doordarshan was fired after referring to the Chinese president as "Eleven Jinping". The announcer had read "Xi" as the Roman numeral "XI".[20] Chinese postings on social media indicate that Chinese understanding of India is no better.[21] Governments in both countries are wary of reporters that they do not control. They deny permissions and visas to each other's media as a way of showing displeasure. After President Xi's visit, the Indian government withdrew "political clearance" for a group of prominent Chinese journalists to attend a conference in New Delhi, partly, it appeared, to express annoyance at another brush between Chinese and Indian troops in Ladakh.[22]

The Book

This book is both a reference work on Chinese and Indian media and a repository for a variety of perspectives and voices. It seeks to understand the commercially driven structures of mass media in China and India, how practitioners go about their work, how mass media influence society and politics, and how these complex media systems interact with each other and affect international relations. The chapters range across two enormous countries and move from the bird's-eye views of outside analysts to the daily concerns of editors and reporters in pressured newsrooms.

We have organized the book in four parts. The four chapters in Part I, "Structures," provide an overview of media institutions in the two countries. In Part II, "Reporters," four chapters zoom down to the level of individual journalists and what they do, both in their own countries and when they work as "foreign correspondents". In Part III, "Practice," five chapters discuss the way media organizations go about their work in China and India, today and in the past. The final section, "Dissections," contrasts disaster reporting in China and India, compares aspects of burgeoning social media and concludes with reflections of a foreign journalist with long experience in both countries.

Underlying these chapters are questions about political history, culture and language. How deep are the foundations of each country's media worlds? In China, "Beijing frets constantly about the disobedience of local fiefdoms outside the capital." There is an expectation (often unfulfilled, but nevertheless expected) of central authority. At the core of Chinese history is the idea of a central government and the fact of a single language written in one script intelligible throughout the country. The newspapers of Guangdong can be read in Beijing, even though spoken language may not be understood. In the ideal world of the Communist Party of China, officials in the regions would follow to the letter, the policies and the directives emanating from Beijing.[23]

India, on the other hand, has 22 official languages. Yet in spite of language differences, a sense of cultural unity is widespread. The gods and goddesses of Hinduism make epic journeys from the Himalayas to Sri Lanka. Political unity has been rare—perhaps a hundred years under the British, a patchy unity of the north for two hundred years under the Mughals and a period of about 40 years under Asoka more than 2,000 years ago. Under its constitution of 1950, independent India was embodied as a federation, and the units of the federation have been continually adjusted to coincide with languages and regional identities (see Figures B and 2.1). Flexible federation accommodates the immense social and linguistic diversity out of which Indian media grow. *"Dilli dur hai"*—Delhi is far away—is an Indian

proverb that suggests that the idea of an ill-defined central government ... somewhere. The expression is in Hindi, a north Indian
language; there is no equivalent in the languages of the south. A
Chinese equivalent—"The mountains are high, and the Emperor is
far away"—recognizes that there *is* an emperor, even if it is possible to
evade his directions.[24]

China has a tradition of adjectival injunctions made famous by the
Communist Party's regular use of such phrases in political campaigns
like the Four Olds of the Cultural Revolution (Old Customs, Old
Culture, Old Habits and Old Ideas—all bad and to be banished).[25] As
we reflected on the encounters between Chinese and Indian media
workers and analysts, we discerned attitudes and discoveries that
might be called the Four Sames and the Three Differents. These tags
provide a way of summing up aspects of this book and highlighting
themes.

The Four Sames

The most obvious, yet under-appreciated, of the Four Sames is the
vastness of the media industries in both countries. The fact that China
supports 2,000 daily newspapers, 1,000 radio stations and close to
3,000 television channels is largely unknown in India and, indeed, not
much understood elsewhere.[26] Such a host of voices, even in a one-
party state, makes variations and opportunities to push boundaries
not only possible but likely.[27] Similarly, the Registrar of Newspapers
for India (RNI) reports that the country has 87,000 newspapers and
magazines (though only 16,000 filed returns with the RNI in 2012).[28]
India's Audit Bureau of Circulations (ABC), a better guide to major
newspapers, had more than 400 paid-up members in 2013;[29] there
were close to 900 registered television channels and 60 per cent of
Indian households had a television.[30] In both countries, these "old
media" were still expanding, unlike circumstances in the West, where
newspapers closed and old-style television networks struggled to
adapt. An electronic world of mobile phones made it possible for all
citizens to be ceaseless consumers of information as well as broadcasters and news transmitters in their own right.[31]

Governments in both countries struggled to cope with "new" or "social" media. China was far ahead of India in the penetration of the Internet (420 million users in 2010 to India's mere 137 million by 2012) and the use of sophisticated mobile devices.[32] But India in 2014 had 800 million active mobile phone subscribers,[33] and their ingenuity in using basic 2G phones for many purposes is illustrated in the chapter by Benney and Rangaswamy in this book. Chinese governments strove to tame telecommunications and domesticate blogs, but "the speed and ease of access of microblogs, combined with the very large user base, have made them difficult to censor."[34] Another scholar argued that "low-cost mobile communication" had enabled "spontaneous and ... self-organized political participation" to confront "the inertia and systematic obstructions in the entrenched bureaucracy in Chinese society."[35] In India, attempts at tight control were impossible. Service providers "simply do not possess the tools required," wrote an experienced telecom journalist.[36]

The Second Same, which surprised Indian participants at our workshops in Singapore, was the dependence on advertising. From the 1990s, advertising revenues for Chinese media grew rapidly, increasing by 10 times between 1990 and 1995, according to one estimate.[37] In 2012, advertising expenditure was estimated at $108 billion annually.[38] In India, it was widely—and wrongly—believed that Chinese media were financed by an all-controlling government. Chinese governments, however, had begun to end subsidies as early as 1978, and by 2003, only three newspapers and one journal were still subsidized.[39] The Party skilfully retained a stranglehold on media content at the same time as making China's thriving advertising industry the paymasters of most media. "Party propagandists," one scholar concluded, "have succeeded in marketing dictatorship."[40]

Chinese media people, knowledgeable about the economics of media in Hong Kong and Taiwan, were less in doubt about the financing of Indian media. They saw Indian media as commercially driven, forced to satisfy advertisers' search for high-income readers and viewers with hungry consumer habits. Indian advertising in 2012 was modest by Chinese standards—estimated at a mere $6 billion at most.[41] Media people in both places knew two truths of modern media: the need for advertising revenue to pay bills and the need to attract high-value readers and viewers whose spending capacity attracted big-budget advertisers.

What we find in both countries, and what readers will discover in this book, is a common love of entertainment, fuelled by the growth of advertising and consumerism. In China, the state and the Party are happy to approve benign and banal entertainment that keeps consumers occupied and makes money for media producers and telecom companies. At the same time, authorities struggle to prevent "vulgar" entertainment, like the talent show, *Super Girl*, driven by "the source of all evil,"[42] viewership ratings, which determine advertising revenues. In India, too, advertising and entertainment join hands in GupShup, a low-tech, mobile-phone-based message service which gives owners of humble 2G handsets the chance to exchange jokes and information and promote products.[43]

The Third Same lay in the experiences of journalists themselves. The hierarchies, pressures and tensions of newsrooms could be surprisingly similar. Struggles to get one's stories into the publication or onto the broadcast were common to journalists from both countries, as were stories of obtuse editors and erring sub-editors. "They wrecked the story on the copy desk" is a lament-without-borders. Ideas of deadlines had also changed in ways familiar to both Chinese and Indian journalists. Users of media now required 24-hour news and entertainment, and journalists in both countries were called on to update reports and sometimes to write blogs or communicate through Twitter or its Chinese equivalent *weibo*, estimated to have 500 million users in 2012.[44] People who gather news for dissemination have a lot in common when they discuss the rewards and pitfalls of their daily tasks.[45]

The most ominous of the Four Sames was the degree of suspicion and hostility that media in China and India could display towards each other. The Hong-Kong-based scholar Simon Shen analyzed perceptions of India in Chinese social media in an essay that identified pitiless stereotypes held by Chinese Internet users. India was racially and militarily inferior, economically backward, allied with the West to encircle China, and a country with which China should not partner.[46] We do not have a comparable survey of Indian attitudes to China, but Srinjoy Chowdhury, a senior Indian television editor and foreign affairs analyst, suggests that a "fog of distrust ... shrouds India–China ties,"[47] which he attributes in part to the lack of openness of China. "The Chinese media are hobbled by their political system," he concludes. Among both Chinese and Indian practitioners, there was agreement that knowledge of each other's country was limited to a remarkably tiny segment of each population. Prejudice, on the other hand, could be generated widely and rapidly.

The Three Differents

The First Different was language. China has a common written language that people can read from north to south and east to west. China in 2013 was reported in official statistics to be more than 90 per cent literate. To be sure, spoken language may be so notably different as to be unintelligible as one moves around the country; but every literate citizen can read the signs, newspapers, books and bus timetables. Chinese has another apparent advantage in the new world of personal communication devices. As Benney and Rangaswamy write in this book:

> …compared to non-character-based languages, it is possible to say more in a single Chinese *weibo* post than in an English Twitter post, even though both are restricted to 140 characters: roughly four times more content can be conveyed per post [in Chinese].[48]

The contrast with India could not be greater. Literacy in India was less than 75 per cent in 2011. India's 22 official languages (plus English) are written in 11 different scripts (See Figure 2.1). A literate traveller from Kerala crossing the border into neighbouring state of Tamil Nadu will be unable to read street signs or bus timetables. Hindi, the official (but not the "national") language of the Indian Union, is spoken by about 40 per cent of the population across north India. India sustains major newspaper industries in 12 different languages, each language generating hundreds of thousands of newspapers a day. Television is comparable: there are about 800 registered channels for entertainment and news in all the major languages.[49]

English occupies an anomalous place. More daily newspapers are sold in English than in any language except Hindi, and English-language schools are sought anxiously by ambitious parents. But north Indian politicians since 1947 have frequently advocated the eradication of English. English is the language of elites and those who aspire to join the elites. Perhaps 5 per cent of Indians (60–80 million people) read English comfortably,[50] and the Roman script of English and most computer keyboards is only one of the 11 scripts in daily use. The multiplicity of scripts has meant that SMS messaging in India has been less popular than in places like Indonesia, the Philippines or, indeed, China. SMSing in the Indian scripts is possible but ponderous. Though the familiarity of millions of Indians with English provided advantages in a globalized world, the complexity of India's language environment placed limits on the ambitions of the vast majority who did not know the Roman alphabet.

The Second Different lies in control and regulation. All mass media work under controls of some kind, including traditions of English law governing defamation and libel. In India, proprietorial and social controls play a larger role in shaping the output of media than government regulations. In China, one could argue that the reverse is true: regulation and control by the government and the Communist Party determine how mass media behave. As well as having Party members in every media organization, the state retains control of 51 per cent of Chinese media outlets, though the remainder may be sold and traded as shares.[51] The State Administration for Radio, Film and Television (SARFT) oversees and censors Chinese media. It enjoys powers that the politicians and bureaucrats of India's Ministry of Information and Broadcasting would relish. It dictates to television channels, for example, and requires them to limit the number of reality shows and other forms of what the Party-state deems vulgar entertainment. The General Administration of Press and Publication (GAPP) exercises similar controls over print and Internet publications.

In India, a toothless Press Council receives complaints about print media and passes judgement, but it has no enforcement powers.[52] Indian television broadcasters have no legally empowered regulator, and they struggle to develop codes of practice that would provide reasonable guidance at times of fast-moving crisis. The absence of such guidance was obvious in November 2008 during the terrorist attack on Mumbai when television channels broadcast live feeds that briefed the killers about the activities of the forces deployed against them.[53] A system of self-regulation was set up in the aftermath of the attack, but its effectiveness was questionable.[54] What constrained Indian media were commercial, social and administrative pressures. Big advertisers can organize advertising boycotts. Newspaper offices, television studios and their employees can be assaulted by gangs sponsored by offended individuals or organizations. Politicians and bureaucrats can launch court cases to harass annoying media outlets.[55]

In China, all media workers are indirectly employees of the state, and members of the Communist Party are in every newsroom. Journalists know what is expected, and self-censorship is widespread. Self-censorship, of course, occurs in many media organizations. Probing analysis of Rupert Murdoch's global empire will not be found in Murdoch media outlets, and Indian editors and reporters know their proprietors' preferences and prejudices. Proprietors who receive complaints from friends, advertisers and politicians may choose to "counsel" (or sack) their editors and journalists. Sometimes collisions end in public storms over "media freedom" and "proprietorial control." Such flurries are less likely to become widely known in China, though some Chinese outlets venture onto risky ground in pursuing stories that Party or government officials find embarrassing. *Investigative Journalism in China,* for example, presents eight studies of Chinese media outlets taking on local officials and pursuing controversial issues and injustices.[56]

In China, editors and journalists who offend higher authority sometimes end in jail. *Southern Metropolis Daily* of the Southern Media Group earned an unchallenged comment in Wikipedia that "the paper is known for its investigative reporting, which often gets it into trouble with the Beijing authorities."[57] *Southern Metropolis Daily* played a key role in the notorious case of Sun Zhigang, a student who did not have an urban residency card and was beaten to death in police custody in 2003.[58] Media reporting of this case eventually led to the abolition of the system that detained and deported back to their villages urban immigrants who lacked credentials.[59] In the following year, however, the editor of *Southern Metropolis Daily* was imprisoned for five months "on trumped-up charges of corruption."[60]

In India most stories can get broadcast or into print, though tough stories may have to search for an outlet or use the Internet. On matters of "national security"—questions of external borders and internal insurgencies—the Indian government does not get unquestioning obedience. An Indian foreign affairs journalist argues that government sometimes has tried to downplay boundary-dispute stories; but his television channel highlighted them anyway.[61] On the other hand,

Indian media tiptoed around the family of Sonia Gandhi, the Italian-born president of the Congress Party and widow of Rajiv Gandhi, the assassinated ex-prime minister. Her illnesses and foreign hospital treatment were treated as if they were state secrets and rarely alluded to.[62] Similarly, the Ambani family, the wealthiest in India, was capable of suppressing books it did not like and of engineering favourable media treatment.[63] Indian media proprietors and their employees did deals with politicians to provide flattering coverage in return for payment—so-called "paid news."[64] In China, similar paid news deals came to light and were punished with much fanfare.[65] Normally, however, the power equation was straightforward: "The instructions [the propaganda department] issues to the media are secret."[66] The Party got its way in the end, though there could be contests before the propaganda department won out.

Even in the control of "new" or "social" media—the Internet and mobile devices—there were differences, though both Indian and Chinese governments struggled to regulate the immensely powerful information-transmitting potential of the technologies. In India, police and intelligence agencies developed modest capacities to monitor digital traffic. Spectacular episodes highlighted the vulnerability of individuals who believed the mobile phone and Internet provided privacy.[67] Attempts of Indian authorities to exercise surveillance were haphazard and subject to a legal system that required judicial authorization before snooping could be legally conducted. If Indian governments sensed the brewing of big trouble, their response was a clumsy closing of all mobile-phone traffic for a fixed period.[68]

In China, on the other hand, monitoring of new media became an occupation for tens of thousands of government-sponsored workers.[69] Computer specialists created programs to identify digital chatter of dissidents.[70] There was clarity about the official Chinese position on electronic censorship. "Because Web sites can be used for activism," wrote Guobin Yang, "state censorship of worker Websites seemed especially tight." Yang pointed out that worker dissent was the most feared source of protest among Chinese authorities.[71] What was the result of increased oversight and "guidance" of new-media activity? "Compared to other countries," writes Benney and Rangaswamy in this book, "users are more likely in China . . . to use the Internet for 'entertainment'." Guobin Yang, a scholar with a particular focus on the Internet, concluded that "Party propaganda departments and marketing firms have taken a special interest."[72] One could argue that new media were being cleverly used to encourage vast Chinese publics to avoid precarious topics and amuse themselves to death.[73] To run afoul of the authorities could lead, one victim asserted, to "a vicious online smear campaign."[74]

The contrasting ability of each state to control new media emphasized the Second Different. Though Indian authorities wished to have greater access to conversations on mobile phones and the Internet, their capacity to do so was inadequate. Governments recognized the mischief and discomfort that uncontrolled new media could bring, but they struggled to exercise scrutiny and control. With nothing like the huge workforce deployed in China to monitor social media,[75] Indians could use the technology to organize political activity largely without fear. In 2007, widespread use of mobile phones played an important part in bringing a Dalit-based political party to power in Uttar Pradesh, the biggest state in the country.[76] Political parties preparing for subsequent elections aimed "to use mobile phones aggressively" to link up with voters and induce them to vote.[77] High-tech phone-based strategies were not a magic recipe for political success, but in the hands of dedicated workers, technology could enhance organizational strength. What was important was that in India, such practices were largely uncontrolled and open to anyone with a cheap mobile phone—and that competing political organizations were legal.

The most notable of the Three Differents lay in perceptions of media professionals about the duties of media and of the people who worked in media. During workshops in Singapore when the question was asked, "What are the responsibilities of media in your country?" Chinese participants would often respond, "To promote development and harmony." Indian participants, if they were feeling especially moral, might reply, "to search for truth" or, less grandly, "to keep politicians honest." The contrast can be seen in the way specific events are reported by journalists and influenced by the state.

Ming Xia in this book describes the temporary media thaw in China that followed the Wenchuan earthquake in 2008. He quotes an account of the "thaw", during which "a 'tectonic change' happened to the news reporting and coverage. The Chinese official media launched the 'most intense', 'most open' and 'longest news bombing' in Chinese history."[78] However, "the temporary 'thawing' in media control," Xia writes, "ultimately fell into a trite formula, namely, a 'ten-step flow chart of disaster management with Chinese characteristics'."[79] Anup Kumar's chapter in this book examines reporting of an Indian disaster—the 2013 floods and landslides in the Himalayan state of Uttarakhand in which more than 5,000 people were killed. Local newspapers and television channels had staffers and stringers throughout the state, but the role of local media was not as noble as admirers might have wished. The state government was slow to react and influenced the local media to downplay the disaster for more than two days (Landslides had destroyed telephone towers and disrupted mobile-phone communication). Only after national and international organizations reported the magnitude of the disaster did local newspapers and TV channels deepen and magnify their coverage. Indian media organizations had far less need than their Chinese counterparts to worry about intimidation from embarrassed politicians when they reported disasters and official failings; but local reporters and outlets could be too friendly with local authorities to break tough stories. For a journalist in China or India, there could be advantages in having outsiders tread on toes in one's own locality: outsiders would be out of range when trodden-on feet kicked back.

Insights: Seeing Each Other

In the second half of 2013, Indian media organizations had four correspondents in China, none doing television.[80] Chinese media were represented in India by about 15 salaried staff.[81] There were, however, half a dozen Indians working in editorial positions in Chinese English-language television and newspapers.[82] Social media of course meant that hundreds of thousands of Chinese and Indians could exchange information and express opinions about each other's countries. But if the exchanges were mostly of ignorance and acrimony, they could become merely aggressive and deeply prejudiced entertainment.

As well as acquainting readers with the Four Sames and the Three Differents, the chapters in this book present the perspectives of news gatherers and analysts on the workings of media in China and India. Li Yang, who has distinguished credentials as a scholar and journalist with the *China Daily*, provides an insider's account of the growth of Chinese media from the revolution of 1949. He argues that "in any society, government wants to control the media; differences lie only in degree of control and ways of control." He emphasizes the effects of commercialization on Chinese media—a process insufficiently appreciated outside of China—and concludes that "Chinese media's overreaction to Indian media's critical reports on China exposes Chinese media's unfamiliarity with India's media landscape and the basic national conditions of India." One of China's most India-experienced journalists, Tang Lu of the Xinhua News Agency and a long-time student, traveller and reporter in India, agrees. She writes:

> In China, many reporters do not have much knowledge about Indian culture and history, and have difficulty understanding the complexity of the cultural and political situation in India. They use their own value standards to gauge the behavior of India and Chinese cultural standards to judge Indian affairs. They treat the pre-conceived idea of India that they have in their minds as reality. This can only mislead the common people's perception of India.

Her analysis contains an essential aspect of Chinese media practitioners' sense that the role of media is to educate the people. The idea is not exclusive to China or the media of one-party states. John Reith, father of the British Broadcasting Corporation (BBC), guided the organization in the 1930s towards education, improvement and what might be called "high culture". The Nehru governments of independent India in the 1950s made similar efforts—and drove listeners away from All India Radio in the process.[83]

Indian media people were open about the way they pursued their work and the questions they faced when reporting China. Srinjoy Chowdhury, a senior editor and foreign affairs analyst at Times Now, the leading English-language television news channel, was sceptical of suggestions that

> the fog of distrust that shrouds India-China ties would vanish ... if there were more Indian journalists in Beijing. This version of the "Blame it on the media" argument steers clear of the fact that the handful of Indian reporters [in China] find the doors locked and cannot go much beyond picking up anti-India blogs, newspaper reports and stiff foreign office briefings.[84]

In Chowdhury's view, "the Chinese media are hobbled by their political system." He describes the adrenalin rush felt by a story-hunting Indian journalist able to call on favours, seek out leaks and question ministers. His descriptions of a top-rating television news-room clarify the goals of producers and the requirements of television journalists in India.

The perspective of an Indian *newspaper* journalist suggest less need for the "sense of excitement" so important for television. Subhomoy Bhattacharjee, a deputy editor specializing in business news with the *Indian Express*, once (though no more) India's most widely available daily newspaper, detected three stages in the development of Indian interest in Chinese business news. It began in a substantial way only with the Asian economic crisis of 1997, sparked by the conspicuous effects in India of Chinese economic activity. Cheap imports from China grew, Indian governments drew on Chinese experience to experiment with "special economic zones" and Indian businesses collided with Chinese competitors in foreign countries. Bhattacharjee judged that "Indian media initially responded with predictable jingoism," taking their cue from government attitudes and corporate briefings. By 2012, he argued that Indian business media "were more diverse in their approach and did not take an unvaried, nationalistic position." However, the nature of mass media made it likely that certain patterns would continue. Interest in China among readers was growing, but this often meant

> sensational events get precedence over the mundane. And lack of expertise about China, including a paucity of Mandarin-speaking Indians, creates a bias in favour of secondary news sources, such as the global wire agencies.

More coverage by better-prepared journalists would enable "the media to recognize which stories are merely politicians at play and which involve solid economic issues that need to be explained to the citizens of each country."[85]

Insights: Seen by Others

Both China and India fared poorly in the 2014 index of the World Press Freedom compiled by Reporters without Borders. China ranked at 175 out of 180 countries; India was surprisingly only a little better at 140, behind countries such as Chad and Libya. Methodology may explain India's showing. Reported violence against journalists lowered a country's rating, and Indian media people are diligent in reporting deaths and injuries of their own kind. Such comprehensive reporting may have contributed to India's low ranking. Nevertheless, though the index may be flawed, it shows that outsiders' impressions differ notably from the view of Chinese and Indian media people themselves.

In its growing interest in news from China, India was following the rest of the world. Reuters, the global news agency, attempted to satisfy this demand by making an agreement with China Central Television (CCTV), the government television apparatus, to subscribe to CCTV stories for distribution by Reuters "without filtering... through the Reuters editorial process." This in effect gave Reuters' endorsement to CCTV stories. John Jirik, a practitioner, scholar and teacher of media, observed the relationship at first hand. What he saw recalled the Global Poll Center survey of 2013: CCTV contributed positive, "soft" stories to Reuters. "Politics, accidents and disasters ... were handled in a way that balanced negative impact with a government or institutional response, resulting in predominantly soft news." Stories from Reuters' own correspondents were mostly "hard news"—politics, business and breaking events, focusing on political leaders who rarely appeared on CCTV except giving speeches and presiding at public events. Jirik concluded that

> Reuters' embrace of CCTV Content was overdue acknowledgement that China's state-controlled media have a legitimate role to play in providing the world a more balanced picture of a country as important as China than traditionally was made available by the agencies.

He argued that many CCTV editors and journalists welcomed the tie-up with Reuters as a way of starting to change what it meant to be a journalist in China "from the Leninist to the objective news paradigm." In all this coverage, India and Indians barely figured. Jirik speculated, however, that Chinese media, as they searched for ways of coping with commercialization, might look to India for clues about how diverse commercial media developed in an equally huge, rapidly changing and potentially explosive country.

Media managers in China search for ways to seize the most powerful methods and technologies and adapt them to the ends of the

Party-state. Danny Geevarghese's chapter in this book notes two levels of censorship in the newsrooms of CCTV. In the international centres in Africa and the United States, some stories get covered that are not broadcast in China itself. To the world at large, the Party-state aims to present its most liberal, all-encompassing face (It shows very little interest in India). In India, on the other hand, no single force or authority is able to control and present the nation's persona.

This book provides a place where the media worlds of India and China encounter each other and confront the values of British and American journalism.[86] Simon Long, writer of the Banyan column for the *Economist* and a long-time analyst of China and India, noted the tendency among Indian and Chinese journalists when they met abroad: "Chinese journalists said that, in writing about relations with India, they had a duty to help foster them. Indian journalists felt their role in bilateral relations was simply to report them."[87] Long argues that in both China and India, media reported about the other country in ways that increased suspicion and were prone to "inaccuracy, alarmism and partiality". He dismisses the Chinese suggestion that Indian opinion about China results from Indian dependence on Western media as "simply preposterous."[88] Meeting face-to-face in a leisurely way in a foreign country, Chinese and Indian media practitioners often found much in common; but from the perspective of pressured newsrooms, or the cloistered keyboards of microbloggers, incomprehension and spontaneous stereotypes were more likely to emerge.

Examples of the frailties of journalists and journalism are well known—from the Ems dispatch that helped provoke the Franco-Prussian War in 1870, to the naive coverage of the Soviet show trials of the 1930s and the credulous reporting of "Iraq's weapons of mass destruction" in 2002. Journalists in the old world of media could be corrupt, incompetent or malicious. In the age of "new media," news organizations, successful in former times, now search anxiously for ways to retain readers and viewers and make a profit. Ultimately, in information gathering, there is no substitute for well-informed, honest people with the time, resources and knowledge to probe, record and explain—and the freedom to disseminate their findings. Tang Lu records how Indian and Chinese media worked themselves into a fever in 2009 over reports of a speech by the Indian prime minister. She understood the context of the speech, knew how to find the full original and took the time to read it. She found it "positive" and "measured"[89] and succeeded in getting her analysis into a Xinhua weekly publication, though she had to struggle to do so. The incident illustrated both the difference an informed reporter can make *and* the internal contests that go on inside media organizations in China, India and everywhere. Improved understanding does not necessarily lead to amity, but it may lead to better judgement and a capacity to perceive diversity.

Insights: Two Stories

Two biographical chapters in this book lend weight to the argument that journalists—fulltime news gatherers—have essential roles, even in a digital world where citizens with a mobile phone can be both consumers and broadcasters of information. In 2014, John Zhou and Anshuman Tiwari were leading journalists in mid-career. Neither came from metropolitan environments nor made his initial mark there. As the maps accompanying their chapters make clear (see Figures 5.1 and 6.1), they were born, raised and educated far from the elite circles of the national capitals: Tiwari in Kannauj in the state of Uttar Pradesh about 350 km east of New Delhi and Zhou in Hubei province, 1,110 km south of Beijing.

Tiwari works in Hindi, India's largest spoken language. He was an editor with the two largest Hindi dailies, *Dainik Jagran*, which origi-nated in the city of Kanpur, and *Dainik Bhaskar*, which grew from Bhopal. Though both newspapers now have headquarters in New Delhi, their origins were in provincial cities. Tiwari too moved to the national capital to follow the economic stories that became his spe-cialty and led him to write a popular book in Hindi on the Indian economy. In 2014, he became the editor of the Hindi edition of India's largest news magazine, *India Today*. Zhou began his career with the *Guangzhou Daily*, "the party mouthpiece of the Guangzhou Municipal government," in his words. He moved to the *Southern Metropolis Daily*, the major newspaper of Guangdong province but with "national influence nowadays."

Zhou and Tiwari have similar reflections about being journalists, though they work in very different political environments. In Tiwari's experience, it is the family that owns the publication or the TV channel that calls the shots. For Zhou, power and authority lie with the Communist Party, though the Party's grip appears to be less tight than outsiders might assume. Both Tiwari and Zhou know their audiences and know how these audiences have grown, because they come from similar backgrounds—from what in India would be called the *mofussil,* the regions outside the great cities. Vast numbers of media consumers live there—half of China and two-thirds of India. Tiwari and Zhou know this fact and understand these audiences. So do their bosses and the accountants who work for their bosses.

◌୫◌

The structure of India's media world is probably changing more rapidly and fundamentally than China's. In China, Party control, though heavily financed by advertising and commercialization, is unlikely to change radically. "The real clash," Ying Zhu writes in this book, "is between the mandate of a cultural tradition and political system dictated by morality and political control and the demand of a market system dictated by profit maximization." In India, however, the absence of a powerful government presence in media and the reality of hungry corporations suggest a keen struggle to control the riches and the messages of the digital revolution. The result is likely to be a loss of ownership diversity and a consolidation of Indian media, including telecommunications, in the hands of a few great corporations. Even more than in China, the driving forces will be audiences, advertising and profit. In such a fast-changing future, we hope this book will help observers, whatever their interests and from wherever they come, to make greater sense of media at work in China and India.

Notes

1. Jianfu Chen, *Chinese Law: Context and Transformation* (Leiden: Martinu Nijhoff, 2008), pp. 16–19. Hassan Bashir, *Europe and the Eastern Other* (Lanham, MD: Lexington Books, 2013), pp. 64–65.
2. Benjamin A. Elman, *A Cultural History of Civil Examinations in Late Imperial China* (Berkeley: University of California Press, 2000), p. 20.
3. Amartya Sen, *The Argumentative Indian. Writings on Indian History, Culture and Identity* (London: Allen Lane, 2005), p. 348.

4. Mao later attended a normal school, worked in the Peking University library and acquired his reputation as a writer, theorist and calligrapher.

5. Richard McGregor, *The Party. The Secret World of China's Communist Rulers* (London: Allen Lane, 2010), p. 6 and Sen, *Argumentative Indian. Writings on Indian History, Culture and Identity* (London: Allen Lane, 2005), p. 33.

6. Edward S. Herman and Noam Chomsky, *Manufacturing Consent: The Political Economy of the Mass Media* (New York: Pantheon Books, 1988).

7. David Shambaugh, "China's Propaganda System: Institutions, Processes and Efficacy," *China Journal*, no. 57 (January 2007): 29.

8. M. K. Gandhi, "My Incapacity," *Young India*, 2 July 1925.

9. Yuezhi Zhao, *Communication in China: Political Economy, Power and Conflict* (Latham, MD: Rowman and Littlefield, 2008), pp. 26–28. Ying Zhu, *Two Billion Eyes: The Story of China Central Television* (New York: The New Press, 2012), pp. 4, 26–27. Li-Fung Cho, "The Emergence of China's Watchdog Reporting," in *Investigative Journalism in China*, eds. David Bandurski and Martin Hala (Hong Kong: Hong Kong University Press, 2010), pp. 169.

10. Nalin Mehta, *India on Television* (New Delhi: HarperCollins, 2008), p. 28.

11. John Fitzgerald, "The Origins of the Illiberal Party Newspaper," *Republican China* 21, no. 1 (April 1996): 13. Joan Judge, *Print and Politics. "Shibao" and the Culture of Reform in Late Qing China* (Palo Alto: Stanford University Press, 1996).

12. The *National Herald*, intended as the English daily of the Congress Party, never took off, though it stuttered along from 1938 till 2008. Communist newspapers in local languages were more successful, notably *Deshabhimani* in Kerala and *Ganasakti* in West Bengal.

13. *Hindu*, 30 April 2013, http://www.thehindu.com/features/metroplus/radio-and-tv/beating-the-wardrums/article4660836.ece?homepage=true.

14. *Global Times,* 21 August 2013, http://www.globaltimes.cn/content/805332.shtml (accessed 30 September 2013).

15. Reshma Patil, "The China vs. India News War," *The Diplomat*, 29 September 2013, http://thediplomat.com/2013/09/29/the-china-vs-india-news-war/ (accessed 30 September 2013). Patil was the *Hindustan Times* correspondent in China from 2008–2011.

16. See Sen's chapter (Chapter 9) in this book.

17. Susan L. Shirk (ed.), *Changing Media, Changing China* (New York: Oxford University Press, 2010), p. 28.

18. BBC News, 15 November 2012, http://www.bbc.com/news/world-asia-china-20338586 (accessed 22 September 2014).

19. See especially Tang Lu's chapter (Chapter 7) and Danny Geevarghese (Chapter 11), but also Srinjoy Chowdhury's scepticism in Chapter 10.

20. *Times of India*, 19 September 2014, http://goo.gl/LemJej (accessed 22 September 2014).

21. Simon Shen, "Neglected Constraints on *Chindia*: Analysing Online Chinese Perception of India and its Interaction with China's Indian Policy," *China Quarterly*, no. 207 (September 2011): 541–560.

22. *Hindu,* 22 September 2014, http://goo.gl/S8ppNX (accessed 22 September 2014).
23. McGregor, *The Party*, p. 173.
24. Ibid.
25. Consider too the Three Closenesses set out for Chinese journalists by President Hu Jintao. Qian Gang and David Bandurski, "China's Emerging Public Sphere: Commercialization, Professionalism, and the Internet in an Era of Transition," in Shirk (ed.), *Changing Media*, p. 43.
26. Li Yang's chapter in this book. Shirk (ed.), *Changing Media*, p. 7.
27. Li-Fung Cho, "The Emergence of China's Watchdog Reporting," pp. 170–171, on the practice of *yidi jiandu* or "extra-regional media supervision"—reporting risky stories from other administrative regions, not one's own.
28. http://rni.nic.in/(accessed 17 September 2013).
29. http://www.auditbureau.org/about.htm (accessed 17 September 2013).
30. Nalin Mehta's chapter in this book.
31. Jun Liu, "Mobile Communication, Popular Protests and Citizenship in China," *Modern Asian Studies* 47, no. 3 (May 2013): 995–1018.
32. Guobin Yang, *The Power of the Internet in China: Citizen Activism Online* (New York: Columbia University Press, 2011), p. 236. See also Benney and Rangaswamy's chapter in this book.
33. Telecom Regulatory Authority of India, Press Release No. 66/2014, 14 October 2014, http://www.trai.gov.in/Content/news/61152_0.aspx (accessed 22 October 2014).
34. Benney and Rangaswamy in this book.
35. Jun Liu, "Mobile Communication, Popular Protests and Citizenship in China," *Modern Asian Studies*, 47, no. 3 (2013): 1008.
36. Shalini Singh, *Hindu,* 26 September 2013, http://www.thehindu.com/news/national/isps-lack-tools-to-block-communal-content-on-web/article5168432.ece (accessed 26 September 2013).
37. Li Yang's chapter in this book.
38. *China Daily*, 28 February 2012, http://www.chinadaily.com.cn/business/2012-02/28/content_14712566.htm (accessed 17 September 2013).
39. Susan L. Shirk (ed.), *Changing Media, Changing China* (New York: Oxford University Press, 2010), pp. 177–178, and Li Yang's chapter in this book. See also Qian Gang and Bandurski, "China's Emerging Public Sphere," pp. 40–43.
40. Anne-Marie Brady, *Marketing Dictatorship: Propaganda and Thought Work in Contemporary China* (Lanham, MD: Rowman and Littlefield, 2008), p. 202. Yuezhi Zhao, *Communication in China*, p. 235.
41. *E-Marketer*, 13 June 2012, http://www.emarketer.com/Articles/Print.aspx?R=1009114 (accessed 17 September 2013) and Robin Jeffrey's chapter in this book.
42. Ying Zhu's chapter in this book and Yuezhi Zhao, *Communication in China*, p. 347.
43. Benney and Rangaswamy's chapter in this book.

44. John Ong, *TNW*, 21 February 2013, http://thenextweb.com/asia/2013/02/21/chinas-sina-weibo-grew-73-in-2012-passing-500-million-registered-accounts/ (accessed 17 September 2013).

45. Ying Chan, "The Journalism Tradition," in *Investigative Journalism*, pp. 4–5.

46. Simon Shen, "Neglected Constraints," pp. 541–560. For the numbers and vitriol that China's Internet users can muster, see Murong Xuecun, "Beijing's rising smear power," *International New York Times* (Singapore), 22 September 2014, p. 6, and Ying Jiang, "China's netizens rail against Western media 'bias,'" *Asian Currents*, February 2013, pp. 30–32, http://goo.gl/d3nv7y (accessed 23 September 2014).

47. Srinjoy Chowdhury in this book.

48. Jack Linchuan Qiu, *Working-Class Network Society: Communication Technology and the Information Have-Less in Urban China* (Cambridge, MA: MIT Press, 2009), p. 69.

49. Robin Jeffrey's and Nalin Mehta's chapters in this book. See also Vanita Kohli-Khandekar, *The Indian Media Business*, 4th edition (New Delhi: SAGE, 2013) for an encyclopaedic treatment.

50. In 2010, the Registrar of Newspapers for India put the number of English dailies on the street each day at 21 million; Hindi dailies were put at 72 million.

51. Shirk, *Changing*, p. 177.

52. http://presscouncil.nic.in/(accessed 11 October 2014).

53. *New York Times*, 7 January 2009, http://goo.gl/29C6iq (accessed 30 September 2013). India's television channels set up a self-regulating body after the Mumbai attack of 2008, but its authority and effects have been limited. In 2014, regulation of television was a matter of debate but little action.

54. *Self-Regulatory Content Guidelines for Non-News and Current Affairs Television Channels* (New Delhi: Indian Broadcasting Foundation, n.d. [2011]), http://goo.gl/xp7RIV (accessed 1 October 2014).

55. *Hindu*, 18 September 2013, http://www.thehindu.com/news/the-hindu-will-not-be-intimidated/article5139221.ece?homepage=true (accessed 18 September 2013).

56. *Investigative Journalism in China*, eds. David Bandurski and Martin Hala (Hong Kong: Hong Kong University Press, 2010).

57. http://en.wikipedia.org/wiki/Southern Metropolis Daily (accessed 18 September 2013).

58. Yuezhi Zhao, *Communication in China*, pp. 246–270.

59. Qian Gang and Bandurski, "China's Emerging Public Sphere," pp. 62–71.

60. *South China Morning Post*, 13 October 2012, http://goo.gl/YchfB3 (accessed 8 September 2014).

61. Srinjoy Chowdhury in this book.

62. *India Today*, 8 August 2011, http://goo.gl/AEWbWr (accessed 8 September 2014).

63. *Sydney Morning Herald*, 8 August 2008, http://www.smh.com.au/news/world/oh-brother-spare-me-the-time/2008/08/01/1217097529489.html?

page=fullpage#contentSwap2 (accessed 4 September 2014). For the Ambani attempt to prevent dissemination of Paranjoy Guha Thakurta *et al.*, *Gas Wars: Crony Capitalism and the Ambanis* (New Delhi: FEEI Books, 2014), see http://kitaab.org/2014/04/20/kitaab-interview-with-paranjoy-guha-thakurta-gas-wars-and-crony-capitalism-in-india/ (accessed 11 October 2014).

64. P. Sainath, *Hindu*, 21 April 2010, http://www.thehindu.com/opinion/columns/sainath/paid-news-undermining-democracy-press-council-report/article407201.ece (accessed 4 September 2014). Paranjoy Guha Thakurta, *Media Ethics: Truth, Fairness and Objectivity*, 2nd edition (New Delhi: Oxford University Press, 2012), pp. 212–257.

65. *International New York Times* (Singapore), 12 September 2009, p. 15.

66. McGregor, *The Party*, p. 235. China had its own "paid news" scandal. BBC News, China, 5 September 2014, www.bbc.com/news/world-asia-china-29074042 (accessed 8 September 2014).

67. Robin Jeffrey and Assa Doron, *The Great Indian Phone Book* (London: C. Hurst, 2013), pp. 202–203.

68. As in Kashmir or before the Ayodhya judgement of 2010. "India Ink," *New York Times,* 21 September 2012, http://india.blogs.nytimes.com/2012/09/21/telecom-services-blocked-to-curb-protests-in-kashmir/?_r=0 (accessed 1 October 2013).

69. Guobin Yang, *The Power of the Internet in China. Citizen Activism Online* (New York: Columbia University Press, 2009; paperback 2011), p. 51.

70. *Economist*, 21 April 2013, http://www.economist.com/blogs/economist-explains/2013/04/economist-explains-how-china-censors-internet (accessed 18 September 2013).

71. Yang, *Power of the Internet in China* p. 230.

72. Ibid., p. 239.

73. Neil Postman, *Amusing Ourselves to Death* (New York: Viking, 1985) warned against the pitfalls of television.

74. Murong Xuecun, "Beijing's rising smear power," *International New York Times* (Singapore), 22 September 2014, p. 6.

75. The "Fifty-cent party"—people paid for posting favourable comments online. Guobin Yang, *Power of the Internet*, p. 51.

76. Robin Jeffrey and Assa Doron, "Mobile-izing: Democracy, Organization and India's First 'Mass Mobile Phone' Elections," *Journal of Asian Studies*, 71, no. 1 (February 2012): 63–80. Dalit is the term used to identify people once called "untouchables."

77. *Livemint*, 16 September 2013, http://www.livemint.com/Consumer/5HG6oz PQITQ9LHM6MhOfzN/The-BJPs-mobile-strategy.html (accessed 19 September 2013).

78. Li Hongbing, "The Earthquake Shook Out the Openness of News" (李泓冰, "震"出来的新闻公开, 新闻记者), *The Journalist Monthly*, no. 305 (July 2008), http://xwjz.eastday.com/eastday/xwjz/node271090/node271092/ula3694635.html (accessed 21 September 2012). McGregor, *The Party*, p. 192.

79. Ming Xia's chapter in this book.
80. *Hindu, Hindustan Times, Times of India* and the Press Trust of India. Email from Ananth Krishnan, *Hindu* correspondent, 21 September 2013.
81. Email from Tang Lu, Xinhua News Agency, 20 September 2013.
82. Email from Ananth Krishnan, 22 September 2013.
83. Robin Jeffrey, "The Mahatma Didn't Like the Movies and Why It Matters: Indian Broadcasting Policy, 1920s–1990s," *Global Media and Communication,* 2, no. 2 (2006): 207–227.
84. Srinjoy Chowdhury's chapter in this book.
85. Subhomoy Bhattacharjea's chapter in this book.
86. Never forgetting Evelyn Waugh, *Scoop* (London: Penguin, 1938) or Humbert Wolfe, "The British Journalist," http://izquotes.com/quote/279265 (accessed 22 October 2014).
87. Simon Long's chapter in this book.
88. Ibid.
89. See Chapter 7.

PART I

Structures

1

Development and Communication: The Evolution of Chinese Media

Li Yang

Born in 1982 in Jinan of Shandong province in China, Li Yang got his doctorate in development communication studies from the Beijing-based Communication University of China in 2010 and has worked as a reporter for the Opinion Department of *China Daily* ever since. His interest is in history of ideas of Chinese intellectuals and cross-cultural communication. This chapter analyzes the interaction of politics, communication, society and economy in China from 1949 to 2013. It describes a fast-changing media landscape and its social, political and economic backdrop through the eyes of a working journalist and scholar. [Li Yang thanks Zhu Yinghuang, former chief editor of *China Daily*, for his assistance in writing this chapter.]

As a working journalist with the *China Daily*, I think it is important to explain how we see the development of media in China since 1947. Media have played an important, yet constantly changing, role in the rise of Communist Party of China and its regime in the Chinese mainland since 1949. People tend to divide China's history since 1949 into the first 30 years and second 30 years with 1978 as the demarcation line, the year is seen as the beginning of China's reform and opening-up. We can also apply this division of time to the development of China's media, as changes in media are so closely related to the development of the country.

The First 30 Years, 1949 to 1978

When the new republic was established in 1949, the country started its "rebuilding after the war" and got on the road to socialist reconstruction. Remember what Mao Zedong once said about how the Communist Party could seize power? "By relying on a gun and a pen." Chairman Mao Zedong compared the newspaper reporters' pens to the soldiers' guns in the anti-Japanese war (1937–1945) and Chinese civil war (1945–1949). Under his regime from 1949 to 1976, he regarded the state-owned media as a tool to unify people's thoughts. The "pen" provides the means of communication to inform, educate and mobilize the people. The Party would never give it up.

In the days after 1949, newspapers, radio and books were the main media forms. China was a backward agricultural country and most of its agricultural population was illiterate. The central government's policies, Mao's thoughts and a few items of other news composed the main contents of media, and media content was passed down from the top to the base in a pyramid structure of communications. Feedback was rare, even during the Great Famine of China from 1960 to 1962.

Learning from the Party's own experience and from the "Communist press theory" of the Soviet Union, the Party started to build up its own mainstream of state-owned media organizations headed by the *People's Daily*, Xinhua News Agency and Chinese People's Broadcasting Station. The Party media began to dominate, though there were some private publications in the early 1950s. In 1950, there were 336 newspapers, out of which around 58 were privately owned. But they were soon transformed into "joint public–private ownership," which actually meant the end of private media in China. The prevailing idea at that time was "the media should work for the party and for the people." And there was no notion of "media being independent."

In those days, the higher an official's rank, the more information from the West in forms of books, films and inside materials he or she could obtain. For example, a daily newspaper published by the state-run Xinhua News Agency named *Reference Information*, which was a digest that carried news articles translated from foreign media, was only available for officials above county-level. Only civil servants above certain levels, and intellectuals in state-run institutes and universities, had access for reference to certain literature and philosophy books from the West, which was regarded an ideological enemy of China. Some of these political and cultural elites as well as their children cherished such privileges. Some of them were actually very critical of Mao's thoughts and deeds, especially after a series of political campaigns from mid 1950s to the 1970s.

China's media closely followed the country's political twists and turns. In 1956, when Chairman Mao declared, "Let a hundred flowers blossom and a hundred schools of thought contend," there was a strong call for media reform, which emphasized "more information, freer discussion and better writing style." However, the growing cry for more democracy and freedom led the authorities to believe there was a "rightist" campaign against the Communist rule, resulting in a political movement called "anti-rightists struggle." Many journalists were punished as "rightists."

In 1957, the "Great Leap Forward" campaign led to a temporary booming of media. The number of newspapers reached 1,325 in 1957 and 1,776 in 1958. More radio stations were set up, and China began to have TV stations in 1958. By 1961, there were 19 TV stations. However, the media then also fanatically joined in the campaign by untruthfully propagating a story of "great achievements far exceeding the reality." The slogan then was, "the land can yield as much as you dare to think," resulting in a lot of false, exaggerated and fabricated reporting.

In early 1960s, China was plunged into huge economic difficulties by both the natural and man-made disasters. And the media also suffered. The number of newspapers dropped to 289 in 1963, radio stations to 84, and only five TV stations survived at that time. It was only after the economic situation improved that the media began to pick up again.

The Chinese had not had too many "good old days" before the notorious Cultural Revolution broke out in 1966. "Class struggle" became the guiding ideology of the whole party and society. The media naturally became the main battlefield for "class struggle." Anything considered "bourgeois or feudalistic" was criticized, and many journalists were humiliated and persecuted. Some newspapers became tools in the hands of "the Gang of Four" to fool the people. The number of newspapers dropped again to only 42 in 1968, with only four national newspapers. For a time, all the radio stations were under military control, and TV stations stopped broadcasting except those in Beijing, Shanghai and Guangzhou. The 10-year Cultural Revolution was a huge catastrophe for the country, as well as for Chinese media. The Cultural Revolution came to an end in October 1976 with the downfall of the "Gang of Four." In 1978, with Deng Xiaoping gaining power, China entered a new era of development, and so did the Chinese media.

When we look back at the first 30 years, we see that although media in China grew in scale, in number, in technology and in functions during the period, it experienced ups and downs in parallel with political climates of the time. Media were basically for one-way communication, more as a tool used by the Party or the ruler, than a tool for information dissemination and public expression. Media were used mainly for informing the people what the government wanted the people to know, to educate officials and the public to "serve the people," and to mobilize the people to contribute to socialist construction.

The Second 30 Years, from 1978 to 2013

The year 1978 marked the beginning of China's reform and opening up when a nation-wide discussion started on "What is the criterion for truth?" Deng established his pragmatism as the ruling principle for the Party through a debate with Hua Guofeng, a successor designated by Mao, who stuck to Maoism, after the "cultural revolution." Most state-owned media, such as the *Guangming Daily*, *People's Liberation Army Daily*, *People's Daily* and China National Radio supported Deng and his allies like Hu Yaobang,[1] and only individual provincial newspapers, and the *Red Flag* magazine, sided with Hua in the debate on the criteria of the truth. Deng pointed out that practice is the only criterion to test the truth. Hua maintained that whatever Mao had said was the truth and must be implemented. Deng's pragmatism won wide support from the public, who were desperate to recover normal life after decades of political movements.

This discussion led to a consensus in the party and society that "practice is the only criterion for truth," which means, "We are seeking truth, but the truth is not what one person (Mao) said it was. It must be proved by practice, or reality, or by what people really feel." This was regarded as the first round of "emancipation of mind," casting away the old dogma and "leftist ideology," and leading the country onto a more pragmatic road of development. The third plenary session of the 11th Central Party Committee at the end of 1978 officially abandoned the policy of "taking class struggle as the guiding principle," and pronounced that the whole party and nation was shifting to "taking economic construction as the central theme." Since then Chinese media have been growing at a speed unprecedented in history, with dramatic changes in media's attributes, concepts of journalism, ownership structure, functions and daily operations.

Deng restarted the national college entrance exam in 1977 and initiated China's market economy reform after the third plenary in 1978. The exam, which had been suspended for 10 years, gave the people a chance to change their lives through education. Thanks to Deng's foresight, many of today's Chinese leaders are college graduates who passed the exam from 1977 to 1980. Market reform in the cities and land reform in the villages started the fast growth of Chinese economy. Meanwhile, books about art, literature, sociology and philosophy were allowed to be published and sold to the general public. Films from the West were permitted to be shown. Some old translators and young people, who had taught themselves foreign languages, participated in the translation projects. Cultural elites started openly organizing activities in the form of exhibits, recitations, seminars, forums and lectures in parks, squares, campuses and even their homes. These were very popular. They formed various clubs, salons and circles to study and discuss literature, poetry, art, photography, music, philosophy and sociology.

Attribute: From "Ideological Weapon" to a Commodity in the Market

While media in China are still regarded as having educational functions, they are now regarded more as commodities in the market. As early as 1978, the government approved eight major media organizations to experiment with "running as enterprises." Advertisements became the main revenue source for many local media at the provincial level. Paid news appeared during this period when some opinion leaders chose specific media as outlets through which to sell their opinions. Years later in 2003, the government announced it would end subsidies to all the publications in China except three papers and one journal. This process was still going on in 2013 with several hundred Party and government newspapers being transformed into "enterprises" or suspending publication. By 2013, nearly all media organizations had become enterprise entities competing in the market. For them, catering to the needs of the audience and surviving and winning in the market became their major concern. This commercialization largely changed the nature of media in China.

Concept: From "Tool of Class Struggle" to "Tool of Public Opinion"

On 5 May 1980, the Chinese Communist Youth League's magazine *China Youth* carried a letter from a non-existent reader called Pan Xiao, supposedly a young worker. The letter was edited from two letters from two young people, whose family names were Pan and Xiao. In the letter, Pan Xiao boldly asked the editor why the path of his life became narrower and narrower, as he found that people only focussed on personal gains and losses, in spite of the education in collectivism education that they had received. This letter caused a great stir among readers. Tens of thousands of letters flooded the postal box of the magazine, and the chief editor opened a special zone to publish readers' letters. The public discussion, the first of its kind since the 1950s, on the value of human life that was triggered by Pan Xiao's letter lasted for several months. It showed that people were reshaping their outlooks and values gradually after they had the freedom and conditions to consume information from different sources.

This cultural fever in China, which is seen as a period of new enlightenment, lasted till 1983 when CPC leaders realized it was necessary to clean the spiritual pollution and be cautious about bourgeois liberalization at home. But once cultural and opinion markets are opened, it is not that easy to exert control over them. One reason was that the people's consciousness of their rights, particularly in the realm of politics, was awakened in a liberal social and cultural environment in the early 1980s.

In 1985, the then Party General Secretary Hu Yaobang called for the media "to be the mouthpiece both of the party and of the people." Two years later in 1987, The 13th National Congress of the Party called for giving the media the supervisory role, saying "The major issues should be made known to the people and should be discussed by the people." In 1998, the then Chinese Premier Zhu Rongji, while visiting CCTV, wrote what he believed should be media's role: "A supervisor through public opinion, a mouthpiece for the people, a mirror for the government and a vanguard in pushing forward reforms." The 16th Party Congress in 2002 called for media to exercise the "three getting close to-s," which means the media should be close to reality, life and people. Today, media are considered two-way communication tools and to have both an educational function and a watchdog role in society.

Ownership: From All State-owned to Diversification

In the 1990s, the Chinese government reformed the state-run media. China's media landscape became more plural than before. Some media were encouraged to participate in market competition and earn their own livings. Previously, all the media were state-owned and subsidized by the state. With the policy opening up, the situation changed. While the number of party papers declined, the number of non-party papers had increased rapidly. Some of them are attached to government departments or institutions, but are actually owned by individuals or a group of people. And some have contracted out their publishing licenses to business investors. Even foreign investors, such as News Corporation, Viacom, Sony Pictures and some film production companies from the United States have got into China's media sector. Theoretically, they are not supposed to be directly involved in the editorial content of the publications, but in reality, for the sake of their investment returns, they are capable of influencing the editorial policy and helping produce content. Thus, there are de facto privately run publications in China (Here, I do not include the New Media, a great part of which are privately owned).

Function: From Being Educational to Being More Informative and Entertaining

Popular songs from Hong Kong and Taiwan and translated TV series and films came into common people's homes along with the spread of cassette recorders and players and televisions from early 1980s. The bell-bottom trousers, jeans, sun glasses, perms, rock music, Coca-Cola and fast food became the fashion overnight in the cities. People realized that life was much more than a revolution or a struggle among classes and life could be fun. But the sharp contrast between extreme collectivism, which was an official ideology, and individualism left many people puzzled and bewildered.

Media in China have become diversified in function. While some people believe media should continue to have an educational function, it is generally believed the media should have more functions than that. Going to any newsstand in the street, you will find many varieties of publications, catering to different needs. You also find a lot of popular foreign consumer magazines. The TV programmes with highest audience ratings are often those that are entertaining and recreational, such as *Super Girl* (超女) on Hunan TV, *If You Are the One* on Jiangsu TV, *Chinese Talent Show* on Shanghai TV and *The Voice of China* on Zhejiang TV. For media people, their everyday concerns are more about what audiences need and whether they like to read and watch their stories and programmes.

Operation: From Rigid Control to More Freedom in Editorial Decisions

The newspapers from Guangdong province, which was influenced by Western culture more than the other places in China because of its long history of being open and its closeness to Hong Kong, became famous for their critical, liberal stands from the middle of 1990s. This tradition was maintained, in spite of the government's obvious dislike.

The relation between the people, especially opinion leaders and the new Party leadership led by Deng, was always precarious. In the late 1970s, as victims of former political movements, they were united behind Deng's pragmatism. However, the weakness of the economic reforms started catching people's attention, especially some opinion leaders, from the mid-1980s. Privatization of some state-owned assets caused huge, corrupt losses of public wealth. The immature and short price reform approved by Deng, which proved to be a bold action to transform China's planned economy to a market economy, in 1988 caused serious inflation. In these circumstances, Deng was vigilant about the possible politicization of activists, though he granted considerable freedom for people who were culturally and spiritually thirsty. The demolishing of the Democracy Wall in Xidan in Beijing demonstrates Deng's vigilance. Some people posted big-character posters on a wall in Xidan, a downtown shopping centre in Beijing in 1979, attacking the political system of China. More posters appeared, catching attention of the government. The wall, called Democracy Wall, soon disappeared.

The tension between cultural elites and the ruling Party exploded in a violent form across the country in 1989 after the death of Hu Yaobang, a liberal-minded Party leader. Despite strong reaction from the international community, the Party succeeded in silencing dissidents with limited cost till the Internet spread in early twenty-first century. The cultural elites became divided in the early 1990s. Some became more liberal; some became the New Left. The former believed China should copy the political system from the West and organize direct elections. The latter, more popular among the political authorities, maintained China had different and more complicated national conditions and each nation deserved the freedom and independence to explore its development path and model. Such a divide remained. Large-scale privatization of state-owned enterprises in the 1990s, which made tens of millions of workers lose their jobs, and China's entry into the World Trade Organization in the early twenty-first century gave the divide an economic and social context. Debates on the legitimacy of the market, consumerism, nationalism, etc. appeared in academic journals, like *Dushu*, an intellectual monthly published in Beijing and founded in 1979.

There has always been a tug of war between those who want to control and those who want more freedom. But in 2014, China's media people enjoyed freedom of reporting and expression in a way never seen in modern Chinese history. On the one hand, people, including government officials, realized that the right to know, the right to participate and the right to express opinions are basic human rights that government and society should respect. It is in the interest of the country's future that the media should continue to open up in a way that people have more access to information and have more freedom to express themselves. On the other hand, with the new financial independence of the press, the proliferation of media outlets, and with the availability of Internet, it is becoming extremely difficult to control what people are seeing and saying. In any society, government wants to control the media; differences lie only in degree of control and ways of control. Now in the age of the Internet, total control is out of the question. On sensitive issues, the government still tries to control, in a way of "giving guidance" to the media, for the sake of social progress and stability. But most of the time and for most of the issues, the media people do have full freedom in reporting and commenting. However, editors and reporters have their own self-censorship, as they have a consensus that the media should help the country to promote economic development and social harmony.

The great changes in Chinese media since the country's reform and opening-up have been part of the changes in the political, economic, cultural and social life of China. These changes are still in progress, which means the media will continue to evolve with the growing maturity of China's political, economic and social systems.

Media Landscape: China in 2014

A Booming Media Industry

The policy of reform and opening-up, success in economic development and flourishing cultural activity, all helped China's media industry grow rapidly in scale, strength and influence. Media outlets proliferated. In 2013, China had around 2,000 newspapers, more than

9,000 magazines, 1,000 radio stations and 200 TV stations broadcasting more than 2,900 channels. By the end of 2009, the population covered by radio and TV broadcasting was 96 per cent and 97 per cent, respectively.

According to one estimate, advertising in all media forms increased 35-fold between 1981 and 1992. Print ad revenues jumped 10 times between 1990 and 1995—from 1.5 billion Yuan to 15 billion Yuan. And recent years have seen steady increases in revenue for China's media industry. The revenue of broadcasting, film and TV industries on the Chinese mainland amounted to 195.95 billion Yuan (about USD 30 billion) in 2009, growing by 17.53 per cent from 2008. The film industry of the mainland market has expanded at over 25 per cent for six years consecutively till 2009, when it saw the biggest rise to 10.67 billion Yuan, growing by 26.5 per cent year-on-year. It is predicted the entertainment and media industry revenue of the Chinese mainland will hit $133 billion by 2014, increasing by 12 per cent every year, much higher than the global average rate of 5 per cent.[2]

In short, the Chinese media industry, called a "sunrise industry," was one of the most prospering sectors in China's economy.

New Media and Their Impact

The Internet was introduced to China in late 1995. *China Daily* was one of the first to put its newspaper on its website, and soon nearly all media outlets set up their own websites, followed by thousands of privately owned websites. China witnessed the fastest growth of the Internet use in the world to become number one in the world in the number of Internet users. By June 2012, China's netizens had reached 420 million, with an Internet penetration of 31.8 per cent, which was above the global average. And Internet broadband coverage reached nearly 100 per cent. The time Chinese netizens spent on the Internet continued to increase, and the 30th Survey Report issued on 28 September 2012 by China Internet Network Information Center found that each Chinese netizen spent 19.8 hours a week on average on the Internet.

From 2003, the mobile phone became the "fifth medium" following newspapers, radio, TV and Internet. By the end of 2012, the number of people who used the Internet by mobile phone reached 233 million. In 2013, there were more than 2.79 million websites, nearly 1 million Bulletin Board Systems (BBS) and 231 million bloggers.[3] But most Chinese netizens only logged onto Chinese-language websites. Facebook and Twitter were blocked on Chinese mainland, and the Chinese netizen community remained largely isolated from the world. The agenda of the large, yet isolated, online community was set by a few large commercial websites headquartered in Beijing, Guangzhou, Shenzhen and Shanghai, which generated their contents from different media of various ownerships and provided platforms for social media discussion. Some of the contents, though generated by the netizens, were edited and repackaged by website editors.

The Internet changed the country's media landscape. It provided ordinary Chinese a public platform which enabled them not only to be better informed, but also to enjoy greater freedom in expressing their opinions. With a judicial system lacking independence and a traditional culture of complaining to higher authorities to punish lower levels for misconduct, the Internet became one of the most popular channels for the public. Citizens could air discontent about district and county governments' misconduct (for example, in enforced demolition and land acquisition) in a bid to catch attention of the superior authorities.

The Internet ushered in a public discourse that had been absent for almost half a century. It also enabled direct communication between ordinary citizens and government officials. It was said that top leaders read opinions from the websites every day. People.com.cn started a channel called Access to Zhongnanhai, through which netizens could write directly to President Xi Jinping and Premier Li Keqiang and other leaders and government departments. Xi indeed won people's support with some refreshing policies and actions. He launched the harshest attack on senior corrupt officials and vowed to limit power through transparency and establish institutions and rule of law. He took a clear-cut stand in eradicating the rumor fabricators and cleaning the cyber public sphere, which had been a problem for a long time. There were some public relation companies making illegal profits from blackmailing or fabricating rumors. Many of the rumors took advantage of the tensions between the people and the government as well as local governments' poor ability to cope with a media crisis. Xi was clear-headed that dealing with rumor fabrication and slander had some important prerequisites, one of which was that there should be space and freedom for different voices, because it was not easy to tell right from the wrong. To clean the opinion market was not to shut the people up, but to create an environment in which every participant knew the rules.

The Chinese media landscape gradually developed into a two-track model with the new commercial media and the state-run traditional media. The big newsy web portals and forums were divided from right to left as well—platforms for opinion leaders who took different stands. The left criticized Deng's pragmatism, the immature market reform and China's entry into the WTO. The right criticized the authoritarian regime and called for direct election and constitutionalism. The divide within new media and the seemingly unified front of the state-run media constituted a sharp contrast. In most cases, the state-run media participated in the online realm as a mediator between the left and the right in a bid to defend the government's interests, because many media crises and debates were caused by grass-roots authorities' malpractices or abuses of powers. One interesting phenomenon was the multiple identities of traditional media staff and government officials, who became individual network users once they got off work. Their personal views on many issues were not necessarily the same as their media and departments. The interactions among the participants and mediators in debates attracted hundreds of millions of onlookers, including the governments of various levels. The debaters and mediators knew that their ultimate purpose was not to win over opponents, but win support from the silent majority of online onlookers.

The Internet was changing the way people got information and had their voices heard. However, the Internet was regarded as a double-edged sword. It gave people access to information, freedom of expression, supervision over the government and participation in state affairs, while government officials could directly hear voices from the grass-roots. On the other hand, it could also be abused by people who spread rumours, launched personal attacks, sent defamatory or obscene messages, or violated the law. That led to a worldwide debate on whether and to what degree Internet flow should be regulated. In China's case, while the government encouraged the development of the Internet, it also worked hard to control content to ensure relatively clean and healthy operations.

Media as a Watchdog?

Chinese decision-makers drew lessons from 10 years of dealing with social problems. Stability did not refer to absolute stability but to a dynamic stability in which the people should have the freedom to raise different voices to solve their problems. Chinese leaders were fully aware of the necessity of ruling by law and for further reforms of the state's powers and operations. Otherwise, the widening income gap and serious corruption would threaten national stability and the Party's status.

The Chinese government promoted the transparency of its administrative affairs. It promulgated and implemented the Decree of Government Information Openness of the People's Republic of China, improved its system of spokespersons and opened government information according to the law. These measures safeguarded people's right to know, participate, comment and supervise. In 2009, the State Council Information Office, other ministries and provinces, ethnic autonomous regions and municipalities held 1,646 press conferences.[4]

With the government acting towards more openness in information, encouraging media to play a supervisory role and with media vying to be competitive in the market, there was more investigative reporting, mostly exposes or negative news. While "positive reporting" was still the guideline from the authorities, media played an increasing role of a watchdog for the government, especially where the Internet was concerned. According to a calculation made by people. com.cn, in 2009, 30 per cent of the most influential social incidents were exposed and disseminated by websites. There were many cases, such as official corruption, abuse of power by the police, neglect of basic human rights. These were reported on the Internet, followed by the traditional media, which later led to government actions in punishing wrongdoers. Many people believed that media provided the most cost-effective supervision of the government.

Internet and Good Governance

As information technology developed and spread around the world, people had more access to information from various sources. Everyone could become an information source on the Internet. These changes also promoted the evolution of governance models in many countries, especially the ones, such as China, that did not have a diversified information market before.

In 2012, China had about 500 million network users, making it one of the most networked countries in the world. But most of the traditional media like newspapers, radio and television were still largely state-owned and mostly represented the government's points of view. The Internet became the most active stage for public discussion. For example, *weibo*, or micro blog, replaced the forum, which characterized web1.0, as the most popular platform for Chinese network users. More Chinese relied on *weibo* for information about the latest news stories and public opinion. Traditional media also took part in online discussions and regarded Internet as an important field to attract audiences.

Everyone was equal on the network. This flat network communication structure entitled each participant to join on an equal footing and witness the discussions. The flat landscape helped to form public opinion that was in contrast with the opinion of the government, especially when people's interests were not in line with those of the government. This two-track communication model, made up of the civil journalism of the network on one hand and the state-owned media on the other, made it more difficult for the government to continue the former governance model which was based on the state-owned media system.

Under the old system, which existed till the Internet became widespread in the late 1990s, the authorities could not get feedback from the people fast and accurately. But the Internet ensured that the authorities heard the response from the public immediately after an incident happened or a new law was passed. Then the government could make necessary changes to win more support from the netizens.

There existed a strong populism and nationalism on the network. Although many farmers and migrant workers did not have access to the Internet, they had plenty of representatives online. Sometimes, the netizens' criticisms of the government were rude and open. Some fabricated and spread rumours to demonize Chinese authorities. This small group of activists labelled themselves as fighters for democracy and freedom. Their extreme style won them considerable support from the silent majority and some liberal scholars on the Internet.

They also had civil opponents. Some people sharply pointed out that China should stick to its own socialist path with Chinese characteristics and that most problems of modern China could be solved by reforms. State-owned traditional media gradually established their identity as reliable information sources, as people discovered that some information provided by the netizens was not reliable.

The Chinese government knew about the split among Chinese netizens and closely followed, and even joined, discussions through its state-owned media. For example, the *People's Daily*, CCTV and *Global Times* were supposed to be important channels for the government to convey its ideas and steer the direction of public discussions. These efficient interactions between the government and the people indicated Chinese authorities cared very much about the people's feelings. This was the precondition for the continual progress of Chinese governance from an authoritarian style to an open and flexible one. Governments at various levels and important functional departments, opened websites or *weibo*. Citizens could get official information and a hearing from the authorities much faster than before.

Chinese Media and the World

A Changing "Identity" for China in the World

The financial crisis, the renewed emphasis of the United States on Asia-and-Pacific strategies, which instigated Japan and the Philippines to provoke China, the US' hegemonic wars in Iraq, the Arab Spring and the lasting Syrian civil war helped the Chinese people gain a keener insight into the nature of the US democracy and the importance of constantly improving China's comprehensive national powers. The debates in the public sphere before 2012 when President Xi took up his position were fundamental. It was revolutionary for Xi to divert the focus of government from purely promoting economic growth to a more balanced development between the environment and the people. And Xi has the ability to unite the people around him to struggle for the common good of the nation. He did not propose any governance theories as his predecessors had done (e.g. Mao Zedong Thought, Deng Xiaoping Theories, Jiang Zeming's Three Representatives and Hu Jintao's Scientific Development). As the first leader of China who suffered severely from the political movements of the twentieth century, Xi empathized more deeply than his predecessors with the common people's sufferings from the setbacks of political movements and the people's hatred of corruption.

China's rapid economic growth impressed the world. In 2012, China had surpassed Japan to become the world's second largest economy and moved from being "marginalized" to the centre of the world stage. This identity change meant more opportunities and challenges, as China faced a more complex environment due to the readjustment of relations between China and the world. In this situation, China needed not only to continue to reform its systems to ensure stable and sustainable development, but also to have better communication with the world to ensure a favourable public opinion environment. It was against this background that China is making unprecedented efforts to push Chinese media to "Go Global."

Chinese Media Begins to "Go Global"

As early as the 1930s, there were some media outlets exclusively for overseas audiences, some controlled by the KMT and some by the CPC. Xinhua News Agency started its English broadcasting from Yan'an in 1944. In the first 30 years after the founding of New China, besides Xinhua News Agency, there appeared several foreign language magazines such as *Peking Review*, *China Reconstructs*, etc. When I was an English major at college, the only English radio we could listen to was Radio Peking.

Starting from 1978, Chinese media took bigger steps to go overseas. That year, Radio Peking was separated from the Central People's Broadcasting Station and set up as China Radio International (CRI). China News Service, a second news agency which existed for a short period in early 1950s and was later merged into Xinhua News Agency was restored as a news agency, especially for Chinese readers overseas. In 1981, the *China Daily*, the country's first and national English-language newspaper, was founded and came to be seen as a symbol of

China's commitment to open wider to the outside world. By 1983, Xinhua announced it would build itself into a world-class news agency, setting up more branches around the world. In 1985, the *People's Daily* began to publish an edition for Chinese overseas. In 1992, CCTV also started its Channel 4 for overseas Chinese, and in 2000 CCTV launched the Channel 9 English service.

In the 10 years after 2002, such efforts to strengthen Chinese media for overseas audiences accelerated. For a time, some Western media played up the story as to how, "China intends to invest 45 billion yuan to build up several state media giants to compete with the Western media." While the story was denied by the Chinese officials, the tendency for Chinese media to go global was obvious as well as necessary.

In 2010, Xinhua News Agency launched its 24-hour English TV station (CNC) which covered many areas of the world. CCTV added French, Spanish, Russian and Arabic language channels to its CCTV–9. CRI also aimed to transmit to a growing number of regions. The *Global Times,* a popular newspaper attached to the *People's Daily,* launched its English *Global Times* and became the second national English newspaper in China. *China Daily* started a North American edition and planned for a European edition.

All these efforts were seen as China's determination to build up its media power as part of its growing soft power. It could be anticipated that someday the Chinese media would gain their due share in the world media market and help counterbalance, to a certain degree, the dominance of the Western media. But that day won't come soon. China for the next several decades will remain a country with a big media industry, but not a country with strong media influence in the world.

Challenges for Chinese Media on the Way to "Go Global"

China in 2013 had a long way to go in global communication. Chinese media's overreaction to Indian media's critical reports on China exposed the unfamiliarity of Chinese media with the Indian media landscape and the conditions of India. Although Chinese media had strong financial support from the government, it needed to improve its understanding of the international environment. Chinese media needed to learn about their targeted audiences, then implement well-focussed communications to inform foreign audiences better about China.

As more Chinese media went abroad, foreigners would acquire more diverse ways to get to know China better. But Chinese media needed to remember that the international communication arena is dominated by the United States. For decades, overseas readers and audiences had been fed with one-sided stories about China. Once Chinese media began to go abroad, they would face discrimination and biased viewpoints about China. They need to slowly correct long-entrenched prejudices developed by some Western media. To do this would require Chinese media to pay more attention to the skills of international communication. They were expected to tell the right stories in the right manner to foreigners and provide reliable information of about a fast-developing China.

The US had a publicity portfolio for foreign countries. Its films, books, businesses and media closely cooperated with each other with the aim of forming a favourable opinion environment for the US to implement its foreign policies around the world. These factors are important components of the soft power of the United States. China should draw lessons from the US. China will not spread so-called universal values by force like the US. China simply needs to struggle for the right to speak for itself in the international community, and its ability to speak should correspond to China's international status. It is more and more difficult for the US to maintain its dominance of the international communication field as more emerging countries rise. Global governance will replace the US hegemony as the only way out in a world facing all kinds of global issues. If humans cannot solve the issues, we cannot survive in the future. And the solution lies in international cooperation, but not in the hands of the only super power. So, the field of international communication will become more plural.

Conclusion

Media played different roles in the past 60 years in China. Before 1976, in a planned economy, media were used as a tool to unite and mobilize the people to accomplish economic and political plans. After the People's Republic of China was established, it was necessary for the authorities to use the media to unite the nation and construct a strong sense of belonging and national identity to better defend a new country's independence.

Televisions came into Chinese families from the early 1980s together with popular culture from the outside world. The reform and opening-up policies also injected vigour into Chinese media. Watching TV and reading books were popular as the main entertainment. Science and literature replaced political concepts in people's minds. From the late 1990s, more and more Chinese were connected to the Internet and learnt to make use of the Internet as an effective platform for public discussions. Media took the role of watchdogs for the governments. To some extent, the new media have become a public sphere in Chinese society in which the political authorities and common citizens are communicating with each other. This unprecedented interaction is mostly constructive and promotes good governance.

On the other hand, Chinese media in 2013 had more responsibilities than before in explaining China to the world, as China was increasingly recognized as an important power in the international community. This publicity work had been done by state-run media. To present a multifaceted and fast-developing country, China needed more civil diplomacy that involved various media and civil organizations from home and abroad to contribute to China's international publicity project.

China does not have a two-party election as the United States. That does not mean the ruling party of China does not have supervisors or challengers. Instead of muffling people's mouths and muffling the media, as it is typically reported by some Western media, the Chinese government did its best to promote constructive communications within society. It regarded public opinion as a mirror that enabled it to adjust its policies and improve its governance. From the late 1990s, such a communication model proved necessary for China's development and fitted China's national conditions. Media will play bigger roles in China as the country becomes more developed at home and more important to the world.

Notes

1. Hu Yaobang (1915–1989) was a leader of the People's Republic of China. He achieved his most senior status within the Communist Party of China from 1981 to 1987, first as Party chairman from 1981 to 1982, then as General Secretary of the Communist Party from 1982 to 1987.
2. State Administration of Radio, Film and Television, Statistical Report, 2012.
3. China Internet Network Information Center, 30th Survey Report, 28 September 2012.
4. The annual report on Chinese government's progress in information transparency of 2009 issued by the State Council Information Office of China.

2

Newspapers in India: Diversity, Ownership and Future

Robin Jeffrey

Robin Jeffrey's first job was as a sports writer on a small-town Canadian daily in the 1960s. He taught in a school in India, became an academic and wrote *India's Newspaper Revolution* (2014) about the growth of the Indian-language press. His interest in media, especially in India, continues. In 2013, he and Assa Doron published *The Great Indian Phone Book* about the rapid spread of cheap mobile phones. The following chapter analyzes the diversity of the Indian press and assesses its financial base and long-term future.

The Indian newspaper industry is the most diverse in the world. It is also one of the largest and one of the few that grew in the twenty-first century—not merely steadily but spectacularly. In 2014, it had another almost unique characteristic: the prospect of continued growth of print-on-paper for another 5 or 10 years.

Large newspaper businesses in India operated in 13 languages and 11 different scripts. In Europe, one could travel from Lisbon to Helsinki (4,000 km) and still read newspaper headlines in Roman script. In India, a comparable journey from Thiruvananthapuram in Kerala state to Srinagar in Jammu and Kashmir (3,700 km) would take a traveller through the territory of seven different scripts, each needing to be learnt.[1] The challenges for printing technology and newspaper distribution are obvious.

The contrast with China could hardly be greater. In China, a single writing system united people whose spoken languages may have been unintelligible. In India, different scripts divided people whose spoken languages may have been fairly similar (Figure 2.1).

Figure 2.1:
Languages of South Asia with scripts

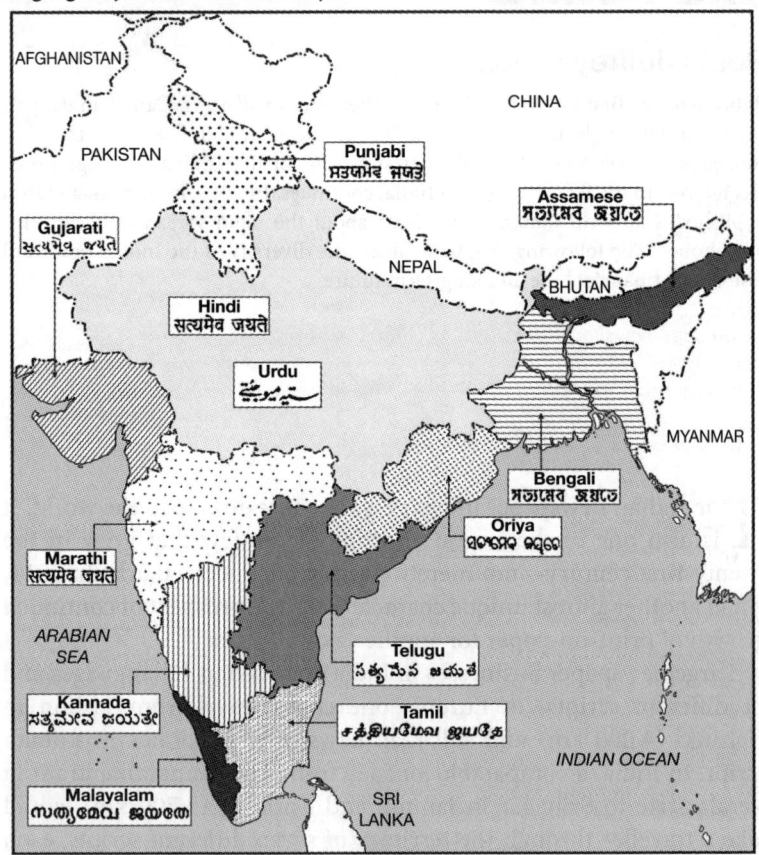

Source: Drawn by Lee Li Kheng, Geography, National University of Singapore, for the Institute of South Asian Studies.
Notes: 1. Each script says: "Satyameva jayate"—let truth prevail.
2. This figure is not to scale. It does not represent any authentic national or international boundaries and is used for illustrative purposes only.

Circulation and Language

India does not have a "national" language. The constitution provides for Hindi, spoken by about 40 per cent of the population across northern India, to be the "official" language of India, but each of the 29 states of the federation is permitted to designate its own "official" language. Literacy grew slowly in India, and circulation of Hindi daily newspapers surpassed the circulation of English dailies only in 1979, 32 years after independence. Even in 2010, English dailies continued to hold second place in circulations with about 13 per cent of all daily sales; Hindi claimed 45 per cent[2] (Figure 2.2). Twelve of the official languages had newspaper industries that sold two million or more papers a day[3] (Table 2.1).

The linguistic complexity of India, its language policy and the expansion of literacy were reflected in the development of the newspaper industry. Readership surveys[4] in 2012 identified the 10

Figure 2.2:
Indian daily newspaper circulations, 1957 to 2010
(Total, Hindi and English)

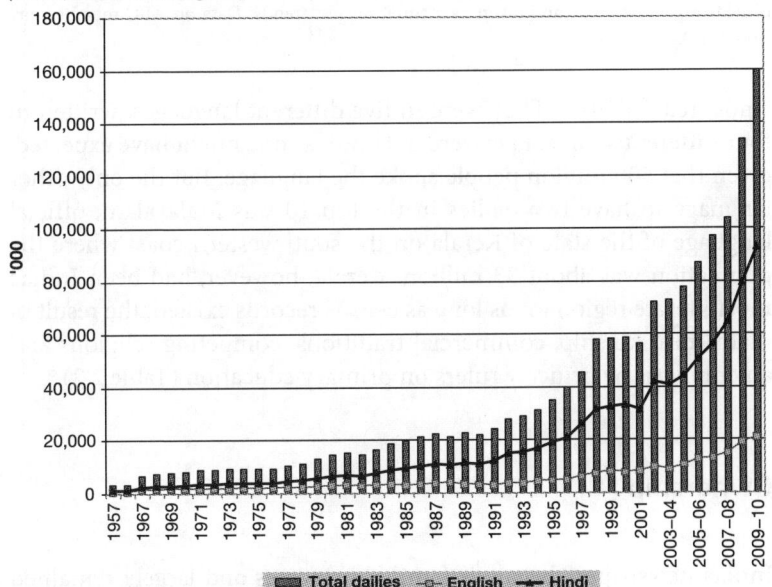

Source: Registrar of Newspapers for India, *Press in India* for relevant years.

Table 2.1:
Major Indian languages, daily newspaper circulations and number of members of the Audit Bureau of Circulations

Language	Circulations 2010 (millions)	Number of ABC Member Dailies 2012
Assamese	0.8	6
Bengali	3.6	14
English	21.1	26
Gujarati	6.4	3
Hindi	71.9	24
Kannada	3.6	7
Malayalam	4.3	4
Marathi	9.5	20
Oriya	4.7	3
Punjabi	2.0	4
Tamil	6.6	4
Telugu	11.3	4
Urdu	14.2	3
TOTAL	**160**	

Sources: For circulations, *Press in India, 2011–2012*. The figures are inflated, but they provide a general guide and taken over time, suggest trends. Data on ABC members are from the ABC website.

"most read" dailies. They were in five different languages, written in four different scripts. Five were in Hindi, as one might have expected, given that 500 million people spoke the language. But the only other language to have two dailies in the top 10 was Malayalam, official language of the state of Kerala on the southwestern coast where the population was about 33 million. Kerala, however, had been India's most literate region for as long as census records existed, the result of matrilineal kinship, commercial traditions, competing religions and an emphasis by princely rulers on primary education (Table 2.2).[5]

Ownership

India's newspapers began as family businesses and largely remained so in 2014 (Table 2.3). Indian governments did not run daily newspapers, though political parties had tried to conduct newspapers, but

Table 2.2:
Literacy in India and Kerala, 1951 to 2011

	1951 (%)	1961 (%)	1971 (%)	1981 (%)	1991 (%)	2001 (%)	2011 (%)
India	18	28	35	44	52	65	74
Kerala	47	55	70	79	90	91	94

Source: http://planningcommission.nic.in/data/datatable/0904/tab_160.pdf (accessed 10 September 2013).

without great success.[6] In the years after independence, the Congress governments of Jawaharlal Nehru discouraged consumerism and advertising, and newspapers grew slowly. Penetration of daily newspapers for the country as a whole was fewer than 30 newspapers per 1,000 people as late as 1991(Table 2.4). The family-owned newspapers that existed at independence grew slowly, but capital was scarce, and profits were not so great as to encourage grand plans. Moreover, at least a few of the proprietors were products of the Gandhian freedom struggle and were genuinely sceptical of crass drives to increase circulations and advertising revenues. To expand circulations meant taking newspapers to small towns and villages where most of India lived. Nowhere in the world had mass newspaper circulations been built on morning delivery to rural populations. Poverty, low literacy, a paucity of consumer goods and the technical difficulties of printing in Indian languages combined to retard the spread of newspapers.[7]

Of the 10 "most read" dailies in 2012, all were controlled by families; none was a fully public company controlled by its shareholders. Four had a limited number of publicly traded shares. Only two of the 10 originated in one of India's great metropolises (the *Times of India* in Mumbai and *Hindustan* in New Delhi; Table 2.2).

The story of *Dainik Jagran*, the Hindi daily with the country's largest readership, illustrated the resilient family-business nature of Indian newspapers and the circumstances in which they began to grow. Founded in Jhansi in central India in 1942 by a merchant-caste family with commercial antecedents, the paper moved its headquarters to Kanpur after independence. It was more than 20 years before they ventured an additional production centre in Gorakhpur, a remote town in eastern Uttar Pradesh in 1975. A younger generation of the family moved into the business in the 1980s and introduced modern management techniques. They recognized that new opportunities to

Table 2.3:
Ten "most read" newspapers, 2012

Newspaper	Language	Original Headquarters	Founded	Ownership	Readership 2012 (millions)
Dainik Jagran	Hindi	Kanpur	1942	Family with limited stock exchange listing	16.4
Dainik Bhaskar	Hindi	Bhopal	1958	Family	14.4
Hindustan	Hindi	New Delhi	1936	Family with limited stock exchange listing	12.2
Malayala Manorama	Malayalam	Kottayam	1889	Family	9.8
Amar Ujala	Hindi	Agra	1948	Family	8.4
Times of India	English	Mumbai	1838	Family	7.6
Daily Thanthi	Tamil	Madurai	1942	Family	7.3
Lokmat	Marathi	Nagpur	1957	Family	7.3
Rajasthan Patrika	Hindi	Jaipur	1956	Family	6.8
Mathrubhumi	Malayalam	Kozhikode	1924	Very limited shareholders; family	6.3

Source: Indian Readership Survey, 2012, fourth quarter

Table 2.4:
Dailies per 1,000 people, 1951 to 2011

Years	Population in Millions	Circulation of Dailies in Thousands	Dailies per 1,000 People
1951	361	2,500	7
1961	439	5,300	12
1971	548	9,041	16
1981	683	15,184	22
1991	846	24,145	29
2001	1,029	56,323	55
2011	1,210	159,708	132

Source: Census reports and *Press in India* for relevant years.

produce larger numbers of more attractive newspapers would allow them to enhance advertising revenue. Realizing that other proprietors saw the same opportunities, families with foresight understood that they had to expand to keep pace with rivals and remain viable. Enterprising publications set up new production centres to bring the paper closer to populations in large towns and the surrounding countryside. By 2014, *Dainik Jagran* published from more than 30 centres and was credited with more than 16 million readers.[8]

Ownership in 2014 was remarkably diverse, though beginning to show signs of concentration. The two largest circulating and most read dailies,[9] *Dainik Jagran* and *Dainik Bhaskar*, were family-controlled companies, competing with each other in the Hindi-language areas of north India. India's diversity of languages and scripts fostered diversity of ownership. It proved culturally difficult for a newspaper based in one language region to move into another language area. Of the top 10 dailies, only *Dainik Bhaskar*, *Hindustan* and the *Times of India* belonged to companies that ran successful dailies in other languages. *Dainik Bhaskar* had broken into the Gujarati market with *Divya Bhaskar* and *Hindustan* was part of the Hindustan Times Group, which produced a major English daily. The *Times of India* was the flagship of Bennett Coleman and Co. Ltd (BCCL), publishers of dailies in Hindi, Marathi and Kannada.

As the biggest media organization in India, the Times of India group (more accurately, BCCL) had interests in television, radio and films. Its remarkable commercial achievements in the 1990s were

attributed to one of the members of the owning family, the idiosyncratic vice-chairman, Samir Jain. The entry on Jain in Wikipedia
captured qualities often ascribed to him:

> His business proposition was simple: he would connect sellers of goods
> to this vast market of consumers. He was the first in media industry to
> dispense with the post of an Editor.[10]

This business strategy proved highly successful and saw BCCL
become the most valuable media company in the country, owner of
the most successful television news channel in English, as well as the
largest selling English daily newspaper (India does not have regulations against cross-media ownership). Critics claimed that its relentless focus on profit had led it to sell its columns to anyone who could
afford to pay and to aim its content at a market hungry for gossip and
titillation. The directors of BCCL could reply that the eyes of millions of readers and the rupees of advertisers justified their business
plan.

Planning and organization were important. The rapidly changed
possibilities for Indian media from the late 1970s meant that it was
essential to carve out audiences and serve them. Otherwise, old thun-
derers could become pipsqueaks. Of the newspapers publishing in
2014, the oldest was *Mumbai Samachar* in Gujarati, founded in
Mumbai by a Parsi in 1822 and serving mobile Gujarati families ever
since. In 2013, its sole edition still sold 90,000 copies a day, mostly in
and around Mumbai.[11] On the other hand, the *Statesman* of Kolkata,
once India's premier daily, was a shrivelled remnant.

Of the ten "most read" dailies in 2012, each was owned by a different family. Another dozen families, owners of major publications such
as the *Indian Express* chain or *Ananda Bazar Patrika* in West Bengal,
were close on their heels. India had more than two dozen families
running substantial newspaper businesses. Indian governments, for
their part, produced departmental magazines and reports, but nothing in print to rival the daily newspapers. And Indian political parties,
other than the Communist Party of India (Marxist), had given up
running party dailies. Ownership of Indian newspapers recalled the
patterns of contending proprietors that were found in Britain or the
US at the beginning of the twentieth century—except that India

worked in many languages. And Indian proprietors could look forward to 300 million illiterates who were expected to become literate in the next 20 years and thus swell the pool of potential readers.

Technology

Expanding capitalism played a part in newspaper growth, but the nature of India's written languages had required new printing technologies to free them from the straitjacket of individual metal types and the Gutenberg press. To be sure, India's scripts were elegantly phonetic. If you could read a word, you knew how to pronounce it, unlike English where words like "power mower" and the perils of "th" and "ph" torment newcomers. However, to achieve this congruence between the symbol and the sound could require up to 900 different letter-shapes. In English, fewer than 70 are sufficient. When printing required the creation of individual metal letters, which then had to be assembled into words, coated with ink and pressed against paper, 900 different shapes were too many to deal with—expensive to make and complicated to put together. Though fonts in the Indian languages were created in the nineteenth century, they were severely limited in their ability to capture every facet of a language. Because they were costly to make, they were available in only a few sizes and styles, and they were ponderously slow to compose. A single newspaper page could take hours to set in type.[12]

From the late 1970s, computer technology and offset printing changed the possibilities. Software programs allowed any letter of an Indian language to be created in the computer's memory. There was no longer a need for hundreds of boxes of different metal letters. Offset printing presses transferred ink to paper by a chemical process, not the physical contact of paper against inked metal. The growing availability of relatively cheap, robust offset presses from the 1980s enabled newspapers to set up production centres closer to their readers. The goal of 7 a.m. delivery even to towns and villages hundreds of kilometres from a newspaper's home base became attainable.

Advertising

Newspapers are the cutting edge of capitalism, as Ben Bagdikian, the US media analyst, argued long ago. He also pointed out that in eighteenth-century America, the most common name for a newspaper included the word "advertiser."[13] One can see the correlation in Figure 2.3 below. While the liberation of many scripts was provided by offset printing and computer technology, the fuel that unleashed the technology was economic—increasing possibilities for the sale of consumer goods and the need to advertise them.

Advertising drove newspaper expansion. In 2013, the cost of Indian newspapers was ridiculously low—rarely more than ₹5 or US 10 cents. Circulations had grown through vicious competition in which newspaper proprietors struggled to demonstrate high circulations in order to woo the biggest advertisers and extract the highest rates for advertising. Controls on India's economy loosened in the 1980s, and newspapers grew as advertising revenues increased. After the beginning of economic "liberalization" in 1991, the pace quickened as

Figure 2.3:
Indian advertising expenditure, 1990–1991 to 2012
(capitalized billings in crores of rupees)

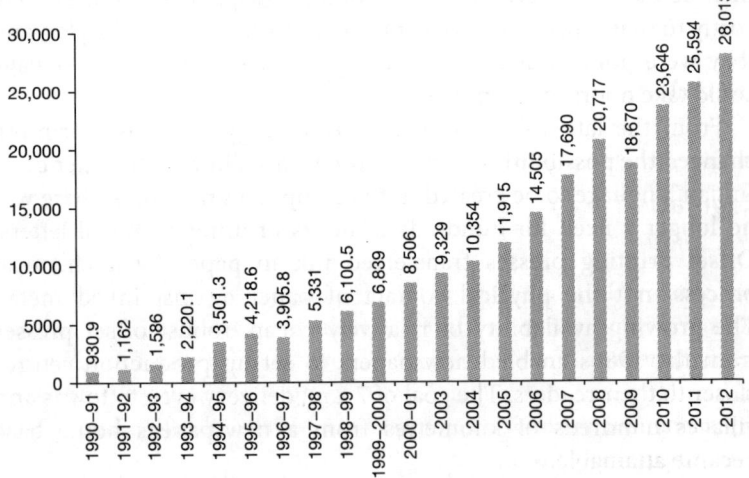

Sources: 1990–1991 to 2000–2001 data from A&M Agency Reports for relevant years. 2003–2011 data from Pitch Madison Media Advertising Outlook Reports for relevant years. 2012 figure is a projected estimate.

consumer goods, from video recorders to refrigerators, became available. Advertising agencies and advertising budgets expanded. And until the mid-1990s, newspapers faced little competition from television, which was severely constrained by government controls and technical limitations. Print media feasted on growing advertising expenditure that had almost nowhere else to go. Estimated ad expenditure increased by six times between 1991 and 1999 before major competition from television began to gobble up a large share (Figure 2.3).

Publishers of Indian-language newspapers suffered from the suppositions of marketers and advertising agencies. The English-language press was judged to be where readers with higher incomes were to be found, and the big advertising campaigns for expensive consumer goods went to English newspapers and magazines. Indian-language newspapers battled to convince the sellers of cars, air tickets and other expensive products that the readers of Hindi, Bengali, Gujarati, Tamil, Telugu, Malayalam and Marathi publications also wanted drive, travel and own refrigerators. Indian-language publications set out to discover and nurture local advertising. They developed classified sections and prided themselves in "educating" their readers about the virtues of advertising births, deaths, marriages and real estate. Many stringers who reported news from small towns were also called on to sell advertisements. And at the level of top management, some owners and their senior employees sold "advertorial" space to those who wanted to pay. Such material was sometimes labelled in small print as "advertisement," but in elections in 2009, some candidates bought favourable coverage depicted as genuine news, as is explained below.

Regulation

For critics of Indian newspapers, the "paid news" scandal of 2010 and 2011 was simply further evidence of how far the press had strayed from some imagined golden age of journalism. From the time that Indian-language newspapers began using big headlines, unpretentious language and colour pictures in the 1980s, old elites had fretted over "dumbing down." When the country's most powerful media organization, the *Times of India,* drove up its circulation with relentless and ruthless marketing and cricket-and-film-star coverage, many Indian-language newspapers copied its formula. Critics complained about "half-clad girls" on page 3 and called for regulation to preserve "Indian cultural values."

The first amendment to the Indian constitution limited freedom of the press; the first amendment to the American constitution guaranteed it. From the time the printing press arrived in significant numbers in India in the eighteenth century, governments struggled to control its products. As foreign rulers, the British feared that the printed word could stir and coordinate resistance. Newspapers that preached nationalism too fervently were required to pay good behaviour bonds or forced to close, though pre-publication censorship was rare. It became common, however, during the 19 months of Indira Gandhi's "emergency" in 1975–1977.[14]

In the tumultuous years after independence, Jawaharlal Nehru's government attempted to set up institutions to ensure "standards." A Press Commission in 1954 to inquire into the workings of the press led to the creation of two institutions, the Registrar of Newspapers for India (RNI) in 1956 and the Press Council in 1966. The former was intended to maintain a register of newspapers, allocate newsprint and foster small publications. The Press Council heard complaints and set standards. By 2013, the Registrar's office was a hollow shell that produced much-delayed compilations of wobbly data. The Press Council, abolished by Indira Gandhi during the "emergency" in 1975–1977, was reconstituted in 1979. It heard complaints about newspapers and gave decisions on their validity, but it had no power to enforce rulings, and newspapers could simply ignore its decisions. The chairman of the Press Council was selected by a committee of three—the presiding officers (speakers) of the lower and upper houses of parliament and a representative of the members of the Press Council at the time the chairmanship became vacant. In 2011, a new, voluble chairman with controversial opinions about many matters gave the Council a brief notoriety it had not had before.

In the Nehru and Indira Gandhi eras, governments aimed to reduce the influence of English-language newspapers owned by big capitalist families and to ensure coverage broadly in line with the wishes of governments. This was attempted through the award or the revoking of government advertising, through housing concessions for journalists and through gentle or heavy-handed coercion, including tax raids and investigations. It was later said that Indira Gandhi's interest in reducing the big English-language newspapers cooled after the "emergency" because she had discovered it was easier to deal with a few large and fairly complacent media targets than with hundreds of small operations each with its own idiosyncratic goals and needs. Later, Rajiv Gandhi's government got an "anti-defamation" bill passed by the lower house of parliament in 1988, but had to drop it in the face of widespread protests and an uncooperative upper house. A somewhat similar effort, linked to Rajiv Gandhi's son and prime-minister-in-waiting, Rahul, was quickly dropped after being mooted in 2012.[15]

The constraints on Indian publications do not, however, come solely from governments or state-sanctioned bodies like the Press Commission and Registrar of Newspapers. Threats to a free press also come from self-censorship and cupidity. Indian newspapers tend to follow an accepted official line when reporting insurgency and unrest in India's border states, notably Jammu and Kashmir and the small states of the northeast. The "paid news" scandals—favourable editorial content in exchange for cash payments from politicians—involved some of the largest daily newspapers. A sub-committee of the Press Council concluded in 2010 that a "huge amount of circumstantial evidence" suggested that "the pernicious practice of 'paid news' has become widespread across media (both print and electronic, English and non-English languages) in different parts of the country."[16] Candidates in the 2009 elections to the national parliament appear to have been asked by senior officials of large newspapers to pay hefty sums for publication of favourable stories about themselves. So, crude was the coverage that "a hagiographical article" on a candidate appeared "word for word in three major rival publications. In two of them, on the same day, in all of them under different by-lines."[17]

There was nothing new in trying to buy favourable stories. At the bottom of the news-gathering chain, lowly paid stringers have long been susceptible to purchase or coercion by local notables who want their fame proclaimed or misdeeds suppressed. But the more recent "paid news" scandals involved conscious policy of managements to generate revenue for the cash-hungry companies.

Tension between governments and journalists was inescapable in a democratic, election-fighting India. In efforts to find ways to control the press, the Indian government and the hyperactive chairman of its Press Council in 2013 floated ideas about requiring journalists to pass government tests in order to acquire a "licence."[18] Though greeted with derision, the suggestion illustrated a continuing struggle by politicians, police, corporations and bureaucrats to have the press dance to pre-agreed tunes.

Another "control" on Indian newspapers was the threat of organized violence. Especially in smaller centres, newspaper offices and printing centres are vulnerable to attack by crowds, roused or paid for by people objecting to particular stories. These tend to be related to religion or social practices, and the destruction is justified on the grounds that a particular group's "psyche" has been wounded by a story.[19] Managements must take the safety of their employees and the security of their assets into account when choosing how they will treat news. Newspapers have large fixed investments in printing presses and computer technology. The Punjab insurgency of the 1980s and early 1990s began in earnest with the murder of a newspaper proprietor, Lala Jagat Narain, of the Hind Samachar group, publishers of the big Hindi daily, *Punjab Kesari*, in September 1981. In the next 12 years, more than 50 newspaper hawkers who sold targeted newspapers were murdered, along with Jagat Narain's son in 1984.[20] It is, however, at the lower levels of the news-gathering chain that journalists are most vulnerable to blandishments, threats and violence intended to influence coverage. One report counted six Indian journalists killed in the first six months of 2013, a number exceeded only by eight deaths in Syria,[21] and four journalists were said to have been killed in the state of Uttar Pradesh in a single week in August 2013.[22] Small-town correspondents are most at risk, since they do not have the obvious support of a big organization and a host of colleagues.

Journalists

Journalists' unions and associations are relatively weak. The Indian Federation of Working Journalists (IFWJ) was formed in 1950, but internal conflict led to theformation of a new organization, the Indian Journalists Union (IJU) in 1989; it claimed more than 23,000 members in 2013.[23] A rival National Union of Journalists (India) dated from 1972. From the 1950s, the salaries of journalists were laid down by a wage board appointed periodically by the central government. Though the system survived in 2013, it was increasingly bypassed by newspaper managements who employed journalists on contracts or kept them dangling as stringers who were paid for individual stories and sometimes given a small retainer. Multi-edition Indian-language dailies were particularly careful not to inflate their salary bills by hiring too many full-time employees.

No training was required to become a journalist. Small-town stringers often had other jobs as teachers, shopkeepers or news agents and were sometimes expected to sell advertisements as well as report stories. From the 1960s, however, courses for journalists and media professionals had been established. The government-sponsored Indian Institute of Mass Communications (IIMC) dated from 1965 and was intended to train media people and research media issues. The expansion of television in the 1990s imparted a new glamour to "careers in media," and journalism programmes in universities and independent journalism schools proliferated. A website that provided information about such schools listed more than 220 in 2013, most of them charging substantial fees.[24]

India's journalists were overwhelmingly upper-caste Hindus. Even though 15 per cent of the population were Dalits (once derisively referred to as "untouchables") and 7 per cent *Adivasi* (or "tribals," indigenous people living in remote areas), there appeared to be no Dalit or *Adivasi* in any significant editorial position on any major daily newspaper as late as 2014. Indeed, there were virtually no Dalits or *Adivasis* in Indian newsrooms at all.[25] Cursory surveys suggested that upper castes made up more than 70 per cent of journalists on substantial newspapers, though upper castes might account for no more than a quarter of the total population. "Diversity in the newsroom" was an issue for American newspapers from the 1970s, but in India, the question rarely got a hearing or was brushed aside with remarks such as, "We don't ask a person's caste." In practice, of course, if there were no Dalits or *Adivasis* in newsrooms, the likelihood of knowing about stories involving them was greatly reduced, as was the access to Dalit and *Adivasi* sources. The reasons for their absence were economic and social. They constituted a large proportion of India's poorest people and consequently had little interest for advertisers; they were disproportionately illiterate; and galling social prejudice still existed against them, in spite of more than 60 years of "reservation" or "positive discrimination" in government institutions.

Future

Unlike most of the world's old-style newspapers, India's dailies in 2014 had a medium-term future printing news on paper. Elsewhere, newspapers cut their staffs, stopped printing on some days of the week or wound up altogether. Everywhere, newspapers explored ways of going online, digital and electronic. In India, too, newspapers and magazines experimented with online methods of selling their wares to readers and their readers to advertisers. But the nature of India meant that print on paper had an expectation of life as far ahead as 2025. Poverty, illiteracy and poor communications helped to explain why.

Though India had more than 900 million mobile phone subscribers in 2014,[26] most of these were users of inexpensive 2G phones. Frugal users carefully bought prepaid talk time. Smart phone prices began to fall steeply in 2014 to about ₹2,000 or 35 US dollars.[27] However, until prices fell to 20 US dollars, the temptations of news and entertainment in colour on one's own phone would remain unattainable for most people. And even when handheld devices came within budgets, the providers of telecom services would still need to find bandwidth and content to make it worth spending portions of meagre incomes on the experience. Print-on-paper newspapers, on the other hand, had developed ways of reaching most parts of rural India. Newspapers did not depend on electricity to charge their batteries or radio frequency that might fail when cellular transmission towers broke down. Newspapers lay around for days and could be read when convenient; old newspapers were useful and could be sold for recycling. And as long as newspapers remained cheap—one could usually recover the purchase price by selling the paper back to a recycler—circulations would stay strong, and advertisers would continue to buy space and thus subsidize the production costs. Finally, the fact that 25 per cent of adult Indians were illiterate in 2011 gave newspaper proprietors the prospect of an emerging market: the 300 million new readers that future adult-literacy drives might produce. Indian print had a future, but it was not unlimited.

Notes

1. Malayalam, Tamil, Kannada, Telugu, Urdu, Hindi and Gurmukhi. India has 23 official languages, excluding English.
2. Sevanti Ninan, *Headlines from the Heartland. Reinventing the Hindi Public Sphere* (New Delhi: SAGE, 2007) is the seminal study of Hindi-language newspapers and their growth from the 1980s.
3. Any one of those languages therefore had daily circulations equivalent to that of the entire Australian newspaper industry which sold about 2.3 million newspapers each day in 2006. (Australian circulations fell thereafter) http://www.abcdiamond.com/newspaper-circulation-figures (accessed 7 June 2013).
4. *Readership* is different from *circulation*. The latter represents the number of newspapers sold each day. *Readership* is estimated on the basis of surveys and questionnaires.
5. Under the British, the southern portion of Kerala was left in the control of two Indian rulers, the Maharajas of Cochin and Travancore.
6. The Communist Party of India (Marxist) runs viable dailies in Malayalam (*Desabhimani*) and Bengali (*Ganasakti*).
7. The growth of Indian-language newspapers is explained in Robin Jeffrey, *India's Newspaper Revolution: Capitalism, Politics and the Indian-Language Press*, 3rd edition (New Delhi: Oxford University Press, 2010). Vanita Kohli-Khandekar, *The Indian Media Business*, 4th edition (New Delhi: SAGE, 2013) provides comprehensive recent data.
8. Jeffrey, *India's Newspaper Revolution*, pp. 83–85.
9. "Circulation" is the number of newspapers printed and sold each day. The most reliable source for circulation figures is the Audit Bureau of Circulation, of which most of the major newspapers are members. "Readership" is the estimated number of people who read a newspaper each day, based on sample surveys carried out by the Media Research Users Council, an organization of advertisers, advertising agencies and other organizations with an interest in media penetration.
10. http://en.wikipedia.org/wiki/Samir_Jain (accessed 26 August 2013).
11. ABC July–December 2012.
12. Jeffrey, *India's Newspaper Revolution*, pp. 33–45.
13. Ben Bagdikian, *The Information Machines: Their Impact on Men and the Media* (New York: Harper Colophon Books, 1971), p. 76.
14. J. Natarajan, *History of Indian Journalism. Part II of the Report of the Press Commission* (New Delhi: Publications Division, 1955) provides a detailed account of Indian newspapers from British times to the first years of independence.
15. *India Today*, 4 May 2012, http://indiatoday.intoday.in/story/print-and-electronic-media-standards-and-regulation-bill-rahul-gandhi-meenakshi-natrajan/1/187347.html (accessed 11 September 2013).

16. Press Council, *Sub-Committee Report "Paid News": How corruption in the Indian media undermines democracy*, 2010, http://presscouncil.nic.in/home. htm (accessed 4 September 2013).

17. *Hindu*, 29 January 2013, http://www.thehindu.com/news/national/yes-we-spent-money-on-paid-news-ads/article4354575.ece (accessed 4 September 2013). This story and a series that broke the "paid news" scandal were by P. Sainath, one of India's most redoubtable journalists.

18. *Mail Today*, 20 August 2013, http://indiatoday.intoday.in/story/manish-tewari-license-system-for-journalists-criticism-social-media-india-today/1/300390.html (accessed 4 September 2013).

19. *Hindu*, 4 March 2010, http://www.hindu.com/2010/03/04/stories/20100304 55750600.htm (accessed 4 September 2009). *Hindu*, 18 January 2012, http:// www.thehindu.com/news/national/tamil-nadu/aiadmk-activists-attack-nakkheeran-office/article2782907.ece (accessed 4 September 2013).

20. Robin Jeffrey, *What's Happening to India?* 2nd edition (London: Macmillan, 1992), p. 94. Jeffrey, *India's Newspaper Revolution*, pp. 201–202.

21. Killing the Messenger—January–June 2013. An analysis of news media casualties carried out for the International News Safety Institute by Cardiff School of Journalism, http://www.newssafety.org/images/KTM2013_Jan-June.pdf (accessed 4 September 2013).

22. *Times of India*, 28 August 2013, http://timesofindia.indiatimes.com/city/lucknow/4-journalists-killed-in-past-45-days-in-Uttar-Pradesh/article-show/22108719.cms (accessed 4 September 2013).

23. http://www.indianjournalistsunion.org/aboutus.asp (accessed 11 September 2013).

24. http://www.way2college.com/JournalismColleges.php (accessed 4 September 2013).

25. J. Balasubramaniam, "Lack of Diversity in the Newsroom," *Economic and Political Weekly*, 12 March 2011, pp. 21–23. Per Stahlberg, *Lucknow Daily. How a Hindi Newspaper Constructs Society* (Stockholm: Stockholm Studies in Social Anthropology, 2002), pp. 137–147. Robin Jeffrey, "[Not] Being There: Dalits and India's Newspapers," *South Asia*, 24, no. 2 (December 2001): 225–238.

26. The Telecom Regulatory Authority of India (TRAI) calculated there were 868 million active phone subscribers on 31 March 2013. *TRAI Annual Report, 2012–13*, p. 14, http://goo.gl/Oq9ZQU (accessed 16 January 2015).

27. *Business Standard*, 26 August 2014, http://goo.gl/2m2MrQ (accessed 19 September 2014), reported on the "the launch of the world's cheapest smart phone at ₹1,999," the Intex Cloud FX using Mozilla Firefox as its operating system.

3

India on Television: Owners, Politicians and Debate in a Democracy

Nalin Mehta

Nalin Mehta is a social historian, writer and journalist. He is an associate professor at Shiv Nadar University, consulting editor at the *Times of India* and adjunct faculty at Indian Institute of Management, Bengaluru. He edits the *South Asian History and Culture* book series and journal and has held senior positions at the UN and the Global Fund in Geneva. His books include *Behind a Billion Screens: Inside Indian Television* (2015) and *India on Television: How Satellite Channels Changed the Ways We Think and Act* (2008), which won the 2009 Asian Publishing Award for Best Book. He has been managing editor at Headlines Today and taught at universities and institutions in Australia, Switzerland and Singapore.

Why Indian Television Matters

In September 2009, India's prime minister, army chief and national security advisor launched a coordinated attempt to douse television speculation about alleged Chinese military incursions on the disputed eastern border. All three leaders issued denials after days of intense focus by India's private TV news networks which had accused the government of hushing up Chinese aggression. Such reports were not restricted to television alone. In fact, matters came to a head when the English daily, the *Times of India,* reported that two border guards had allegedly been injured in a skirmish. Many analysts, however, noted that the general tone of the aggressive media discourse was set

by what one newspaper editor called "war-mongering TV channels."[1]
Both governments denied the incidents,[2] but the story had created
such heat that the then National Security Advisor M.K. Narayanan
appeared on a television interview on CNN-IBN with a dire warning:

> I don't know what the reason is why there is so much reporting ... but I
> think this is a national security issue ... the more you raise people's con-
> cerns, the tensions could rise and we would then be facing a situation of
> the kind that we wish to avoid [sic] ... It could create a problem of a kind
> and I have been through [in] [the] 1962 [war] ... then of course we didn't
> have the media of this kind...
>
> What we need to be careful of is that we don't have an unwarranted inci-
> dent or an accident of some kind, that's what we are trying to avoid. But
> there's always concern that *if this thing goes on like this someone somewhere
> might lose his cool and something might go wrong*.[3] (emphasis added)

That this statement came in a television interview was no accident.
The government was asking India's TV networks to tone down. This,
at least, was the majority view in Delhi's newsrooms. Television was
seen to have largely led the debate; print was seen to have followed.
Anecdotal evidence certainly supported this view. Among others,
B.V. Rao, a former TV news editor and media columnist, noted that
the government was asking the media to "back off" because "this time
the frenzy seemed to have spread even to print [from television]."[4]

Whether the allegations about border incursions were true or not is
outside the scope of this chapter. Such shadowboxing between the
media and the government on tricky issues is part of every democracy
and India is no exception. It is pertinent for our purposes, however,
that this was the second time in the year that India's TV news networks
were accused of side-tracking bilateral relations with another country.

When a group of Indian students were injured in a racist attack in
Melbourne in May 2009, the story was initially virtually ignored in
the national newspapers. It was first given prominence on Times
Now, the Times of India Group's 24-hour English news channel,
which ran an emotional campaign around it. The network made the
story its first headline and ran a sustained campaign about injured
Indian pride. Times Now has for several years been the most watched
English news network in India, and its commercial success has been

built on an aggressive policy of pursuing stories with a nationalist angle—especially those involving non-resident Indians; a hard line on security, especially on Pakistan and China; and the notion of a powerful India, an India that is no more a pushover. Television ratings show that its audiences like that tone, and this in turn affects its choice and treatment of stories. The Australian racism story fitted its template very well. Once it got traction and the Ministry of External Affairs was forced to react, every other media group, television and print, followed the suit. This is the nature of the media—the story had become too big for others to ignore.[5]

The intense focus meant that every attack on an Indian thereafter— even ones that were part of general crime patterns and not racist— were framed through the same lens. Once such reports would have been relegated to the inside pages of newspapers or, at best, would have made it to a box item on the front page. Now, they became part of an ongoing media discourse about a resurgent India that would not take things lying down.

At a time when Indo-Australian relations had been on the upswing after years of historical mistrust, the story upset the trajectory of bilateral relations, with the Indian Foreign Minister, facing middle class anger in television studios, issuing warnings to Australia. The central role of television in this discourse was best summed up in a tongue-in-cheek account published in the *Hindustan Times*:

Other countries have think-tanks, India makes do with prime-time chat shows...

To media consumers who got initiated into Australian society this past week, that country must seem formidably scary, almost the fastness of Ming of Mongo. There was discussion on a "white Australia" policy that went out of business 30 years ago. Clips of Australian cricketers sledging or arguing with Indian, West Indian and Sri Lankan cricketers were juxtaposed with reportage of attacks on Indian students, as if one were dealing with a nation of all-purpose bigots.

On one television show, an anchor said Australia had been preceded by attacks on Indians in Germany, the United States and Idi Amin's Uganda and wondered why the world hated Indians. This is a happy universe of nuance-free non sequiturs.

Even so, India's television-propelled middle class opinion is a clear and present reality. It will shape discourse that will hassle and harangue governments, demand instant action and colourful rhetoric. In some senses, the drama outside the Delhi airport during the IC-814 hijack was a teaser trailer. This is the new India. Now even Kevin Rudd [Australian prime minister] knows that.

For our purposes, it is immaterial whether the television coverage was right or wrong, nuanced or simplistic, and sensationalist or measured. The point is that both the examples cited earlier underlined the centrality of 24-hour private satellite news as a new factor in the Indian political and social matrix. In both cases, the discourse of Indian television had serious consequences for domestic policy imperatives and an impact beyond India's borders. A detailed study of Indian news television's impact on foreign policy is still to be written, but it is important to reiterate how recent the phenomenon of private TV news is.

This is a country where as late as 1994, a prime minister cancelled the launch of a new state TV channel because it promised to show live current affairs programmes. Narasimha Rao's reasoning couldn't have been clearer: "We cannot have live broadcasts. It is too dangerous," he said, while cancelling the launch of DD 3 in October 1994.[6] The fear was that there would be no way of controlling anybody from saying anything against the ruling Congress on live programming. Historically in India, control over television has been central to the state's self-image—broadcasting's principal objective was to "display and enact government control"—and live television threatened to break down the edifice on which Indian television had been built.

Despite the best efforts of the Indian state to resist the forces of change in the 1990s, India has gone in two decades from just one state-owned television network to over 800 licensed private satellite channels. In 2000, India had 132 TV channels, by 2013 this number had gone up to over 877 in various languages.[7] The first Indian 24-hour news channel only started broadcasting in 1998, but by 2013, more than 150 channels were broadcasting news in 15 languages and more than a hundred (in 11 languages) were 24-hour news channels.[8] The numbers illustrate the massive changes in Indian broadcasting.[9] There has been a simultaneous expansion in reach and penetration. In 1992, if you divided India's population of 846,388,000[10] by the total number of television sets in the country,[11] the number of people clustering around a set would have been a little over 26. By 2011, that ratio had come down substantially to just about 10 people per television set, despite a substantial increase in the population.[12] In a little over a decade, the total number of Indian television households more than tripled to reach an estimated 145 million.[13] It made India the world's third largest television market, just behind China and the United States.[14]

The figures tell a story of the TV boom. But it is only half of the story. Within India, the growth of the medium unleashed new battles over control, media ownership and who ultimately controlled the public sphere. These questions are especially important for a profession, whose very existence depends on the rhetoric of public service and probity. Its rise has had significant implications for Indian democracy, and its daily travails as a business, as a cultural commodity and as a significant lever of society offer an unparalleled view into the daily theatre of India. Immense changes are engulfing Indian television. Global TV companies increasingly turn to India, not just for its growth potential but as a new primary market. Television is emerging as the preeminent cultural force in the country.

Television touches virtually everyone in Indian society, but in the din of daily headlines, it is important to start with some fundamental questions. Who really owns Indian television? What are the patterns of control nationally and across regional languages? Are there any commonalities across languages and regions? Can we discern underlying trends that drive the business and what are the politics? At a time when many believe, on one side, that corporate India is buying up Indian television and, on the other, that ownership is irrelevant because digital media have created an information revolution which no one can control, these questions are at the heart of the debate about modern media.

The Reign of Five: Two Models of Indian Television

For its first 15 years, the Indian private broadcast industry expanded like the American Wild West. Canny local entrepreneurs rode into uncharted territories and planted their stakes in the ground. They then used their first-mover advantage to build walls and defended themselves against ambitious newcomers. The complexities of language and the challenge of India's regional peculiarities meant that the regional players in the initial stages remained protected from predatory outsiders or from big media groups looking to expand. Television still operated like a cottage industry until the early-2000s and the initial big players—whether in Hindi or in the regional languages—remained largely intact in their splendid isolation.

Since 2008, though, India's television map has changed significantly with a spate of buyouts and moves towards consolidation. This phase has coincided with a greater corporatization of the industry, the availability of greater capital for expansion, and with a realization that it is the regional markets where the primary growth lies. It started with Zee's first hesitant forays into regional languages, turned into a trend with Star's determined push into the non-Hindi space and was cemented by Sun TV's underrated tactical brilliance in buying up channels in the non-Tamil south Indian languages. Sony belatedly joined the rush with its acquisition of the Telugu language Maa TV.

The first thing that stands out when one looks at the ownership map of India is that five players dominate the TV entertainment business: Star, Zee, Sony, Sun and Viacom. Between them, by 2012, these five big players ran about 10–12 per cent[15] of all channels in the country and controlled about 61 per cent of the viewing market (Table 3.1). By June 2012, for example, Maa TV remained the only major TV channel which still enjoyed a significant viewing share in any language and was not owned by one of the big five: until it too sold a significant stake to Sony.[16]

The second thing that stands out is how *little* they control. The 61 per cent viewing market share of the big five companies might seem like a lot, but not when one knows that this is the lowest when compared with other countries with big television industries. The top five companies in the United States control as much as 69 per cent of the cable TV market (and the top six companies almost 80%, if you calculate by revenue share);[17] the top five in the United Kingdom and Australia over 80 per cent, and the top five in Canada almost 80 per cent. In Japan, this is as high as 92 per cent, in Brazil, 77 per cent and in Italy and Mexico, the top two companies control almost everything (Figure 3.1). In international terms, Indian television remained a highly competitive and tough market, despite the trend towards consolidation.

Table 3.1:
Percentage viewing share of TV market, 2012: Big five

Network	All India	Hindi	Andhra Pradesh	Karnataka	Kerala	Maharashtra	West Bengal	Tamil Nadu
Star	19.0	22.5	4.4	13.7	32.8	21.6	25.5	7.6
Zee	14.0	16.7	11.5	9.6	1.3	19	21.8	3.2
Sony	12.1	15.8	3.2	3.5	1.7	15.3	10.5	1.6
Sun	10.5	0.2	26.3	36.9	28.5	0.5	0	47.9
Viacom	6.6	8.8	1.6	1.9	0.9	7.6	5.7	0.4
TOTAL	61	64	47	65.6	65.2	64	63.5	60.7

Source: TAM CS4 data for January–September 2012.[18]

Figure 3.1:
Why India is better off: Country-wise percentage viewing share of top five companies (select countries)

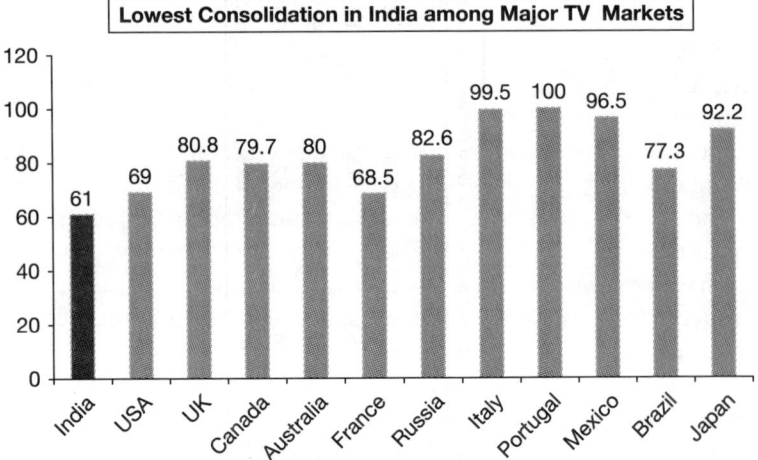

Source: International figures from Analysis Group, *Vertical Integration in TV Broadcasting and Distribution in G8 Countries and Certain Other Countries,* 7 August 2012, http://dwmw. files.wordpress.com/2012/08/analysis-2012-vertical-integration-tv-canada.pdf (accessed 30 September 2012).

Looking deeper into the Indian figures, no one network controls more than 20 per cent of the national market. Only Star approached this mark in 2012, while the other four hovered between 6–14 per cent (Table 3.1). The share of the big five is distributed across nearly 100 individual channels, and if you drill down by language and by channel, the picture gets much more complicated.

Two distinct models emerge. The first is marked by intense competition and fluctuating fortunes. Four language groups have remained locked in close contests where leads are slim: the Hindi-speaking market, Kerala, West Bengal and Maharashtra. Star is the leader in these languages, but its next-best competitor in each group is within 5–6 percentage points. This is especially true in Maharashtra where Star has remained neck-and-neck with Zee. The key feature here is that, with the exception of the Asianet channel in Kerala, which alone accounts for one-fifth of the local market for Star, no single channel (as opposed to media group) in any language is so decisively ahead of its rival to be uncatchable. For example, the largest channel in Hindi hovers between 6.5–8.5 per cent of the market share, in Marathi between 5–7 per cent and in Bengali between 12–15 per cent.

Leadership in these languages is less about having one big dominant channel and more about building it incrementally by running a diverse line-up of different kinds of programming: general entertainment, music, movies, children-focussed channels. This is where conglomerates with diverse offerings and deep pockets have a built-in advantage and this is why standalone channels are difficult to sustain.

The second model is one of the complete network dominance. This is the case in Andhra Pradesh, Karnataka and Tamil Nadu where Sun has held unparalleled sway. It is six times the size of its nearest competitor in Tamil Nadu and more than twice the size of the second-largest networks in Karnataka and Andhra. In contrast to the states with close competition, Sun's dominance in its three big states is powered by the *numero uno* status of its flagship channels. In Andhra, Sun's Gemini TV is nearly twice the size of the next big network Zee Telugu. The same applies in Karnataka, where Uday TV is nearly double its challenger Suvarna TV. And for historical reasons, which go to the heart of how its politics has evolved, Tamil Nadu is a class apart. In 2012, Sun TV's astounding 31.5 per cent share in its original home-ground dwarfed the next best of Vijay TV which stood at a mere 6.5 per cent.

Linguistic boundaries and cultural and political nuances give Sun such leadership in these states, but it is precisely these boundaries and nuances that prevent it from expanding outside its southern bastions and keep its national share where it is.

What does all this amount to and how does Indian ownership diversity match global trends? This is an important question and concerns about consolidation are genuine. Yet much of this debate has so far been conducted more with emotion and ideology and less with facts. The data show that with the exception of Tamil news, even the most concentrated language markets in India still remain more diverse than those in most other countries where television is widespread.

To measure owner concentration in industries, policy makers and scholars around the world have, since the early-1980s, used a statistical measure developed by two economists. The Hirfindal–Hirschman index (HH-I) measures owner concentration. Its use became widespread after the US Department of Justice and the Federal Reserve began using it to analyze the competitive effects of mergers. The higher points a market scores on the index, the more concentrated is its ownership, the lower the points and the more diverse the ownership. It is not perfect, but it provides a universally accepted method to measure market diversity.

By this measure, ownership concentration in all Hindi news and entertainment channels as well as English news channels in India is moderate and remains among the most diverse in the world. A 2008 study for the Ministry of Information and Broadcasting, which examined five language markets, found that the real problem was in Malayalam, Tamil and Telugu, which showed very high levels of concentration. The Malayalam TV industry was similar to the situation in Britain, but better than in Sweden, Germany, Italy and Ireland. Tamil news and Telugu entertainment were undoubtedly among the most concentrated globally, but Tamil entertainment appeared fairly diverse. The Telugu news TV industry is similar to Britain, Sweden and France—at least by these standards. Data for other Indian languages are not available but seeing the available Indian figures side-by-side with international comparisons provides the perspective (Figure 3.2).

Yet statistical analysis of this kind provides at best an incomplete and at worst a misleading picture. To understand this, we must turn to the third key feature of Indian television: news television. The trends in the business of news TV are remarkably different from those in the larger entertainment industry.

"I Must Have Been Crazy": The News, with Politicians, Builders and Businessmen

In 1999, the then-ruling Left Front government of West Bengal wrote to the Ministry of Information and Broadcasting in Delhi asking for permission to set up a TV channel. The request was rejected on two very sensible grounds. The first was the Supreme Court judgement of 1995 which had freed the airwaves from government control, arguing that "government control in effect means the control of the political party or parties in power for the time being" and was bound to colour

Figure 3.2:
Problem yes, but not so bad after all: How TV ownership concentration in five Indian languages compares internationally (H–I index: Less is good)

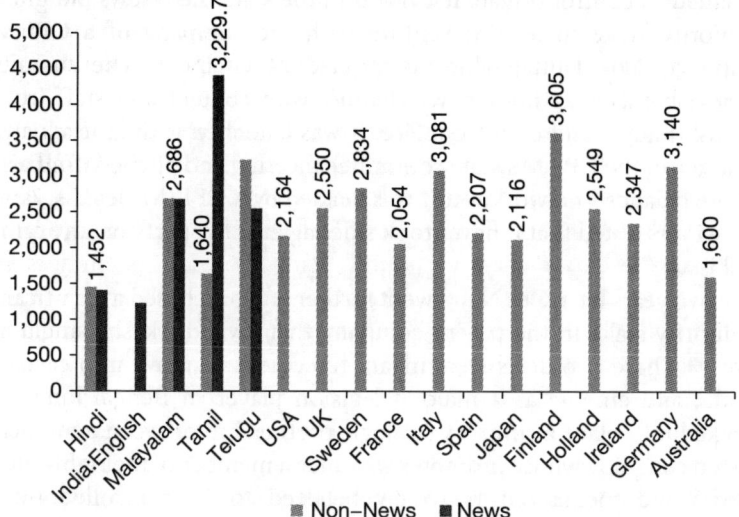

■ Non–News   ■ News

Sources: Indian figures from report for Ministry of Information and Broadcasting by Administrative Staff College of India, *Study on Cross Media Ownership in India: Draft Report.* International figures from Elie Noam, *Media Ownership and Concentration in America.*

free expression. Second, such a propaganda channel would distort the level playing field between political parties and third it would have opened "a Pandora's box" of various public-funded bodies and political parties wanting their own personal channels.[19]

The official request may have been denied but the Communist Party of India-Marxist (CPI-M) was not to be thwarted. If it was to be denied a government-owned TV channel, it would get a party-controlled one. Just before the 2001 assembly election, Akash Bangla was launched with funds from city businessmen and with the CPI-M's media face Avik Dutta as its Managing Director. The idea reportedly came from Anil Biswas, the late party secretary in West Bengal, and Akash Bangla started life as the first politically-coloured TV network in the state.[20] But the story soon got even more interesting.

By 2006, Zee News, looking to shore up its expansion into eastern India, decided to join hands with the avowedly CPI-M men who seemed to control private television in the state. Zee News bought a majority stake in a joint venture with the company of a CPI-M support, Avik Dutta, which controlled 24 Ghanta.[21] The channel began life as a 24-hour news channel with content and staff from Akash Bangla and cash from Zee. It was launched with an exclusive telecast of the CPI-M's state committee meeting and pitched itself as a more balanced network, yet it was headed by a CPI (M) loyalist, and observers noted that it never took sides against the party on any critical issue.[22]

Two years later, Zee News went further and purchased a significant minority stake in the parent company that owned Akash Bangla as well.[23] These two deals were meant to cement its move into eastern India and emerge as a major television player in Bengal but also locked into place a complex strategic partnership between a publicly listed company whose promoter was once a member of the right-wing RSS[24] and media outfits widely believed to be controlled by a Communist Party.

Zee's business moves were not ideological. These were tactical alliances to further its viewing reach, irrespective of the politics of its news partners. The best illustration of this is the story of Zee in Andhra Pradesh, where it entered into yet another politically loaded deal, this time with a Congress leader. Plagued by losses in its Telugu news channel, Zee Ghantalu, the company announced in August 2012 that it was closing it down. Channel officials pointedly told journalists that Ghantalu would be shut down because its 14 competitors in the state were "politically driven" and it did "not make sense to continue" in such a market.[25] Yet within weeks, newspapers were reporting that a deal had been struck. Instead of closing down, Zee would sell a major share in the channel to the family of the president of the Andhra Pradesh wing of the Congress Party, Botcha Satyanarayana. The minister confirmed that his brother, a cable operator, would buy a controlling stake and assume control, while Zee would retain a minority share.[26]

These alliances were typical of the way business houses operating in the TV space functioned, given the subtle political influence exercised at ground level by local political leaders. These were only micro-examples, and more benign ones at that, of larger trends within the news industry.

A New Indian Power Elite:
Who Owns the News and Why?

As a genre, news attracts less than 10 per cent of viewership in India and only about 16–17 per cent of advertising.[27] Yet more than half of the over 877 licensed TV channels in the country are news channels, and one-third of these beam 24-hour news.[28] This is a bizarrely high ratio compared to other countries. It is especially so when everyone in the industry agreed that news channels had turned into financial black-holes and enjoy a negligible market share. Yet news channels kept getting launched and money pumped into them.

Hardly any news channel in India made money. With the exception of a handful of channels, most news channels had never made money across their whole life cycles. Financially, the business of TV news was so broken in 2013 that if you invested your money in a fixed deposit, you would get a better return than if you invested it in a news channel. As film-maker Prakash Jha, who started Maurya TV in Bihar, told an interviewer, "I was crazy to have entered the media business. It was the love for my state that inspired me to launch the channel. But I am bleeding right now. My revenues don't even cover one-third of the cost of running it."[29]

Three kinds of people have been major investors in news television in the past decade: politicians, real estate, chit fund and money market companies and large corporations. These three categories now have deep stakes in the majority of the news TV business in most Indian states. My research shows that between them such companies make up over 80 per cent of the news TV business in Andhra, Karnataka and Odisha and between 60–70 per cent in Punjab, Maharashtra, West Bengal, Tamil Nadu and the North-East (Table 3.2). A decade ago, only a handful of states like Tamil Nadu had channels like Sun TV or Jaya TV, which were set up as propaganda arms of rival political parties. By 2013, this was the norm across India.

Politicians got into the television business for obvious reasons: to gain a platform to relay their messages to voters. In Andhra Pradesh, only 2–3 of the 14 news channels are not controlled by politicians or their proxies. The growth in news was not driven by companies looking to create new platforms for serious coverage but by power players looking to spread their own propaganda and views. From Sakshi TV

Table 3.2:
Television news companies owned by politicians, corporations and real estate/ chit fund/personal-finance companies in selected regions and language areas

Region	Language	Percentage
Odisha	Oriya	90
Former Andhra Pradesh	Telugu	83
Karnataka	Kannada	82
Maharashtra	Marathi	70
Tamil Nadu	Tamil	66
West Bengal	Bengali	60–65
Northeastern states	Assamese, Manipuri, Mizo	60–65
Kerala	Malayalam	56
Punjab	Punjabi, Hindi	60
North Indian states	Hindi	40

Note on sources: The calculations are based on the Ministry of Information and Broadcasting records, publicly available information on listed TV companies, media reports and industry interviews in select states. The numbers were accurate in January 2013. There are limitations in such calculations because of the opacity of data on non-listed companies, but interviews confirm that the numbers reflect an accurate picture of ownership trends.

of Jagan Reddy of the YSR Congress to Captain TV of the Tamil actor Vijaykanth, it was almost an unwritten rule for new entrants on the political stage to announce their arrival by launching their own TV channel.

By itself, this should not necessarily be a problem. Politicians have a right to free speech, and in theory at least, various propaganda voices should cancel each other out. The trouble, however, was two-fold. First, this trend loaded the democratic field in favour of those with access to big, under-the-table funding and crowded out less wealthy players. Second, the easy money that politicians brought into the game distorted the market and drove out all serious, neutral players. In a market where virtually no one made money anyway, the arrival of new rivals rich with cash and with no need to make money squeezed out genuine players or forced them to make dubious alliances to survive. This partly explained some of the alliances made by Zee. This also explained why institutional investors, with no political axe to grind, were reluctant to invest in news television. As one heavy investor in news TV in Andhra Pradesh told a newspaper reporter,

"What began as an opportunity has become a liability. There are too many news channels in the market, mostly run in an unprofessional manner by owners who have interests beyond media."[30] And there was, of course, the question of what happened to news when "politicians convert the newsroom into their party office," as one news editor put it?[31]

One of the most under-analyzed ways through which politicians control the news is by controlling cable operators. States like Chhattisgarh and Punjab have evolved their own model where television is controlled by the ruling party through its own private TV networks, as well as a cartelization of the cable industry. In Chhattisgarh, for example, broadcast journalists encountered a peculiar kind of censorship during the run-up to the state's first election in 2003. Every time any of the news channels broadcast a news item that was even mildly critical of the then chief minister Ajit Jogi, it was blanked from the air. Chhattisgarh viewers watching that particular broadcast would suddenly find their television sets going blank and the pictures would return only 15 minutes or so after the offending news story was over. This unannounced censorship would happen only within the territorial boundaries of Chhattisgarh; television viewers in the rest of India did not encounter this problem. This was because supporters of the Chief Minister had set up a state-wide private television network—Akash (Sky) TV—that bought over, or took control of, cable distribution networks across Chhattisgarh, and this provided an easy mechanism for controlling the broadcast of national news channels within the state's borders. The national networks could be turned off each time their product did not suit the ruling establishment. It was an ingenious form of censorship: it wasn't officially announced, it technically did not come from the state and there was nothing any of the channels could do about it.[32] The uses, or misuses, of Akash Television became an important part of the BJP's electoral campaign against Jogi in 2003 and within hours of his losing power on December 4, its television studios were taken over by a triumphant crowd of the party's supporters.[33]

Similarly, in Punjab, the ruling Badal family on returning to power in 2007 started their own PTC television network (owned through a complex web of companies) and took control of cable companies which distributed television.[34] In August 2007, the Cable Operators Federation of India complained to the Ministry of Information and

Broadcasting of physical threats and arrests of cable operators in the state. Similar to Jogi in Chhattisgarh, Sukhbir Singh Badal [President, Akali Dal] denied the charges; but the parallels were undeniable.

Before the Akalis came to power, the Congress Chief Minister Amarinder Singh had patronized the Punjab Today channel. Within hours of his losing the election in 2007, this channel went into oblivion, and many cable operators in the state were forced to replace it with the new Akali-friendly channel PTC on their prime frequencies.[35] Detractors complained that any channel that broadcast anti-Badal stories would be blanked out. As one cable operator from Patiala said after being released from prison on charges of violence, "This is state terror being used against us and the police are being used freely and scores of false cases are being filed."[36]

In middle of 2013, when the Managing Editor of the Punjab news channel Day and Night News resigned, he publicly blamed his channel's financial problems on a "powerful political entity in Punjab," which aimed at snuffing out "fair and free journalism". In a speech to his employees on YouTube, he sarcastically congratulated the politicians and "a group of news and entertainment channels... behind the cartel that controls the cable network in Punjab" for succeeding in driving them out. In his view, Day and Night News failed financially because the dominant cable company in the state, Fastway, which controlled 95 per cent of subscribers, had been "abusing its dominance to deny us access to the Punjab market."[37] This was not an empty accusation: it was upheld by the Competition Commission of India, which a year earlier had imposed a hefty fine on the cable network for denying access to Day and Night News.[38] Yet the end result was that the news channel was driven to the ground.

Power and television were intrinsically combined in this Punjab model. The PTC network became popular not just by forcing cable operators to relay it, but by suddenly getting the rights to broadcast live daily *gurbani* from the Golden Temple. These rights had been sold to another channel, ETC Punjabi, for 11 years but were transferred in a deal with PTC overnight once the Akali Dal came to power.[39] Along with this, despite being so new, PTC received a large amount of state advertising—₹78 lakh in its first year of operations—from a government controlled by the Badal family. Badal denied allegations of favouritism, but other channels seem to have got similar amounts only over a five-year period. The Competition Commission of India ultimately registered a case against the cartelization, calling it an "unfair trade practise." Similarly, there were over 20 cases being examined by TDSAT and TRAI.[40] Yet Congress accusations against the Akalis of cable control rang hollow, as they had done the same thing when in power.

India is not the only country where television censorship has been practised indirectly through control of cable distribution networks. It is widely documented that during the civil rights protests of the 1960s in the American south, most of the local press and television stations did not report the news of protests against racism accurately because of their owners' opposition to racial desegregation. They would often ignore coverage of the civil rights movement and sometimes black out—citing technical problems—telecasts by the national networks that focussed on the issue.[41] The best example is that of the local television station WLBT in Jackson, Mississippi, which would occasionally interrupt the NBC's national flagship news programme, the Huntley Brinkley Report, when it was covering civil rights. Sometimes, prior to news reports on the Today Show, a WLBT announcer would warn, "What you are about to see is an example of biased, managed Northern news. Be sure to stay tuned at seven twenty-five to hear your local newscast"—which would either not include the undesirable news about the civil rights protests or present a WLBT version.[42]

The case of politicians being in television is simple enough: a voice for their political interests. But it is the capture of news television by big businesses and real-estate and chit fund kinds of financiers that complicates the picture far more. Their dominance of the news space and the influence it gives them tells us a great deal about the new power structures of India. There is nothing abnormal about businesses owning the news: business houses and news have been intertwined the world over. Within India itself, some of the biggest newspapers have been owned by industrial barons with deep pockets and multiple interests in other sectors—the Birlas with *Hindustan Times*, the Jains with *Times of India*, the Goenkas with the *Indian Express* and so on. What is striking is the kind of businesses that began to get into TV news in India and their similarities.

The first variety includes companies with interests in real estate: construction, housing development, hotels and infrastructure. A large number also run chit funds and collective investment schemes.[43] These are businesses which require a great deal of political patronage, as anything to do with land in India does, and also generate a great deal of black money. "*Ab to builder chala rahe hai news channels* [builders are running news channels now]," said Arun Jaitley, a senior BJP leader and then the leader of the Opposition in the upper house of parliament. This has serious implications for what the channels actually show. As Jaitley observed:

> The economic model of news channels is still not adequate. Therefore— barring a few channels, or some channels which have a very large regional base, and a handful of national channels—news channels per se are not a profitable business. In fact most of them are making losses. That compulsion is pushing the concept of paid news and some recent cases are far more disturbing than even paid news.[44]

For many of these channels, the boundaries between them and politics are often so porous that they are almost impossible to map. "A news channel is a useful asset. It brings influence and access, and opens doors in politics and in government," says one senior television manager. "A news channel is relatively cheap to launch, can further your business interests and also give you bragging rights."[45]

With technology getting cheaper, it is possible to set up a basic channel with capital expenditure of 50–60 lakh (excluding license fees) and run it on a shoestring budget of 1.5–2.5 crores annually. Of course, serious news channels cost a great deal more to run—some more than 20 times as much. But these are average running costs of many functional news channels in Punjab, for example. "It is that cheap," says one channel head.

For many businessmen, the driving force seems to be ego as much as political influence. As one consultant who specializes in setting up these small regional channels said,

> Many of these investors have a *keera* [an itch or bee in the bonnet]. They are all dying with ego [sic]. It is not much money and they run a news channel like this for 2-3 years, finish their *shauk* [hobby], then sell it forward to the next guy. It also brings them many other benefits in their business, like in real estate.

The cost-dynamics are entirely different in south India, where production values are generally higher and average capital expenditure on launching a small news channel can be anything between 10–50 crore (not counting licenses) and average annual running costs estimated to be well over 20 crores.[46] Much like the politicians, people invest in the news business because they see it as a tool for furthering their other interests. As one senior executive who headed a TV channel launched by a real estate company said,

> Soon after I joined, there were elections in Uttar Pradesh. I was busy launching our channel in north India but found that my owner was doing all kinds of deals with candidates about coverage and a lot of money was flowing in without any accounting. They were even going to launch an IPO and I had to sign some papers. I showed to my lawyer first, and he said, if you don't want to go to jail, don't sign this. I resigned the next day.[47]

The second category includes large corporate companies. The most striking example was the deal that gave India's largest corporate entity, Reliance Industries Limited, ownership of one of the country's largest regional language news enterprises, Eenadu TV, and Network18—and its subsidiary TV18—the listed entity which controls channels such as CNBC-TV18, CNBC Awaaz, CNN-IBN, IBN7 and IBN-Lokmat.[48] In effect, it initially combined two major media groups to create what many thought was India's largest media conglomerate.[49] It was initially forged by Reliance money through a complex financial arrangement that was permissible under the rules but raised a great deal of speculation. Eventually by mid-2014, Reliance took full management control of Network18 by converting its optional debentures into equity shares. The fact that Reliance, India's biggest corporate entity, had moved into the news space in 2008 by investing in the country's largest regional news networks, remained hidden from public view at first. Early information came into the public domain when the widow of former Andhra Pradesh chief minister Y.S.R. Reddy filed a petition in the Andhra High Court in October 2011 seeking a probe into the assets of a former chief minister of Andhra Pradesh, N. Chandrababu Naidu. It was alleged that Mukesh Ambani of Reliance had come to the rescue of a Naidu backer and local media owner who had run into financial difficulties.[50] Reliance denied any wrong-doing,[51] and in January 2012 put out a press release which for the first time detailed the financial structuring that gave Reliance a remarkable presence in media. Ambani became, in the words of *India Today,* a "new media mogul."[52]

Mukesh Ambani's acquisition of a big share in the TV news market—ostensibly to gain content for Reliance's mobile phone service Jio—was not the only manifestation of a wider trend. In May 2012, another major Indian conglomerate with deep interests in telecom, the Aditya Birla Group, announced that it was acquiring a 27.5 per cent stake in Living Media India Limited,[53] the company which runs the India Today Group, including several channels such as Aaj Tak and Headlines Today. In this case, though, full control remained in the hands of India Today chairman Aroon Purie. Similarly, in December 2011, Oswal Green Tech acquired a 14.17 per cent shareholding in New Delhi Television in two separate deals from the investment arms of Merrill Lynch and Nomura Capital.[54]

In 1956, C. Wright Mills argued in his classic *The Power Elite* that a small social class of influential people was taking over the key institutional "command posts" of American society, the places where the decisions are made and which have the most direct influence on the course of events in society. Arguing that the power of wealth was not nearly as important as the "institutional powers of wealth," Mills showed that a small coalition of big businessmen and ascendant military men had come to control the levers of power in the American social system with no effective counterweight.[55] The key insight of this argument was that the idea of democracy, where different viewpoints competed in the marketplace of ideas and the best argument eventually won, was more a fairy tale than a useful approximation.[56]

India in the twenty-first century is a very different place from the United States of the 1950s, but the example of news television shows us that we may be seeing a similar move on to the strategic command posts of society. Such a move came from politicians and businesses with interests in real estate, chit funds or personal finance schemes. News TV channels have emerged as vital platforms and crossroads of Indian society and one of its most influential lightning rods in the public sphere. The power elite that emerged in the 1990s understood this and staked a claim to this powerful social lever.

A new media-industrial complex was coming into being, somewhat like the military-industrial complex that emerged in the United States in the 1950s. The structure of the news TV business changed in the first decade of the twenty-first century. It led to a furious public debate about media ownership, regulation and content with various bodies like the Telecom Regulatory Authority of India, the Law Commission and various ministries weighing in with their own views on what should be done. Most of these founder on the question of whether old regulations based on traditional categories of print, television and Internet remain relevant in the age of convergence and the mobile phone. The debate is far from resolved, and the past experience shows that it is difficult to trust governmental bodies—of any ideological persuasion—to be neutral arbiters on media matters. One thing though is certain: media plurality remains the best defence against media capture. As Mao said, let a hundred flowers bloom, let a hundred schools of thought contend.

Notes

1. S. Gupta, "Stop Fighting the 1962 War," 19 September 2009, *The Indian Express* (internet), http://www.indianexpress.com/news/stop-fighting-the-1962-war/518975/0 (accessed 20 September 2009).

2. China Foreign Ministry, Spokesperson Jiang Yu's Regular Press Conference on 15 September 2009. http://www.fmprc.gov.cn/eng/xwfw/s2510/t584510.htm (accessed 20 September 2009).

3. CNN-IBN, "NSA Says Media Hype on Chinese Intrusions Risky," (internet) 19 September 2009. http://ibnlive.in.com/news/nsa-says-media-hype-on-chinese-intrusions-risky/101741-3.html (accessed 19 September 2009).

4. B.V. Rao, 2009, "Madam Minister, Please Read the NBA's Unwritten Code of Collective Silence," 25 September. http://www.exchange4media.com/e4m/news/fullstory.asp?news_id=35997&section_id=6&pict=5&tag=31896

5. M. Wade, "Serious Damage as 'Racist Australia' Airs in India," 4 July 2009. *Sydney Morning Herald.* http://www.theage.com.au/world/serious-damage-as-racist-australia-airs-in-india-20090703-d7u4.html (accessed 30 September 2009).

6. B. Ghose, *Doordarshan Days* (New Delhi: Penguin/Viking, 2005).

7. Estimate is by Uday Shankar, CEO, Star India. Quoted in Tanna, "Invest in Innovation."

8. http://www.mib.nic.in/ShowContent.aspx?uid1=2&uid2=84&uid3=0&uid4=0&uid5=0&uid6=0&uid7=0 (accessed 6 December 2009).

9. I have detailed the reasons behind the remarkable rise of private Indian satellite television elsewhere. Mehta, *India on Television,* 2008.

10. Registrar General of India, *Projected and Actual Population of India.*

11. India had 34,858,000 TV sets in 1992. S. R. Joshi and Bela Trivedi, *Mass Media and Cross Cultural Communication: A Study of Television in India* (New Delhi: Development and Educational Communication Unit Indian Space Research Organisation, 1994), p. 16.

12. There were estimated to be 120 million TV sets in India by 2011. The population had gone up to 1.2 billion according to the 2011 Census.

13. The National Readership Survey 2006 estimated 112 million TV sets in the country. Industry estimates currently place the number of TV sets at 120 million. Telecom Regulatory Authority of India, *Consultation Paper on Policy Guidelines*, p. 5.

14. Pricewaterhouse Cooopers, *The Indian Entertainment Industry*, 36.

15. In October 2012, Star TV broadcast 17 channels, Viacom 6, Sony 9, Sun Network 21 and the Zee Network 38. This is a total of 91 which is 31 per cent of the 831 channels officially licensed at the time. This figure does not include the news channels controlled by Network 18.

16. *Hindu Business Line*, "Sony Ventures South; Picks 30% Stake in MAA TV," 9 April 2012.

17. Eli Noam, *Media Ownership and Concentration in America* (New York: Oxford University Press, 2009), p. 101.

18. Data from TAM, compiled and supplied by R. Padmasri, Star TV.

19. Ministry of Information and Broadcasting, "Background Note on Permitting State Governments to Enter into Broadcast Activities," reproduced in Annexure A, TRAI, *Consultation Paper on Issues Relating to Entry of Certain Entities into Broadcasting and Distribution Activities* (New Delhi: TRAI, 25 February 2008), p. 52.

20. *The Indian Express*, "The Party Live," 23 May 2007. http://www.indianexpress.com/news/the-party-live/31596/0 (accessed 25 October 2012). Also see http://thehoot.org/web/Politics-and-media-control/6047-1-1-2-true.html (accessed 19 October 2012).

21. The channel was launched on 1 April 2006. Zee owned 60% of the joint venture, Zee Akaash News Private Ltd. *Zee News Annual Report, 2009–10*, p. 28.

22. *The Indian Express*, "The Party Live," 23 May 2007. http://www.indianexpress.com/news/the-party-live/31596/0 (accessed 25 October 2012).

23. In 2008, Zee News reported to the Bombay Stock Exchange that it had bought a 26% stake in Sky B (Bangla) Pvt. Ltd., the company that runs Akash Bangla. The company reported a 12.8% stake in 2009 and a 16% stake in Sky B (Bangla) in 2012. 2008 figures from: http://www.nseindia.com/marketinfo/companyinfo/eod/announcements.jsp?symbol=ZEENEWS and *Business Standard*, "Zee News India acquires 26% stake in Sky B," 1 November 2008, http://www.business-standard.com/india/news/zee-news-india-acquires-26-stake-in-sky-b/48693/on (accessed 4 November 2012). 2009 figures from *Zee News Limited Unaudited Final Results 2009–10*, pp. 1 and 2012 figures from "Zee News Ltd's Q4 Ebitda stays strong, slips into net loss due to Akash Bangla," 17 May 2012, http://www.indiantelevision.com/headlines/y2k12/may/may138.php (accessed 18 May 2012).

24. Zee TV's founder and Chairman Subhash Chandra has often publicly talked about being a RSS swayamsevak and spoke as an honoured guest at at least one high-profile RSS gathering near Agra when the Vajpayee-led NDA

government was in power. For his assertions on being a swayamsevak in his youth see for instance, Vidyottama Sharma, "Zee's back with good, bold shows: Subhash Chandra," *The Economic Times*, 2 August 2003, http://articles.economictimes.indiatimes.com/2003-08-02/news/27529728_1_subhash-chandra-trendz-nri-status.

25. Zee News announced on 18 August 2012 that the channel would close by 20 September. Indiantelevision.com, "Zee News Ltd to Shutter Telugu News Channel," 28 August 2012 http://www.indiantelevision.com/headlines/y2k12/aug/aug232.php

26. The Congress minister's brother Satish Narayan runs Citivision a cable operating company. "AP Minister's Family May Take over Zee Telugu News Channel," *Business Standard*, 12 September 2012, http://www.business-standard.com/india/news/ap-ministers-family-may-take-over-zee-telugu-news-channel/486137/ (accessed 30 September 2012).

27. FICCI-KPMG, *Hitting the High Notes: FICCI-KPMG Indian Media and Entertainment Industry Report 2010–11*, p. 20.

28. Of the 877 channels, licenses were cancelled for 61 in 2013 by the Ministry of Information and Broadcasting due to non-fulfilment of license conditions. Data on channels from Ministry of Information and Broadcasting. Information on cancellations from "Ministry Cancels License of 61 Channels," *Cablequest*, 28 June 2013, http://www.cablequest.org/news/government-news/item/2680-ministry-cancels-license-of-61-tv-channels.html.

29. Quoted in Archana Shukla, "We also Make TV News," *The Indian Express*, 19 August 2012.

30. Ibid.

31. Mahendra Mishra, TV 9 Karnataka and News 9 Director in http://www.indiantelevision.com/special/y2k12/Mahendra_Mishra_yearender.htm

32. Interview with Sanjeev Singh, Principal Correspondent, STAR News. New Delhi: 25 January 2004.

33. Interview with Sanjeev Singh.

34. The PTC channels are owned by Gur-Baz Media Pvt. Ltd and G-Next Media Pvt. Ltd. Both companies are wholly owned subsidiary companies of Orbit Resorts Pvt Ltd. However, according to his lawyers in the Punjab High Court, Sukhbir Singh Badal is neither a shareholder nor a director in the media companies but has substantial shareholding in Orbit Resorts Pvt Ltd. See reporting by Raman Kirpal, "Not on TRP Radar, Yet Govt Windfall for Badal Family Channel," 20 January 2012. http://www.firstpost.com/politics/not-on-trp-radar-yet-govt-ad-windfall-for-badal-family-channel-188878.html (accessed 30 January 2012). Also see Raman Kirpal, "Punjab CM's Family in Higher Orbit," 19 January 2012, http://www.firstpost.com/politics/badal-inc-how-punjab-first-familys-wealth-moved-to-a-higher-orbit-187252.html.

35. Interview with a senior TV consultant in Punjab who has worked with several TV networks but declined to be named.

36. Sujit Chakrabarty, "Akali Dal Accused of 'State Terror' on Cable Ops in Punjab," 8 August 2007, http://www.indiantelevision.com/headlines/y2k7/aug/aug105.php (accessed 9 August 2007).

37. Quoted in Chander Suta Dogra, "TV Channels under Political Squeeze, Managing Editor Quits," *Hindu*, 5 August 2013, http://www.thehindu.com/news/national/other-states/tv-channel-under-political-squeeze-managing-editor-quits/article4989567.ece (accessed 1 September 2013).

38. Abida Hasan, "Fastway Transmissions to Pay Penalty of ₹8.40 cr to CCI," 5 July 2012, http://www.exchange4media.com/47106_fastway-transmissions-to-pay-penalty-of-rs-8-40-cr-to-cci.html (accessed 5 September 2013).

39. Express News Service, "Ahead of Polls, Cong 'Proves' Ownership of Badals in PTC," 4 October 2011, *The Indian Express*.

40. Raman Kirpal, "Not on TRP Radar, Yet Govt Windfall for Badal Family Channel," 20 January 2012. http://www.firstpost.com/politics/not-on-trp-radar-yet-govt-ad-windfall-for-badal-family-channel-188878.html (accessed 30 January 2012).

41. Robert J. Donovan and Ray Scherer, *Unsilent Revolution: Television News and American Public Life, 1948–1991* (Cambridge: Cambridge University Press, 1992), pp. 7–9. Also see an excellent account of the politics of the media in the civil rights disturbances of 1960s America by the veteran journalists Gene Roberts, Hank Klibanoff in the *Race Beat, The Press, the Civil Rights Struggle, and the Awakening of a Nation* (New York: Alfred A. Knopf, 2006).

42. Fred W. Friendly, *The Good Guys, the Bad Guys and the First Amendment: Free Speech Versus Fairness in Broadcasting* (New York: Random House, 1975), p. 91.

43. Also see, Archana Shukla, "We Also Make TV News," *The Indian Express*, 19 August 2012 and "News, Uninterrupted" 8 November 2009, *The Indian Express*.

44. Interview with Arun Jaitley, senior BJP leader, 21 October 2012.

45. Interview with a senior TV consultant who has launched several regional TV networks but declined to be named.

46. Ibid.

47. Interview with the senior executive who now runs a national TV news network. He declined to be named.

48. Network18 is a media company promoted by Raghav Bahl. Through its subsidiary TV18 Broadcast Ltd the group operates news channels—CNBC-TV18, CNBC Awaaz, CNBC-TV18 Prime HD, CNN-IBN, IBN7 and IBN-Lokmat (a Marathi regional news channel in partnership with the Lokmat group). TV18 also operates a joint venture with Viacom, called Viacom18, which houses a portfolio of popular entertainment channels—Colors, Colors HD, MTV, SONIC, Comedy Central, VH1, Nick. Nick Jr. and Nick Teen—and Viacom18 Motion Pictures, the group's filmed entertainment business. TV18 also operates HistoryTV18 in a joint venture with A+E

Networks. TV18 and Viacom18 have also formed a strategic joint venture called IndiaCast, to drive domestic and international channels distribution, placement services and content syndication. Through Network18 Media & Investments Ltd., the group operates its digital, publishing and e-commerce assets including moneycontrol.com, ibnlive.com, in.com and firstpost.com. "Network18" also operates e-commerce properties like HomeShop18 and bookmyshow.com and publishes Forbes India, in collaboration with Forbes Media. http://network18online.com/ (accessed 5 September 2013).

49. In an article in the *Economic and Political Weekly*, the journalists Paranjoy Guha Thakurta and Subi Chaturvedi argued that this combined new entity would be larger than the Rupert Murdoch-controlled Star TV and the Bennett and Coleman Company that controls the Times of India Group. Paranjoy Guha Thakurta and Subi Chaturvedi, "Corporatisation of the Media: Implications of the RILK-Network18-Eenadu Deal," *EPW*, 47, no. 7 (18 February 2012) 10–13.

50. Anusha Subramaniam, "Bailout Saga," *Business Today*, 5 February 2012, http://businesstoday.intoday.in/story/ril-network18-deal-conversion/1/21776.html

51. Thakurta and Chaturvedi, "Corporatisation of the Media," pp. 10–13.

52. Sandeep Bamzai, "A Network of Reliance," *India Today*, 14 January 2012, http://indiatoday.intoday.in/story/bailout-for-raghav-bahl-network-18-signals-mukesh-ambani-willing-to-bet-big-money-on-media/1/168680.html (accessed 1 September 2013).

53. Aditya Birla Group Press Release, "Aditya Birla Group to invest in Living Media India," 18 May 2012. Retrieved from http://www.adityabirla.com/media/press_releases/Living-Media-India

54. Thakurta and Chaturvedi, "Corporatisation of the Media," p. 12.

55. C. Wright Mills, *The Power Elite* (New York: OUP, 1956). Also see review by Rudolf E. Morris, *The American Catholic Sociological Review*, 17, no. 3 (October 1956): 255–256. Talcott Parsons, "The Distribution of Power in American Society," *World Politics*, 10, no. 1 (October 1957): 123–212.

56. C. Wright Mills, "The Structure of Power in American Society," *The British Journal of Sociology*, 9, no. 1 (March 1958): 39–40.

4

China's Cultural War against the West*

Ying Zhu

Ying Zhu is a leading scholar on Chinese cinema and media studies. She has published eight books, including *Two Billion Eyes: The Story of China Central Television*. Her writings have appeared in leading academic journals, edited book volumes and journalistic publications such as the *Atlantic*, *Foreign Policy*, the *Los Angeles Times*, the *New York Times*, the *Wall Street Journal*, ChinaFile and CNN. Her works have been translated into Chinese, Dutch, French, Italian and Spanish. Zhu is a recipient of a National Endowment for the Humanities Fellowship (2006) and an American Council of Learned Societies Fellowship (2008). Zhu also produces current affairs documentary films, including *Google vs. China* (2011, with the Netherlands National TV) and *China: From Cartier to Confucius* (2012, with the Netherlands National TV).

In July 2014, Chinese media reported that the State Administration of Press, Publication, Radio, Film and Television (SAPPRFT) had been considering a plan to impose a quota system on the licensing of imported programmes by popular Chinese video websites such as Sohu, Youku Tudou and Tencent[1] which collectively stream about 400

---

* Parts of this chapter appeared in several short online opinion pieces: "How U.S. Soft Power Won the Chinese Box Office," *Foreign Policy* (accessed 6 September 2014): http://www.foreignpolicy.com/articles/2014/09/06/how_us_soft_power_won_chinas_box_office_transformers_4_hollywood; "After 'Big Bang Theory' Censorship, No Mass Viewer Revolt," *Wall Street Journal* (19 May 2014) http://blogs.wsj.com/chinarealtime/2014/05/19/after-big-bang-theory-censorship-no-mass-viewer-revolt/; "Why Frank Underwood is Great for China's Soft Power," ChinaFile (27 February 2014) https://www.chinafile.com/Frank-Underwood-Great-Chinas-Soft-Power

American and British TV shows including *Sherlock* and *The Vampire Diaries*. Rumor started to circulate in China since October 2014 that SAPPRFT was mulling over whether to follow the movie-import system by applying a quota system to TV shows. The bread-and-butter impact of such a policy could be devastating to Chinese video websites as imported programmes have been their major attractions among the well-educated young audiences, the core web users. Sohu, for one, is known for licensing popular US TV shows in the likes of *House of Cards*, *Saturday Night Live* and *The Ellen DeGeneres Show*. It is also home to, until recently, the most popular show among the Chinese viewers, *The Big Bang Theory*, which was banned in April 2014, together with *The Good Wife*, *NCIS* and *The Practice*.

The ban in April left Western media abuzz and China watchers scratching their heads. After all, the banned TV shows pale in their depictions of violence, sex and/or political scandal when compared to other foreign shows that can still be streamed online on Sohu. *House of Cards*, for example, is by far the most transgressive when it comes to violence and scandal, yet it has so far evaded the honour of being banned.[2] But for those who have followed the moves of China's censors more closely, the ban should not come as a surprise. In March 2014, SAPPRFT reissued two Internet content regulation notices that it had previously rolled out, which aimed to root out excessive violence and sex in online programming. Though the online content guidelines were mostly targeted at domestic programming, Chinese social media users quickly voiced concerns that their access to the US shows might be next to be jeopardized. The media backlash against a speculated ban was clear in an online poll conducted by Sina in March in which more than 130,000 respondents—or 95 per cent of those polled—voted against banning the US TV dramas, which prompted the government to explicitly state that the regulations would not apply to foreign programmes. However, the regulator's inaction on foreign exports agitated domestic content providers, who appealed to censors for equal treatment so that they could better compete with foreign content providers. Foreign TV shows are viewed as a threat to state-owned broadcasters who have seen new media undermine their revenue streams. It is a further threat to the Chinese Communist Party (CCP) which is wary of Western culture influence. From March 2014, authorities required that US and UK shows obtain approval from censors before they were posted on video streaming sites. In April, Chinese President Xi Jinping launched a campaign to rid Internet of porn, rumours and other unruly contents, domestic and imported, which soon precipitated the ban of four US TV dramas. At the same time, a sanitized version of *The Big Bang Theory* was scheduled to run on China Central Television, the state-run TV network with close financial ties to SAPPRTF.

This chapter teases out the political economy of China's culture war against the West by tracing China's recent incidents of backlash against Western cultural and entertainment products. I argue that the battle against the West initially launched on political and ideological grounds has been complicated by an all-encompassing market force. The patronage between the party and the state-run enterprises means that they more often than not act in unison to protect their mutual interest in keeping the masses and profits on a short leash. So, while fending off Western culture influence, the battle is fought on the home turf, between the privately owned new media and the state-controlled broadcast media, both vying for preferential policies from the state. Meanwhile, the West continues to serve as a punching bag and a convenient archenemy for the CCP to rally popular support against in the name of patriotism.

On the Home Turf

The ban of four US TV shows in April 2014 caused a stir among the shows' loyal Chinese followers who took to social media to openly mock and ridicule censors.[3] Western media too responded with the usual hysteria, speculating a harsher time down the road. The outpouring of disbelief and outrage from both sides recalled another incident three years ago, when censors removed *Avatar* from China's 2D theatres to make room for China's heavily promoted domestic film, *Confucius*. Chinese fans rose to Hollywood's defense, publicly snubbing *Confucius*.

Pulling the 2D version of *Avatar* to make way for *Confucius* was not quite the overanxious political move that was commonly perceived by Chinese audiences and Western media, which suggested that the state removed *Avatar* because it felt threatened by the film's anti-violence theme that promoted ethnic freedom and autonomy. In fact, it was unusual for a Hollywood blockbuster to secure a release window so close to the Chinese New Year holiday, which was normally reserved for major domestic releases. So, ending *Avatar's* run about a week ahead of the holiday's start was more or less according to the usual practice. Nevertheless, the state's action was so abrupt, and the film was so popular, that audiences were considerably miffed. Miffed and moved to action, going online and on social media sites in huge numbers to express their passion for the blue people of Pandora and against poor Confucius.

The response was quick, widespread and intense. As *China Daily* reported, the backlash had unintended consequences—

> Amidst the outpouring of anger and frustration toward movie industry manipulations are the voices that point to the thoughts of Confucius as a negative force in Chinese history. The anti-Confucius sentiment runs counter to the State's trend of promoting Confucius and his teachings as a quintessentially Chinese alternative.[4]

The article went on to comment, facetiously, that

> what serious scholars could never [succeed] in demystifying, and whom former chairman Mao Zedong, Lu Xun and all the revolutionaries failed to topple from the pedestal, the film authorities did with one simple stroke— by throwing a boomerang at Pandora ... and instead hitting the man they had crowned with a halo.

The Chinese audiences had a key ally during that episode: the market. Many theatres driven by bottom-line considerations simply ignored the government's order to remove *Avatar*. The government eventually backed down, restoring *Avatar* to more screens.

Yet in April 2014, the outrage of Chinese fans over the ban of four US TV shows failed to bring the same victory. This time around, the Chinese fans were caught in a domestic market turf war. China's local content providers want to carve out a lion's share of the massive domestic online content market and to cultivate their own fans instead of siding with the fans of imported shows. According to a research cited by *The South China Morning Post*, revenue from online video was worth 12.8 billion Yuan ($2.07 billion) in 2013 and is expected to double by 2017.[5] The economic dimension of China's battle against Western and entertainment cultures adds complexity to the political and ideological dimension of control and censorship.

In October 2011, Chinese authorities banned scores of racy and overtly materialistic entertainment shows on prime time television. A Chinese dating show from Jiangsu Provincial Satellite TV, *If You Are the One*, is frequently cited as an example of "excessive entertainment."[6] In this programme, provocatively dressed young women publicly embrace materialism, opting for wealth and affluence over love and romance, all of which evidently defies traditional Chinese morality. This and similar reality shows featuring material girls and boys became a real eyesore for the party and cultural guardians. Beginning on 1 January 2012, the Chinese State Administration of Radio, Film and Television (SARFT) enacted a mandatory cap on the number and duration of entertainment shows that would be allowed during prime time (7:30 to 10:00 PM).[7] The order restricted the number of entertainment programmes that satellite channels can broadcast to two per week, with a maximum of 90 minutes of content defined as entertainment. Programmes promoting "traditional virtues and socialist core values" were encouraged. While Western reports of Chinese prime time TV's cultural cleansing focussed mostly on political and ideological control, a close look at the unique structure and control mechanism of Chinese television industry brings to light a more intricate economic tussle between the national and local broadcasters.

China has a so-called four-tier television structure in which TV stations are set up at the national, provincial, county and city levels. Both national and local regulators operate their own TV stations and serve audiences within their own administrative boundaries. Stations are expected to remit a percentage of their annual revenue to their respective regulators. So, the economic interest of state regulators is intricately linked to that of the broadcasters they purport to regulate, which leads to state control and monopoly, the foundation of the so-called China Model. As a result, television stations, broadcasting bureaus and governments at the same administrative level are closely linked in economic and political exchange—local TV stations depend on the local government to protect their local market. Meanwhile, local governments rely on television stations to maintain their political influence and to bring in financial revenue. China Central Television (CCTV) is the only broadcaster allowed nationwide coverage, although the arrival of cable and satellite TV complicated the neat structure.

The regulator overseeing CCTV is the State Administration of Radio-Film-TV (SARFT), which is now part of SAPPRFT. SARFT is motivated to maintain CCTV's monopoly for both political control and profit share. To ensure local support, SARFT mandated that local stations must carry CCTV-1's programmes in full, including commercials. SARFT emphasizes that guaranteeing CCTV-1's national coverage is a political mission, an "undeniable" obligation and responsibility of local broadcasting bureaus and television stations. CCTV is further granted exclusive coverage rights to major national and international events, and the CCP regularly leaks exclusive information to CCTV, making it the go-to source for insight on the party. In addition, CCTV has the exclusive coverage rights to national and international sports events, including the Olympics and the World Cup, which bring in huge profits.

SARFT has been consistently criticized for suppressing attempts by provincial TV stations to expand regionally and nationally, thereby securing the network's national monopoly. As the financial stakes grew huge, discontent over SARFT's preferential policies mounted among the local broadcasters, especially local satellite TV channels. In China, each provincial TV station is allowed to operate one satellite TV channel with signal coverage capable of reaching the entire nation technologically; yet because of the administrative boundaries and local protectionism, each provincial TV station must negotiate with other provinces to bring its satellite channel to their local cable networks. Most provincial broadcasters have managed to extend their regional reach via independent satellite and cable distribution deals with other provincial broadcasters. The youth and entertainment-oriented Hunan Satellite TV (HSTV), in particular, have become a formidable CCTV challenger in recent years. HSTV's *Super Girls*, a singing competition show modelled on *American Idol* with mobile phone voting became an overnight rating sensation when it debuted in 2004. Feeling the heat, CCTV launched a campaign to attack HSTV, calling it a rogue broadcaster with vulgar taste.

As I traced in *Two Billion Eyes: The Story of China Central Television*, the overnight sensation of a singing competition show, *Super Girls*, from a provincial TV station in 2004 sent a shockwave through CCTV's leadership, which promptly denounced the show as *a* "rogue programme" produced by "the rogue broadcaster." Feeling the heat for becoming increasingly irrelevant to the masses, especially the youth, it was mandated to reach and unify, CCTV aired a story in June 2005 to criticize the prevalence of entertainment shows modelled on foreign programmes and their detrimental impact on Chinese society. On 19 July 2005, CCTV sponsored a much publicized industry summit attended by top propaganda officials and television hosts from major broadcasters around the country. Three of its anchor hosts spoke at the summit and criticized *Super Girls* for being vulgar and condemned ratings as "the source of all evil." Wang Taihua, general director of SARFT, complained that there were too many low-quality and lowbrow reality shows that cater to the least common denominator and that the government must strengthen supervision of entertainment programmes and restrict the number of reality shows allowed on TV. CCTV pledged to adhere to its vocation of "spreading advanced culture" and "actively advocate mainstream values in line with the times." As CCTV condemned *Super Girls,* it aggressively launched its own talent quest show, *Dream China,* in 2005; but the show failed to generate the same sensation as *Super Girls.* In private, the network lobbied the central propaganda department to put a lid on Hunan STV. The SARFT eventually announced a ban on airing talent shows during prime time starting in October 2007. Under the new rules, the programmes must be no more than 90 minutes and offer no prizes to attract contestants.

After a year of siesta in 2008 when the Beijing Olympic Games preempted all other events, Hunan TV made an attempt to re-launch Super Girls under a different name, *Happy Girls,* in 2009. Hunan TV submitted to SARFT conditions that the show would only last for two months and each episode would air only after 10:30 PM. The draconian directives of the SARFT were astonishingly amusing: judges must hold themselves to some decorum; publicity revolving around the private lives of contestants was banned; and text-based and online voting systems were no longer allowed. Finally, competitors were forbidden from hugging each other or expressing extreme emotions on stage, and no fan groups were allowed to cheer for contestants in the studio.

The same pattern of political control and economic negotiation is reflected on recent tightening of internet programming, a result of the state-commerce cronyism rooted in China's TV and Internet structure in which the state agency regulating China's media industry is financially linked to state broadcaster and politically reliant on the broadcaster to serve as the party's mouthpiece. The Party keeps CCTV on a short leash as it lobbies for policies protective of its own market share, which has been eroded in recent years by entertainment shows on provincial television, and more recently by online competitions. TV remains the party's most manageable vehicle for cultural engineering, yet the Chinese state cannot control consumer behaviour. The tightened regulations on TV have converted more viewers into web surfers. China in 2014 had 400 million online video viewers, 250 million of whom were watching videos through mobile devices.[8] The number was expected to grow further, especially in China's third- and fourth-tier cities.

The rapid audience erosion prompted TV stations to plead for a tougher online video censorship policy. Chinese video websites had enjoyed a relatively open environment regarding content choice.[9] Online contents used to be entirely unregulated, being subject to no direct examination of the SAPPRFT. No quota restriction existed when it came to imports, leaving websites free to go for popular US and UK TV shows. For programme diversification and localization, websites also started to experiment with self-made programmes that took advantage of lax online regulations. Sohu, for one, made the popular miniseries, *Diors Man,* that satirizes pop culture as it touches on pressing social issues with daring humour. Tencent video and iQiyi.com produced ghost-themed miniseries that were banned on broadcast TV. Under the intense lobbying of traditional broadcasting companies and conservative cultural guardians, a new policy of "censor first, broadcast later" was instituted in the spring of 2014 that required online content to be examined by qualified personnel who "have been trained by state or provincial Internet video and audio programs industry association." The supervision of video websites now involves both SAPPRFT and the Ministry of Industry and Information Technology (MIIT). While the SAPPFT regulates content, the MIIT oversees network flow; and the two are not always on the same page, which makes a concerted effort in policing online programming difficult. Nonetheless, the restrictive policies signalled the end to an unrestrained era for online programming and will have an impact on China's audiovisual landscape.

Culture as Enlightenment and Indoctrination

Local economic turf war aside, the CCP has maintained that the biggest threat to China is Western cultural erosion. China's cultural regulators and guardians have always been vigilant against Western encroachment. Culture in China ultimately serves to maintain stability and solidify one-party rule. The subservience of media to politics remains China's official ideology today, though such an ideology is not entirely the invention of the Chinese Communist Party. It is rooted in a longer tradition of Chinese aesthetics that desires culture to represent the "good and the beautiful," that is, to deliver uplifting images devoid of criticism. This perspective can be traced to a moral and ethical fabric grounded in Confucianism, which leads to an interventionist cultural policy that frequently resorts to censorship as a control mechanism. Compared to Western traditions which view culture as a critical vanguard, the Chinese tradition emphasizes the responsibility of culture in the normalization of society. In China, culture is supposed to teach moral lessons and indoctrinate the masses, not to push boundaries or expand market, though the market has emerged as a major force for the state to contain and appropriate.

CCP's cultural policy has been decisively interventionist since the party established the League of Left Wing Writers in 1930 to promote art and literature at the service of the Communist Revolution. The result of such a policy has been cultural centralization, homogenization and anti-Westernization. The CCP has consistently singled out Western culture as a source of China's spiritual pollution and moral corruption. The party has further charged the West with pursuing a policy of "peaceful evolution" by infiltrating Chinese society with destabilizing Western political and cultural values. Thus, the Chinese state has frequently waged cultural wars against Western cultural influence. The Anti-Spiritual Pollution Campaign of the mid-1980s and the anti-Bourgeois liberalization Campaign of the late 1980s to early 1990s are two classical post-Mao instances of CCP's efforts in battling Western culture. By the late 1990s, the surface of the term "cultural security" equated the party's campaign against Western culture with protecting Chinese cultural security. Cultural policy in the post-Mao reform era might have moved away from overtly didactic propaganda, but the notion that literature and art must serve the party in the name of people endures as a first principle, reinforced by successive Chinese leaders, from Deng Xiaoping to Jiang Zemin, Hu Jintao and the new leader Xi Jinping.

Deng Xiaoping proclaimed during the early stage of reform and opening up in 1979 Four Cardinal Principles that China should adhere to: the principle of upholding the socialist path, the principle of upholding the dictatorship of the proletariat, the principle of upholding the leadership of the CCP and the principle of upholding Mao Zedong Thought and Marxism–Leninism. The Four Cardinal Principles aim to undermine the influence of Western political and cultural values. Jiang Zemin, who succeeded Deng following the Tiananmen Square protests of 1989 that ousted the pro-democracy Zhao Ziyang as General Secretary, reiterated in the early 1990s the popular line that the US is a "hostile foreign force" that had many times interfered in China's "internal affairs."

The historical sensitivity towards foreign interference makes Chinese society susceptible to anti-imperialism rhetoric. Fanning the nationalistic rhetoric, the CCP has been quick to link any Western criticism about China with infringement on Chinese sovereignty and evoking the historical memory of the Opium Wars in the 1840s. During a 1993 anticorruption campaign, Jiang appealed directly to Chinese nationalism by asserting that "some forces in the West have never relaxed their 'peaceful evolution' plot against China."[10] He called for the Chinese to be ready "at any time" to "counter 'peaceful evolution' and combat corruption and wholesale Westernization." "Peaceful evolution" by means of cultural values rather than direct military force pointed to the urgency of China's political and ideological control.

The notion of "peaceful evolution" is frequently coupled with "bourgeois liberalization," a term surfacing in the mid-1980s aiming to put a lid on an increasing vibrant cultural scene in China that called for political reform for a democratic society. In September 1986, a CCP Plenum defined "bourgeois liberalization" as "negating the socialist system in favor of capitalism." At the core of bourgeois liberalization are both Western political values and popular culture. In November 1986, the CCP suppressed student demonstrations that called for greater political openness. Early in January 1987, the party organ *People's Daily* published several articles denouncing "bourgeois liberalization" and defending Deng's Four Cardinal Principles. The anti-bourgeois liberalization campaign eventually brought down the pro-student General Secretary Hu Yaobang and several prominent intellectuals, journalists and writers. Hu died in mid-April 1989, setting off the fire of new student demonstrations that led to the military suppression in June 1989. The term "anti-bourgeois liberalization" is still in use in the Communist Party's Constitution, which states that party objectives include "combating bourgeois liberalization," which is in line with Deng's four cardinal principles.[11]

While the CCP's charge against the Western political values aims at preserving China's socialist market economy, its charge against Western culture is said to help root out moral corruption caused by unwholesome Western popular culture. In 1997, amidst rampant corruption, Jiang Zemin launched a campaign to promote spiritual civilization, blaming foreign influences for a cluster of social issues including corruption, never mind that the Chinese had been masters of corruption long before the Westerners arrived in the nineteenth century. As Robert Elegant puts it, "every imperial dynasty ended in a welter of graft, special privileges, exploitation, civic disobedience, banditry and revolt."[12]

The new millennium ushered in a new round of anti-Western campaigns. Jiang Zemin introduced his legacy-carrying theory of "three representatives" on 25 February 2000 as the CCP's new guiding principles. The hazy party-speak "Three Representatives" stipulated that the CCP should represent advanced social productive forces, advanced culture and advance the interests of the overwhelming majority. Advanced culture here refers to socialist culture antithetic to Western culture. At the 16th National Congress of the CCP on 8 November 2002, Jiang further delivered a report entitled "Build a Well-off Society in an All-Round Way and Create a New Situation in Building Socialism with Chinese Characteristics." Chinese characteristics or not, corruption continued to be virulent, and nefarious officials ran amok by the time Jiang stepped down in the early 2000s. The campaign for "socialist spiritual civilization" seeking to inculcate and elevate personal and civic morality while deceptively scapegoating Western culture failed to deliver a better society to Chinese people, and to Hu Jintao, Jiang's successor.

Hu Jintao nonetheless followed the same tactics, singling out Western culture as a destabilizing force seen as a grave threat to the CCP rule. Hu warned in a 2006 speech that "some powerful foreign nations wish to use culture as a weapon against other nations... ."[13] He warned further that "The one who takes commanding point on the battlefield of cultural development will gain the upper hand in fierce international competition."[14] In October 2011, at the annual plenum of the party's Central Committee, Hu delivered another speech, reasserting the need for the party to tighten its grip over culture and ideological affairs and to fend off Western Culture inroads.[15]

Hu's speech was later published in *Seeking Truth*, the party magazine. In the article, Hu pleaded for the CCP leadership to "clearly see that the international hostile forces are stepping up strategic attempts to westernize China, and ideological and cultural fields are a focus for long-term infiltration." Hu's speech served as a warning against the rapid uprisings in the Arab world at the time. With *Avatar* dominating the Chinese box office and Lady Gaga serving as a popular icon among Chinese youth in 2011, a prevailing sense of cultural anxiety among Chinese cultural guardians echoed Hu's assertion that "the West is trying to dominate China by spreading its culture and ideology and that China must strengthen its cultural production to defend against the assault."[16] Pitting Chinese culture against Western culture, Hu declared that an escalating culture war between the two sides had begun. Certain passages in Hu's *Seeking Truth* essay register a Cold War tone. Hu urged Chinese cultural policy makers to,

> clearly see that international hostile forces are intensifying the strategic plot of westernizing and dividing China, and ideological and cultural fields are the focal areas of their long-term infiltration... We should deeply understand the seriousness and complexity of the ideological struggle, always sound the alarm and remain vigilant and take forceful measures to be on guard and respond.

He summed up: "The overall strength of Chinese culture and its international influence is not commensurate with China's international status."

The campaign against Western cultural "infiltration" only intensified under China's new President, Xi Jinping. A leaked party memo issued in April 2013 titled *Briefing on the Present Ideological Situation* listed a number of ideological "perils" that included constitutional democracy, universal values of human rights, press freedom, and complaints about the undisclosed personal wealth and financial ties of government officials. The memo warns that,

Western anti-China forces and internal "dissidents" are still actively trying to infiltrate China's ideological sphere, and have made a fuss over asset disclosure by officials, fighting corruption with the Internet, media supervision of government, and other sensitive hot-button issues, all of which stoke dissatisfaction with the Party and government.

In May 2013 in a state-run *Guangming Daily* editorial, the People's Liberation Army (PLA) general Zhu Heping warned against the influence of Western "cultural colonialism," particularly on Chinese youth. "Western cultural infiltration techniques are very clever in their deception and hidden nature," Zhu wrote, "Western hostile forces seize every opportunity to sneak attacks against us, and they are pressing harder and harder." In October 2013, a Chinese film *Silent Contest*, which was co-produced by the PLA and the Chinese Academy of Social Sciences identified the Hollywood movies and the US educational programmes and organizations such as the Fulbright Program, the Ford Foundation, the Asia Foundation and the Carter Center as tools of Western infiltration that work to undermine Communist Party rule, brainwash Chinese citizens and impose on China American cultural values.[17] By 2014, Western "cultural threat" escalated to be one of several types of "unconventional security threats" under China's new National Security Committee's surveillance. The PLA senior colonel Gong Fangbin singled out the US as a particularly dangerous source of Western culture infiltration and Hollywood movies and the Internet as lethal tools for disseminating Western cultural values.[18] Chinese youth were perceived as particularly vulnerable to such Western cultural influence.[19]

Yet the Chinese censors were losing the war, judging by the success of Hollywood products in China, particularly the smashing Chinese box-office hit of *Transformers-4, The Age of Extinction*, a film with little artistic credibility or box-office muscle in the US. A record number of Chinese captivated by Hollywood's "spectacular junk" was the ultimate victory of US-led Western popular culture. Hollywood scored a further victory in the film: Chinese sponsors paid to have their products and landmarks shown and China's beloved pop stars contributed cameos, all of which were so haphazardly thrown together that they were at worst insults and at best satire, neither of which cast China in a particularly glowing light. Hollywood ridicules as it seduces. In typical Hollywood fashion, as the entire earth and human race are in danger of being annihilated, the film has a renegade Texan chasing the enemies to the Far East to save the earth and the human race.

PLA generals are right to point out the mesmerizing power of Hollywood cinema in disseminating the myth of triumphant American individualism and selling the image of a hero at war with the state. Joseph Stalin once marveled: "If I could control the medium of the American motion picture, I would need nothing else to convert the entire world to Communism." The fear of the CCP of being reversely converted might have some validity. Ironically, it was the brilliant production assistance and marketing campaign of Hollywood's Chinese partners, the monopolistic China Film Group, and its sister company, the equally monopolistic China Central Television's Movie Channel that enabled Paramount to conquer China's massive market. The state-owned China Film Group has decisive control over that market—at the expense of China's smaller and private film companies. Here again, the conflicting mandates of political control and market incentive could work to weaken the party's war against the West. The battle is back on the home turf, between the all-powerful state-run enterprise and small private firms, both vying for favourite policy while catering to the lowest common denominator.

Conclusion: Whose War and to What End?

The Chinese-versus-Western rhetoric in successive CCP leaders' charges of amoral Western influence is misguided, if not downright deceptive. After all, *House of Cards*, a US show with plenty of unwholesome elements, ranging from political assassination to erotic asphyxiation and threesomes, did not bother the Chinese censor. The Chinese censor's scrutiny of media content in its repeated campaigns against sex and violence and political transgression is not really about morality as it is about politics. Sex and political violence do not transgress so long as they serve to make the US look bad. The current cultural clash is not China versus the West but a top-down cultural control imposed by the state and conservative cultural guardians versus the vernacular pop culture ushered in by a market economy. The real clash is between the mandate of a cultural tradition and political system dictated by morality and political control and the demand of a market system dictated by profit maximization.

As China faces the challenge of generating more appealing indigenous content to combat Western programmes, the paternalistic Chinese cultural guardians have yet to come to terms with the reality that pop culture is the logical extension of a market economy, which the Chinese state has embraced. Instead of blaming the West for eroding its cultural mores and political stability, China would need to take ownership of its self-induced cultural and political dilemma. Western culture is not the real culprit in the withering of China's once-upon-a-time, high-minded culture. Marketization and globalization have opened the Pandora's box of the vernacular. The cultural war is internal, between China's own vernacular and the genteel as well as the monopolistic state media institution and smaller private media industry, both skirting the discredited propaganda culture.

Though the cultural tightening in China is the continuation of a top-down control, which is further tempered by market forces, it nevertheless reflects a bottom-up response to Chinese society's loss of moral grounding and Chinese society's ambivalent march towards a market economy. Historically, the infiltration of the market and its profit logic into every fabric of a society has triggered society's protective mechanism in preserving its social and cultural integrity, through means of state legislation and other forms of societal intervention. In addition to the state intervention, what we witness in China is also a spontaneous moral response to the shocks of a free market that threatens to tear apart China's moral fabric. So, the resistance comes from a grass-roots level as well, though such a popular sentiment is often framed by the state as resistance towards the evil West, which leads to the frequent eruption of Chinese nationalism. The moral panic of Chinese over vulgar content on national television is no different from what the US Federal Communications Commission chairman Newton Minow registered in 1961. He referred to American commercial television programming as a "vast wasteland" and advocated programming in the public interest.

It is worth noting that though imported Western shows may be popular, they are preferred not by the masses, but by sophisticated urban elites. The latter are wealthier, better-educated and pride themselves on having cultivated a taste for quality Western programmes, as opposed to the East Asia pop culture devoured by what the elites see as viewers with less discerning tastes.[20] And of course for elites,

Chinese domestic TV dramas are further down the food chain still. Social snobbery is the very fabric of the global elite, which ascending members of China's elite society yearn to be a part of. The backlash against the ban on the four U.S. shows was more about a desire to connect with cutting-edge global trends than it was an effort to demand more political openness within China. The motivation was similar to wanting access to French wine and cheeses, Italian fashion and German cars—access to such goods brings about instant status and gratification. Seen from this angle, the CCP and its army generals had nothing to worry about, as jaded Chinese youth mesmerized by Western shows were not interested in political dissent but in economic conformity.

Notes

1. Han Bingbin, "Quotas may limit more foreign TV shows online," *China Daily*, 31 July 2014, http://www.chinadaily.com.cn/culture/2014-07/31/content_18222556_2.htm
2. Zhu, Ying, "Why Frank Underwood is Great for China's Soft Power," *ChinaFile*, 14 February 2014, http://www.chinafile.com/Frank-Underwood-Great-Chinas-Soft-Power
3. The view count of US TV series represents one-fifth of the website's total and is expected to continue to grow.
4. Raymond Zhou, "Confucius loses his way" *China Daily*, 29 January 2010, www.chinadaily.com.cn/cndy/2010-01/29/content_9395429.htm
4. Patrick Boehler, "Shutting out 'Sherlock,' 'House of Cards'? Outcry over reports China's censors are restricting foreign TV series," http://www.scmp.com/news/china-insider/article/1457860/shutting-out-sherlock-house-cards-outcry-over-reports-chinese
5. Edward Wong, "China TV Grows Racy, and Gets a Chaperon," *New York Times,* 1 January 2012.
6. China sees culture as a crucial battleground 10:03 AM EST, Thursday 5 January 2012, http://www.cnn.com/2012/01/05/world/asia/china-western-culture/
7. Han Bingbin, "Battle for the Small Screen," *China Daily* USA, 4 October 2014, http://usa.chinadaily.com.cn/epaper/2014-04/10/content_17424653.htm
8. Ibid.
9. Orville Schell, "The Jiang Zemin Mystery," 23 September 1999, http://www.chinafile.com/library/nyrb-china-archive/jiang-zemin-mystery
10. CPC Constitution, CPC English Website, http://english.cpc.people.com.cn/65732/6758063.html

11. Robert Elegant, "Anti-Western Beijing Touts 'Socialist Spiritual Civilization', " http://www.nytimes.com/1997/04/17/opinion/17iht-edrob.t_0.html (accessed on 17 April 1997).
12. "Soft Power: China Takes Measures to Bolster Its Global Cultural Prowess," China Media Project Online, 19 December 2007, http://cmp.hku.hk/2007/12/19/797
13. "Hu Jintao Speech to Literary and Art Circles," Renmin Ribao, 12 November 2006.
14. David Bandurski, "All in favor of culture, say 'Aye' China Media Project," 26 October 2011.
15. Edward Wong, "China's President Lashes Out at Western Culture," *New York Times*, 4 January 2012.
16. A previous (2012) party statement from the CASS Institute of Marxism likewise identified the Fulbright Program, the Ford Foundation, and the Rockefeller Foundation in addition to Hollywood movies and major US news organizations as threats to "Chinese culture" and to Communist Party rule.
17. http://www.scmp.com/news/china/article/1404926/cultural-threats-among-five-focuses-new-national-security-panel-colonel.
18. Mark C. Eades, "China's Foreign Policy," 15 January 2014.
19. Known as a Korean entertainment hub, Youku Tudou has branded itself as the go-to place for South Korean TV series and entertainment shows.

PART II

Reporters

PART II

Reports

5

Portrait of a Chinese Journalist

John Zhou

John Zhou was born in a small village in Huanggang county of Hubei province, located in the centre of China (Figure 5.1). His father was an accountant and his mother a housewife. He has a brother and a sister and is the youngest in the family. His father had served in the army. After retiring from the army, he worked in a state-owned factory in a small city. His father was a member of the Communist Party and was a typical Chinese.

The primary school and middle school I attended are unknown ones. But I did meet some good teachers. An English teacher in middle school aroused my interest in English. Later, I went to a high school named after Li Siguang, who was a famous Chinese geologist. After high school, I went to study at a normal university in Hubei. Later, I went to the southern city, Guangzhou, to pursue a master's degree. I decided to be a journalist when I graduated from Guangdong University of Foreign Studies (GDUFS) in 2000.

At that time, my aim was to find a well-paid job. The Guangzhou Daily Group was at its peak in 2000 when I joined. It boasted that the circulation was more than 1 million. It was the leading press group in China with the highest advertising revenue at that time. Li Yuanjiang, the former chairman and president of *Guangzhou Daily*, was regarded as the most powerful figure across the industry in China (in the sense of business). It was the good old days of printed media in China. Later Mr Li was put in prison on criminal charges.

Figure 5.1:
Huanggang region

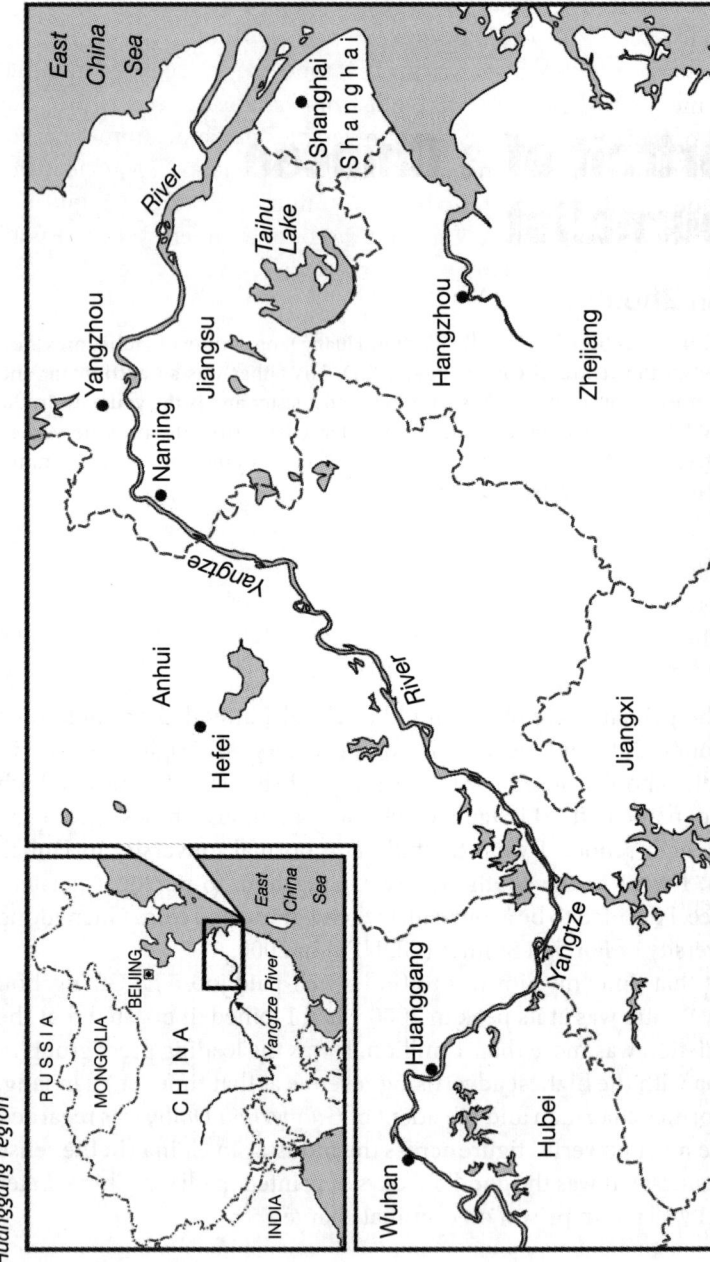

Source: Drawn by Lee Li Kheng, Geography, National University of Singapore, for the Institute of South Asian Studies.

Note: This figure is not to scale and does not depict authentic boundaries.

I got some training when I was employed at *Guangzhou Daily*. Several professors from the Missouri School of Journalism gave lectures to us for a week. That was the first time I got journalistic training. Like me, many beginners were not from schools of journalism. But most of them were from leading universities in China. Some refer to the phenomenon as "high consumption of the talents." I learnt how to be a journalist mostly by "on the job" training. Experienced journalists or editors gave instruction to interns or newcomers. I started as an editor at *Guangzhou Daily* where my duties were to cover the news from the Pearl River Delta.

I turned to *Southern Metropolis Daily* (*SMD*) in 2001. In my early years as an editor, I was particularly influenced by Cheng Yizhong, the former chief editor of *SMD*. He was an upright man with a strong sense of justice. He was awarded UNESCO/Guillermo Cano World Press Freedom Prize 2005 because, as a testimonial stated, "Mr. Cheng represents Chinese journalism at its best; he speaks out for the weak and checks the strong. His courageous outspokenness has contributed to raising public awareness in China." He had influenced a lot of people.

Cheng laid the foundation and set the direction for the newspaper. He adopted the principle of separation of news collecting and editing and the separation of editing and business management. This principle was new for media in China at that time. They developed the editorial policy after many months of discussion involving the editorial staff. Bearing the concept of "to be the best newspaper in China" in mind, *SMD* insists on objectivity and fairness when reporting news. *SMD* is known for its investigative journalism. Since 2003, its reports, such as those on the SARS flu outbreak and the "Sun Zhigang Incident," have had great impact at home and abroad.[1] With a high reputation, *SMD* has been called "a paper with conscience."

SMD says it has the largest circulation (more than 1.83 million) in Guangdong province. In 2012, the advertising revenue, based on cars, real estate and jobs, amounted to more than RMB 350 million or about USD 60 million (http://corp.oeeee.com/nfdsb.html). It targets people living in the Pearl River Delta, but enjoys national influence nowadays.

I was an international news editor for several years at *SMD*. After 2009, I chose to be an international reporter. As an editor, my morning started at noon and my job started in the afternoon. Usually our rush hour was at night. When in the office, we must surf all important foreign news websites and find the important news. Later at around 5 PM, there would be a meeting at which editors commented on the newspaper of the day and discussed what topics and news should be put in tomorrow's paper.

To be a reporter, however, is quite different. I usually work at home like a freelance, and I often go abroad to cover big events. For example, in March 2014, I was sent to Malaysia to cover the disaster of flight MH370 of Malaysian Airlines.

The biggest story I wrote in my early years as reporter was Nepal's transition from monarchy to republic. I spent nearly a month in Nepal with a photographer on this assignment. We joined the final press conference by the last king of Nepal. We interviewed some important figures such as Maoist leader Prachanda. We were among the few journalists to step into jungle to visit the mysterious Maoist military camp. It was an unforgettable experience.

We often use Xinhua News Agency and China News Service. For international news, we cover some important events by ourselves. We also use photo services of some foreign agencies. I surf various Western media including CNN, Reuters, AP, *New York Times*, *Time*, *Guardian*, etc. Occasionally, I surf the *Times of India*.

I had an opportunity to travel in India. I visited the famous Golden Triangle, the Ganges at Varanasi and Mumbai. I saw the ancient side of India. The way Indians treated life and death impressed me greatly. It is a land of contrast. It seems to me that there are two Indias: a rising, democratic and bright India, and a stumbling one with millions struggling for the least means of life.

My newspaper covers India, but not as much as other topics. That does not mean we do not care about India. For example, we seldom cover New Zealand, except when there is a big event or something related to China. When there was something wrong with the milk from New Zealand, Chinese media covered it en masse. We get Indian news from agencies, though occasionally we cover it by ourselves. Generally, media in China are not so interested in India, but I do not think that is right. We should pay more attention to our neighbours including India, Nepal, etc. We could learn a lot from India.

Our choice of news depends on the importance of the story itself and whether our readers are interested in it. Chinese media often turn to India when the topic is concerned with our security, defense, border issues, etc. For example, India launched its Mars orbiter on 5 November 2013. It became a favourite topic. For example, if a reporter chooses the topic and there is no objection, the reporter goes ahead. On some occasions, if the topic is sensitive, more consideration is needed in order to avoid taking risks. The principle is that we should follow our editorial policy and make the most out of a story at the lowest possible cost.

I believe many of the journalists at *Southern Metropolis Daily* are the best in China. They showed great courage during their coverage of China in the transitional period. For example, Wang Lei covered Sun Zhigang whose death caused huge storm in China. The story led to the abolition of the 21-year-old detention and repatriation system. Long Zhi covered the black jails in China. The story had tremendous repercussions.[2]

Journalists like the two mentioned above will definitely have a niche in the history of China's journalism.

Now *Southern Metropolis Daily* is attempting to blend traditional media with new media and build an all-media pattern. The result of these efforts remains to be seen. Generally, many are pessimistic about the future. Compared with my colleagues, I am not a good user of social media. Some of them have tens of thousands of fans at the Chinese micro-blog Sina Weibo. They are able to find clues for their stories and conduct polls. It is an important source of information. Given the present atmosphere of press freedom, social media such as Weibo are an important channel for their voice. Some even become opinion leaders.

My aim as a journalist is to write good stories like those excellent ones of the past. Most Chinese journalists, especially international journalists, are fully aware that China and India could become good neighbours. But the two countries should cultivate mutual under-standing. Media on both sides have been playing very important roles in this aspect. A lot of Chinese experts, scholars as well as journalists, have good insights into India and are committed to promote the Sino-India friendship. Above all, I believe people-to-people exchange is the most important thing for the Sino-India relationship.

Notes

1. Sun Zhigang was a migrant worker, beaten to death in detention. The outcry over the case resulted in the abolition of laws permitting the arrest and return to their homes of migrant workers. See, for example, *South China Morning Post*, 14 May 2013, http://goo.gl/3p9sOM (accessed on 6 August 2014).
2. See his in-depth report: "An Yuan Ding: Investigation on Beijing 'Black Jail'." An Yuan Ding is a company whose business is to put the petitioners in jail or escort them back to their home county.

6

Portrait of an Indian Journalist

Anshuman Tiwari

Anshuman Tiwari was born on 25 March 1970 in Kannauj, a historic town in central Uttar Pradesh, which today has a population of about 100,000 people (Figure 6.1). He has one sister, but lost a beloved younger brother in a tragedy a few years ago. He belongs to a family of teachers. His father has retired as a professor and is also a noted author and poet. His mother had been an eminent teacher and is now retired. He completed his primary and secondary education as well as graduation in Kannauj. He completed his postgraduate studies in Kanpur, a much bigger city, also in Uttar Pradesh.

Journalism is the only profession I ever wanted to be a champion in. "I'll become a journalist," was a decision I took while I was in school. But journalism wasn't considered an outstanding profession at that time. It didn't enjoy the kind of recognition and respect it is accorded now. Apart from the profession of a doctor or a teacher, government jobs were the most respected and highly sought after. Because of these attitudes, my relatives and friends were highly sceptical and surprised by my decision to be a journalist. But my parents have supported me to the hilt because they understood the significant role played by journalists in society. They were well aware of the worth of the fourth estate.

My first institutional training in journalism was from Bharatiya Vidya Bhavan, Kanpur, which was one of the few media training institutions in the country in those days. I did a post-graduate diploma in journalism from this college. Senior local journalists used to teach us,

Figure 6.1:
Kannauj region

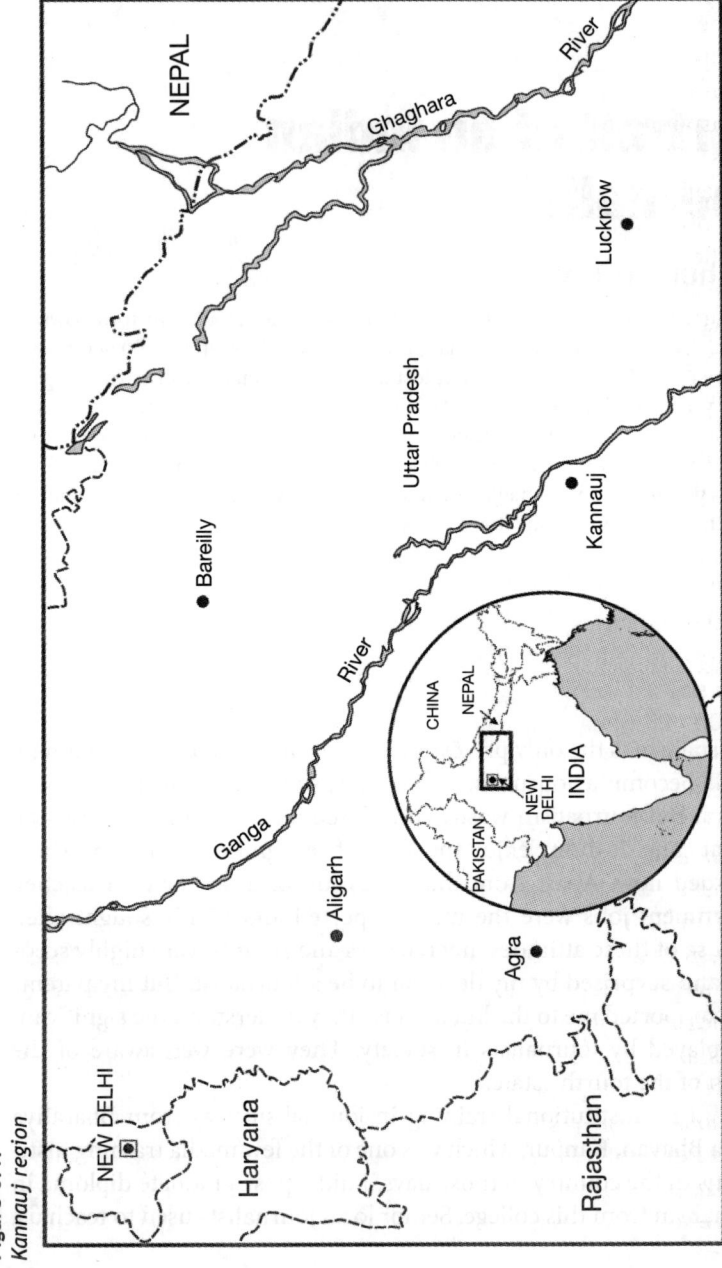

Source: Drawn by Lee Li Kheng, Geography, National University of Singapore, for the Institute of South Asian Studies.
Note: This figure is not to scale. It does not represent any authentic national or international boundaries and is used for illustrative purposes only.

and this enabled me to understand the practical aspect of journalism, but the course structure was not that evolved. It was very theoretical— swamped with theories, history, laws, etc. On-the-job training was the only way for someone to grind himself into a journalist. I derived my inspiration from a host of renowned journalists and authors of the 1990s. The late Rajendra Mathur (a legendary editor of Hindi-language newspapers) influenced me with his impeccable, innovative style of analysis. The writings of Prabhash Joshi (another highly regarded Hindi-language editor), Nikhil Chakravarty, Shekhar Gupta (English-language editors) also influenced and trained me. All these journalists had their own peculiar USP (unique selling point), and by observing theirs, I could develop my own.

I started my career in 1991 as a business correspondent with *Amar Ujala*, a regional Hindi daily in Kanpur. I covered the stock exchange of Kanpur and was responsible for writing business stories. I have worked for four media organizations, including the one I am associated with since 2014. These are *Amar Ujala*, *Dainik Jagran*, DB Digital—*Dainik Bhaskar's* digital division and the India Today Group.

Let me explain a little about these newspapers. *Amar Ujala* in 2014 is India's fourth largest Hindi daily, founded in Agra in Uttar Pradesh, but now having its headquarters in New Delhi. It has 18 editions in seven states and a union territory. It claims a staggering readership of over 30 million people and a circulation of 2.2 million. Those figures make it the leading daily in the states of Uttarakhand, Himachal Pradesh, Jammu & Kashmir and a very strong No. 2 in India's largest state, Uttar Pradesh.

Dainik Jagran is the flagship Hindi daily newspaper of the Jagran Prakashan Ltd (JPL) media organization, which for many years was based in Kanpur, where I did my media trading and postgraduate study, in Uttar Pradesh. Its claimed readership of 56 million has made it the largest read daily newspaper in India for more than 10 years of the Indian Readership Survey (IRS). Its 37 editions covered 11 states. It was also once declared by the World Association of Newspapers (WAN) to be the largest read daily in the world.

Dainik Bhaskar, promoted by the DB Corp Ltd, is a 50-year-old Hindi newspaper. I joined DB Digital, the online division of *Dainik Bhaskar* in February 2014. *Dainik Bhaskar* was started in 1958 from Bhopal, the capital city of Madhya Pradesh. It circulates in 12 states with 37 editions. The group's Gujarati daily *Divya Bhaskar* has seven editions in Gujarat and Maharashtra, and the Marathi daily *Divya Marathi* has seven editions in Maharashtra. The group entered English publishing through a joint venture with the Zee television organization to publish the Mumbai-based daily *DNA*.

I write about economics, and my job at *Dainik Bhaskar* was to use electronic media to conceptualize and deliver business and economic content in Hindi, Gujarati and English for common readers and investors. We launched the first product, *Money Bhaskar*, in record time of 120 days (http://money.bhaskar.com/). We got resounding traffic from the very first day by offering fresh, de-jargonized content with plenty of guidance and background for people who are developing their understanding of finance and large markets.

Being the editor of the website, I was responsible for every single story uploaded on the page. My duties included identifying stories, supervising headlines and deciding on priorities. The day started at 7:30 before market opening. Indian stock markets open at 9:15, and before that, I discussed the day's plan with my team members. Team meetings were held three or four times a day. Ours was a running, live newsroom. We endeavoured to provide real-time updates on markets via our website during market hours, and we worked on analysis, opinions and other catchy, exclusive stories which we ran 24/7.

The biggest investigation which I have written was on the Commonwealth Games held in India in 2010. I was honoured with a Ramnath Goenka Excellence in Journalism Award for those stories. My story, titled "Commonwealth Games: Excuse us, Delhi is not ready!" revealed how unprepared the city was to host this mega sports event. It was my first scoop from the six-part series that shed light on the haphazard work in the run up to the games. The onslaught of consecutive stories triggered a debate in media and among policy-makers. It established that the organizing committee comprehensively failed to meet deadlines. The stories were pursued and recognized by other national and global media as well.

The stories came about when I happened to visit Jawaharlal Nehru Stadium in New Delhi where the event was to be organized. Curiosity drove me to concentrate on preparations. I was shocked by the sheer nothingness of what I saw. Delhi seemed utterly unprepared to host the event. I decided to dig deeper. My search led me to sources in the office of the Comptroller and Auditor General of India. The CAG had just completed an audit of Commonwealth Games preparedness. I substantiated my stories with CAG reports. With the help of credible sources, I could effectively expose the failure of management and governance. My background in financial journalism came in handy. I did these stories while working with *Dainik Jagran*. The newspaper played it big. The impact these stories made would not have been possible without the support of *Dainik Jagran's* management.

2013 was the pinnacle of policy paralysis and scandals in India. The scam over allocation of coal blocks came to the surface, at the same time that the Commonwealth Games and 2G telecom scams were already hitting headlines. The coal scandal, which involved allegations of favourites and bribery in the grant of the right to mine coal, was the biggest ever because even the integrity of the country's prime minister was being questioned. A report of the Comptroller and Auditor General accused the Prime Minister's Office (PMO) of involvement. Later, the Central Bureau of Investigation (CBI), the country's national investigation agency, revealed that the government was trying to suppress scam-related information. Such scandals and their treatment in the media were the major reason behind Congress Party's rout in the 2014 Lok Sabha election.

A journalist does not have a completely free hand. There have been a couple of instances in my career when I got hold of pretty provocative scoops, but the organization I was working for was unwilling to run with those stories. Professional editors work in tandem with the management and with broad editorial guidelines. Higher authorities—aka newspaper owners—are definitely consulted before putting out a big story or giving a certain angle to stories.

In my position at *Money Bhaskar*, I consumed foreign media throughout the day thanks to apps like Google Currents and Zite. These aps provide a consolidated package of major international news sources. China is my area of special interest. I have been to China twice and have visited Shanghai, Chongqing and Guangzhou. I read a lot about China. The *South China Morning Post* and Xinhua's English version are my principal sources. Apart from those, I also follow international news brands such as the *Financial Times*, *The Economist*, Quartz (http://qz.com/), etc. At *Money Bhaskar*, we used Indian news agencies like the Press Trust of India (PTI), United News of India, Cogensic and international news agencies like Reuters, Associated Press (AP) and Agence France Presse (AFP).

As my website focussed on business, we did China stories as part of our daily tasks. It is the second largest economy in the world. Apart from covering Indo-China trade relations, border skirmishes and visa issues, we kept an eye on China's internal economic challenges and also how China is affecting the world economy. No business news source can afford to avoid China. News agencies were the major source for our China-related stories.

Soon after my stint with *Money Bhaskar*, I got an opportunity to work with the India Today Group, India's most prestigious media house, as the editor of the Hindi-language edition of India Today magazine. This is India's most credible and highest circulated weekly and has been for many decades. Holding a key leadership position in the organization, my responsibilities include editorial planning and delivery of content across the India Today network. I also conceptualize and execute digital initiatives to promote in-house news content. Being a senior executive, I also have synergy with TV news channels and other verticals as part of my job. My sole ambition has been to keep practising quality and unconventional journalism with immaculate integrity.

7

Experience: Understanding and Reporting India

Tang Lu

Tang Lu first went to India to study international relations at Jawaharlal Nehru University in Delhi in 1996. She returned to India in 2004 as a visiting scholar at Sardar Patel University in Anand, a town in the western state of Gujarat. She has travelled widely and experienced the surprise of people in rural India when they encounter a Chinese face for the first time. She has written analysis and feature articles about a wide variety of Indian affairs. As a scholar and a journalist, one of her research interests is media coverage and public opinion in India and China. In 2010, she published an essay on Indian English-language reporting of China in the Chinese journal, *South Asian Studies*. She returned to India in early 2015 as the bureau chief of the Xinhua News Agency in Mumbai.

About two decades ago when I graduated from Peking University, India had not captured the world's attention. At that time, many Chinese scholars thought faster and better academic progress would be found in American, European and Japanese research, but I chose to go to India. As a student, I first visited India in 1996 and studied at the School of International Studies of Jawaharlal Nehru University (JNU) based in New Delhi. Eight years later, I went to India again, and went to Gujarat as a visiting scholar, to study Indian politics and society at Sardar Patel University situated in the heart of a rural countryside.

It was my good fortune around this time also to be selected as vice-governor for a year in Baishui county, recognized as a Chinese National Poverty County, located in Shaanxi province of China. This meant that I was placed in charge of various programmes, including media, tree planting, road building and cultural activities, in one of

China's poorest counties. I spent a lot of time interacting with farmers. These experiences helped me to understand the rural reality in both India and China. There are quite a number of Chinese journalists and scholars who have worked and studied in India. However, very few people have had my experience of studying and conducting research in India as a journalist and a scholar, as well as having worked as a senior local official at the grass-roots in China.

To be honest, any Chinese reporter can work in India and write clearly and logically. However, whether they objectively report on India is a different matter. Due to the present limitations on visits between India and China, the majority of people have to rely on the media to get to know the other country and to learn about Sino-Indian relations. The problem is whether media reports on each country are accurate.

I still remember what my supervisor Professor Harbans B. Patel said when he first met me in Gujarat in 2004: "It is difficult for foreigners to understand Indian politics, even Indians themselves would not be able to catch the key." Prof. Harbans told me a story:

One day, an Indian teacher required three foreign students go to a nearby village to investigate the life of the local people. Student A just stayed for a while in the morning at the village and told the teacher:

"The people of that village live a very hard life, probably they are terribly hungry, I saw lots of villagers eating wooden sticks." Student B spent the morning and afternoon at the village. He said, "The village seems to be quite wealthy, I saw lots of villagers sitting in a greenhouse to eat and drink." Students C who lived at the village for two full days told the teacher, "I did not see the discernible difference in the lives of ordinary people of this village and nearby villagers." Student C did not think that the teacher would praise him, but the teacher did: "This is the best observation. It is consistent with reality. Student A and Student B are practicing *seeing is believing*, but the village is not as poor as A said. The villagers are not eating sticks. They are washing their teeth with special twigs (from the neem tree) which not only act as a toothbrush to clean the mouth, but also are able to treat a variety of diseases. The village is also not as rich as B described. What he saw happened to be a wedding being held in the village. In accordance with custom, all villagers participate in celebration of weddings and enjoy a free lunch."

I understand what my supervisor thought. He was hoping that I would carefully observe what I saw in India and not rush to conclusions. Over the years, I have been bearing his words in mind. As a scholar, I do more in-depth research on India than many reporters; as a journalist, I have an advantage over most scholars, I publish my views of India frequently in official Chinese media. Some Chinese readers think my pieces on India are more objective and balanced, without personal emotion. I think, in addition to my long-term observation and thinking, my stories benefit from my unique experiences in India, as well as many in-depth exchanges with Indians of different backgrounds.

I once wrote in an essay describing my impressions of India:

> Many Chinese often judge a book by its cover, and the dirty, poor and backward aspects of India are exposed on the surface. Without in-depth interactions with Indians and careful observation, the Indian image that stays in a person's memory may be only that of poverty and backwardness. There are many Indian slums scattered in the most prosperous areas of large cities. There are fewer skyscrapers and international shopping centers than in China, and more beggars and poverty-stricken people, narrower roads, and an overwhelmingly chaotic and polluted urban environment. However, beneath the surface India is a young and vibrant country. Beneath the surface, we see the heartfelt pride and self-confidence for their motherland through interaction with Indians.[1]

Study Tour: India and Bharat

I heard the story of "The Blind Man and an Elephant" in my childhood. This Indian fable is the best cautionary guide when observing India. Whenever I felt frustrated in India, I would think of the famous Chinese saying by the great ancient philosopher Mengzi: "When Heaven is about to place a great responsibility on a great man, it always first frustrates his spirit and will, exhausts his muscles and bones." This motivational Chinese saying could be a good guide to action research in India. In addition, patience and a good attitude are necessary. Below I detail some commonly held observations on India that most Chinese people tend to have. I too had them.

(a) Many Chinese who visit India believe that the developments and changes in India progress far less rapidly than in China. I agree with this view if you only look at the urban scene. However, through a decade's observation of India, I feel the change in India. If people ask me which aspect of India was most affected by the economic liberalization in 1991, I would say: the mindset of India. One can see this change even in watching Indian movies.

When I first came to India in 1996, I was witnessing the early stages of economic liberalization and the general living standard in the country was relatively low. The clash between Western popular culture that came with liberalization and the traditional Indian value system had just begun.

I recall an interesting incident. A popular Hollywood production, *The Bridges of Madison County*, was playing at the Priya Cinema (it was yet to be taken over by PVR, India's largest movie exhibition chain). However, when I tried to catch it merely five days after its release, I was told it had been taken off because "extramarital affairs do not comply with Indian traditional values." I was puzzled. China and India have similar family values. *The Bridges of Madison County* had not caused strong, negative reactions among Chinese audiences. Why was it banned in India? Were young Indians conservative? When I discussed this matter with my neighbour, she was very clear: "The movies reflecting extramarital affairs are absolutely not allowed in Indian society. Of course, the authorities cannot allow this idea to expand through publicity in films." Ten years have passed, and in 2013, not only are extramarital affairs in India no longer a taboo subject, a spate of Bollywood productions have exploited this theme and tasted success.

In 1996, I watched a romantic Hindi movie *Dilwale Duhania Le Jayenge* (The Brave-hearted will Take Away the Bride). The movie tells the story of a young couple who fall in love while on vacation in Europe and relates how the boy tries to win the girl's parents' approval so that she can marry him rather than the boy that the girl's father has chosen for her. In this movie, the boy (Shahrukh Khan) loves the girl very much, but he refuses to run away secretly with her. He hopes to get the formal marriage recognized by the girl's family. However, in another movie *Rab Ne Bana Di Jodi* (A Match Made by God) starring Shahrukh Khan in 2008, the hero encourages the heroine to run away with him if she is unhappy with her marriage. Movie scripts exaggerate, but they imitate life. In 1996, Shahrukh Khan, the hero, refuses to elope with his girlfriend, but by 2008, his role has him convincing another man's wife to elope with him in order to pursue happiness. Big changes! But this is just a small example of the changes, depicted in films and occurring in real life that I have seen in Indian society.

(b) My imagination of Gujarat before I moved there was very different: I did not realize how different life was for people living far away from the big cities and from the elite in New Delhi, Mumbai, Chennai, etc. I also did not realize that English was not the language spoken by all Indians and that English-language newspapers were India's elite newspapers. Most Indians only read newspapers in Hindi, Gujarati and other vernacular languages.

During my first stay in India, my residence was at JNU in New Delhi, where many people spoke English, and English-language newspapers and magazines were always available. Train tickets were obtainable at the counter for foreigners at railway stations. The basic necessities of life were conveniently available. I was not bothered by any lack of conveniences until I went to live in Gujarat at the Sardar Patel University (SPU), known as India's first rural university, close to Anand, the Milk City of India. The life there was pretty tough compared to what I had in Delhi. In smaller townships, sometimes basic necessities come as luxuries.

Gujarat is one of the most economically developed states in India and has opened widely to the outside world. I assumed the English environment in SPU would be acceptable, though not comparable to the standard at JNU. For years, I had believed that people could go anywhere in India if they spoke English. But this belief was proven wrong by my encounters at SPU. At that time, I simply went back and forth between classrooms, my boarding house, restaurants and internet shops. I seldom took a scooter, even though it took at least twenty minutes to walk to any of these places. The reason was very simple: the drivers could not understand me when I spoke to them in English. I was once even taken to a restaurant when I asked to go to the railway station! After making several trips to more remote areas, I realized that English was far less widely spoken in India than most Chinese assume. For instance, at SPU not many teachers and students could speak English. When I gave a lecture in English at the Department of Politics, only one-third of the audience could understand me. The remaining two-thirds relied on the translated transcript of my lecture in Gujarati. If SPU was like this, how could we imagine that India had 100 million people who could speak English, as we were often told in Chinese media?

As a media person, reading newspapers is my daily work. When I was at JNU, the postman would deliver at least four different English newspapers to my room daily. But things were totally different in SPU. The newsstand of the main campus received fewer than 10 copies of English newspapers each day. The majority of newspapers and magazines were in Gujarati. I had to get up early everyday so I could grab a copy of the English newspapers at the newsstand. How can I forget waking up in the wee hours to get hold of the absolutely limited copies of the *Times of India* and *Indian Express* from my neighbourhood stall? Five minutes of extra sleep and they would all be gone.

In Gujarat, the most fun I had was when I travelled to New Delhi, Mumbai and other cities for conferences or to meet friends. I would first enjoy non-vegetarian food in a restaurant, then watch a movie and look around bookstores, where I would purchase many English newspapers and magazines before returning to Anand, which is 6 km away from SPU. As Anand is a small railway station, few trains stop there. It was difficult to get train tickets at suitable times: most trains arrived at Anand about 3 AM. There was no facility to announce upcoming stations, most passengers were asleep, and usually I was the only person to get down at Anand station. In order to be sure to get off during the short stop, I practiced opening the door of the train repeatedly. I also needed to carefully count the number of stations passed. I used to spend the night counting them out. If there were any unscheduled stops (which in fact were many), I would mess up my counting and get down at the wrong station.

Life was better in New Delhi, but I still enjoyed my time in Gujarat. I loved the wonderful roads, the constant electricity with no blackouts, and the helpful local people. It greatly enriched my awareness of India. I got to know that there are two different Indias. One is called India, which displays modern life, as in cities such as New Delhi, Bangalore and so on. The other is Bharat, which envelops more Indian people living in rural areas. I am happy to have witnessed the life of both India and Bharat as few foreign journalists have.

(c) During my stay in Gujarat, I participated in a 26-day walk to celebrate the 75th anniversary of Mahatma Gandhi's Salt March. The march was initiated and co-organized by the Mahatma Gandhi Foundation. The event was not only an experiential journey to re-explore Gandhi; it also made me feel the profound impact of the Gandhian spirit. At the same time, I witnessed a political mobilization which gathered many political organizations and parties.

Originally I planned on spending one or two days at this great event. I feared I was too weak for a long walk and also had some pending research. But I soon knew I would be able to go to the end. I was quickly infected with ordinary Indian people's enthusiasm for Mahatma Gandhi. Whether we walked in cities such as Ahmedabad, or in the township of Anand, or at the poorer villages, we constantly experienced a warm welcome from common people who spontaneously lined the streets. Smiling faces suggested that they were taking part in a pious and holy event. Those of us who participated in the Salt March were just a group of Gandhi believers out to explore the Gandhian spirit. Waking daily at 4 a.m. and under a sun blazing at 45 degrees Celsius, and then having to catch up on the day's news and file stories under the streetlights because the makeshift tents had no source of power, contributed greatly to my spiritual experience during this journey.

I recall what a Congress leader said to me when he noticed that I was worried about the 26-day journey: "You can do your studies anytime, but you won't come across such a big political event very often." He was absolutely right. Before I attended the Salt March, I had not realized that the Congress Party had invested huge political capital in this event. The walk gave me the opportunity to get a closer look at how Indian political parties conduct political promotion. During the entire journey, the Congress Party drew on charismatic leaders. Congress President Sonia Gandhi and the then Prime Minister Manmohan Singh were present at the opening and closing ceremonies, and other central and state leaders visited the team almost daily. There were massive propaganda and agitprop scenes with banners and slogans of the Congress Party accompanying the march every day. Mass rallies gathered thousands of people from the grass-roots. There was at least one mass political rally at each day's destination. No wonder Tushar Gandhi, the great grandson of Mahatma Gandhi, president of the Mahatma Gandhi Foundation, frankly admitted in an interview: "The event is with political overtones. As many Indian media pointed out, it borrows from the past to relive the history. The Congress-led commemoration of the Salt March is pure political propaganda, which is also the party's largest propaganda activity in recent years." Participation in this political event gave me the opportunity to meet and interact with various leaders of the Congress Party.

During the event, I also met some young Indian political leaders of the future. There were "78 Warriors"—marchers—during the Salt March in 1930. All were selected by Mahatma Gandhi. In the commemoration march 75 years later, the most sought after place was to be chosen as one of the "78 Legionnaires," who came from the Youth Congress Party drawn from India's states. Each state nominated only two or three candidates, while Sonia Gandhi made the final decision on membership. Because of the selection process, the young political leaders cherished this rare opportunity and tried their best to get close to the party's top leaders. They seized every opportunity to show their political talents. Within a year or two, some young leaders who were with me on the Salt March were already prominent figures in Indian politics.

(d) I travelled extensively in remote rural areas to see first-hand local farmers' living conditions. But it was not until I was assigned to the government of Baishui county in Shaanxi province, an underdeveloped rural area of China, that I saw the fundamental differences between life in the countryside of China and of India.

There are more than 2,000 counties in China. Baishui is a poor agricultural county. However, in terms of its rural infrastructure, such as roads, electricity, water facilities and rural school buildings, they are all better than many rural areas in India, especially the northern states. In 2005, together with a few Indian journalists and NGOs, I visited a malaria-infected village near the border area between India and Bhutan. The farmers told us that they had not seen the government doctors for many years. In Baishui county, we have at least one health care centre at each village, and they are fully supported by the local government.

I noticed a very interesting phenomenon in both countries— slogans. The slogans posted in Chinese villages are more focussed on the government's priorities. Banners such as, "To get rich, first build roads" and "The family planning policy is great and girl children are as good as boys" were ubiquitous. In contrast to China, most of the posters seen in India's rural areas are related to elections, and bear slogans like "Vote for me" beneath the symbols of political parties—a bicycle, an elephant, a water cup, a lotus.

The other interesting contrast was the leaders' motives in going to the village. As a local top leader in Baishui, I had to go to the village almost every day so that I could personally understand the needs of farmers and offer them help. I could never forget the old woman with tears in her eyes when I delivered a wheelchair to her in cold weather with heavy snow. As I observed in India, however, most politicians think about farmers only during times of elections when their votes are needed.

But something that distinguished India from China was the active role NGOs play in helping local farmers. There are many in India that do all they can to help farmers acquire new knowledge and practical farming techniques. When natural disasters such as tsunamis or earthquakes occur, these NGOs immediately step forward to support and give help to the poor. I witnessed how their warm-hearted efforts made a significant difference to the material and cultural life of local farmers.

I do not presume to be different from others' writing about India. What I hope is that what I write about India should be objective. However much a page-turner a report is, if it deviates from reality, it is a blasphemy of my profession. I dare not say that my reports about India are absolutely correct in every respect. There is a limitation to anyone's ability to capture reality. However, my experience has led me to think twice before I write a report about India. In recent years, along with the rise of India in the world, more and more Chinese people have an increasing thirst for information about India. India has thus become a hot topic with Chinese media. Whatever happens in India will end up in reports in small and big media or websites in China. Some of them are merely relaying erroneous information. As a reporter with the state media, I not only express my views on Indian issues on a personal blog, but also write news analysis, commentaries and interviews for the Xinhua News Agency about India or Sino-Indian relations. The aim is to deliver a sober perspective on India.

Many Chinese elites seem to have heard of Nehru's notion in *The Discovery of India* that India aspires to be a major world power. "India's dream of world power" has been a hot topic with Chinese media. Whatever happens in India, whether good or bad, media persons tend to link it to India's dream of world power and highlight it with eye-catching headlines.

On 26 November 2008, a severe terrorist attack took place in Mumbai, which became big news for international media. Many in the Chinese media linked the attack with India's dream of becoming a world power. In this context, my editor assigned me to write a report about how the terrorist attack in Mumbai destroyed that Indian dream of world power status.

I was informed that since the line of almost all international media reports was that the terrorist attack in Mumbai destroyed India's world-power dream, I should follow suit. However, according to my observation of India over the past 20 years, similar terrorist attacks have confronted India, but India still kept developing. The major difference was that former attacks mainly targeted the poor, while this was the first time a terrorist attack had targeted India's elite and foreigners. Another key characteristic was that the three-day attack was broadcast live to the world.

Through the camera, we witnessed the ferocity and cunning of the terrorists, the bravery and resolution of the Indian police, the anxiety of Indian politicians, and the fury and helplessness of Indian citizens. I could not draw the conclusion that the terrorist attack in Mumbai destroyed India's dream of world-power status. Just as a world power cannot be created through one or two incidents, it cannot be destroyed by a single terrorist attack. My conclusion was that even with the best preparations, India could not be certain that nothing bad would happen. However, the pace at which India moved towards becoming a world power would not be slowed down by terrorist attacks. At last my editorial team agreed that I could contribute according to my own judgement. It seems that my report, "The Terrorist Attack in Mumbai Can't Destroy India's Dream of World Power," turned out to be the most original voice among all the reports of Chinese media about the incident in Mumbai.

At the end of July 2012, the power grid in north India collapsed, which was also a hot issue for Chinese media. Countless articles highlighted the opinion that the collapse of the power grid in India impacted the life of 670 million people and shattered any pretensions about India becoming a world power. Naturally, I received a request for a contribution.

I wrote about the things that lay behind the power failure. I noted that "though outsiders all read news about the power failure in India, many Indians are not as severely impacted as they thought." Since a great section of the media strained every nerve to exaggerate that "670 million people stumble in the dark," what I wanted most to deliver to Chinese readers was "how many people on earth are impacted by the power failure." According to my experiences, though theoretically the power failure covered 670 million people, there were not so many in reality. The houses of middle-class Indians were mostly equipped with emergency electricity equipment, usually powered by diesel motors. Therefore, the power outage would not have affected them too much. I once went to villages in Gujarat and Bihar and found no power there at all. In other words, a proportion of people among the 670 million had never been covered by the national power grid. They had no idea that the power grid had collapsed.

I did not draw rapid conclusions about whether the incident would destroy India's dream of becoming a world power, as many Chinese media outlets did. Instead, I left my observations about daily life in India to the end of the article:

> It is said that the nature of Indian people is that they just make things do. Like a shabby carriage, as long as it can move forward, slight tinkering will do. Only when the carriage can't move at all, Indians will stop and make an overhaul. Maybe the power failure this time really will awaken India. It's time for it to fix the power sector that impacts the economic development of the country.

The powerful advertisement "India Shining," the catch line for the Bharatiya Janata Party's election campaign in 2004, became the most discussed popular slogan of that year. It penetrated TV channels, newspapers and general discussion and was picked up and commented on in Western media. This meant, of course, that it drew the attention of Chinese media.

The resulting treatment illustrated how the media of one country influence the media of another. In 2004, Chinese media virtually copied American reporting which was along the following lines: "after 56 years since it got rid of British colonial rule, India is now heading for a 'shining' era". When such reports were published in Chinese media, an Indian correspondent in China wrote a story about Chinese media reports, which got headlined: "Chinese Media Claim India Really 'Shining.'" Indian media loved it, and there were various commentaries with striking titles such as "China Weekly Appraises India's 'Shining' Movement" or "Chinese Uphold So-called 'Shining' in India."

During that period, many Chinese friends would ask me "Is India really developing that fast that it will soon surpass China?" To present Chinese readers with the truth about "India Shining," I contributed an article "India 'Shining' in the Election Year," which argued that "India Shining" was more of a domestic and overseas publicity initiative by the Vajpayee government. I wrote:

> To avoid too many unfavorable opinions from appearing in western media, the Indian government hired American public relations companies. Through the power of publicity Vajpayee not only made Indian people confident about the prospect [of a Shining India], but also made western media keep posting about India.

I also wrote that "the publicity campaign of the Vajpayee government not only ignores the long-standing problems of domestic poverty which brought some criticism, but also evoked a lot of doubts from Indian economists." At the end of the report, I quoted the words of an Indian journalist: "In fact India hasn't seen substantial change now compared with the first half of the year. However, it suddenly jumps into the vision of the world. Does it profit from the publicity of 'India Shining'?"

In Chinese media, the idea of India cooperating with Japan, the United States, Australia and other emerging powers to restrain China is a common headline. For many Chinese editors, only such a headline can attract the attention of readers. However, it is sometimes far-fetched.

Indian Prime Minister Manmohan Singh visited Japan, Malaysia and Vietnam from 24 to 26 October 2010. The main newspapers in Japan made a great effort to stress the special significance of the visit when Sino-Japan relations were strained. They pointed out that both India and Japan were threatened by Chinese military, so the two sides should strengthen strategic cooperation to contain China. This had been the consistent view of Japanese media and the issue was whether India would also take that line. Perhaps having seen the banner headline on the front page of a well-known Chinese newspaper, "Indian Media Advocate Uniting with Japan to Contain China," an editor of another Chinese media outlet hoped I could explain how the Indian media could advocate joining with Japan to contain China.

I read Indian newspapers every day, but I had not noticed the Indian media giving much attention to Manmohan Singh's visit to Japan. The fact was that they talked more about the other two countries in his three-state visit—Malaysia and Vietnam. Malaysia is a Muslim country, and a few years back, it had been the strongest opponent to India's entry to ASEAN as a dialogue partner. Vietnam's importance to India was clear and natural. So I broke the editor's assumptions and wrote a report, "Why Indian Media Are Not Interested in Singh's Visit to Japan." I wrote:

> India also has territorial disputes with China just like Japan, and the Sino-India relation has been strained recently. We expect the Indian media will naturally pay much attention to Singh's visit to Japan and they will advocate joining Japan to contain China just as the Japanese media have done. However, the expected situation did not occur. We can see by reading Indian newspaper articles, though the main English newspapers ran pages about Singh's visit to Japan, the reports were limited and many reports were replicated from other media. In other words, Prime Minister Singh's visit to Japan did not become the focus of reporting for Indian media. In Indian reporters' eyes, only American President Barack Obama's visit to India in November will be news.

Both Chinese and Indian media love the topic of which country is more powerful: China or India? The media of the two countries will not therefore pass up the sensitive issue of navy competition. The real comparison of Chinese and Indian military forces remains to be carefully analyzed. However, in their respective reports, it is always their own military that wins in the Sino-Indian navy competition.

After the 2009 Spring Festival, several pieces of news on the Sino-Indian navy rivalry in the Gulf of Aden were widely spread on Chinese and Indian media. According to the Chinese media, the Chinese naval escort fleet adopted tactics to force the Indian Sindhughosh class submarine to emerge from under the water in Bab el Mandeb on 15 January 2009. At the same time, Chinese media stressed that the *Times of India*, the *Hindu* and other mainstream newspapers reported as headline news on 2 February that an Indian submarine had followed a fleet of "a certain nation" for seven days and launched simulated attacks against it 39 times.

In fact, the initiator of the news, *Qingdao Morning News*, had faked it! The frequently mentioned news that the *Times of India*, the *Hindu* and other mainstream newspapers ran big headlines on 2 February about an Indian submarine following the fleet of "a certain nation" was hard to believe. When I did the research, I found, as I suspected, that the front pages of the two Indian newspapers did not run any news concerning China on 2 February and there were no similar articles several days before or after that day. Based on this, I wrote a story that was headlined "After the Fake News of Sino-Indian Navy Competition" to ensure a correct understanding of the facts.

It was not the first time that the Chinese media fabricated or exaggerated news about India, but the previous influence had been limited to China, and especially on the Internet. However, the *Qingdao Morning News* story on Sino-Indian navy competition was spread by the *South China Morning Post*, an English publication which retains great public trust and influence in Asia. The episode turned into an international joke and caused negative feeling among the Indian and Chinese publics. Indian media unanimously highlighted the Indian naval spokesman's statement "denying there are any Indian submarines conducting activities in the mentioned waters." Some newspapers even referred to this as cat-and-mouse game between one Indian submarine and two Chinese warships. The event showed media representing the interests of their respective country and the influence of nationalism on perception of each side through its media.

In 2012, the then Minister of Environment & Forests in the Government of India, Jairam Ramesh, on a visit to China, criticized the Ministry of Home Affairs for forbidding purchase of Chinese telecommunications equipment. He thought the decision was "a delusional disorder." A stir resulted, and Indian media blamed Ramesh for commenting on a subject outside his portfolio and for criticizing India while in a foreign nation—seen as the larger shame. However, Chinese media could not understand why Ramesh was "besieged politically" in his own country simply because he spoke well of China.

I have been friends with the straightforward Ramesh since 2005, when he had just coined the word "Chindia." I could understand why he openly criticized the Home Ministry of India, and I knew how the majority of Indian elite groups perceived this too: perhaps some of them supported China silently, but they seldom made such pro-China remarks openly and directly.

To help Chinese readers to learn about Ramesh and the complicated Indian political environment, I wrote a piece headlined "The Pro-China Minister of India is in Minority," which introduced the economic and political background of Ramesh and the political culture of the Indian Congress Party, which "does not allow a minister to go too far on his personal ambition." I pointed out that Ramesh's remarks on China had triggered a stir in India, reflecting the political status quo of Indian perceptions of China. As a minister, Ramesh had insisted that China and India are competitors and not rivals. The problem was that the Indian government, Indian Congress Party and others could not fully accept Ramesh's ideas, which went against the security creed of New Delhi. The Chinese should realize that in India not only the Ministry of Home Affairs and other intelligence and security organizations doubt China, but also the middle class elites. High-ranking politicians like Ramesh are in a minority in India. China would like India to draw a clear line between the business objectives of a company like Huawei and the strategic and diplomatic purposes of the Chinese government. However, in India where doubt over China is widespread, no distinction between a great company and the Chinese government is made. The Indian government would rather believe the allegations from its military and intelligence department that Chinese companies pose a threat to Indian security. With this understood, it is easy to see why Ramesh belongs to the minority.

Speaking in parliament in June 2009, Prime Minister Manmohan Singh said that India would step up defense preparedness along the borders with China and would increase its military strength. He referred to additional troops and combat aircraft. The prime minister's hard-line stance on China in his speech became a heated topic for many Chinese media outlets. Some noted that the timing of Singh's address coincided with increase in military strength, and several Chinese newspapers and websites posted such reports. The Chinese media's response quickly came back to India: news appeared in major Indian newspapers about China's official media reporting India's hard-line stance.

Having seen the media was increasing the hype over the event, I found the original of Singh's address in parliament. About the border issue, he said:

> There are, of course, issues which are complex, such as the boundary question. But we have agreed upon a mechanism to address this matter... We wish to build a strong and stable relationship with China. Whether it is China or any country, we will ensure the territorial integrity and unity of our country and protect the security in every manner necessary. The House should have no misgiving on that score.[2]

I thought the tone of Singh's remarks was positive and his stance on sensitive issues was measured. More importantly, Singh's address was for the domestic parliament members and had nothing to do with India's increase of military forces along the border with China and there was not a word mentioning this in his address.

However, Chinese media were condemning the hard-line speech on China by the Indian prime minister, and nobody noticed what Singh actually said or in what context. Perhaps because the two declarations were close in time, some Chinese media editors wrote about Prime Minister Singh's remarks based on hearsay, not evidence. In this situation, I wrote "Is Prime Minister Singh's Address Related to India's Increase of Military Forces in South Tibet?" for the *International Herald Leader*, the weekly newspaper attached to the Xinhua New Agency. I learnt that some Indian experts noticed this article. One commented: "In contrast to the general media trend so far in China to criticize Manmohan Singh, the piece from *International Herald Leader* tried to project the Indian Prime minister in a positive light."[3]

The cases I have just discussed result from my own experience in writing reports about India. In China, many reporters do not have much knowledge about Indian culture and history, and have difficulty understanding the complexity of the cultural and political situation in India. They use their own value standards to gauge the behaviour of India and Chinese cultural standards to judge Indian affairs. They treat the pre-conceived idea of India that they have in their minds as reality. This can only mislead the common people's perception of India.

Why are Sino-Indian relations in the media so negative? This is a question I have been trying to answer. About a decade ago, while studying Sino-Indian relations, it would have been sufficient to focus only on bilateral official statements. But that is not possible now. Political relations are close and stable; officials from both sides have made use of various international occasions to communicate. The trade volume between India and China has reached a new high. However, the common people do not seem to share these perceptions. I am asked why China–India relations always appear very tense and nervous. It is mostly due to people receiving their knowledge of Sino-Indian relations from media coverage. Relations between India and China in the media are seldom depicted in the friendly way that government officials from both countries describe them. For example, in May 2013, a standoff between Indian and Chinese soldiers in border areas received a lot of media attention. But officials from both sides maintained harmonious communication and the "crisis" passed. It is no wonder that the media are often criticized by officials and scholars for hyping news or for being "irresponsible." In fact, there are positive stories about the relationship in the media, but they tend to get overshadowed by the negative.

Complex factors affect India and China's negative media coverage about each other. These include the mindset of media persons and elites in both countries, business and commercial considerations, Western media reports and other contributing factors, common in both countries. Apart from that, there are special factors in India and China. For instance, the shadow of the 1962 war and the Pakistan factor affect Indian media coverage of China. In China, the government has controlling influence over domestic media, which the Indian government does not possess.

Furthermore, a relatively new trend is the interactive media coverage about each other. This factor links to the mindsets of media persons and elites. In general, Indian media (mainly the English media) pick up more negative stories in the Chinese media about India than the other way round. While Chinese media tend to look down upon India, as is evident from their reports, Indian media reports on China try to convince readers that China is hostile to India and therefore

China is not to be trusted. When news or comments from Indian newspapers are translated or rewritten in Chinese media, they are often exaggerated or inaccurate. They reflect the state of mind of Chinese editors who have their own preconceived ideas about India and the way in which stories about India should be treated.

A few years ago, one Chinese netizen wrote to me after he read my article on India–China relations. He said: "Some of our media are always looking down upon India with extreme nationalism and contempt. I don't know whether the Indian public is aware of that?" He asked me whether Indian media report these feelings from China? He said: "I really worry, and just hope the Indian reporters cannot understand Chinese, so that they cannot read these bad feelings." I answered: "There are a number of English-speaking people in China who can read Indian English newspapers. However, few Indians are fluent in Chinese and that includes Indian reporters. Thus, Chinese media persons are more likely to gauge India's attitude toward China from Indian English newspapers, but Indians will gather information from Chinese media more slowly because they have fewer people with language capability."

In 2013, things have changed a lot. As I mentioned earlier, a few years ago, the coverage of each other's country mainly came from the Western media. However, the media in both countries are beginning to turn to each other. Many Chinese newspapers, and some online media, now publish or reproduce news or viewpoints from Indian media, such as the *Times of India* and the *Hindu* to name a few. At the same time, Indian correspondents based in Beijing often gather information from *China Daily*, Xinhua News Agency, the *Global Times* and other English media. Apart from that, some Indian experts who are fluent in Chinese pick articles from Chinese websites and introduce them to India. Therefore, an interactive paradigm is emerging.

This interactive media coverage is a positive trend. Media persons in India and China have begun to focus on their counterparts' perceptions and are not merely following Western media reporting. However, because the mainstream media reports on each other tend to be negative, particularly the Indian media's reports on China, and since mainstream media tend to set the tone, the interactive media coverage is often likely to disseminate negative and incorrect information.

Let me try to illustrate how such interactivity may work. For instance, the *Times of India* reported that India was going to add to its armed forces along the Sino-Indian border. This would be considered as negative news in China, so we can give the negative degree of this original report a single "+." However, the negative degree of the same news when presented to Chinese readers may rise to two "++" after re-editing by Chinese media persons who have a prejudice against India. If Indian correspondents based in China write about the Chinese media reaction based on the Chinese report, then the degree of negativity may become "+ + + +" on the Indian media. Since India is a democratic country, politicians and officials must respond to the stories and show a tough stance. That begins a new round of interactive reports, and in the end, the negative degree may be further increased to 6 "+" or 7 "+".

The problem is that readers fully accept negative news about China or India that appears in their media. Very few people are inclined to question, or able to verify, authenticity. Thus, interactive media coverage may sometimes lead the other side to make hostile judgements causing the apparent hostility between the two countries to spiral. It seems difficult to turn this situation around because of the many misperceptions about each country are held by people working in their respective media.

Let me outline some of those misperceptions. In China, people do not know that there will be 101 opinions among 100 Indians, and they may consider the view expressed by an Indian in the media as the majority view. Chinese people are unaware that the majority of Indians do not read the English-language newspapers. Chinese people do not know that Indian media opinions are not equivalent to the stance of the Government of India, and they are unaware that the Indian media are influenced by domestic politics and the market. Chinese people do not understand this complex background when they read Indian media reports

In India, people believe that the Chinese government can control the media and therefore all the opinions published in the media reflect the government's stance. According to my observations, the commentaries by Indian media and Indian experts on China are quite often based on Chinese English media, such as *China Daily*, *Global Times*, and *People's Daily online*. However, those media views are not necessarily those of the government. The editorials of the *Global Times* are written by a small team. *China Daily* cannot be regarded as the government's mouthpiece: the expert opinions are the personal views of the authors and do not represent the official stance. Although *People's Daily online* is attached to the *People's Daily*, the columnists' opinions have nothing to do with the *People's Daily*. Some Indians also regard the critical views of India published on websites as a reflection of government thinking—if not planted, at least authorized.

In 2009, for example, a Chinese online think tank called the "China International Institute for Strategic Studies"[4] published a blog entitled "China must break up India." It was written by a nationalist netizen calling himself "Zhan Lue" (or "Strategy"). It pointed out that "If China takes a little action, the so-called Great Indian Federation can be broken up into 30 pieces." The controversial article was translated into English and quoted many times in Indian media. The Indian reports mentioned that "this article could not be published, unless it was recognized by the Chinese authorities." Indian media even speculated that the author, "Strategy," might be a senior official of the CPC. Some of the confusions resulted from the fact, that the name of organization of which "Strategy" claimed to be a member (i.e., the China International Institute for Strategic Studies) was almost exactly the same as that of one of China's leading official think-tanks—the China Institute for International Strategic Studies (CIISS), which is attached to the Defence ministriny. "Strategy's" group was simply a military forum without any government backing.

The root cause of this misunderstanding was due to the fact that Indians did not understand that the voices of the Chinese media are diverse. In fact, Chinese media can publish their own exclusive opinions, although all media are under government regulations. The views do not represent the government's stance. It is more or less the same as the complicated Indian media: Chinese media never speak with one voice. The *People's Daily*, *QiuShi* magazine, *Study Times*, Xinhua News Agency, *Southern Weekend*, the *Global Times*, all of them represent different voices.

The factors mentioned earlier do not exist in isolation. Because these factors are intertwined, the coverage of the two countries will be complicated and will deviate from the actual situation of Sino-Indian relations at a government level. As long as China–India relations do not reach a genuine breakthrough, it will be difficult to change the negative tendency of media coverage of each other in both counties.

Notes

1. *International Herald Leader,* 4 January 2007.
2. "PM reply to the debate on in the Lok Sabha on the president's address," http://pmindia.gov.in/speech-details.php?nodeid=760
3. http://intellibriefs.blogspot.com/2009/06/china-media-anger-on-arunachal-pradesh.html
4. The Chinese for "China International Institute for Strategic Studies" is 中国国际战略研究网. Its original IP was www.iiss.cn. It changed to a new IP as http://www.chinaiiss.org/after the events involving India referred to earlier.

Notes

8

Media, Messaging and Misperceptions in India–China Relations: Reading the Tea Leaves

Ananth Krishnan

Ananth Krishnan was the Beijing-based China correspondent of the *Hindu*, India's third largest English daily, from 2009 to 2014, covering a range of issues from India–China relations and domestic Chinese politics, to the economy and religion in China. Focusing on Sino-Indian relations, Ananth's reporting has taken him to all but 5 of China's 34 provinces and administrative regions and has included dispatches from the Kashmir–Xinjiang border, Tibetan monasteries at the centre of self-immolation protests, forgotten Hindu relics in Fujian and the old Communist Red bases of central China. Before moving to Beijing, Ananth worked for the *Hindu* at its headquarters in Chennai and in Mumbai. Ananth holds a master's degree, focusing on Tamil Nadu politics, from the University of Chicago.

In August 2009, a day after India and China held their thirteenth round of talks on the long-running boundary dispute, a think-tank in Chennai, the capital city of the state of Tamil Nadu in southern India, published a paper detailing what it described as a "Chinese strategist's plan to break up the Indian union."[1] The briefing paper, issued by the Chennai Centre for China Studies, had been inspired by a post that first appeared on an obscure Chinese online forum, which rather presumptuously called itself the International Institute of Strategic Studies (although it had no relation to the reputed military-affiliated

Chinese think-tank, the China Institute for International Strategic Studies).[2] The online forum in question specialized in publishing posts by anonymous bloggers, who often tended to articulate extreme, nationalistic views that did not find space in the Chinese state-sanctioned official media. The tenor of commentaries appearing on the forum was largely in line with the views of the rising class of Chinese "netizens" often derisively referred to in China as the "fenqing," or "angry youth". The post in question was authored by an anonymous blogger who called himself "Zhongguo Zhan Lue", which translates literally as "Chinese strategist." In the article, the blogger hypothesized that if China "took little action, the so-called Great Indian Federation can be broken up." Describing India as "a Hindu religious state," he suggested that India could be torn apart from within—presumably to China's advantage—along ethnic or religious lines.

On any given day, the increasingly vibrant Chinese Internet is filled with similar postings. Most are directed at the United States—China's new great rival—or at Japan—China's old historical adversary. The extreme ravings of anonymous Chinese bloggers are, for the most part, disregarded by most serious China-watchers in Washington or Tokyo, rightfully seen as noise that does not merit space in the mainstream public discourse which shapes public opinion and provides the backdrop to the conduct of diplomatic relations between any two nations.

In India, however, one blog post by an anonymous Chinese blogger managed to stir such media outrage as to force a statement from the highest levels of the country's foreign policy establishment, and effectively paralyze the conduct of public diplomacy for a matter of a few weeks on account of public anger fanned by the media. How did one anonymous Chinese blogger manage to dominate the narrative of the China discourse in India at a time when both countries were, that very same week, negotiating at the highest levels a solution to their vexed border dispute? The entire episode merits analysis, as it exposes in stark terms the alarming inadequacy and confusion that pervades India's media and strategic community when it comes to reporting on and analyzing China—a limitation that, this chapter argues, distorts and severely restricts the mainstream discourse that shapes public perceptions in India and China. The failure of an effective public diplomacy response from both New Delhi and Beijing has compounded the problem, leading to a situation where misperceptions, alarmism and hype are setting the media agendas on both sides of the Himalayas in the absence of robust and fact-based on-the-ground reporting.

The controversy surrounding the blog post is a useful case study in analyzing how the current China discourse in the Indian media is formed and shaped. While the storm of media coverage triggered by the blog post merits careful analysis, the number of articles that were published over the span of that one month in 2009 is far too large for them all to be analyzed. Yet underlying most of them were key assumptions that often wrongly inform Indian media coverage of China. In the brief disseminated by the Chennai think-tank, which triggered the ensuing outrage among media outlets, the think-tank's director, D. S. Rajan, who is a widely respected and long-time Indian "China hand" and a former official of the Cabinet Secretariat of the Government of India, wrote that the blogger's "write-up could not have been published without the permission of the Chinese authorities." Rajan's argument was, unquestioningly, taken at face value and faithfully reproduced by many media outlets, leading to widespread perceptions that the Chinese government had some role in the blog post. The suggestion was that the Chinese government was sending a negative signal ahead of the border talks, although the boundary negotiators themselves did not appear to suggest that was the case, as officials later clarified.[3]

The assumption that everything that appears on the Chinese Internet, which is today a thriving space for comment and debate despite censorship regulations, is vetted and approved by Communist Party censors, is one that surely would not have stood scrutiny against a well-informed public discourse on China. But once the subject of Rajan's commentary made it into the prime time evening talk shows of India's rambunctious television channels, there was no stopping the ensuing spectacle of media outrage.[4] India's newspapers began to rage against an ostensible Chinese plan of "murdering with borrowed knives". The *Economic Times*, India's most read business newspaper, said the fears were well-founded. The newspaper described the online forum, where the anonymous blog post first appeared, as "a leading Chinese think-tank whose views count with the Beijing's Communist administration."[5] It identified the author as Zhan Lue, not realizing that it was merely an often-used pseudonym ("zhan lue"), literally meaning "strategist", assumed by members of China's *fenqing* with a passion for strategic affairs. Most Indian media outlets followed their lead, assuming that Zhan Lue was some well-informed Beijing strategist at an official think-tank (which, it is to be remembered, did not exist in the first place).[6] Barraged with interview requests from television channels and newspapers when preoccupied with the far more serious issue of the thirteenth round of boundary talks, the Ministry of External Affairs (MEA) was forced into making a public statement to respond to the blog post, saying it continued "to maintain that opinions and assessment on the state of India–China relations should be expressed after careful judgement based on the long-term interests of building a stable relationship between the two countries." MEA spokesperson Vishnu Prakash pointed out, albeit in vain against the storm of outrage, that the article in question was "an expression of individual opinion and does not accord with the officially stated position of China on bilateral relations conveyed to us on several occasions, including at the highest level, most recently by the State Councillor Dai Bingguo during the visit to India last week [for the border talks]."[7]

What shapes the Indian public discourse on China, and what are the elements of a well-informed and robust public discourse? India's English-language newspapers, which enjoy far less readership than their regional language counterparts, continue to command influence in setting the news agenda when it comes to foreign policy issues. News stories published in the English-language media are often picked up by television channels—English, Hindi and other regional languages—and help set the 24-hour news cycle on any given day. When it comes to China, stories that involve the disputed border are usually the ones picked up by television channels, which often focus on reports of transgressions by Chinese troops across the disputed Line of Actual Control. Other China stories rarely get air-time on India's electronic media, which operate in an intensely competitive environment where the all-abiding objective is securing the highest ratings. "Other China stories don't sell. It's as simple as that," one senior level editor of an English-language television language said in an interview.[8] Discussions on China—which usually mean discussions on the boundary issue—tend to follow a standardized format, led by a studio anchor, and involving a panel of two or three experts for commentary and analysis. These experts are usually drawn from the select pool of security or foreign affairs correspondents of major newspapers or television channels, who are usually based in

New Delhi, as well as Indian strategic affairs experts who are usually retired foreign service officers or former military officials. Discussions almost never involve voices from China. The television channel editor attributed this to two reasons: firstly, the logistics and costs involved of bringing in a Chinese expert through, for instance, a satellite link-up; secondly, the concern that an input from China would disrupt the flow of panel discussions, which are, for the most part, intense and free-flowing events where panelists are encouraged to express themselves in the strongest terms possible to create the impression of a heated and passionate debate, which, television channels have concluded, is an accepted formula for securing high ratings.

What emerges is that there is little room for on-the-ground perspectives from today's China in Indian debates. This is compounded by the fact that in 2014 there were only four full-time Indian correspondents reporting out of China. They were all from English-language print media outlets—from the Press Trust of India (PTI), the *Times of India*, *Hindustan Times* and the *Hindu*—and they were all stationed in Beijing. No television channel or regional media outlet had correspondents based in China. Reporting out of China—whether this includes dispatches from resident Indian journalists or analysis by Chinese scholars or experts—is no doubt a crucial element in fostering a well-rounded public discourse. This was also a missing element in the coverage of the blog post, where context about how to read a post by an anonymous blogger against the backdrop of China's rapidly changing Internet landscape was clearly missing. This was context that would have, in all likelihood, framed the debate in a more informed way, and perhaps questioned the assumptions that permeated most reporting in India.

How did the China-based Indian correspondents report on the blog post? Here I will consider reportage by the *Times of India* and *Hindustan Times*, the most widely read and second most-widely read English newspapers in India, respectively. The latter failed to shed new light or background on the blog post or the forum where it first appeared, instead adopting similar assumptions and tropes that characterized much of the other reporting from India. This included conflating the views of the one anonymous blogger with that of the Chinese government and entire Chinese strategic community, which itself is often embroiled in heated debates. The *Hindustan Times* report observed that, "It is rare to hear *the Chinese* advocate an active policy of helping split up India," suggesting the anonymous blogger was representing the views of all of his compatriots.[9] The *Times of India's* Beijing-based correspondent provided a detailed report debunking most of the claims made in the Chennai think-tank's write-up. The newspaper interviewed the person running the forum which published the blog post, who was identified as Kang Lingyi. Kang is a well-known member of the online "fenqing" crowd. He started out as a hacker,[10] and later ran a website for Chinese "military fans" which routinely published articles taking extreme positions against the United States and Japan. Needless to say, most of Kang's utterances have not received prominent attention either in Washington or Tokyo. Kang himself appeared amused by the storm of attention, and, perhaps, by the absurdity of a former hacker having a role in dominating the China discourse in India and overshadowing boundary negotiations. "It is simply a piece written by an ordinary netizen," he said. "The Indian scholar," he added, referring to Rajan of the Chennai centre, "said it is a study by a government-run think-tank. This is ridiculous."[11] Chinese foreign policy experts also rubbished the blog post. "No responsible scholar in China will say such things," Wang Chungui, vice president of the Association of Foreign Diplomats of China, told the *Times of India*.[12] Zhou Gang, a respected former Chinese Ambassador to India, described the blog post in uncharacteristically blunt language as "nonsense." "This is not the thinking in China," he said.[13] The *Times of India* report should have ended the storm of controversy about the blog post. It did not, however, stop other commentaries from lambasting the Chinese government's supposedly secret plan of "murdering with borrowed knives."

The *Hindustan Times* report was revealing in its suggestion that the anonymous author was speaking for "*the Chinese*." This was very much in keeping with Rajan's original assertion that the "write-up could not have been published without the permission of the Chinese authorities." Both descriptions suggested a widely prevalent perception in India that everyone in China—whether they be former hackers, anonymous bloggers or the Chinese president—speak in the same voice. This perception feeds into a larger confusion about interpreting news and views that come out of today's China. China-watchers in the 1960s and 1970s had few sources of information to analyze. Energies were spent poring over the front page of the *People's*

Daily, the Communist Party of China's (CPC) official newspaper, examining carefully the sequence in which Politburo members were named in articles, or how they posed in photographs, for any clues to lift the veil on internal politics.

Chinese politics may still be opaque, but the information landscape in China has changed dramatically. Besides authoritative official newspapers, from the *People's Daily* to the English-language *China Daily,* which is under the State Council Information Office, there are today a host of other media outlets in China which do not necessarily speak for the CPC or the government, even if they are state-owned and subject to censorship regulations. For instance, there is the *Global Times,* which is published out of the *People's Daily* stable, but is not an official newspaper in the strict sense. The newspaper is known for articulating usually nationalistic positions. Unlike the *People's Daily,* the *Global Times* does not represent the views of the Party or the State and is often described by Western media reports as a tabloid that adopts populist positions. Also unlike the *People's Daily,* the *Global Times* operates with commercial considerations in mind, not unlike its Indian counterparts. Unlike its sister newspaper, it does not have a blank check from propaganda authorities. Like most other Chinese newspapers, it depends on circulation and advertising revenues to sustain its operations and is not a generously funded flagship newspaper in the sense that the *People's Daily* is by the Party's propaganda department, or the *PLA Daily* is by the People's Liberation Army. Hence, Western scholars and diplomats often read the *People's Daily* and *Global Times* in entirely different ways: the former is seen as an authoritative voice of the CPC, while the latter is seen as representing a certain segment within the Party that often adopts nationalistic and hardline views that are populist. In India however, this distinction is often lost, and the *Global Times* is routinely described as "an official daily"[14] or as "a State-run daily."[15] Both descriptions feed the confusion about interpreting different voices.

Compounding this confusion is the emergence of a vibrant Chinese blogosphere. There are hundreds of thousands of independent Chinese blogs, and the rise of Twitter-like microblogs such as Sina Weibo has dramatically altered the nature of debate and discussion in China. Blogs and microblogs are subject to the expansive system of censorship that is in place; posts discussing sensitive political issues are removed on a daily basis. At the same time, there is an increasingly wide diversity of views that was hitherto unseen in Chinese debates, whether on politics, reform or for that matter, foreign policy. There are more than 500 million users of Sina Weibo, and half a billion Chinese blogs. While there are red lines that bloggers cannot cross, the idea that every post is vetted by Chinese authorities is far-fetched: Chinese censors simply do not have the wherewithal to track every single post. Yet the notion persists among Indian journalists and strategic experts that blog posts "could not have been published without the permission of the Chinese authorities."[16] Twitter-like microblogs are filled with rants aimed at a host of countries, with special ire reserved for Japan and the United States. Chinese microbloggers are no different from their counterparts in India or the United States; the very nature of social media lends itself to serving as a platform for extreme views. Yet the extreme anti-American or anti-Japanese comments on Sina Weibo are rarely reported on by the US or Japanese mainstream media outlets, rightfully seen as noise that characterizes social media in any country and does not necessarily merit careful scrutiny or media attention. In India, however, even comments by microbloggers are assumed to have been posted with "tacit official encouragement," as the *Times of India* suggested, reinforcing the questionable notion that every voice on the Chinese Internet is that of the state.[17]

This confusion leads to an uninformed and skewed Indian media discourse on China. Whether this confusion stems from a failure to grasp the changed media landscape in China, or whether it is driven by the more practical impulse of playing up a story in the face of competition, is unclear. There have, however, been numerous instances where Chinese voices have been deliberately misrepresented to play up a story. One such example was a rather routine opinion piece authored by Chinese strategic expert Shen Dingli, a professor at Shanghai's Fudan University, in 2010. Shen was responding to a long-running debate among Chinese strategic scholars on whether or not China should consider setting up a military base overseas. Shen wrote, expressing his view in a general sense, that "setting up overseas military bases is not an idea we have to shun" and that "it is our right."[18] The day after Shen's piece appeared, the *Times of India* published on its front page a report headlined "China mulls setting up military base in Pakistan."[19] The first sentence declared that "China has signaled it wants to go the US way and set up military bases in overseas locations that would possibly include Pakistan." The report said "the obvious purpose would be to exert pressure on India as well as counter US influence in Pakistan and Afghanistan." The report was clearly based on Shen's article, from which it quoted extensively, although Shen's article did not even mention Pakistan. Interestingly, the *Times of India* report did not name Shen, but only described its source as "an article published ... at a Chinese government website." By doing so, the *Times of India* conflated the views of one Chinese strategic scholar with that of the entire Chinese government, thereby adding legitimacy to its front page report. The report did not seek a comment from the Chinese Foreign Ministry to verify its claims. Unsurprisingly, the report caused a storm in India, picked up by television channels and debated on talk shows, although none questioned its flawed basic premise.

On occasion, reports published by the Indian media have borne absolutely no relation to their source material, but have, all the same, gone on to trigger heated debates on China. When the error is committed by India's major news agency, the Press Trust of India, the effect is all the more magnified: PTI's dispatches are carried by most Indian newspapers and websites, and even translated into regional languages. One such instance was a PTI report that claimed to break the news that China was seeking to expand mining explorations in the Indian Ocean—an issue that had been seen as a sensitive one for India as it brought Chinese interests right into India's backyard. The PTI report from Beijing wrote that China planned to "expand its seabed mineral explorations in the Indian Ocean after an international authority approved its bid to mine for polymetallic sulphide ore, much to the surprise of India."[20] China had, earlier that month, already acquired approval to explore a 10,000 square kilometre area in the southwest Indian Ocean. The PTI report was significant as it suggested China planned to expand this already sizeable area. The report did not, however, specify the source of the new information. Its only detail was a quote from Liu Cigui, head of the State Oceanic Administration, who told an ocean technology meeting in Beijing that China planned to "expand the depths and scope of 'oceanic research' and improve our understanding of the ocean, with special focuses on the polar regions and deep sea environments."

It emerged that the source for the PTI story was a report issued by China's official Xinhua news agency, detailing Liu's speech at the conference. Curiously, the Xinhua report had no mention of mining rights, or even the Indian Ocean. It merely featured Liu's quote, which was reproduced by PTI, and only said China planned to expand "oceanic research" in "polar regions and deep sea environments."[21] The PTI report was promptly picked up by television channels and framed as the latest Chinese snub to India's interests. The PTI report prompted the *Times of India* to carry a front page report the next day, datelined from New Delhi. The report was headlined "India, China square off for sea fight," and declared that the oceans were the "new theatre of India–China competition."[22] The *Times of India* report failed to see the glaring discrepancy in the PTI report. The *Times of India's* correspondent also reproduced Liu's comments as reported by Xinhua—which carried no reference to either the Indian Ocean or mining rights—and, like the PTI copy, claimed that China had said that "It would expand its exploration of 10,000 sq km of seabed in southwest Indian Ocean," although there was no reference to any such plan either in Liu's comments or in any other Chinese media outlet.

This pattern of news making has become par for the course for Indian media outlets. The absence of rigorous fact-checking in Indian newspapers and an abiding media culture where newspapers do not report on their competitors' stories—even if to issue a correction—allows such misrepresentations to remain unchecked. It can be argued that intense competition and the emergence of 24-hour television news is forcing news agencies and newspapers to devote more energies towards producing "breaking news," and look beyond routine reports. The pressure to do so, however, comes at a cost: breaking news can often mean giving short shrift to fact. As the earlier examples show, reporters are free to interpret and analyze news as they see fit, even on news pages. This is, needless to say, not a China-specific issue. At the same time, it results in an uninformed discourse on China, as the need to sensationalize news stories—from inventing Chinese military bases in Pakistan to new mining plans in the Indian Ocean—means there is no distinction between fact and fiction, making it impossible to have a meaningful and informed public debate on China.

There are no quick fixes to the problem of improving Indian reporting on China, as it is merely symptomatic of the larger malaise that is plaguing Indian media, where sensationalism is undermining credibility. As far as reporting on China is concerned, the biggest obstacle towards improving the level of debate and addressing mis-perceptions is the lack of on-the-ground perspective. This would require more Indian media outlets to invest in posting foreign correspondents who can provide the necessary context—and, on occasion, help fact-check the often misguided assumptions prevalent in media coverage. This would also require investment in training reporters in Mandarin. Most Indian media rely on English-language Chinese media outlets, such as Xinhua, the official *China Daily* and the *Global Times*. It is hence no coincidence that the often extreme and nationalistic positions adopted by the *Global Times* receive predominant attention in the Indian media, further skewing an already unbalanced debate.

It must also be stressed that public diplomacy efforts from both New Delhi and Beijing have been inadequate in helping lay the foundation of informed engagement. The Indian Ministry of External Affairs (MEA) is often slow to respond to wrong reports—if it, at all, responds—and has only recently begun to attempt to come to terms with the fast-changing 24-hour news-cycle media environment. China, on the other hand, remains reluctant to engage with foreign journalists, with spokespersons rarely venturing beyond the official script when responding to queries from reporters. While Chinese strategic experts and think-tanks have begun to open up to foreign media, the persisting lack of engagement from Chinese officials remains an obstacle in understanding Chinese viewpoints. In May 2013, both countries took a long overdue first step in recognizing the problem, by agreeing to set up a media forum with representatives from both countries, when Premier Li Keqiang visited New Delhi.[23] The forum offered the prospect of a platform for journalists from both countries to begin to engage directly with each other—the first step towards creating a meaningful public discourse where the extreme does not dominate over the moderate, where fiction does not trump fact, and where the wrong messages are not gleaned from reading the tea leaves.

Notes

1.   D. S. Rajan, "China Should Break up the Indian Union, Suggests a Chinese Strategist," Chennai Centre for China Studies paper, 9 August 2009. http://www.c3sindia.org/india/719 (accessed 1 January 2014).

2. "China's top think-tanks." China.org.cn. http://www.china.org.cn/top10/2011-09/26/content_23491278_2.htm (accessed 1 January 2014).

3. "China should break India into 20–30 states," Zee News. http://zeenews.india.com/news/nation/china-should-break-india-into-20-30-states_554432.html (accessed 1 January 2014).

4. "Break up India: Chinese think-tank," Headlines Today. http://indiatoday.intoday.in/video/Break+up+India:+Chinese+think-tank/1/56111.html (accessed on 1 January 2014).

5. "China's India policy: Murder with borrowed knives," *Economic Times*, 12 August 2009. http://articles.economictimes.indiatimes.com/2009-08-12/news/28387859_1_india-china-relations-china-s-india-state-councilor-dai-bing-guo (accessed on 1 January 2014).

6. "Government Downplays Suggestion that India should be Split," *Indian Express*, 11 August 2009. http://expressindia.indianexpress.com/story.php?storyId=500816 (accessed on 1 January 2014).

7. "Government Downplays Suggestion," *Indian Express*.

8. Interview conducted by author in New Delhi; subject spoke on condition of anonymity as was unauthorized to speak on the record about editorial policy.

9. Patil, Reshma. "India Easy to Break up, says Chinese strategist," *Hindustan Times*. http://www.hindustantimes.com/india-news/india-easy-to-break-up-chinese-strategist/article1-442340.aspx (accessed 1 January 2014). Emphasis added.

10. "The World Wide Web of Deception," *China Daily*. http://www.chinadaily.com.cn/china/2011-12/30/content_14354316_3.htm (accessed 1 January 2014).

11. Saibal Dasgupta, "Chinese Website Denies Being Government Think-tank." *Times of India*. http://timesofindia.indiatimes.com/world/china/Chinese-website-denies-being-govt-think-tank/articleshow/4886609.cms?referral=PM (accessed 1 January 2014).

12. Ibid.

13. Ibid.

14. "Japan India Ties Irk China," Press Trust of India, 13 May 2013, http://archive.thedailystar.net/beta2/news/japan-india-ties-irk-china/ (accessed 1 January 2014).

15. "State-run Chinese Daily Lauds Indian Tech Power," Press Trust of India, 23 August 2013, http://archive.indianexpress.com/news/staterun-chinese-daily-lauds-indian-tech-power-as-ins-vikrant-is-launched/1158232/ (accessed 1 January 2014).

16. Rajan, "China Should break up the Indian Union."

17. Saibal Dasgupta, "China Twitterati Fuming against India on Ladakh," *Times of India*, 27 April 2013, http://timesofindia.indiatimes.com/world/china/China-twitterati-fuming-against-India-on-Ladakh/articleshow/19748364.cms (accessed 1 January 2014).

18. Shen Dingli, "Don't Shun the Idea of Setting up Overseas Military Bases," http://www.china.org.cn/opinion/2010-01/28/content_19324522.htm (accessed 1 January 2014).

19. Saibal Dasgupta, "China Mulls Setting up Military Base in Pakistan," *Times of India*, 28 January 2010, http://timesofindia.indiatimes.com/world/china/China-mulls-setting-up-military-base-in-Pakistan/articleshow/5510235.cms?referral=PM (accessed 1 January 2014).

20. Press Trust of India. "China Announces Plan to Expand Sea-bed Mining in Indian Ocean," 17 September 2011, http://m.economictimes.com/news/politics/nation/china-announces-plan-to-expand-seabed-mining-in-indian-ocean/articleshow/ 10019208.cms (accessed 1 January 2014).

21. Xinhua. "China to Invest More in Oceanic Science," 16 September 2011, http://www.chinadaily.com.cn/china/2011-09/17/content_13724796.htm (accessed 1 January 2014).

22. Indrani Bagchi, "India, China Square off for Sea-fight," *Times of India*, 19 September 2011, http://m.timesofindia.com/india/India-China-square-off-for-sea-fight/articleshow/10033781.cms (accessed 1 January 2014).

23. Joint Statement on Li Keqiang's State Visit to India, point 17. http://www.mea.gov.in/bilateral-documents.htm?dtl/21723/Joint+Statement+on+the+State+Visit+of+Chinese++Li+Keqiang+to+India (accessed 1 January 2014).

PART III
Practices

9

China in the *Times of India*

Ronojoy Sen

Ronojoy Sen is a political scientist who has spent over a decade in journalism. He is Senior Research Fellow at the Institute of South Asian Studies and Asia Research Institute, National University of Singapore. He was earlier with the *Times of India* where he was a senior assistant editor for the editorial page. He is the author of *Articles of Faith: Religion, Secularism, and the Indian Supreme Court* (2010) and co-editor of *More Than Maoism: Politics, Policies and Insurgencies in South Asia* (2012), *India of Ideas* (2013) and *Being Muslim in South Asia: Diversity and Daily Life* (2014).

In 1838, the first year of publication of the *Bombay Times and Journal of Commerce* (the predecessor to the *Times of India*), there was a mention of China and it was unsurprisingly in reference to the opium trade. The report said that the "question of crushing the opium trade is again being mooted in China."[1] The next year there was a passionate debate in the paper on the merits of opium trade. On 8 June 1839, the newspaper published a letter by the chairman of the Bombay Chamber of Commerce. The chairman, H. G. Gordon, wrote about the consequences of the "destruction" of the opium trade in the prelude to the first of the opium wars in China. He made a plea for using the opportunity to put commercial relations with China on a "sure and stable footing, more consistent with the honour of the British character."[2]

In this chapter, I examine how China has figured in India's consciousness by looking at the coverage of China—from the opium trade to the Communist revolution to the rise and fall of Indo-Chinese friendship—over roughly a century from the late 1830s to 1964, the year of Nehru's death, two years after the Indo-China war which marked a decisive break in India-China relations. I do so by looking at the *Times of India* (TOI), one of India's oldest English-language newspapers and currently India's and the world's highest-circulated English-language daily.

The *Bombay Times and Journal of Commerce*, which was originally published twice a week, changed its name to *Times of India* in 1861. The then editor and proprietor of the newspaper, the legendary Robert Knight (who later started the *Statesman* in Calcutta) wrote:

> The Bombay Times this day loses its modest title to become the Imperial Times of India ... It is to the Bombay Press that the home public must look for intelligence from all parts of India, and upon it must the Indian public wait at no distant period for news of the world.[3]

This was not an empty boast since cable wires would connect London to Bombay in 1865.[4] Though circulation figures are not known for that period, the TOI was robust enough to acquire in the 1860s two other Bombay newspapers, the *Bombay Standard* and the *Telegraph and Courier*.[5] In 1893, Thomas Bennett (who also became the editor of the newspaper) and F.M. Coleman jointly founded the Bennett, Coleman and Company Limited, which became the owner of the *Times of India*. To this day, the name of the group that publishes the TOI and its sister publications remains Bennett, Coleman and Company Limited (BCCL).

Till the 1940s, the newspaper was British-owned and largely staffed by British journalists and this naturally coloured its reports. This was in contrast to other English dailies such as *Hindustan Times* and *Amrita Bazar Patrika* which were wedded to the Indian nationalist cause. Though the TOI's readership was mainly British in the first half of the twentieth century, it was read by Indians too. Many Indian families, especially in the port cities, have been fluent speakers of English for more than six generations, tracing their familiarity with the language back to the early nineteenth century. Such families, particularly in western India, have had the *Times of India* or its predecessors as part of their reading matter from the 1850s.

Thus, Arvind N. Das reminds us in his introduction to a book published on the occasion of TOI's sesquicentenary that "events shaped *The Times of India* but *The Times of India* played an important part in shaping the memories of these events." This chapter is not an exhaustive catalogue of the major China-related events but a brief survey of items that were reported in TOI over roughly a century and the responses that they evoked in India. It aims to document not only the significant milestones in the media coverage of China but to also give a flavour of how the events were reported and in a few cases of who reported them.

The Long Nineteenth Century

Opium was a major money-spinner for the British empire in India. A publication from 1839 stated that the trade benefited England to "an extent of 6 million pounds yearly without impoverishing India."[6] By one estimate, the total quantity of opium stock in China in 1839 was 20,000 chests valued at 2,000,000 sterling.[7] According to another estimate between 1805 and 1839, imports of opium into China increased more than ten-fold from 3,159 to 40,200 chests.[8] By the late nineteenth century, opium exports contributed to 16 per cent of the total revenue in India.[9]

That opium and China trade figured prominently in the pages of *Bombay Times and Journal of Commerce* is not surprising. Bombay's business leaders founded the newspaper in 1839 and for many of them, the opium trade was crucial to their interests. Jamsetjee Jejeebhoy, a Parsi merchant with substantial interests in China, was a member of the syndicate that owned the *Bombay Times and Journal of Commerce*.[10] Jejeebhoy was a major partner in Jardine, Matheson & Company in Canton, which traded in large quantities of opium and had himself made five voyages to China between 1799 and 1807.[11] Trading ties in the modern era between India and China went back to the mid-eighteenth century. It was as early as 1756 that the appropriately named Parsi merchant, Hirji Jivanji Readymoney, ventured to China. His brother Mancherji set up a branch of the family at Canton and was soon followed by several other merchants, a majority of whom were Parsi.[12] Most of them purchased stocks of opium as well as cotton and consigned it to commission agents in Canton. In 1835, there were 52 Parsis involved in the China trade as opposed to 35 English traders.[13] In fact of the 20,383 chests of opium surrendered to the Chinese in 1839 in the run-up to the first opium war, 5,315 belonged to Parsi merchants alone.[14]

Not surprisingly, 10 days after Gordon's letter in the *Times of India*, the newspaper published a petition by a group of Parsi merchants imploring Governor-General Lord Auckland to compensate for losses sustained due to the surrender of the opium stock in China. Their letter emphasized that the issue affected the "Commerce of both England and India with China," but was also of "most vital importance to the properties and credit of those merchants immediately and directly engaged in the trade, but concerns intimately every person employed in Mercantile pursuits at all the Presidencies."[15]

Views against the opium trade were, however, not entirely absent from the newspaper. An editorial from the *Friend of India,* published in the *Bombay Times and Journal of Commerce*, brought up the question of morality and ethics of the opium trade:

> Perhaps it is too much to exact of the faith of a Christian Government, that they should believe there is a God existing, to whom good and evil is not indifferent—who has powers sufficient in the world to see the loss sustained in doing what is good in his sight shall be compensated, as well as that profit made by disobedience to Him shall be useless.[16]

Indeed, the opium trade dominated much of the discussion in British India on China in the nineteenth century.

The first opium war that resulted from Chinese efforts to suppress the opium trade ended in 1842 with the Treaty of Nanjing. Indian troops played a major role in the war though this did not find any mention in the newspaper. The *Bombay Times and Journal of Commerce* published the order of the governor general of India which said:

> The Governor-General has sincere satisfaction in announcing the termination of the war with China, by a Peace honourable to Her Majesty's Crown, and durable in its provisions, which was concluded in the British Camp, under the walls of the Imperial City of Nankin, on the 29th of August.[17]

The peace however did not turn out to be durable. By 1857, when India would be shaken by the Great Uprising against British rule, war drums were beating again in China. The second of the opium wars (also known as the Arrow War after Chinese officials boarded the *Arrow* ship and lowered the British flag) began in 1857. British and French troops combined to defeat the Chinese and yet another treaty was signed at Tianjin (or Tientsin) in 1858. The *Bombay Times and Journal of Commerce* reported that the treaty "seems to be a great improvement on the last one, providing for the residence of an envoy at Pekin, the opening of additional ports, and liberty to travel to the interior."[18] This too proved short-lived and another agreement, the Peking Convention, was signed in 1860 to reaffirm the conditions of the Tientsin Treaty.[19] This did not however stop periodic tensions between Britain and China which were reported in the newspaper.

Opium continued to be a running theme in the nineteenth century in discussions of China. In 1889, the newspaper, by now the *Times of India*, carried a report of a debate in the House of Commons where a motion against the opium trade was sought to be passed. The motion said:

> That the House views with deep regret the history of our opium policy towards China and regards the traffic in that drug as repugnant to the true interests of that country; that it calls upon the Government of India to take steps looking to the final extinction of the trade and urges upon her majesty's Government to intimate the Chinese Government that, in the next revision of the Treaty of Tientsin, full power to extinguish the trade in opium if its thinks fit.[20]

Predictably the resolution was defeated with opponents pointing out that it would deprive the "people of India their most profitable crop." Besides they said stopping the opium trade from India would "open the door to native-grown opium and that which was grown in Persia." The Royal Commission on Opium endorsed the majority opinion of the House of Commons. The commission's report, which was presented to Parliament in 1895, was carried in a summary form in the TOI.[21]

The war between China and Japan in 1894–1895 was given considerable coverage in the *Times of India*. A report stated that Japan declared war on 1 August 1894 after "two severe engagements had been fought between Chinese and war vessels."[22] A report later that year said Port Arthur had fallen to the Japanese. In a precursor to the events of the late 1930s, the Japanese committed atrocities in early 1895 at Port Arthur. The TOI reported "horrible butchery of unarmed Chinese" by Japanese troops. The two countries ceased hostilities with the Treaty of Simonosaki in 1895 of which the TOI wrote that it was "neither a cruel nor a crushing peace" for China.[23]

The end of the nineteenth and the beginning of the twentieth century was marked by the Boxer Rebellion, a significant event in modern Chinese history. A long report by the *Times of India's* correspondent, titled *Letter from Tientsen*, explained the situation well. The correspondent listed several reasons for the rebellion including a poor harvest. But the disruptive presence of foreigners and modern technology, notably the railways and telegraph, was a primary cause of the rebellion. The correspondent also reported that the Chinese felt a "smoldering feeling of anger at the missionaries for their denouncement of ancestor worship."[24] Besides missionaries, native converts to Christianity were also the targets of the Boxers. An earlier report spoke of Christians having "recanted to save their lives" and "forced to crawl to the temple idols."[25] The Boxer Protocol, signed in January 1901, to bring about cessation of hostilities, did not find much mention in the newspaper though a report in 1908 spoke of the "long negotiations and squabbles" following the peace protocol.[26]

The Early 1900s and the TOI's Men in China

The first three decades of the twentieth century saw momentous events in China, including the rise of the Republican movement, led by Sun Yat-sen, the fall of the Qing dynasty, the ascendancy of the Kuomintang under Chiang Kai-shek and the founding of the Communist Party by Mao Zedong. Some of these events were covered for the *Times of India* by a remarkable man, Bertram Lenox Simpson, who wrote under the pen name of Putnam Weale. During this period, Stanley Reed, the longest serving editor of the TOI (1907–1923), was in charge of the newspaper. Reed ushered in many changes, including extending the deadline for printing news from 5 PM to midnight. He also reduced the cover price of the newspaper from four annas to one, boosting the paper's circulation. To cope with the increased circulation, the paper installed rotary printing machines.[27]

Weale was a member of the Chinese Maritime Customs service and a correspondent for several publications, including the *Daily Telegraph*. He was a prolific writer on China, having penned several books. He later worked for the political section of the office of the

Chinese president and got involved in local politics.[28] He died in 1930 at the hands of unidentified assailants. One of his reports for the *Times of India* was titled, *Soul of a Mob*, where he described in 1927 the situation in China thus: "The problem is not clear cut or simple as in olden days, but has become an intangible devilish thing with Bolsheviks inspiring it, Russian cunning and devilishness staining Chinese yellows a crimson hue which cannot but inspire fear."[29] Weale wrote in detail about the rise of the Kuomintang. He reported on the situation in Hankow: "Everywhere along the British bund is the Kuomintang flag and the National flag."[30] In one of his last reports, Weale identified three main players in China: Feng Yu-hsiang (or Yuxiang),[31] Chiang Kai-shek and the Chinese Communists whom he preferred to refer to as a "composite person" called Hankow.[32] Weale's assessment of the situation was that "Chiang Kai-shek, no matter what allies he may have, can never defeat the composite man called Hankow because that stands for Soviet Russia and all the striking-power that foreign powers can mobilize."[33]

A Reuters report on Weale's killing was carried in the TOI. It said, "Three Chinese gunmen motored to the house of Putnam Weale at Tientsin and asked him for an interview." While Weale was escorting them to his study, "one of them whipped out a revolver and fired twice."[34] Weale had apparently fallen foul of the Nationalists who did not want him to carry on as Customs Commissioner at Tientsin and that could have been the reason for his death. An earlier report stated that the Nationalist government had protested to the British about Weale's appointment.

Weale was not the only person reporting for the TOI on China. Everard Cotes, an Anglo-Indian journalist, reported from China around the turn of the century. What appears to have been his first report appeared in 1906 on the Hanyang steel factory.[35] In a later article, where Cotes is described as the newspaper's special correspondent, he wrote of the current situation in China:

> There is no lack of intelligence in the ruling classes. Only honesty of endeavour in the interest of the public, instead of behalf of themselves, is required… China is only in the position from which Europe has emerged. Her ultimate regeneration is looked for confidently by the best informed of her residents.[36]

His despatches to the newspaper were published in a book titled, *Signs and Portents in the Far East*. In a review of the book, the TOI wrote of Cotes,

> He saw the great and growing part the Chinese played in the development of Singapore; witnessed the commencement of railway enterprise at Canton; traversed the broad reaches of the Yang-tse river to Hankow, and journeyed over from the new trunk line from that port to Peking; inspected Port Arthur in the hands of the Japanese, and rode over the battlefields of Manchuria…[37]

Though no Indian journalist was yet to report from China, the poet and philosopher Rabindranath Tagore in 1924 visited both Japan and China. The tour itself was not much reported in the TOI but a speech in Calcutta on his return was. Though he greatly admired the "industry and frugality" of the Chinese, the Chinese were, according to Tagore, "Mere automatons in their own country, who worked for the benefit of other nations who had established factories and workshops."[38] The speech reflected the disappointment that Tagore must have felt at the hostile reception in many places in China to his message against uncritically accepting Western modernity.[39]

The Communists

The famous Long March of Mao Zedong's Red Army in 1934–1935 did not find much mention in the TOI. Neither did the Nanjing massacre of 1937–1938 where the Japanese killed thousands of Chinese. However, reports by Madame Chiang Kai-shek (Meiling Soong) datelined Nanking were carried in the TOI in 1937. In one of them, she wrote that the Japanese were "trying desperately to demoralize the nation [China] by murderous bombing of inhabited centres under the guise of aiming at military establishments."[40] The Japanese responded to Madame Chiang Kai-shek's reports with the Japanese consul M. Ishikawa writing a letter to the editor where he pointed out that it was "evident that China is cunningly attempting to shift the responsibility of her ruthless actions and the consequences of them on to Japan."[41]

This was also the time when the Indian nationalist movement was at its peak. The *Times of India*, which completed its centenary in 1938, was still very much a "British newspaper whose senior editorial and production staffs were exclusively British."[42] According to Frank Moraes, who joined the newspaper in 1936 and later became the editor, he was the only Indian assistant editor in TOI at the time. By 1940s, however, a column written by an *Indian Political Correspondent*, who was a serving assistant editor, was being published in the newspaper. In his memoirs, Moraes writes, "*The Times of India*'s political policy, though more liberal than that of the raj, moved broadly in step with it."[43] Moraes adds that while the TOI "gave cautious support to the advancement of Indian self-government it believed in the durability of British rule."[44] At the same time, the "majority of Indian journalists even on British newspapers were nationalist in outlook."[45] Since British-owned newspapers, such as the *Times of India* and the *Statesman*, "exerted considerable influence and patronage" Indian nationalist leaders read them with interest. Mohandas (Mahatma) Gandhi for one was not averse to writing letters to the editor if he disagreed with the TOI's opinions.

One of the early contacts between the Indian nationalist movement and the Chinese Communists occurred when Nehru himself visited China in 1939 and even experienced a Japanese air raid in Chungking.[46] One year earlier, the Indian National Congress had sent an Indian medical unit to China. A brief report in 1939 mentioned Mao's letter to Nehru recording his appreciation for the medical unit which he said had "made a profound impression on all who came in touch with them."[47] An earlier report spoke of the Congress Chinese Ambulance Unit led by Dr Atal and having as one of its members Dr Dwarkanath Kotnis. The report said that the committee to choose the medical team had received an astonishing 700 applications, including one from a journalist who wished to accompany the team as information officer and even pay for all his expenses. Later that year, the team sailed from Bombay in the *SS Rajputana* with 54 cases of medicine and surgical equipment. The Congress leader, Sarojini Naidu, was present at the send-off along with the Chinese vice consul. A group of Chinese boys sang on the occasion.[48] Dr Kotnis was the subject of a film, titled *Dr Kotnis Ki Amar Kahani* (the Immortal Story of Dr Kotnis) in less than a decade after the medical mission went to China. That was possibly due to the remarkable life of Dr Kotnis who was in China from 1938 to 1943, married a Chinese Communist and died in a remote corner of north-west China.[49] The film directed by Shantaram was based on K. A. Abbas' book, *And One Did Not Come Back,* and had as one of its technical advisers, Dr B. K. Basu, one of the members of the medical mission. Shantaram himself played Dr Kotnis in the film and an Indian actress, Jayashree, was cast as Dr Kotnis' Chinese wife Chin Lan. Even Madam Sun Yat-sen (Song Qingling) sent a message wishing the film well: "Dr Kotnis and the Indian Medical Mission will be warmly remembered in China for their part in the common struggle for National Liberation."[50] The film had a gala premiere at the Swastik theatre in Bombay in 1946, where "unprecedented scenes of enthusiasm were witnessed"[51] and it ran to packed houses for several weeks.[52]

There was some contact between India and China in an unlikely place—on the football field—in the 1930s. The match between the Chinese Olympic team, on its way to the Berlin Olympics, and an Indian team in Calcutta was described by the TOI as the first "soccer international" in India. The game was played before 20,000 people and fittingly ended in a draw.[53] Another match in Bombay too ended in a draw.[54]

In the midst of World War II, Chiang Kai-shek and his wife arrived in New Delhi "after travelling incognito with a large party of 15 Chinese officers."[55] He spent several days in India meeting prominent Congress leaders. Besides Nehru, Chiang Kai-shek met Mahatma Gandhi for over four hours in Calcutta[56] though there were rumours that Gandhi was not too keen on the meeting.[57] Later in 1945, then war correspondent Frank Moraes met Chiang Kai-shek in Chungking, claiming the "privilege of being the first Indian correspondent to be received by him."[58] Moraes, who was very impressed with Chiang Kai-shek, noticed a picture on the wall of the Generalissimo with Gandhi taken three years earlier.[59] The extensive coverage of Chiang Kai-shek's visit reflected the importance of China in the wartime efforts against Japan.

Mao's rise to the supreme leader of China was covered in some detail. In a lengthy article in TOI titled, "Mao Tse-Tung: China's New Master," a columnist, Robert Greve, likened Mao to a "Yellow Stalin" and wrote: "Like Stalin Mao established his rule within the Party by the ruthless elimination of all those who disagreed with his policy or his methods."[60] The writer had met Mao twice in the past three years and these were his impressions: "Mao looks much younger than his 56 years, and is in good health … He has an almost embarrassing way of looking straight into your eyes all the time. By the end of the interview, I felt almost dazed by this constant direct look." The TOI reported the election of Mao as the Chairman of the Central People's Government of the Republic of China[61] and a few months later wrote that recognition of the new government by the West was "imminent." The report stated that this "will mark the end of the Chiang Kai-shek regime in China and the emergence of a new Communist State controlling one-fifth of the world's population."[62]

Hindi-Chini Bhai Bhai

Just before India was to become independent and when British businessmen were leaving India in droves, the sugar baron Ramakrishna Dalmia bought Bennett, Coleman in 1946. Unlike some other newspapers in independent India, the TOI did not follow any particular ideology or take a particular line. As a senior editor of the TOI wrote in his memoirs, "To Dalmia a newspaper plant was no different from a cement … factory. Making profit … was the sole motivation."[63] The editor might not have got it entirely right since Dalmia had his pet causes, such as a ban on cow slaughter and was not averse to using the newspaper to champion them. Ownership of the TOI passed to Dalmia's son-in-law Shanti Prasad Jain in 1948, after Dalmia was embroiled in financial troubles, and with it the newspaper's approach subtly changed too. A member of the extended Jain family believed that Shanti Prasad Jain did not think of the newspaper "as an industry or as a way of wielding political power or clout like Dalmia*ji*."[64] Historian Gyan Prakash points out that at the time TOI was "sober and elitist" and "carried a whiff of the formality inherited from its colonial past."[65] In 1950, the TOI launched its Delhi edition, giving the newspaper a greater national footprint, as well as three years earlier a Hindi daily, the *Navbharat Times*. This also meant increased coverage of the Congress government under Nehru and parliament. The TOI's Delhi bureau had distinguished journalists such as B.G. Verghese (later the editor of *Hindustan Times* and the *Indian Express*), who was assigned to cover parliament, the Planning Commission and other ministries.[66]

By then, the Oxford-educated barrister Frank Moraes had been appointed the first Indian editor of the newspaper.[67] Moraes, the editor from 1949 to 1957, was described by a fellow journalist as "urbane and suave ... well-travelled, well-to-do and well read."[68] Verghese wrote of Moraes that he "did not bother too much about the nitty-gritty of running the newspaper, which he left to his deputies."[69] N. J. Nanporia (he later edited the *Statesman*), who succeeded Moraes, had a reputation for being somewhat aloof from his colleagues.[70] Both had their issues with the TOI owners and the management.[71] Under Moraes and Nanporia, however, the TOI covered developments in India–China relations in great detail. It also benefited from the newspaper's own journalists visiting and reporting from China. Moraes himself visited China in 1952 as part of an Indian cultural delegation, led by Vijaylakshmi Pandit, and wrote a series of articles on his impressions of China. In his concluding piece, Moraes noted the contradictions of Communist China: "The face of Mao's China is far more resolute, robust and roseate than Chiang [Kai-shek]'s China. The ends are impressive. But what of the means?"[72] Nanporia had a considerable interest in Asian affairs too and reported for TOI from Tokyo in the early 1950s.[73]

The 1950s was marked by independent India's, and particularly Nehru's, embrace of Communist China. The Chinese premier Zhou Enlai conducted a successful visit to India in June 1954. At a state banquet in Rashtrapati Bhavan, Zhou said, "Between China and India there has existed for two thousand years a traditional friendship ... I hope that China and India will co-operate even more closely for the noble aim of safeguarding peace in Asia."[74] It was during that visit perhaps that the *"Hindi-Chini bhai bhai* (Indians and Chinese are brothers)" slogan was possibly first heard. When Zhou visited the Taj Mahal in Agra, members of the crowd shouted, *"Chini Hindi bhai bhai."*[75] Later that year when a 60-member Chinese delegation arrived in Bombay, the slogan—*"Swagat Pyare, Chini Bhai hamare* (A loving welcome to our Chinese brethren)"—was heard. School children also raised the *"Hindi-Chini bhai bhai"* slogan on that occasion.[76] The flurry of visits by Chinese continued with Madame Sun Yat-sen too visiting India as a state guest in 1955.[77]

When Nehru reciprocated by visiting China in 1954, the TOI's reports captured some of the excitement around his visit. The TOI's correspondent, G.K. Reddy (he later moved to the *Hindu* where he spent most of his career), reported from Peking: "It was indeed a "Himalayan" welcome which the Indian Prime Minister received here today. Nearly a million people lined the 12-mile route from the airport, singing and cheering in a tidal wave of exuberant enthusiasm and affection."[78] S. Mulgaonkar reported the next day on the Western anticipation of the meeting between Nehru and Mao. He quoted James Cameron, a journalist in China, who described the meeting as one "representing between them half the population of the world."[79]

It was during this visit that 20,000 Young Pioneers shouted "Hindi Chini bhai bhai" when Nehru arrived in Shanghai from Peking.[80] When Nehru left China, the TOI reported that he "was firmly convinced that at least the present generation of Chinese leadership does not want war."[81] The Sino-Indian ties were further re-affirmed when Zhou again visited India in 1956 and was given a "tumultuous welcome symbolic of the bonds of friendship that had drawn India and China close together since his last visit here in the summer of 1954."[82]

The visit by Nehru allowed Indian journalists to acquaint themselves with different aspects of China, including the Chinese media. In a long article G. P. Jain explained the differences between Indian and Chinese newspapers, including the lack of advertisements and sensational news in the latter. He wrote,

> Crime, sex and sensationalism are missing in the Chinese papers. By Western standards they are dull sheets merely chronicling the construction activities. But they arouse in the Chinese people's hearts pride in the nation's achievements and inspiration for greater efforts to reach yet higher goals.[83]

When Jain asked the editor of a private Chinese newspaper if he could criticize the government, the editor replied: "Yes, we can, but you must remember that we have all agreed to the socialisation of the country under the leadership of the working class."

Hindi-Chini Bye Bye

Soon, however, cracks began to appear in the Sino-Indian relationship. The initial sticking point was Tibet where the Chinese had invaded in 1950 and claimed it as their own territory. From the late 1950s, the Chinese were seen to be meddling with Tibetan autonomy and were on a collision course with the Dalai Lama.[84] In a statement to Parliament, Nehru expressed his sympathies for Tibetans and said India wanted to see "real autonomy" in Tibet.[85] In early April 1959,

Radio Peking announced that the Dalai Lama had taken refuge in India.[86] The very next day, Nehru announced in Parliament to tumultuous cheers that the Dalai Lama had crossed into India.[87] Two days later, Nehru reiterated that India was interested in the autonomy of Tibet and that the government would not place any "undesirable curbs" on the Dalai Lama.[88] Later that month, the story of the dramatic escape of Dalai Lama from Lhasa was front page news in the TOI with the banner headline: "Narrow Escape from Chinese Guns." The report datelined Tezpur (in today's Arunachal Pradesh) said: "The Dalai Lama has informed the Prime Minister, Mr Nehru, that he decided to flee Tibet because the Chinese resorted to force after he had resisted more than once their attempts at whittling down Tibetan autonomy."[89] At the end of April, Nehru told Parliament that thousands of Tibetans had fled into India and had been granted asylum.[90] He decried Peking's claims that India had expansionist aims in Tibet. By September, Nehru was talking about the "growing feeling of irritation, anger and estrangement" between India and China.[91] And by the end of the year, Nehru told a public meeting that while India was ready for a peaceful settlement of the border dispute with China, it had to be ready for "all eventualities, not excluding war."[92]

When Zhou visited Delhi for the third time in 1960, the reception was in marked contrast to his earlier visits. The TOI reported that the crowds greeted him "in silence." Though Zhou paid lip service to the "everlasting" Sino-Indian friendship, Nehru pointedly spoke of the need to "undo much that has happened."[93] Earlier that month, the Chinese government stated that the Sino-Indian border had never been "formally delimited" and repeated its rejection of the McMahon Line, the frontier between Tibet and British India negotiated in 1914.[94] The assessment by the Indian press of Zhou too had changed dramatically by then. A TOI correspondent, who was part of an Indian team that met Zhou in Peking in 1954, gushed: "An hour and half with Premier Chou was an unforgettable experience for all of us." Zhou was described as a man "known for his extraordinary charm and ability to make friends and influence people."[95] Six years later on the eve of Zhou's third visit to India, the tone of the TOI correspondent was very different: "During his earlier visits, Mr Chou en Lai exuded goodwill and friendship... On both those occasions we were too willing to be charmed. Today we cannot afford the luxury of taking the mask for the face."[96]

These fears were not unfounded. Over the next few months, relations steadily deteriorated over the disputed Sino-Indian border. In 1960, a bewildered Nehru was telling Parliament that India had to be prepared for war with China.[97] Soon after Nehru informed Parliament that Zhou had rejected India's position that Chinese troops had entered Indian territory. The Chinese argued that Sinkiang and Tibet had been in their possession for 200 years.[98]

By the end of 1961, relations had degenerated to the extent that there was talk of war in the air. Nehru told Parliament in November 1961 that a "military build-up" was in progress along the Sino-Indian border.[99] He also added that far less than 2,000 square miles had fallen under Chinese occupation in Ladakh. The reports from China were not encouraging either. The TOI's Sudhakar Bhat reported from Hong Kong that China will "always try and maintain a vastly superior military build-up, in relation to India's along the Sino-Indian border."[100]

In 1962, war seemed imminent.[101] India's controversial defence minister Krishna Menon claimed that through "skilful diplomacy" India had "isolated" China.[102] Even if this claim were true, it did not stop China in September of that year from occupying territory that India deemed as its own. Later that year Menon said, "We shall not surrender, nor will we negotiate, whoever may tell us, until the Chinese have vacated our land."[103] Two days later, Nehru told Parliament that the "premeditated invasion" of India by China was a "turning point" in the history of the world. Amid cheers he proclaimed, "We accept the challenge with all its consequences."[104] The Indian Communists too backed Nehru with a Communist Party of India MP Hiren Mukherjee pledging "unqualified support" on behalf of his party. Indeed when Nehru told Parliament of the fall of Se La Ridge in the North East Frontier Agency (NEFA) to the Chinese, there were demands by Socialist MPs to declare "total war" on China.[105]

There were, however, persistent questions about India military readiness. The Indian army was in retreat in the icy mountains on the Sino-Indian border. To boost morale, Nehru addressed Indian troops which had managed to come back to the Indian lines after engaging in combat with the Chinese. He assured them that India's defence was being strengthened against further Chinese incursions.[106] About this lack of preparedness, B. G. Verghese wrote, "The Indian Army was unprepared and surprised and it would have been very strange indeed if the aggressor had not won the initial success he did."[107] The border dispute dragged on for most of 1963 with Nehru saying that China's word could not be trusted.[108] Later that year, he insisted that China withdraw from areas occupied by them in 1962.[109]

The Indo-China conflict was being played out in the larger theatre of the Cold War and Nehru was all too aware of that. In an interview with the Associated Press, he said, "The Chinese are keen on bringing about a situation in which India is no longer considered non-aligned."[110] The great powers regularly weighed in on the conflict. Soviet President Nikita Khrushchev hoped that China and India would settle their "misunderstanding" but refused to put any blame on China.[111] Another report from TOI's correspondent in Washington said that the United States was "fully prepared to commit its own forces to the struggle of Indo-China."[112] Pakistan, with whom India was soon to fight a war and who sided with the US in the Cold War, was also very much part of the equation. According to a TOI report, President Ayub Khan was "seeking to frighten the USA into giving up its arms aid to India by holding out the threat that this might force the smaller countries of Asia to look to China for protection."[113]

There was not much movement on the border issue in 1964 either with a weary Nehru saying that India was prepared for talks but the first move must come from China.[114] Within a few days of the statement, Nehru suffered a fatal heart attack. The TOI reported that the Chinese press had maintained an "organised silence" over the death of Nehru.[115] However, the Hong Kong press was scurrilous in its assessment. The TOI reported that the *Ching Pao* accused Nehru of steering India on a path where it was "unable to live in peace with a single neighbouring country." The *Express Daily* described Nehru as a "double faced person." The *Hong Kong Times* stooped even lower calling Nehru "a small clown on the international stage." The war with China clearly had an adverse impact on Nehru. Nanporia, then editor of TOI, wrote in a tribute to Nehru: "The last years of his life were overshadowed by some particularly acute disappointments the most important of which were Communist China..."[116] The shock of the Chinese invasion was clearly articulated by Krishna Menon in an interview to Michael Brecher: "I think it affected him [Nehru] deeply; it had a very bad effect on him. It demoralised him very much. Everything that he had built was threatened."[117]

Conclusion

Nehru's death is a poignant and fitting place to end a narrative of over a hundred years of coverage of China. The final years of Nehru's prime ministership undermined the ideas of non-alignment and Asian unity that Nehru had so fervently propounded. Though in the post-Nehru years diplomatic relations between India and China once again became cordial, the border dispute continues to haunt Sino-Indian relations. So does the Tibet issue with the Dalai Lama having made India his home since the time he fled Lhasa. China has intruded into India's consciousness in myriad ways including radical movements in rural India taking up Mao's name and ideology.

The TOI has of course continued to chronicle these events, some of the more recent ones having been described in other chapters in the book. During this period, BCCL or the Times Group has grown to become the largest publishing house in the country. It now owns 13 newspapers, published in English, Hindi and regional languages, and 18 magazines. It also owns television channels, including Times Now, the most popular English news channel in India.[118] The TOI itself is now truly a national newspaper with editions in all the metro cities as well as some of the smaller cities. However, the newspaper is no longer the staid "newspaper of record" that it once was. Under the third-generation Jains, the Times Group has led the way in making its own newspapers, as well as rival dailies, more market- and profit-driven. As the BCCL managing director Vineet Jain recently told a journalist, "We are not in the newspaper business, we are in the advertising business."[119]

History has a cyclical quality to it and more than 150 years after the opium wars it is trade, albeit of a different kind, that substantially underpins the discussion about China in India.[120] In the nineteenth century, the opium trade tied together the destinies of India and China. Now, China and India are discussed as economic powerhouses as trade between the two countries continues to burgeon. This is reflected in much of the reportage and editorializing in the TOI on China where the emphasis is on economic competition between India and China, the opportunities for cooperation and admiration for

China's efficiency in achieving economic miracles. At the same time, the border issues of the 1950s continue to hamper Indo-China relations and often provoke a nationalistic response from the TOI. An unsigned editorial from 2006 (written by me when I was with the newspaper), just before President Hu Jintao was to visit Delhi, captures some of these tensions:

> At a time when there is plenty of talk about the joint potential of Chindia, quibbles about the McMahon Line and the Indo-China border seem anachronistic. New Delhi must take the initiative in steering the talks to trade and economic issues that are of much more importance than redrawing the map.[121]

It is this duality that defines the *Times of India*'s contemporary coverage of China.

Notes

1. *Bombay Times and Journal of Commerce*, 24 November 1838. The spellings of names of Chinese people and places have been kept as they appeared in the newspaper.
2. *Bombay Times and Journal of Commerce*, 8 June 1839.
3. Edwin Hirschmann, *Robert Knight: Reforming Editor in Victorian India* (Delhi: Oxford University Press, 2008), p. 67.
4. Reuters set up their office in India in 1866. Knight had set up a Times of India Telegraphic Agency in 1860 to sell news dispatches to other newspapers in India but later sold the service to Reuters.
5. Hirschmann, *Robert Knight*, p. 75.
6. Julia Lovell, *The Opium War: Drugs, Dreams and the Making of China* (London: Picador, 2011), p. 24.
7. *Bombay Times and Journal of Commerce*, 2 November 1839.
8. Lovell, *Opium War*, p. 36.
9. M. Emdad-ul Haq, *Drugs in South Asia: From the Opium Trade to the Present Day* (London: Macmillan, 2000), p. 1.
10. http://www.timesgroup.com/bccl/history.html (accessed on 18 October 2014).
11. Madhavi Thampi, *Indians in China: 1800–1949* (New Delhi: Manohar, 2005), p. 88.
12. Ibid., p. 65.
13. Ibid., p. 76.
14. Ibid., p. 86.

15. *Bombay Times and Journal of Commerce*, 19 June 1839.
16. Ibid., 6 March 1839.
17. Ibid., 2 November 1842.
18. Ibid., 25 August 1858.
19. Ibid., 8 January 1861.
20. *Times of India*, 31 May 1889.
21. Ibid., 6 May 1895. See also Haq, *Drugs in South Asia*.
22. *Times of India*, 20 August 1894.
23. Ibid., 19 April 1895.
24. Ibid., 7 August 1900.
25. Ibid., 11 July 1900.
26. Ibid., 17 January 1908.
27. Sangita P. Menon Malhan, *The TOI Story: How a Newspaper Changed the Rules of the Game* (New Delhi: HarperCollins, 2012).
28. Paul French, *Through the Looking Glass: China's Foreign Journalists from Opium Wars to Mao* (Hong Kong: Hong Kong University Press, 2009), p. 82.
29. Putnam Weale, "The Soul of a Mob," *Times of India*, 4 May 1927.
30. Ibid., "Hankow Under the 'Reds'," *Times of India*, 13 May 1927.
31. Feng Yuxiang, a warlord, was vice-premier of the Republic of China from 1928–1930.
32. Putnam Weale, "How Peace will Come," *Times of India*, 4 October 1927.
33. Ibid.
34. *Times of India*, 13 November 1930.
35. Ibid., 12 June 1906.
36. Everard Cotes, "The China of Today," *Times of India*, 26 September 1906.
37. *Times of India*, 15 March 1907.
38. Ibid., 23 July 1924.
39. For a detailed description of Tagore's visit to China, see Stephen N. Hay, *Asian Ideas of East and West: Tagore and His Critics in Japan, China and India* (Cambridge: Harvard University Press, 1970), Ch. 5. See also Pankaj Mishra, *From the Ruins of Empire: The Intellectuals who Remade Asia* (New York: Farrar, Straus and Giroux, 2012), Ch. 5.
40. Madame Chiang Kai-shek, "Bombing of Nanking," *Times of India*, 28 September 1937.
41. *Times of India*, 15 September 1937.
42. Frank Moraes, *Witness to an Era: India 1920 the present day* (London: Weidenfeld and Nicholson, 1973), p. 43.
43. Ibid., p. 44. Moraes recounts that as an Indian he could not use the senior staff canteen or the "exclusive" lavatory meant for the British staff. He was also initially excluded from the daily morning conference attended by all the other British assistant editors, but upon protesting was invited to take part.
44. Ibid., p. 95.
45. Ibid.

46. *Times of India*, 25 August 1939.

47. Ibid., 14 July 1939.

48. Ibid., 2 September 1938.

49. Ibid., 29 March 1945.

50. Ibid.

51. *Times of India*, 23 March 1946.

52. Ibid., 11 May 1946.

53. Ibid., 6 July 1936.

54. Ibid., 9 July 1936.

55. Ibid., 10 February 1942.

56. Ibid., 19 February 1942.

57. Later Gandhi wrote to Vallabhbhai Patel of the meeting: "I would not say I learnt anything, and there was nothing that we could teach him." See Guido Samarani, "Chiang Kai-shek, Nehru and China-India Relations during the Second World War Period," Working Paper no. 11, 2005, Centre for East and Southeast Asian Studies, Lund University.

58. F.R. Moraes, "Marshal Chiang on India's Great Help to China," *Times of India*, 22 January 1945.

59. Chiang Kai-shek, however, made no reference to Gandhi but asked about Nehru. See Moraes, *Witness to an Era*, 132.

60. Robert Greve, "Mao Tse-Tung: China's New Master," *Times of India*, 13 March 1949.

61. *Times of India*, 1 October 1949.

62. Ibid., 18 December 1949.

63. D.R. Mankekar quoted in Robin Jeffrey, "Mission, Money, and Machinery: Indian Newspapers in the Twentieth Century," in Ravi Sundaram, ed., *No Limits: Media Studies in India* (New Delhi: Oxford University Press, 2013), p. 104.

64. Malhan, *The TOI Story*.

65. Gyan Prakash, *Mumbai Fables* (New Delhi: Harper Collins, 2010).

66. B.G. Verghese, *First Draft* (New Delhi: Tranquebar, 2010), p. 40.

67. It is now little remembered that before Moraes took over, there were two Indian editors who had very short stints as editors of TOI: R. Gopalaswami and Lala Feroze Chand. See Verghese, *First Draft*, p. 35. The last British editor of the newspaper was Ivor Jehu.

68. M.V. Kamath, *A Journalist at Large* (Mumbai: Jaico, 2007), p. 206. For details of Moraes' career see "Moraes lived close to the scene of action," *Times of India*, 5 May 1974.

69. Verghese, *First Draft*, p. 35.

70. See S. Nihal Singh, *Ink in My Veins* (New Delhi: Hay House, 2011), p. 159.

71. The introduction to a collection of Moraes' essays says that his "relations with *The Times of India* management became strained and one not so fine morning he was summarily dismissed," See R.C. Cooper, ed., *Without Fear or Favour: A Selection of Articles by Frank Moraes* (Delhi: Vikas Publishing,

1974). Nanporia was so fed up with the TOI management that he even wrote a confidential letter to Nehru narrating the interference of the owners in the day-to-day functioning of the newspaper. See Malhan, *The TOI Story*.

72. Frank Moraes, "Journey to China X: The Balance Sheet," *Times of India*, 1 July 1952. Moraes also wrote a book on his visit to China called *Report on Mao's China* (New York: Macmillan, 1953).

73. *Times of India*, 26 December 1952.

74. Ibid., 28 June 1954.

75. Ibid.

76. *Times of India*, 18 December 1954.

77. Ibid., 17 December 1955.

78. G.K. Reddy, "Peking's 'Himalayan' Welcome to Mr Nehru," *Times of India*, 20 October 1954. A few years earlier Reddy was at the receiving end of Nehru's famous temper for his reporting of the Chinese invasion of Tibet. Nehru apparently felt that Reddy had taken China's side and said in a press conference, "This man is either a fool or a knave or a combination of both." See Inder Malhotra, "The Great Communicator," *Indian Express*, 11 November 2014.

79. S. Mulgaonkar, "Nehru-Mao Meeting may Change History," *Times of India*, 30 October 1954.

80. *Times of India*, 18 October 1954.

81. G.K. Reddy, "Nehru Convinced China does not want War," *Times of India*, 18 December 1954.

82. *Times of India*, 29 November 1956.

83. G.P. Jain, "The Press in China," *Times of India*, 9 January 1955.

84. John Garver writes that the "Tibetan issue was central to the deterioration of Sino-Indian relations which culminated in the 1962 war." See Garver, *Protracted Contest: Sino-Indian Rivalry in the Twentieth Century* (Seattle: University of Washington Press, 2001), p. 60.

85. *Times of India*, 31 March 1959.

86. Ibid., 13 April 1959.

87. Ibid., 4 April 1959.

88. Ibid., 6 April 1959.

89. Ibid., 16 April 1959.

90. Ibid., 28 April 1959.

91. Ibid., 12 September 1959.

92. Ibid., 29 November 1959.

93. Ibid., 20 April 1960.

94. Ibid., 12 April 1960.

95. G.P. Jain, "An Evening with Mr Chou En-lai," *Times of India*, 31 October 1954.

96. Ibid., "Chou En-Lai: A Shrewd and Patient Negotiator," *Times of India*, 7 April 1960. One wonders whether the writer is Girilal Jain, the legendary future editor of the newspaper.

97. *Times of India*, 24 November 1960.

98. Ibid., 27 April 1960.

99. Ibid., 29 November 1961.

100. Sudhakar Bhat, "Mao wants to arm every Chinese," *Times of India*, 4 December 1961.

101. There are several accounts of the 1962 war, many of them at odds with each other. B. N. Mullik's *My Years with Nehru: The Chinese Betrayal* (Bombay: Allied Publishers, 1971) is an account by an insider who was the director of the Intelligence Bureau. The title of his book betrays his position. The London *Times* correspondent Neville Maxwell in his controversial *India's China War* (London: Cape, 1970) blames Nehru for the war. Other interpretations include K. Subrahmanyam's "Nehru and India-China Conflict of 1962," in B.R. Nanda, ed., *Indian Foreign Policy: The Nehru Years* (Delhi: Vikas Publishing, 1976).

102. *Times of India*, 17 February 1962.

103. Ibid., 7 November 1962.

104. Ibid., 9 November 1962.

105. Ibid., 20 November 1962.

106. Ibid., 7 December 1962.

107. B. G. Verghese, "Report on NEFA: Lessons of the War," *Times of India*, 4 January 1963.

108. *Times of India*, 31 January 1963.

109. Ibid., 11 June 1963.

110. Ibid., 25 September 1963.

111. Ibid., 15 December 1962.

112. Ibid., 22 June 1964.

113. D.F. Thomas, "Hong Kong Press Hurls Insults at Nehru," *Times of India*, 11 July 1963.

114. *Times of India*, 18 May 1964.

115. Ibid., 11 June 1964.

116. N.J.N., "The First Servant Is No More," *Times of India*, 28 May 1964.

117. Interview of Krishna Menon by Michael Brecher. "The Chinese Invasion II," *Times of India*, 12 October 1968. The interview was carried in three parts.

118. Srinjoy Chowdhury writes about Times Now in Chapter 10 of this book.

119. Ken Auletta, "Citizens Jain: Why India's Newspaper Industry is Thriving," *The New Yorker*, 8 October 2012.

120. See Subhomoy Bhattacharjee in Chapter 13 of this book.

121. *Times of India*, 15 November 2006.

10

The View from an Indian Television Newsroom: What Makes Us Different?

Srinjoy Chowdhury

Srinjoy Chowdhury's first story was a feature about a Kolkata juice bar, a favourite haunt of Indian freedom-fighters of nationalist times. National Affairs Editor of Times Now, India's most-watched TV news channel in English, he joined *Sunday*, a leading national news magazine in 1984, and later worked for the *Telegraph*, a Kolkata-based English newspaper and the *Statesman*, a national daily. He has written *Despatches from Kargil* (2000), the story of India's undeclared war with Pakistan in 1999; co-authored, with the plane's pilot, *Flight into Fear* (2000) about the hijacking of an Indian Airlines flight to Kandahar in 1999 and published three quiz books. He went to La Martiniere College and Presidency University in Kolkata. He lives in New Delhi.

An Indian Journalist in a Chinese Square

On a balmy summer afternoon, as children scampered after over-sized plastic balls and parents pushed prams, several hundred armed security men stood shoulder to shoulder waiting for a ragged bunch of protesters with home-made posters and outraged expressions. Photoshop the policemen out and it could be anywhere, but this was Tiananmen Square, Beijing, on 4 June 2007. It could not have looked more different from 1989, but China had not forgotten those days. I was there because China had invited Pranab Mukherjee, then India's external affairs minister. The security men were there because China was alert to a protest, however forlorn.

Nor had the Indian Embassy forgotten the sensitivity about 1989. How distracting would the detention of an Indian television journalist in Tiananmen be before a big ministerial visit? The Indian Embassy pressed ID cards on my cameraman and me. The cards impressively announced our status as visiting journalists in English and Mandarin. The embassy advised caution: "Don't go anywhere without your ID card."

At the Square, a quick on-camera walkthrough about how different the day is from the day in 1989 that appalled the world. The reminder of the horror. The tape was quickly placed in an anonymous jacket-pocket, and the camera got a new tape for a piece-to-camera on the visit. You cannot be too careful: all you need is one eager-beaver security man to confiscate the tape and ruin a story!

Minutes later, the first man in uniform arrived. No TV camera in the Square is above suspicion on 4 June; you did not have to know Mandarin to know he was not happy to see us around, but the Indian Embassy's credentials were a badge of honour. We would not get frog-marched out; we would, minutes later, face another security man, only more senior. Once again, the ID saved the day. Carefully examined this time, the ID bought us a few more minutes, just enough time for another piece-to-camera before the Big Man arrived. So, what exactly was I doing, shooting in the Square? It was all very polite, just conversation between friends. Yes, the ID explained who we were, but why were we shooting here, in Tiananmen?

"When I shoot in the Square, my viewers will know I am in Beijing. So much of your city is just skyscrapers. I could be anywhere—Shanghai, Guangzhou, even Hong Kong or Singapore. I have to explain to my viewers I am here," I replied.

Acknowledging the legitimacy of my argument (good visuals make for good stories) and the fact that I had only arrived that day, he was ready with another question.

"So, what are you going to talk about? What issues? What subjects?"

"I am an Indian journalist. I have come with my external affairs minister. Naturally, this is about India and China and the issues that are going to be discussed," and then, truthfully enough, "Why don't you stand by and listen to what I have to say?"

No statement could have built more trust. "That's fine then. If you have a problem, let me know." He shook hands as he left, but didn't leave a number.

A guilty smile or two were the only interruptions after that, from locals who came up to me and said: "Anniversary! Anniversary!" What if there were demonstrations that day? How close could my camera get to the protesters being dragged away. What would I have managed to shoot? If I did get something out, mobile phones being such a blessing in these circumstances, how long would my visa (if I were Beijing based) have lasted once my story was on air in India?

Reflecting on this, I ask myself how often do foreign correspondents in India ask themselves these questions when they work on stories? Or need to?

Six years later. 2013. It was not even the anniversary, but the iron fist was still showing: shooting in Tiananmen was tougher than it was before. "You have to take permission," an Indian diplomat declared, "several hours in advance". Then you are solemnly "escorted" there by a handler. Mine was polite and perhaps, deliberately economical with his English. He was there, beside my cameraman, while I did my pieces to camera, several of which were almost interrupted by security guards, not quite standing shoulder-to-shoulder but sufficiently prepared for pesky journalists. What is all this about the new media, the new glasnost?

"A Hungry News-gatherer"

It is fair to say the two political systems—a liberal democracy in India (for all its flaws) and a one-party monolith in which capitalism flourishes in China—have bred different kinds of journalists and different views of what the media's role is. That is what many Indian media-professionals believe. There was evidence at a seminar at the National University of Singapore in 2012 when a veteran Chinese journalist declared he would have been silent, and perhaps even, sympathetic, if the launch of India's first Agni-V ballistic missile (range of about 6,000 km, nuclear-capable, considered a counter to China) had failed. Silence, not gloating, he felt, was in the Chinese national interest and his work did not go against his country's desire to have friendly ties with India. Harping about a failed launch would, he said, have been detrimental to Chinese national interest. Journalism, an Indian journalist replied, is not or should not be an extension of national policy. If the launch had failed, the Indian media would have been strongly critical as happened when the Agni-III ballistic missile launch went down in flames in 2006.

If the Chinese media, still relatively tightly controlled, articulate the aspirations of the State, and even their leaps into anti-establishment reporting are kept within cautious boundaries, mainstream Indian voices are almost anarchic by Chinese standards. The Indian media is heterogeneous—more than 800 TV channels and 82,000 registered newspapers and magazines, virtually all privately owned. No doubt there are fat-cat proprietors and plenty of evidence about "paid news"; but Indian media are less trusting, more questioning and never keen to buckle under government pressure.

One "incident," played again and again on the news television channel Times Now has no parallel in the Chinese media. After the Comptroller and Auditor General (CAG) of India's report of a huge scam in the telecom sector, and the Indian government's attempted whitewash, Times Now's editor-in-chief Arnab Goswami asked Manmohan Singh, then Indian prime minister, during a rare press conference, if he believed, "The zero loss claim in the 2G scam." Harish Khare, then Singh's media advisor, cut in immediately. "Goswami. This is not an interrogation of the Prime Minister. Please … show him the courtesy. Show him the courtesy." The testy retort of the media advisor is not just another example of hostility, of stark antagonism. It is evidence that the Indian media can ask the tough question. When was a Chinese Premier confronted this way on television and that too, by a Chinese journalist?

If the foreign policy media beat in India was ever a backwater, away from the mainstream of domestic politics, it isn't any more. Foreign policy doesn't just divide the chattering classes; it can drive domestic discourse. Foreign policy reporting too is much more mainstream today. Stronger economic sinews after the post-1991 embrace of globalization and also, the developments in rocketry and nuclear technology have made India more assertive, a bigger "global player". India wants a place at the international high-table; a permanent seat in the United Nations Security Council is only one demand.

India is also more "aggressive" about protecting its citizens abroad, taking up issues with other countries. India's "hard line" after uproar in the media in 2010–2011 about Indian students being beaten up by belligerent and often, drunken Aussie bruisers in Melbourne and Sydney is a case in point. After a number of attacks, the media spoke out against racist attacks. Responding to this pressure, the Indian external affairs ministry pressurized the Australian government to ensure Indians were protected. Australia was forced to admit that some of the attacks were racially motivated. S. M. Krishna, the then external affairs minister, and his deputy, Preneet Kaur, repeatedly protested, the former announcing that if he were a young man looking to study abroad, he would not go to Australia for degrees in cooking and hairstyling. On several occasions, Times Now hired a reporter in Melbourne to interview battered students in hospital. We would then ask the Australian High Commission in Delhi and the Ministry of External Affairs what they had to say and what they planned to do to stop the continuing attacks.

Aided by the information-technology–telecom revolution (Skype, for example, is very helpful if a TV camera is not available), the Indian media are more proactive today. Foreign policy reporting is not only about arcane policy discussions and cozy handshakes any more: there is a growing belief among reporters that if New Delhi is really the muscular giant-in-the-making, it should surely have the ability to help/protect its citizens, whether they have been captured by pirates, or are being exploited by construction barons in West Asia or even "harassed" by foreign governments. Once, Indian media houses, with honourable exceptions, sent reporters abroad usually on the prime minister's or external affairs minister's plane. Even a decade ago, Indian journalists would not have trooped to Tahrir Square in the numbers that they did during the turmoil: many media houses would not have had the resources and even if they did, would have depended on foreign agencies.

In the imperfect world that is contemporary India, it is not necessary to wake up one morning and decide an anti-establishment position is imperative. When the high-and-mighty flounder repeatedly, a robust media can hardly look away. So, why should India–China ties be any different?

How do the media deal with a relationship that is often dysfunctional, yet both sides pretend that all is well? The Chinese media, particularly the official organs, may turn a Nelson's eye to irksome issues unless there is a specific directive from the authorities. Indian media, on the other hand, will be more news hungry. "If it bleeds, it leads," old newsroom hands once said. The dictum still applies to foreign affairs reporting.

India–China ties are not just about the occasional gaze. Far too much is going on: Soldiers of the People's Liberation Army painting rocks communist red on what India thinks is its side of the Line of Actual Control; Tibet's self-immolating monks; the Dalai Lama's visit to Arunachal Pradesh (an Indian state China claims as its own); China's denying visas to people from Arunachal Pradesh and senior military personnel; aid (including nuclear technology) to Pakistan; and disputes in the South China Sea.

Foreign policy is not alien to the twenty-first century Indian TV viewer. Virtually every middle-class Indian has family abroad; many have studied abroad, many more have travelled abroad to work and for vacations—something unthinkable a generation ago. A Wimbledon final is available live as is the Oscar awards ceremony; the BBC and CNN bring world news to Indian living rooms. Why can't Indian news channels do just as well or even better?

As Indian interest in foreign affairs has grown, life with the Chinese dragon, and an economically and militarily resurgent one at that, has not become easier. Once, the unsettled border divided India and China; it just is not politico-military any more. Rather, there are differences over oil and water and atomic energy, dams on the Tsangpo/Brahmaputra, the South China Sea oil wells and even the Indo-US nuclear deal, over which the Chinese opposed India's efforts to get a clearance from the Nuclear Suppliers Group. Within the Indian establishment, there are growing concerns about economic ties, primarily about the access and strategic power that Chinese firms in India are acquiring.

Fault-lines fuel tough stories. Such stories are not dug out by the Indian government and fed to the media to passively accept. To be sure, the Indian establishment is divided about Beijing. George Fernandes (a former Indian defence minister) told senior journalist Karan Thapar during a TV interview in 1998 that China was India's "potential threat No 1." No doubt there is suspicion about China, but there isn't a black-arts cell in the Indian external affairs or defence ministry waiting with anti-China handouts. Quite the contrary, when there is concern about Beijing, it is privately and discreetly expressed, and whenever possible, played down.

When a government official does leak, it is usually to help a friend (breaking a strict directive about not passing on sensitive information to the media) and always in confidence. Breaking stories invite "trace the leak" inquiries and official frowns. Only India's democratic traditions ensure the media remain a powerful force. Even after stories break, there are attempts at gentle persuasion by government officials to limit their life.

Sometimes, it is not a secret memo that makes a story, but a statement in writing by the defence minister of India, a reply to a question by a Member of Parliament, a tiny gold needle in a haystack of bumf. One such story was about People's Liberation Army (PLA) soldiers breaking down a wall built by Indian troops along the Line of Actual Control (LAC). When Parliament is in session, ministers have to reply each week to questions by Members. The reply to the fruitful question went like this:

> On July 13 this year, a PLA patrol attempted to cross a 200 foot wall of loose stones constructed 250 metres on our side of the LAC (Line of Actual Control) in (the) Yangtse area of Tawang, which was prevented by our troops. The stone wall was partially damaged by PLA, which was reconstructed.[1]

A flag-meeting followed, the Minister continued, and India had made the usual protests. This written reply, stapled together in the usual bunch of answers to written questions which normally had little news value, contained considerable detail. For once, the usually circumspect defence ministry had abandoned its oft-repeated reply that "the information is being collected and will be placed before the House." For this story, you did not need a Deep Throat; it was about persistence, looking through piles of bland replies, twice a week, week after week, and getting it before anybody else. That's one way a hungry news-gatherer works.

Any responsive news desk will gobble up such a story. All it takes for this written reply, which would normally be lost among dozens of others to become breaking news is for the reporter to phone the channel news-editor on duty and then report the story, live on-camera with Parliament in the background. None of this took long: only one phone call to dictate the story at the same time as I jogged to the camera-position. This was not an easy story for TV, however. There were no shots of the PLA breaking down a wall, not even a still photograph of the broken wall, just generic shots of the area. But there is footage of Tawang in Arunachal Pradesh and particularly of the famous monastery. We inserted in the story file footage of A. K. Antony, the Minister, and of PLA soldiers, and imbued the story with a sense of excitement.

Bites of the usually reticent defence ministry/army spokesman were difficult. "The minister has already spoken" was what we heard at first. Immediately after the story broke, there was a phone call (more evidence that there isn't someone in the government spoon-feeding anti-Beijing stories to the pliant media) from a polite and hesitant army officer uncertain about where the story had come from, not having seen the defence minister's reply in Parliament.

"You can see I am quoting the defence minister himself. So, I must be very sure of it," I replied to his first flurry of questions.

Shortly afterwards, I received another call. Was the story based on the Parliament question?

"Yes, it is."

Then, he said, very politely: "It happened several months ago. Why are you doing it now?"

Because, we said, the story hadn't been reported. "Nobody knew about it."

A final question from the officer: "Could you tone it down a bit?"

The Zhan Lue Episode

There is another story that illustrates the new international media environment and the differences between the way "news" becomes "news" in China and India. This story also brought an intervention from a senior official in the Prime Minister's Office, another indication that the Indian government does not feed media with anti-China stories. This story would have had little impact before the Information Revolution. In August 2009, a Chinese think-tank mounted on the Internet a paper saying India should be Balkanized, broken up into 20–30 parts with the help of Pakistan and Nepal. A generation ago, the think-tank would have published a small-circulation journal which would have carried the article. A Western wire service would have chanced upon it and later, filed a story. Only then would it have reached an Indian desk.

However, in 2009, once the essay by Zhan Lue (meaning Strategy), entitled "China can dismember the so-called Indian Union with one little move!" appeared on a Chinese strategic think-tank's website, the Indian Ministry of External Affairs expressed its unhappiness.[2] When it did so, alert media houses quickly downloaded the essay and broke the story. The assumption (and a fair one, considering China's political structure) that the essay had some official sanction (Indian intelligence agencies later told the government that Zhan Lue was a senior Chinese official), and the fact that the Ministry of External Affairs had reacted to it, gave the story more traction. With shots of the Chinese website, an interview with one of the think-tank mandarins, and a report of New Delhi's displeasure, the story was on air.

Minutes after the story broke, the Prime Minister's Office was trying its version of Newspeak. "Why are you carrying this story? It isn't Beijing's official position! Why publicize a radical think-tank's off-the-wall views?" the caller from the PMO asked.

"Of course, this isn't the official Chinese position," I replied.

No one is saying it is. It is an article carried by a think-tank and often, considering the relationship between the establishment and the media, it could reflect the view of a certain section of the Chinese Communist Party or the government. Even if it isn't, it is still an interesting point.

I mentioned we had waited a while and spoken with various people. I added that a senior journalist known for his understanding of international issues had written about it. Exasperated, the PMO official blamed me for following a burnt-out fossil of a story and rang off. The story stood.

Outside Stories

Even earlier, after reports about Chinese "intrusions" into east Ladakh by reporters in Jammu and Kashmir and based on off-the-record interviews with state government officials, I was sent to Leh to investigate what the on-the-ground situation was.

Impossible, the assignment initially seemed to be. The commander of the Army's 14th Corps refused to see me, even though one of his aides (a close friend) advised him to. Local bureaucrats stonewalled adroitly. Neither the army nor the local bureaucracy would allow me to visit Demchok, the troubled area on the LAC. One needed a permit to go to.

I was losing hope until a friend advised me to speak to the local political leaders—members of the Ladakh Autonomous Council. A worried man, Tshering Dorjay, then chairman, regretted that PLA soldiers were not only entering Indian territory but troubling the locals, mostly poor herdsmen.

"On one occasion, they damaged their tents. Then, they came again, and took everything away. I had to buy tents for these people," he complained.

Was he ready, I asked for an on-camera interview?

"Yes, I am," he said, probably not imagining how important his statement would be. This was the first time any Indian government official was speaking about PLA soldiers entering India and harassing Indian citizens!

He had more news for me. Nawang Morbu, the local representative from the contested area, was in Leh, buying gifts for a family function. I could speak with him if I wished.

"Most certainly," I replied and found him, laden with packages outside a shopping centre. He too expressed helplessness about Chinese intrusions. It was all so refreshingly different (and honest) from the bureaucratese of Delhi. There, officials would tell us, "Oh, we have different perceptions about where the Line of Actual Control is—they [the Chinese] come up to where they think the LAC is and our patrols do the same."

This high-octane story could not wait for the reporter to return to New Delhi. Despite the impossible logistics (bandwidth problems, serious power-cuts), the footage finally got through to the newsroom in New Delhi. Our editorial team decided to go with the story immediately; our viewers had a detailed from-the-front exclusive that evening. From the Times Now studios, the anchor called me in Leh for a "phono" (the reporter live with the anchor): "Now, you would have no doubt about the PLA's intrusions?" he asked. I agreed. How could you overlook what the locals are saying?

Inside Stories

Sometimes China stories do emanate from inside government, but they are as likely to be motivated by personal connections as Indian-government scheming. When the Deputy Chief of China's General Staff, General Ma Xiaotian's proposed visit to India was cancelled as the dates were "inconvenient," an official quietly leaked the news. There was nothing Machiavellian about the motive. The official was helping a media friend who was short of a story. After discussions during Times Now's mid-day editorial meeting and because video footage of General Ma was easily available, the story was quickly on air as a headline. Yes, he wasn't coming, A. K. Antony, the defence minister, announced the next day; but it wasn't because relations had deteriorated; it was only because there were other visits on that day and it would not be "convenient."

In ferreting out stories, a "mole" in the ministry who is involved in the paper-flow is gold-dust. Sometimes a mole isn't necessary: the suspicion within the Indian establishment about China is publicly spoken of. A speech by Shekhar Dutt, then defence secretary and the ministry's top bureaucrat, is a case in point. In May 2007, he made a speech at a combined function of the Army and the Confederation of Indian Industry on a slow Saturday with only one TV camera in attendance. The speech lacked the usual measured tenor, and it ensured a reaction from the usually silent Chinese embassy in New Delhi. The speech asserted that:

> China has embarked on a major programme of "informisation." The strategy is to win regional wars under high-tech conditions. China is primarily exploring non-conventional or asymmetric warfare as a method. China's 2004 defence white paper encourages the establishment of a military and national information infrastructure with appropriate military and civil information capability to conduct cyber wars.

Why would a cautious official, working for a government that was uncomfortable about criticizing China, raise eyebrows unnecessarily? It was unusual, except in the context of unease about China within sections of the establishment that is sometimes inadvertently reflected. That he spoke about Chinese strategies to win "regional wars" was the Big Story, and the bites—Dutt reading from a prepared text—were the clincher. This was a classic Indian TV story, built on strong bites. When you have got it, it is played as an "exclusive," which the competition will regret missing and the External Affairs Ministry and the Chinese Embassy will fret over.

Requests for reactions went out to both, but the first sirens went off in the External Affairs Ministry. Did Times Now have a copy of the speech? We did. Dutt was travelling; his office didn't have a copy or hadn't passed it on. One look at the speech and the diplomatic community knew damage control was not possible. No claim that Dutt had been quoted out of context would help. "What do you have to say?" I asked a senior diplomat. "Go with the defence ministry's statement," he replied.

A furious denial from the Chinese Embassy followed the next day; the story was alive again, headlined "China refutes defence secretary's claims." The denial allowed the channel to go with the story another day, along with the previous day's bites for context.

Visualizing Stories

Sometimes, sensational stories are difficult to present as television. An example was the meeting between Wen Jiabao (then Chinese PM) and Manmohan Singh, in Hanoi on 29 October 2010. It was near the end of the latter's tour of Japan, Malaysia and Vietnam. The Indian media looked at how the Chinese media were setting the tone. And there it was, a *People's Daily* editorial arguing that India's Look East Policy was an attempt by Delhi's hawks to "encircle China." This was potentially dramatic—a newspaper of the all-powerful Chinese Communist Party condemning New Delhi's aggressive instincts just as the Indian prime minister was in the neighbourhood meeting with leaders of two countries with which Beijing had problems, Japan and Vietnam.

The challenge was to visualize the story—to make it work on TV. We had shots of Singh with Japanese leaders, but he was still on his way to Hanoi. "Encirclement" was a *People's Daily* phrase; but no Chinese leader had or would say that publicly. As shots of the story would only go so far, the story had to be a bite-based, he-said, she-said story. The on-camera reaction was from the senior MEA official on the PM's flight during a hurriedly arranged briefing. India, he said, did have a Look East Policy to reach out towards Southeast Asia, but it began in the 1990s when P. V. Narasimha Rao was India's prime minister and it wasn't about the encirclement of China. Apart from Indian experts, usually retired diplomats, we interviewed a Hanoi-based Vietnamese strategic affairs expert. He spoke of his country's keenness to have good relations with both India and China and not be involved in power games.

India–China ties are often about the unexpected, and the media have to be ready for it. At the Manmohan Singh–Wen meeting in Hanoi, "encirclement" was set aside. Usually, these meetings begin with cameramen being called in for the photo-opportunity, and then hustled out after a minute or two. On this occasion, as I walked in with a video-camera, I heard a forthright Wen, speaking through an interpreter, announce he wanted to visit India very soon. Bureaucrats on both sides, he said, can iron out differences before that.

Why would Wen, a careful and protocol-conscious man, tell Manmohan Singh what he wanted to do before a roomful of cameramen? Was it a pre-planned gesture before a largely Indian media contingent? Indian officials were convinced it was. They believed the Chinese wanted to tell the Indian media directly and not via Indian officials that at the highest level, there was "maturity and understanding" about India–China ties.

In a world where a minute's lead matters, this was a big "break." The briefing by the Indian national security advisor happened shortly after the meeting ended and was effectively upstaged. On a "phono," I was asked what the talks would lead to. Instead of being a little speculative, I said unequivocally that I had heard Wen tell Prime Minister Singh he wanted to visit India and would the officials get to work on the details of settling and solving issues before he got there. The Chinese interpreter's statement in English was loud enough to be picked up by camera microphones, and we ran it along with the post-meeting Indian statements.

During another Manmohan Singh–Wen meeting in Bali on 18 November 2011, the South China Sea issue surfaced. China spoke against the presence of "outsiders," meaning India. India repeated that its interests in the area were "purely commercial." This was intended to mean that if there were disputes, they were between China and Vietnam or China and the Philippines. India claimed the right of passage—and the right, if invited, to explore for oil.

The occasion for raising the question of the Indian navy in the South China Sea had occurred in July 2011. *INS Airawat* on its way from Na Thrang in Vietnam and about 45 km from Haiphong received a message in Mandarin on the open radio channels. The caller told the ship to stay out of Chinese waters. Despite the "warning," the

Indian warship did not change course. When the story broke in a Western newspaper, every Indian TV channel went for it. It was a story no one could overlook. It was a headline throughout the day, for virtually every major TV channel, gradually picking up pace as reactions came in. The Indian Navy confirmed receiving the message. Of course, it said, there was no eyeball-to-eyeball confrontation. There were enough visuals of the *INS Airawat*. There were reactions from everywhere—India, China and other countries. Even the Vietnamese ambassador to Delhi chipped in, saying Indian warships were welcome to visit any port in his country at any time.

The *INS Airawat* incident might have been a one-off, dismissed as the actions of an over-zealous Chinese naval officer but for Beijing's position on oil-drilling in the area. The Chinese were unhappy about an Indian firm's efforts to find oil in the South China Sea, and the spokesman in Beijing made that clear whenever he was asked about the issue. That got reported in India, where New Delhi kept saying its interests in the area were "purely commercial." The basic positions were so starkly different that even repeating them ensured media coverage.

In 2013, the South China Sea issue was not Breaking News every day, but the media had not forgotten it either. When Admiral D. K. Joshi, then Indian Navy chief, announced during a press conference in December 2012 that if necessary he would send warships to the South China Sea to protect Indian interests, it was big news for national newspapers and the TV channels. It ensured an immediate clarification by Shiv Shankar Menon, then Indian national security advisor, who, embarrassingly for the government, was in Beijing for talks at the time.

Muddled thinking within a government makes for an absorbing story. The differences between India's National Security Council (NSC) and the telecommunications ministry provide a good example. The NSC had warned of the danger of working with Huawei, the Chinese telecommunications firm. A copy of the draft memorandum of understanding between Huawei and India's prestigious Indian Institute of Science surfaced. This time the story was not about the dangers of Huawei infiltrating Indian systems, but of the differences within the Indian government. Times Now had both documents: the two arms of the government appeared to have different views on Huawei. If Huawei were a security risk because its links with the People's Liberation Army made it an arm of government, what was it doing signing MoUs with a premier Indian scientific institute?

The story was not a visually strong story, but had to be done. One way of breaking such "visually dry" stories is to get two reporters to "flash" the documents before live cameras, while telling viewers the story, with the anchor going back and forth to the reporters. There were sound-bites from the government, Huawei and IT experts, and these built up the story through the evening.

Happy Stories?

As all these case-studies relate to conflict, the compelling questions are: "Isn't there any India–China story on cooperation? Are the media that negative?" To the media, a story is a story is a story: media do not measure whether a story is positive or negative and for whom.

There have been headlined stories about India and China working together. A memorable one with dramatic still photographs sent by the Indian Navy was an operation against pirates in the Gulf of Aden. When Somali pirates attacked the *MV Full City* about 850 km off India's west coast on 5 May 2011, the Indian navy sent a TU-142 maritime reconnaissance plane to hover over the mother ship, forcing it to disengage and sail off. After 24 Chinese sailors were rescued, Beijing through the embassy in New Delhi thanked the external affairs ministry. Stills of the encounter, a defence ministry bite and a statement by the Chinese embassy in Delhi made the story.

Depsang and Chumar

All these incidents seem irrelevant when compared with the story of the PLA setting up camps near Depsang, in the Daulat Beg Oldie sector of east Ladakh in April–May 2013 and in Chumar, a little to the south, in September 2014.[3] "Depsang" began with a terse press statement from the Indian Army's Northern Command. That there was a statement, considering how India underplays LAC issues, was almost miraculous on the eve of the Chinese Premier Li Keqiang's first visit to India and just before Indian external affairs minister Salman Khurshid's visit to Beijing. Yet the event is still dismissed by a section of the establishment in Delhi as "four men and a dog."

It was not just four men and a dog, of course, but a platoon of armed PLA soldiers, who entered India on 15 April and set up four tents. Nobody seems to know why. They confronted an equal number of Indian troops till they packed their tents and departed on 5 May 2013. It was a long and tense period.

Other than the initial statement, there was only official silence. Sources—senior armed forces officers, intelligence officials or leading diplomats, people who were helpful for years and also friends—fell silent. "I am sorry I cannot tell you a thing," was the common refrain. A senior official showed me a photograph of the four tents. "That's all I can do," he said, "and of course, I haven't shown you the photograph." When I asked if I could take a photograph with the camera in my BlackBerry, he went silent and pale. "Out of the question," he said at once.

Getting news became a challenge. Reporters sent to Leh, the biggest town in Ladakh, came back with scraps. Several friends helped. One spent an evening explaining how there was a flurry of "deep probes" by PLA patrols in the area before the intrusion. He drew a map, explaining how Indian security forces rarely patrol up to the Line of Actual Control in some areas, preferring to go up to the LOP or the Limit of Patrol. Going any further than the LOP would not be a patrol; the difficult terrain would make it an expedition. "The Chinese have taken advantage of that," he said, giving me breaking news. "They have plans to build a road in the area between the LOP and the LAC!" Another friend tipped me off about a flag meeting. "Nothing much happened beyond a decision to meet again," he said. Just those sentences and a few more details were gold dust when the silence was as stressful as it was.

If someone dared to break the curfew, they were people at the highest levels of government, usually reticent men. One called me to his home on a Sunday afternoon and briefed me about the situation on the ground. A top armed forces officer called me to his office and suggested the face-off would end after another flag-meet. A minister, known for his tactful silence, one day revealed something important. After I had done a lot of frenzied walking around the corridors of power, I noticed some "movement" and realized that he had called a meeting. It would be crucial and provide an understanding of the end-game that lay ahead.

There is a saying about India: "Whatever you say, the opposite is also true." Despite the government's deliberate decision to ensure secrecy, a top official, on several occasions, shared situation reports with one or two journalists he knew. If one part of the government stayed silent, another part generously shared it all. Everyone seemed to know who had leaked the information; everyone complained about it; but no one did anything about it. At a time when newsgathering was so difficult, these leaks were an enormous challenge in an atmosphere of intense media competition.

Equally challenging was getting photographs of the event. Depsang was too distant and difficult to go to. How could we get photographs of Indian and Chinese soldiers waving flags and staring at each other? It was not a visual story, but it was too important to ignore. Stock footage of the area and of troops and leaders of both countries were used along with maps and graphics. There were talking heads every evening. Viewership remained high. Unsurprisingly, the Chinese government had little to say, and the Chinese media had less to report.[4]

The relationship between an Indian correspondent and his government regarding Sino-Indian issues is not any easier in the era of Prime Minister Narendra Modi who came to power in May 2014. The stand-off between the Indian and Chinese troops in Chumar in 2014 was the biggest in decades as nearly a thousand Chinese troops and a slightly larger continent of the Indian army and Indo-Tibetan Border Police faced each other for more than two weeks. A primary objective of the Indian government was to deny information to reporters. The blackout was only partially successful: there is always someone willing to speak or a young officer near the front with news and internet access. It is distressing, one official said, that so many young, well-armed and well-trained officers are virtually eyeball-to-eyeball. They must be only 300 or 400 metres away from each other, he fretted. "We have told China that both sides must reduce troops in the face-off area. Otherwise, there is a risk of escalation." That made quite a story.

You could learn when the next flag-meeting was and later what had happened. Sometimes there was something outrageous. An ailing Chinese lieutenant had landed near an Indian post in Chumar during the stand-off. He was fed, given medication and returned without any fanfare. "How the f… did you hear that?" an army officer asked when I called him for a reaction. Another, after a crucial flag-meet over Chumar took my call. "There is a clamp-down. I am not supposed to speak. The pullback begins tomorrow," he said and rang off.

People emailed photographs of the face-off—groups of flag-waving Indian and Chinese confronting each other—oxygen for a visual-starved

TV channel. Facing a perpetual government blackout, journalists look towards technology as a game-changer, often the humble mobile-phone. How can you stop people from photographing Chinese soldiers pushing and shoving their way past their Indian counterparts on the Line of Actual Control, and emailing it to a TV channel? What "Times Now" aired in 2013, before Chumar, was not studio-glossy, but it was compelling footage. You could hear the grunting, the shouting and an Indian army officer trying to keep calm, ordering his men not to react. The army quickly admitted the footage was genuine, but sniffed that it was not recent. It had to be genuine. Faking that kind of footage would have required a million dollars and Steven Spielberg.

In the middle of all this, Xi Jinping, the Chinese president, arrived in India on 17 September 2014. Prime Minister Modi announced he had asked Xi to move troops out of Indian territory, which was the first unequivocal official confirmation that Chinese troops were in India.

During the Depsang episode in 2013, there was no similar announcement. It was only later, after the Chinese left, that Salman Khurshid, then external affairs minister, memorably called the incursions "acne." In Beijing during the Depsang standoff, he said he had not brought up the issue during discussions with his Chinese counterparts, when in fact he had. Indian officials were appalled and later admitted "a wrong message had been sent."

Seeing Each Other

Just how wary the Chinese establishment is of the Indian media, and how ignorant about its functioning, is evident from its reactions. In July 2014, Chinese soldiers crossed over into east Ladakh, pitched tents and stayed for a few days. They left after two flag-meetings, but before they marched off, they had a terse message for the Indian army. "Make sure the Indian media does not get to hear of it." Days before the Chumar intrusion ended, Le Yucheng, the Chinese ambassador to New Delhi, came to South Block, where the Indian Foreign Office is located, to meet senior officials. I noticed the ambassador's limousine driving in. The flag is a giveaway, besides the CD plates. For any journalist, calling for a cameraman and getting an interview with the ambassador as he leaves is business as usual. After the interview was aired, a Chinese embassy official asked: "Did your ministry of external affairs tell you that our ambassador was coming?" He did not know that—far from tipping off the journalist—the MEA was furious with him for "accosting diplomats" outside South Block.

One view is that all the suspicion that shrouds India–China ties would vanish if there were more Indian journalists in Beijing. This version of the "blame it on the media" argument steers clear of the fact that the handful of Indian reporters in China find the doors locked and cannot go much beyond picking up anti-India blogs, newspaper reports and foreign office briefings. In those circumstances, why bother with the investment in the age of the internet and international flights? If there is a big story, a reporter is only a flight away.[5]

Let me offer five propositions widely held in Indian television newsrooms.

(a) First, India is a liberal democracy with a history of press freedom, except for the period of the "emergency" in 1975–1977. Recent initiatives like the Right to Information Act have strengthened the media, and their ability to be critical of the government, as should be the case in a democratic country.

(b) Second, foreign relations are not overlooked by Indian media houses. Today, they have the resources and viewership. People have more understanding of the world, and Indians in this age of globalization have stronger links with other countries.

(c) Third, when tough stories are reported about the Indian president, why pull punches on foreign-affairs stories? If there are tensions between India and China, they must surely be reflected in day-to-day reporting.

(d) Fourth, if the Indian establishment is divided over China, the voices of both hawks and doves will find their way into the media. There is no deliberate effort by the Indian government to leak stories. Instead, the government downplays stories of China–India confrontation and tries to stop tough stories.

(e) Fifth, the Chinese media are hobbled by their political system.

Are Mandarins in power dealt with more sympathetically by the Chinese media than Mughals in Delhi by their Indian counterparts? Aren't the differences in the way the media in India and China function (Mandarins treated more deferentially than Mughals?) a reflection of the different political systems and ways of life? For all the activism of the fringe media in China, the view from Delhi is that even "dissent" is often deliberately created and controlled by the Party and government establishment.

There may be no better example of the differences than the furore over a "ban" on a TV channel in 2011 by the Congress, then, the political party in government. Deciding that the channel was "too critical," some top Congress Party leaders decided they would not send a spokesman to take part in prime-time talk shows. What it meant was that during the much-watched discussions, there would be no Congress representative to put the party's point of view. The move was unprecedented, and unusual. Debate began within the party. A number of leaders thought this was a bad idea. The ban was on only one channel, but if other channels criticized the party, would they be banned too? How many channels could the party afford to ban? A few days later, "democratic spirit" prevailed. A very senior leader assured the offending channel that he would certainly come to be interviewed.

Could such an episode have occurred in China? Would a Chinese TV channel have been able to offend the Party so seriously? Would the contemplated punishment have been a withdrawal of party participation from that channel's talk shows or something more draconian? In the answer lies an explanation of the differences between the functions of media in the land of the Mandarins and the land of the Mughals.

Notes

1. Defence Minister A. K. Antony, replying to a question in the Rajya Sabha (upper house), 21 December 2011.
2. See Tang Lu's perspective on the "Zhan Lue episode" in Chapter 7 and Ananth Krishnan's view in Chapter 8 of this book.
3. See Danny Geevarghese's discussion of Depsang and Chumar from the perspective of a Chinese newsroom in Chapter 11 of this book.
4. See Danny Geevarghese's account in Chapter 11.
5. For a Chinese journalist's view, see Tang Lu's chapter in this book.

11

Trying Hard to Be Soft: The Chinese State and India in CCTV News

Danny Geevarghese

Danny Geevarghese is Chief News Editor at CCTV News in Beijing, where he has lived since 2011. He is the first South Asian to hold an editorial position at CCTV News and writes on China for the *Economic Times*. Danny began his career as correspondent/producer in India reporting from the Indian Parliament and Supreme Court. He later managed media advocacy programmes at Panos South Asia. He has a master's degree in Media and Politics from the School of Oriental and African Studies (SOAS), University of London, and a post-graduate diploma in journalism from the Asian College of Journalism, Chennai.

Do perceptions of China and India differ in each other's newsrooms? Is India not considered an equal partner by China? China features prominently in Indian newsrooms, but does New Delhi matter to Beijing? Having worked in Indian and Chinese TV newsrooms, I try in this chapter to unravel the idea of India in the Chinese editorial spectrum.

In the autumn of 2014, a public spectacle played out on world television. President Xi Jinping of China and Prime Minister Narendra Modi of India, in mutual admiration, enjoying an evening stroll on the banks of the Sabarmati River in Ahmedabad, were on display. Timed to get the setting sun, the glistening river, and the dancing *garba walis* in their colourful *cholis* in the frame, the leaders—walking shoulder to shoulder—exuded charm and veneration.

India's national public broadcaster, Doordarshan, beamed these images live, which were picked up by its counterpart in Beijing, China Central TV (CCTV), and played on the many channels that the network owned. Chinese TV pundits waxed eloquent about the "close ties" between India and China and how India was a partner in the Asian growth story. Hours later, however, the demands and curiosity of Indian news TV were obvious. Along with the 24 × 7 coverage of President Xi's visit, television newscasters were asking: "Is this charm offensive by China a farce?" and "Why are Chinese troops inside Indian territory while their President is in New Delhi?"[1]

Introduction

China Central Television (CCTV) is China's biggest state broadcaster. With 48 channels, CCTV broadcasts both news and general programming in Chinese, English, French, Spanish, Arabic and Russian. Portuguese and Japanese channels too are in the works. CCTV viewership surpasses 1.1 billion at home, and when combined with its international language channels, is estimated to be upwards of 1.5 billion.[2]

English-language media in China can be traced to the 1920s,[3] and television broadcasting in English to 1979. In 2000, CCTV–9 was launched as the country's first English news channel. It was controlled and run like a Chinese news channel with Chinese producers, Chinese management, and most editorial meetings in Mandarin. The channel began to employ foreigners—news readers and news anchors, mostly of Caucasian and Chinese origin. Copyeditors were hired but given no editorial control. Many of the foreigners had no journalistic experience, and that suited CCTV, as the managers only wanted better grammar, not necessarily better journalism. Consequently, in spite of attempting to "emulate the Western style," becoming "the first television media organisation in Asia that can beam its signals to every corner of the globe," and "being seen in 119 countries," the channel was watched in 2003 mainly by young, English-learning Chinese and a smaller number of non-Chinese viewers in older age groups.[4]

To penetrate foreign markets, the channel underwent makeovers. CCTV–9 began to look outward, rather than serve as only one of the 16 channels of the CCTV network or an eye into China. The channel's marketing tagline was changed from "A Window on China for the World" to "Your Window on China and the World." As one senior CCTV executive explained, "We refined our mission by bringing to the world the Chinese and Asian perspective on Chinese, regional and international affairs."[5] The process coincided with the run-up to the 2008 Olympics in Beijing and gave a semblance of the government loosening its control over public broadcasting.

Meanwhile, by the beginning of 2007, English-language international channels backed by governments had been launched by Russia (Russia Today), France (France 24), Qatar (Al-Jazeera English) and Iran (Press TV). China realized that it had to raise its game to be taken seriously in the international news arena. In April 2010, CCTV–9 was renamed CCTV News. About two months later, David Shambaugh of George Washington University wrote in the *New York Times*:

> [The] State Council Information Office is coordinating China's media and exchange organizations to "go out" (zou chuqu) and establish a foothold in the international media environment and think-tank world. The Chinese government is investing a reported $8.7 billion in 2009–2010 in its "external publicity work"—primarily on the "Big Four": China Central Television (CCTV), China Radio International (CRI), Xinhua News Agency and the China Daily newspaper—while media executives and opinion shapers from various countries are being brought to China for "familiarization" tours.[6]

CCTV News decided to move into the international English news space and broadcast news from outside China. It was decided to separate CCTV America from Beijing-based CCTV News and create an identity distinct from the main channel but from within. CCTV America would have professional American journalists, the latest in technology, and be less controlled editorially than Beijing. CCTV Africa too would emerge a few months later adding to CCTV News's expanded footprint.[7] How did this expansion affect editorial selection and what made CCTV America stand apart from the regular news cycle produced from Beijing?

The Dual System: Selective Censorship

CCTV's international division works as a public broadcaster platform while retaining strong and direct links to the government and state. Let me explore the different kinds of links and how they impinge on journalism at CCTV News.

CCTV News is funded by the Chinese government and controlled by the State Administration of Press, Publication, Radio, Film and Television (SAPPRFT), an arm of the State Council led by the Chinese Premier. Thus, directly under the central government in Beijing, CCTV News is often seen as a mouthpiece of the Chinese state. This caricature, however, ignores the degree of autonomy that CCTV News enjoys in the contemporary global media landscape.

For example, for the 24-hour news cycle, the CCTV News headquarters in Beijing produces content for about 18 hours a day, while the rest is shared between CCTV America (four hours) and CCTV Africa (two hours), based in Washington, D.C. and Nairobi, respectively. In this segregated-broadcasting model (that Al-Jazeera also started out with but later abandoned in favour of a single broadcast centre in Doha), producers at CCTV America and CCTV Africa—both running news bands within the channel—have their own assessment of their respective audiences, different from those in Beijing. As Ma Jing, Director General of CCTV America said in a PBS programme, "We uphold the traditional journalistic values. We consider accuracy, objectivity, truthfulness, and public accountability very important, more important than anything else." In the same programme, Mike Walter, an anchor on CCTV America said, "I don't see people coming and saying, 'Mike you have got to change this script.' It hasn't happened."[8]

This is not the case at the channel headquarters in Beijing, however. CCTV News in Beijing employs senior Chinese editors, through whom all scripts must pass before they are green-lighted. These gatekeepers, whom colleagues refer to as Lǎoshī ("teacher"), have usually spent a few decades in China's print media (Xinhua or *People's Daily*) and have the final word on what goes on air. Very often, they tell news writers that the language is not in line with state policy and needs to be changed. For instance, the Lǎoshīs ensure that references to organizations banned in China—like the Falun Gong—are removed before any script is approved. More often than not, their intervention relates to a word or phrase that cannot be broadcast. For example, the Lăoshīs ensure that every reference to the "disputed Senakaku islands" (as Japan calls them) is changed to "China's Diayou Islands." Similarly, the Lăoshīs at CCTV News in Beijing will not allow the words "separatists" or "rebels" to go on air about those opposed to Beijing's rule in Xinjiang or Tibet; the fighters are almost always classified as "terrorists." The same principle applies to rebels in countries that have friendly relations with China, such as Russia, Syria and Iran. Thus, the Lăoshīs serve as the last line of editorial defence, protecting the interests of the Chinese state.

Uniquely, in the case of China, segregated broadcasting has ushered in separate editorial policies. The CCTV News tagline ("A Window to Asia") remains the same in different geographies, but a dual system of editorial standards operates within the same channel—one set of guidelines and practices in Beijing, and another set elsewhere. In August 2014, when CCTV America reported on the arrest of suspected members of an illegal cult in China, it also mentioned the arrest of Falun Gong members in 1999, even though the source story from Xinhua had not contained any such reference.[9] A *New York Times* blog complained, "CCTV America provided only very limited coverage of the Bo Xilai scandal or the drama surrounding Chen Guangcheng, the blind activist who took refuge in the American Embassy in Beijing and later made his way to the United States."[10] But in Beijing, there was a total blackout on the same stories. A senior producer in Beijing points out, "Who will watch CCTV America in America if we give them content from Beijing? For us to reach them, we have to look like them, talk like them, and maybe even give them a little of what they want." Whatever the raison d'etre behind dual standards, when CCTV America puts out content that is not allowed in Beijing, it implies some degree of autonomy and is perhaps unprecedented in Chinese broadcasting history.

Even though the segregated-broadcasting model has enhanced the space for freedom in CCTV News, its impact among journalists in Beijing has remained largely unchanged. The boundaries are omnipresent and defined at times, as with coverage relating to China's sovereignty and claims of territoriality. Hence, at an editorial meeting, no news writer will raise the issue of the Dalai Lama travelling to Washington, D.C. to meet the US president (The Dalai Lama's pictures are banned on CCTV News). On domestic issues, the boundaries vary according to the topic. Criticism of the Chinese Communist Party is a strict no-go, but stories about corruption at the highest levels are selectively cleared as when Xinhua releases a story. Softer stories critical of China's policies are allowed, such as those critiquing the country's pollution, environmental issues and education reform. The boundaries are thus porous when it comes to much of domestic coverage. Still, no news writer will raise the issue of a human rights activist in China being detained if she believes that the story will not go beyond the table. And if a sensitive story is discussed at editorial meetings, the norm followed in decision-making is "better to avoid and play safe" than push the envelope to see where the boundary lies on that topic. Down the hall, the Lǎoshīs act as censors inside the network; their workload lightened by the self-censorship of younger journalists.

Self-censorship and boundaries at CCTV News do not emerge from the channel's dependence on advertisements. Because unlike many channels on the CCTV network, which are financed largely by advertisements from private and public enterprises, CCTV News is funded almost entirely by the state. The channel carries advertisements (often of public enterprises), but they do not influence editorial priorities. As Jonathan Hassid observed regarding media control in China:

> Although oversight is often hands-off, the fact that the sponsoring units retain ultimate responsibility over the content published by their attached news units creates a strong incentive to set appropriate boundaries. After all, few players in the Chinese bureaucracy want to invite greater scrutiny from the Center.[11]

How much do editorial diktats and self-censorship reflect on news priority? Why does news from Japan take prominence over news from India? I explore these questions in the next section.

India-gazing: New Delhi in the Chinese Newsroom

How is India viewed by China's public broadcaster for international affairs? What kinds of Indian stories have priority and why? It is useful to first learn what CCTV's priorities are in the newsroom. On a regular day, the order of editorial priority is: issues around China's sovereignty (including Japan–China relations), US–China relations, US foreign policy (including US–Russia), Chinese economy or domestic issues, Hong Kong and Taiwan, the Middle East, East Asia and Afghanistan–Pakistan.

Coverage of India is not a priority for CCTV News; on a normal day, India would occupy the ninth or tenth position on the list. News stories from India are carried in the channel's bulletins, but unless it is a world event like the change of central government in New Delhi, a visit of a Chinese leader to New Delhi (the favour is not always reciprocated) or a major natural disaster, it would not be prioritized. India is seen as a regional heavyweight of South Asia and "does not enter our realm in the Northeast Asian spectrum," according to a senior researcher at a think-tank affiliated to China's foreign ministry. This is in contrast to any English-language TV newsroom in India, where China figures prominently and would probably follow domestic politics and Pakistan in a roster of editorial priorities, ahead of SAARC countries. This coverage is mostly limited to issues surrounding the disputed border with China and rarely does one see headlines on Indian TV about Chinese domestic politics, environmental pollution or even corruption, all of which receive much bigger play on channels like BBC World or CNN.

Let us look at India's place in China's news priorities. Up until September 2014, no Indian TV channel, including state broadcaster Doordarshan (DD) had a correspondent based in Beijing, while representatives of three Indian newspapers and one news agency had a correspondent in the Chinese capital. At the same time, until end-2013, CCTV News channel had one correspondent in New Delhi; since then, another has been added to increase the number of India-specific stories. China employs more than half a dozen correspondents in India who write for both English and Mandarin language outlets in China and report for its Chinese-language television stations. This is a far cry from CCTV News in the United States, where the channel employs dozens of journalists in Washington, D.C. and more than 20 reporters across the country. In Japan—with 127 million people, less than 10 per cent of India's population—CCTV News has one full-time correspondent and a few freelancers. Yet Japan dominates news and current affairs talk shows on the CCTV network.

In 2013, in the 100-odd discussions on "World Insight," the flagship world affairs programme, which chooses the channel's top two stories of the week for a 20-minute discussion with international scholars and diplomats, India featured only twice—once on the protests following the Delhi gang rape of December 2012, and the other on Premier Li Keqiang's maiden visit abroad, which began in India in May. To put this in perspective, out of the 100 slots that year, 15 discussed the United States (foreign policy, domestic politics, or economy) and 10 were on Japan (Sino–Japanese ties, Northeast Asian security, Japanese domestic politics or US–Japan ties).[12]

Equally instructive is the tone of coverage on Japan. CCTV News largely spotlights the negatives of Japanese foreign policy: its alliance with the United States and since 2012, the issue of the disputed islands. Japan is to China what Pakistan is to India—a constant threat, and a niggling political and military worry.[13] So the Japanese are covered with appellations, similar to how Indian news TV channels report on an "intruding" Chinese army or "infiltrating" Pakistani troops.

India is so deep in the recesses of the Chinese psyche that she invariably eludes CCTV News managers; they are preoccupied in their editorial logic by Japan, often accompanied by the corpulent presence of the United States. US action in East Asia, including the 2012 announcement by the US State Department about a US "pivot to Asia," created a furore in traditional and online Chinese media.

A third way of understanding CCTV News' approach to India is to study how Indian and Chinese TV channels covered a particular event—for our purposes, the coverage of the Depsang incident of 2013.

The Depsang Incident of 2013

In April 2013, about 30 Chinese soldiers reportedly set up camp at Chumar, inside what India claims is its side of the border in the Depsang sector of Ladakh, 750 kilometres east of Srinagar.[14] This happened a couple of weeks before Chinese Premier Li Keqiang, having taken office in March, was to make his maiden visit abroad, beginning in New Delhi.

As observers of the region know well, media reports about problems on the Sino-Indian border are nothing new. In fact, the 2013 issue looked like a repeat of similar claims of "intrusion" made four years earlier. In 2009, when news reports had appeared, the Indian government initially denied them, complained of "aggressive hype" by the Indian media, and asked media houses not to "overplay" incidents on the border. It even threatened to take "legal action" against the two journalists who had filed a story in the country's most widely read English newspaper.[15] Later, however, Prime Minister Manmohan Singh was forced to indicate "that he was in touch with the 'highest levels' of the Chinese government, and media reports of incidents on the long India–China border were a reflection of the inadequate flow of information from his government."[16] Indian Sinologist Alka Acharya wryly observed that it was probably the first time that the media had been asked to play down an incident on the Indo–Sino border, and that when it came to relations between the two neighbours, "occasional voices of sanity were simply overwhelmed by the course of conflict and contention."[17]

So, when the incident was repeated in 2013, the Indian media had another field day. Leading Indian news channels, including New Delhi TV (NDTV) and Times Now, discussed the issue five days in a row, during the 7 PM–11 PM prime time news band, in the week beginning 22 April 2013.[18] CCTV's counterpart in India, Doordarshan (DD), too was not sedate in its coverage of the issue. In a news slot aired in the evening and headlined "India–China Stalemate Continues," DD said "Chinese troops [had] moved inside Indian territory."[19] Two days later, the *Hindu* newspaper reported India's view that a differing perception about the "disputed boundary, which remains yet to be demarcated" was the cause of the problem.[20] It must be noted here that TV channels, including the nation's public broadcaster, had termed the movement of troops by the Chinese side an incursion "into Indian territory," which, as the *Hindu* said, was yet to be demarcated.

In contrast, across the border, CCTV News largely ignored the issue, which was underplayed at editorial meetings. "World Insight" turned a blind eye to the incident (despite involving China), and the conflagration on evening news in India was ignored. Producers at CCTV were told that the issue was not to be discussed and that it would be "handled" by a brief mention on the daily news segment—not more than a few minutes a day were to be spent on it. When the Indian media coverage was raised by some of the younger (and newer) segment editors at the weekly editorial meetings, they were told that "China had good ties with India" and "We have been told not to cover the issue in depth." Since the news was making waves on social media, one journalist suggested that it could go into the Media Review section (which looked at trends on social and traditional media), but this too was ruled out as it would apparently "only complicate matters." Care was taken, however, to ensure that every piece on CCTV News that talked about the Sino-Indian border would call the boundary "disputed" and "not demarcated," in line with the official statements of the Chinese government (and in this case, the Indian government too). The veteran Lǎoshīs persevered to see that the scripts adhered to this dictum. Meanwhile, outside CCTV News, a Chinese think-tank researcher, who had had official stints in Chinese embassies, said in a private conversation that "there was nothing to worry about on the border" and that "it was just the Indian media making mischief."

To highlight the difference in the Chinese approaches to India and Japan, one needs only to contrast the Sino-Indian border incident with a Sino–Japanese dispute. In 2012, about seven months before the Sino-Indian border incident, Japan "nationalized" the Senkaku/Diaoyu islands in the East China Sea by buying them from a private Japanese owner. Massive and unprecedented protests broke out against Japan in more than fifty Chinese cities.[21] The Japanese ambassador's car was attacked in Beijing. Japanese clothing stores were attacked and the showrooms of carmakers Toyota and Mitsubishi were targeted by mobs. Chinese flags were raised atop Japanese noodle restaurants. The protesters were pacified and sent home, but not before the damage was done. Reuters reported that in China, "the demand for Japanese products is falling across the board. Japanese exports to China for the year through March dropped 9.1 per cent to 11.3 trillion Yen."[22]

Why then did not a single person demonstrate to support Chinese troops in Depsang? Why weren't all of CCTV's news channels discussing the incident on the border, just as the Indian news channels were?

At CCTV, "We Don't Care about India"

I asked a senior Chinese journalist working at CCTV News to explain the channel's approach to the world and India. Yang Rui is the producer and anchor of a daily current affairs talk show on CCTV News called "Dialogue" and has been with CCTV News (including its previous avatars) from the mid-1980s. Yang, a senior editorial decision-maker at CCTV News is a controversial Chinese media personality, not just because he is known to ask indecorous questions of guests but also because of his staccato style of presentation and atypical worldview. His is one of the dominant English-speaking voices on Chinese state TV. The international press based in Beijing love to pontificate about his on- and off-air comments. It is no exaggeration to say that he is a face of Chinese soft power.[23]

During our interview for this chapter, Mr Yang said that he was a "patriotic journalist" and that it was his duty to "safeguard the image of China."[24] He made a crucial caveat, however, by adding that it "is necessary to defend the dignity of China but it is not always necessary when it comes to the government," drawing a distinction between the Chinese state and the Chinese government, and in effect saying that the state was his primary concern. According to him, "China is only re-emerging, and not rising, and that is a crucial distinction that CCTV must make."

Mr Yang, who hasn't been to India "yet" describes it on his shows as a "rising Asian power" and "friend of China." At the same time, he said that India was "not an editorial priority." Producer of more than 300 episodes a year, he recalled that India was talked about "maybe once or twice a month, but not every month." About the Depsang incident of April 2013, he said that there was a lot of Indian "noise about the border, which we chose to ignore ... Honestly, we don't care." This is "partly because India is not a strategic partner or a threat to China."

In his view, China is "held hostage by the rise of nationalism in Japan and the military might of the US" and these are "what Chinese people are most concerned about," not a "1960s border issue with India or about Tibet." He said that his show was "the voice of developing nations, and we compromise sometimes on the principle of impartiality, especially as seen by a Western eye."

Mr Yang's perception that India ranks low among Chinese priorities seems spot on. Even though only a handful of foreign films are allowed to be released on Chinese screens, Bollywood movies, Buddhism and Yoga are the popular clichés attached to India. At CCTV in Beijing, if one were to ask Chinese staffers under 30 to name an Indian movie they had seen, they would most likely say *3 Idiots*. Another? *Slumdog Millionaire*. A third? None.

What about the war of 1962? What do you think of it? Pat comes the reply, "What war?" Unlike in Indian schools, the Sino-Indian border war of 1962 is not required reading in China, and most Chinese do not know of the antagonism in India against China because of the war.

The preceding sections demonstrated the strong ties between the Chinese state and CCTV News, and how that link affects the practice of journalism. Are self-censorship and boundaries within CCTV News significantly different from those that exist in media organizations in other countries? Don't journalists and media houses in other countries—whether run by the state or private actors—practise self-censorship and set boundaries when they deal with stories about their own key investors or sources of finance? To understand the media industry in China or any country, one must go beyond reading the practices and priorities of a particular media organization in isolation. One needs to also identify the systemic behaviour of actors and the economic structure of the media environment in which journalists and organizations are embedded.

Nevertheless, from Yang Rui's interview, one can glean a fundamental difference between Indian and Chinese journalists. While Yang works to "safeguard China's image," an Indian TV journalist, even a senior decision-maker in a state broadcaster, is unlikely to be preoccupied with the "image" of India that they project in their work. This difference is perhaps an outcome of the divergent Indian and Chinese approaches to TV journalism in particular, and "soft power" in general.

Soft Power: Trying Hard to Be Soft

In 2007, Chinese President and General Secretary of the Communist Party of China Hu Jintao incorporated "soft power" in his keynote speech to the 17th National Congress of the Party. He stressed the need to "enhance Chinese culture as the country's soft power," adding that "development of the press, publishing, radio, film, television, literature and art" were part of this.[25]

It would be necessary, according to Joseph Nye, who introduced the concept of "soft power," for Chinese statecraft to use it to "alleviate fears and reduce the likelihood of other countries allying to balance a rising power."[26] Nye outlined the concept:

> A country may obtain the outcomes it wants in world politics because other countries—admiring its values, emulating its example, aspiring to its level of prosperity and openness—want to follow it. In this sense, it is also important to set the agenda and attract others in world politics, and not only to force them to change by threatening military force or economic sanctions. This soft power—getting others to want the outcomes that you want—co-opts people rather than coerces them.[27]

A decade hence, in 2014, soft power has become a booming weapon in China's "peaceful rise" arsenal, with elements ranging from Chinese Nobel laureates in Literature (Gao Xingjian and Mo Yan), through the popular, comedy, martial arts film *Kung Fu Panda* (paradoxically, produced by DreamWorks and distributed by Paramount Pictures, both US firms), to China's 480 Confucius Institutes around the world and Beijing's increasingly large, media footprint.

For China, its slick, English-language international news channel CCTV News is a vehicle of "attractive power."[28] CCTV News executives see the channel as a component of China's soft power. The channel's adoption of a dual system of editorial standards is an acknowledgement of soft power, and a recognition of the strengths and dangers of TV news. As Pierre Bourdieu wrote about TV news in his seminal work *On Television*:

> It suits everybody because it confirms what they already know and, above all, leaves their mental structures intact. There are revolutions, the ones we usually talk about, that aim at the material bases of a society—take the nationalization of Church property after 1789—and then there are symbolic revolutions effected by artists, scholars, or great religious or (sometimes, though less often) political prophets. These affect our mental structures, which means that they change the ways we see and think ... If a vehicle as powerful as television were oriented even slightly toward this kind of symbolic revolution, I can assure you that everyone would be rushing to put a stop to it.[29]

For China, the dual system of editorial standards ensures that CCTV News does not pose a threat to the existing political order at home, even as the channel at the behest of the state attempts to serve as an intercontinental weapon in China's soft power arsenal, suggestive of a smartly "re-emerging" China. CCTV News, thus plays an important part in trying transform the straitjacketed image of China from that of a fire-breathing dragon to that of the clumsy congenial panda.

But since the medium mediates the message, does Beijing's intention end up being the message that viewers perceive and take on board?[30] A crucial element of soft power is that it seeks to make a country's culture, foreign policies and political values more popular abroad.[31] Of the three, the latter two—foreign policy and political values—are more difficult to sell, yet from a Chinese point of view, they are the ones that need to be marketed the most. To this end, Chinese diplomats and foreign affairs scholars use CCTV News to explain Beijing's decisions. For example, after a Chinese veto at the UN Security Council, they draw attention to how sparingly China has historically used its veto compared to the United States or Russia and how no one, especially in the West, gives them credit for this.[32]

Yet if China's aim is to turn unfriendly heads and elicit smiles toward Beijing through cuddly pandas and Mandarin teaching centres (and CCTV News), then the method does not seem to be working. Pew Research Center's Global Attitudes Project, published in 2014, found that "Americans, Europeans and Japanese overwhelmingly believe the Chinese government does not respect the rights of its own people. Also, China's overall image in the United States and Europe is mostly negative."[33] In the same survey, Chinese President Xi Jingping got "mostly poor reviews in the West. Nearly six-in-ten Americans (58 per cent) lack confidence in Xi, as do most in Spain, Italy, Poland, Germany, France and Greece. Xi's ratings are (also) largely negative in the Middle East, especially in Israel and Turkey."[34] The animosity towards China is not new, but what is surprising is that it has become worse, especially in the United States. In a study of soft power in Asia in 2008, the Chicago Council on Global Affairs found that "American feelings towards China have steadily declined since 2004."[35] This was despite the steady escalation of Beijing's efforts to win over the world through multifarious engagements of soft power.

Indians too do not see China in kind light. A survey by the Pew Center in 2012 revealed that Indians took "a more sceptical view of China's role in the international arena. Only 20 per cent of [Indian] urban residents think China is the world's leading economic power. By comparison, across the other 20 nations surveyed by the Pew

Research Center this year, a median of 42 per cent see China as the global economic hegemon."[36] Also, 40 per cent of Indians polled "see Delhi's relationship with Beijing as one of hostility, only 28 per cent see the relationship as one of cooperation" and "about half (53 per cent) of Indians living in cities think China's growing economy is a bad thing for India."[37]

India, on the other hand, has never had a state policy directed at increasing its soft power. In the popular perception, "expressions of Indian soft power now abound: Bikram yoga, Bollywood dancercise gyms, cricket's Indian Premier League. And here is what they have in common: the Indian government had virtually nothing to do with their success."[38] But India continues to reap the unintended consequences of decisions made by those who made the Indian constitution, who thought that a free press and free association benefited government as well as society by bringing those abusing power to public notice.[39]

Conclusion

What conclusions can one draw from this discussion? We have seen that in the evolution of CCTV News, in the forms of state intervention in the channel's functioning and in the journalism practised by individuals associated with the channel, that the Chinese state is omnipresent in the channel's operations. The case of CCTV News thus demonstrates that China's idea of soft power is closely tied to the state. When the instruments of soft power are owned and operated by the state, the vehicles and values are likely to be encoded with coercion and appear manufactured. The result is that they are viewed with suspicion.

In contrast, the elements of Indian soft power, rather than being state-directed or state-owned, have emerged from Indian society and economy, and are hence organic, rather than manufactured to serve a political agenda. Nalin Mehta argues that "Indian TV thrives on programming genres that marry older argumentative traditions with new technology and notions of liberal democracy to create new hybrid forms that strengthen democratic culture."[40] Indian products and Indian soft power are helped further by the fact that even politically, they come encoded with non-coercive values, because the underlying political (democratic) and economic (capitalist) frameworks that facilitated the creation of the products underscore freedom. Perhaps it is due to this organic flavour of Indian soft power, that India polls better than China in world perception surveys.[41]

But what about China? Will China widen and free up the public space that its state-sponsored media operate in? For CCTV be taken seriously in the world of state-sponsored broadcasters, as have recent entrants like Al-Jazeera English, it should commit squarely to the core universal values and standards of journalism, both domestically and internationally.

If CCTV News' move to America is part of its strategy to make its voice heard, and if this has been successfully implemented with minimal oversight from Beijing, as CCTV America's journalists assert, then the same parameters can easily be memed in China too. Will China loosen its controls over CCTV News and other media outlets, especially considering the "reverse wave of democratization" that appears to be underway across the world?[42] This is unlikely in the short term. However, the fact that such structures exist, with the varying levels of editorial controls, as described in this chapter, shows that Chinese newsrooms are more lively and argumentative than would have been thought possible thirty years ago.

As a fellow member of the BRICS group of developing nations and a rising regional power, China must invest more in covering India and its states. As the Chinese Communist Party and institutions have kept up its periodic contact with their Indian counterparts, Chinese and Indian media must also create mechanisms by which media persons from both countries can meet on a regular basis.[43] Short, reciprocal media internships would enable journalists to be housed in each other's media organizations and work and learn from each other.

CCTV News must invest in more reporters in India, and editors in Beijing should be told that they must look beyond Japan and East Asia for a more holistic coverage of the region. It may be difficult, however, for Chinese journalists to see India divorced from its relation with Pakistan and, increasingly, the United States. Both these countries, in the eyes of many Chinese scribes and India-watchers, affect Sino-Indian ties.

In 2014, China became India's largest trading partner. This may provide the impetus for Indian media to look beyond the disputed McMahon line and try better to understand the Chinese people and the Chinese growth story. For that, Indian news television will need to invest in reporters who can understand Mandarin and also invite Sinologists and political scientists to their evening talks shows on China, rather than the ubiquitous sabre-rattler and unctuous former diplomat. The media play an important role in building a nation's perceptions. For China and India to understand one another better, it is imperative that the first steps in relaying a clearer picture be taken by one of the most powerful tools of public perception—television.

Notes

1. "Border Face-Off Shadows PM Modi's Talks With Chinese President Xi," NDTV, 18 September 2014, http://www.ndtv.com/article/india/border-face-off-shadows-pm-modi-s-talks-with-chinese-president-xi-593795 (accessed 19 September 2014).
2. *Advertising Age*, "DataCenter," http://adage.com/(accessed 1 September 2014).
3. Guo Ke, Sang Cuilin and Wang Wei, "Globalizing the Local: The Global Impact of China's English Television," *Media Asia*, 31, no. 1 (2004): 51–60.
4. Guo Ke, Sang Cuilin and Wang Wei, 2004.
5. Jian Heping, "Window on China and the World CCTV-9," in Sucharita S. Eashwar ed., (n.d.), *Promoting Peace and Prosperity in a Globalised World: Asia Media Summit* pp. 173–175, 2005, Kuala Lumpur: Asia-Pacific Institute for Broadcasting Development, p. 173. http://download.aibd.org.my/books/AMS_05_Promoting_Peace_and_Prosperity.pdf (accessed 1 September 2014).
6. David Shambaugh, "China Flexes Its Soft Power," *New York Times*, 8 June 2010, www.nytimes.com/2010/06/08/opinion/08iht-edshambaugh.html (accessed 1 September 2014).
7. Andrew Jacobs, "Pursuing Soft Power, China Puts Stamp on Africa's News," *New York Times*, 16 August 2012, http://www.nytimes.com/2012/08/17/world/africa/chinas-news-media-make-inroads-in-africa.html?pagewanted=all&_r=0 (accessed 1 September 2014).
8. "China's Programming for U.S. Audiences: Is it News or Propaganda?" *PBS Newshour*, 23 March 2012, http://www.pbs.org/newshour/bb/world-jan-june12-cctv_03-23/(accessed 1 September 2014).
9. "China Arrests Nearly 1,000 Members of Illegal Cult," *CCTV America*, http://www.cctv-america.com/2014/08/19/china-arrests-nearly-1000-members-of-illegal-cult (accessed 1 September 2014); "China Arrests Thousand of Cult Members," *Xinhua*, http://news.xinhuanet.com/english/china/2014-08/19/c_133568664.htm (accessed 1 September 2014).

10. Jacob Fromer, "On CCTV America, Some China Stories Recede From View," *The Lede: The New York Times News Blog*, 17 August 2012, http://thelede.blogs.nytimes.com/2012/08/17/on-cctv-america-some-china-stories-recede-from-view/?ref=africa (accessed 1 September 2014).

11. Jonathan Hassid, "Controlling the Chinese Media: An Uncertain Business," *Asian Survey*, 48, no. 3 (2008): 414–430, 419.

12. "World Insight," *CCTV News*, http://cctv.cntv.cn/lm/worldinsight/program_video/index.shtml (accessed 20 September 2014).

13. China loathes the fact that Japan has about 30,000 US troops under Beijing's nose. Sino–Japanese relations are further muddied by Japan's horrific past as China's brutal colonizing power, and many Chinese still see Japan though the narratives of those dark days. CCTV does its part to help. Most afternoons, Mandarin channels CCTV–1 and CCTV–4 broadcast war dramas showing early–twentieth century exploits of the Chinese resistance against Japan. Most story lines are interwoven with the usual ingredients of a TV pot boiler—treachery, lies, espionage, and love—and lead to one ultimate winner, that is, China. Philip Cunningham says,

   > the wartime epithet "guizi," referring to Japanese as devils, repeated on Chinese TV hundreds of times a day, frequently makes the leap into real-world conversation. One only has to ask a Beijing taxi driver, or even a college student about Japan, and the word is bound to follow, sometimes playfully, sometimes not.

   "China's TV War Machine," *New York Times*, http://www.nytimes.com/2014/09/12/opinion/chinas-tv-war-on-japan.html?_r=1 (accessed 1 September 2014).

14. "Chinese Soldiers Return to Chumar," *Hindu*, 19 September 2014, http://www.thehindu.com/news/national/chinese-soldiers-return-to-chumar/article6427294.ece (accessed 20 September 2014). See also Srinjoy Chowdhury's discussion of the Depsang incident in this book, Chapter 10.

15. Nirmalya Banerjee and Prabin Kalita, "ITBP Jawans Injured in China Border Shootout," *Times of India*, 15 September 2009, http://timesofindia.indiatimes.com/india/ITBP-jawans-injured-in-China-border-shootout/articleshow/5011353.cms (accessed 1 September 2014); "Media Asked Not to 'Overplay' China Border Incidents," *Hindu*, 20 September 2009, http://www.thehindu.com/news/national/media-asked-not-to-overplay-china-border-incidents/article22617.ece (accessed 20 September 2014).

16. Neena Vyas, "India in Touch with China on Incidents," *Hindu*, 19 September 2009, http://www.thehindu.com/todays-paper/india-in-touch-with-china-on-incidents/article186992.ece (accessed 20 September 2014).

17. Alka Acharya, "Whither India-China Relations?" *Economic and Political Weekly*, 44, no. 45 (7 November 2009): 8–12.

18. "The Newshour Debate: Will India Defend Itself Against China?" *Times Now*, 24 April 2013, https://www.youtube.com/watch?v=DFgnbYHgSOY; "India asks

China to withdraw troops," *Times Now*, 24 April 2013, https://www.youtube.com/watch?v=m6pJLVJweJE; "China Dares India Again," 24 April 2013, *Times Now*, https://www.youtube.com/watch?v=Z8qrbAhfVro; "Should India's Response to China's Incursion be More Aggressive?" *NDTV*, 22 April 2013, http://www.ndtv.com/video/player/india-decides-9/should-india-s-response-to-china-s-incursion-be-more-aggressive/272185 (all accessed 20 September 2014).

19. "News Night: India–China Stalemate Continues," *DD News*, https://www.youtube.com/watch?v=_1n6Rqc2ZlQ (accessed 20 September 2014).

20. Vinay Kumar, "Ladakh Incursions: Army Chief Apprises Antony of Situation," *Hindu*, 25 April 2013, http://www.thehindu.com/news/national/army-chief-apprises-antony-of-situation/article4653461.ece (accessed 20 September 2014).

21. Ian Johnson and Thom Shanker, "Beijing Mixes Messages Over Anti-Japan Protests," *New York Times*, 17 September 2012, http://www.nytimes.com/2012/09/17/world/asia/anti-japanese-protests-over-disputed-islands-continue-in-china.html (accessed 20 September 2014).

22. David Lague and Jane Lanhee Lee, "Special Report: Why China's Film Makers Love to Hate Japan," *Reuters*, 25 May 2013, http://www.reuters.com/article/2013/05/25/us-china-japan-specialreport-idUSBRE94O0CJ20130525 (accessed 20 September 2014).

23. James Fallows, a veteran China hand and former White House speechwriter says that "Dialogue" aspires "to be seen as a combination of the Charlie Rose Show, the old William F. Buckley 'Firing Line', and Ted Koppel's 'Nightline', with perhaps a dash of the author-interview segment of 'The Daily Show'." James Fallows, "China Soft-Power Watch: The Yang Rui 'Foreign Bitch' Factor," *The Atlantic*, 19 May 2012, http://www.theatlantic.com/international/archive/2012/05/china-soft-power-watch-the-yang-rui-foreign-bitch-factor/257403/(accessed 1 September 2014).

24. All comments by Yang Rui are from an interview with him for the purpose of this chapter.

25. "Hu Jintao Calls for Enhancing 'Soft Power' of Chinese Culture," *Xinhuanet*, http://news.xinhuanet.com/english/2007-10/15/content_6883748.htm (accessed 1 September 2014).

26. Joseph S. Nye, Jr, "The Rise of China's Soft Power," *Wall Street Journal Asia*, 29 December 2005.

27. Joseph S. Nye, Jr, *Soft Power: The Means to Success in World Politics*, New York: Public Affairs, Chapter 1, 2004. See also, Joseph S. Nye, Jr, *Bound to Lead: The Changing Nature of American Power*, New York: Basic Books, Chapter 2, 1990.

28. Joseph S. Nye Jr. and Wang Jisi, "Hard Decisions on Soft Power: Opportunities and Difficulties for Chinese Soft Power," *Harvard International Review*, 31, no. 2 (2009): 18–22.

29. Pierre Bourdieu (Trans. Priscilla Parkhurst Ferguson), *On Television*, New York: The New Press, 1999, p. 45.

30. Marshall McLuhan, *Understanding Media*, New York: McGraw–Hill, 1964.

31. Joseph S. Nye Jr. and Wang Jisi, "Hard Decisions on Soft Power: Opportunities and Difficulties for Chinese Soft Power," *Harvard International Review*, 31, no. 2 (2009): 18–22.

32. Personal conversation with former senior Chinese diplomat. See also, "Research Guides: Veto List," http://research.un.org/en/docs/sc/quick/veto (accessed 1 September 2014).

33. Pew Research Center, *Global Opposition to U.S. Surveillance and Drones, but Limited Harm to America's Image*, July, Chapter 2, http://www.pewglobal. org/2014/07/14/chapter-2-chinas-image/ (accessed 1 September 2014), 2014.

34. Pew Research Center, *Global Opposition*, 2014.

35. The Chicago Council on Global Affairs, *Soft Power in Asia: Results of a 2008 Multinational Survey of Public Opinion*, http://www.thechicagocouncil.org/ UserFiles/File/POS_Topline%20Reports/Asia%20Soft%20Power%202008/ AsiaSoftPower%20Executive%20Summary%20FINAL.pdf (accessed 1 September 2014), 2008.

36. Pew Research Center, *Deepening Economic Doubts in India*, September, Chapter 3, http://www.pewglobal.org/2012/09/10/chapter-3-india-and-the-rest-of-the-world/(accessed 1 September 2014), 2012.

37. Ibid.

38. Bobby Ghosh, "From the Buddha to Bollywood to BPOs: A Brief History of India's Soft Power," *Quartz India*, 25 September 2014, http://qz.com/271585/ from-the-buddha-to-bollywood-to-bpos-a-brief-history-of-indias-soft-power/(accessed 26 September 2014).

39. C. A. Bayly, *Recovering Liberties: Indian Thought in the Age of Liberalism and Empire* (Cambridge, UK: Cambridge University Press, 2011).

40. Nalin Mehta, *India on Television: How Satellite TV Has Changed the Way We Think and Act* (New Delhi: HarperCollins, 2008), pp. 232–236.

41. Pew Research Center, *Deepening Economic Doubts*, 2012.

42. According to Freedom House, which annually tracks democratization, in 2013, "fifty-four countries showed overall declines in political rights and civil liberties, compared with 40 that showed gains. For the eighth consecutive year, *Freedom in the World* recorded more declines in democracy world-wide than gains." Freedom House (2014), *Freedom in the World 2014*, http:// www.freedomhouse.org/report/freedom-world/freedom-world-2014 (accessed 1 September 2014). For "waves of democratisation," see Samuel P. Huntington, *The Third Wave: Democratization in the Late Twentieth Century* (Norman: University of Oklahoma Press, 1991).

43. "Want Contact with BJP at Party Level: Communist Party of China," *Indian Express*, 17 June 2014, http://indianexpress.com/article/india/india-others/ want-contact-with-bjp-at-party-level-communist-party-of-china/#sthash. KUZohQG9.dpuf (accessed on 15 October 2014).

12

The CCTV–Reuters Relationship

John Jirik

John Jirik speaks English, Russian and limited Chinese. A scholar and journalist, he was teaching at Lehigh University, Pennsylvania, when he researched and wrote this chapter. In August 2013, he took up a post as Planning Editor at CCTV News, Beijing. Previously, Jirik has worked as a journalist in Moscow, Hong Kong and Singapore. He also had three extended periods in China, researching and working in media and as a teacher. He has an undergraduate degree from the University of Melbourne and has completed MA from the University of Leicester and PhD from the University of Texas.

Introduction

In early 2011, Associated Press (AP) and Reuters[1] announced that they would begin providing clients a daily feed of stories from China Central Television (CCTV). The material would be provided by CCTV News Content (hereafter "News Content," website: news-content.cctv.com), a video wholesaler set up by CCTV and its commercial arm CITVC (China International Television Corporation). The deals were part of a growing trend at both agencies to distribute unedited third-party material to subscribers. Although the third-party material was branded as such and the agencies made clear that they took no editorial responsibility for the content of the CCTV feed, both agencies were trading on their names and reputations in providing the material. As Christoph Pleitgen, managing director of Reuters, noted, "[t]he extension of this relationship allows CCTV to broaden

its reach into the global broadcasting community while simultaneously satisfying our clients' increasing appetite for news from China."[2]

Although AP and Reuters have long had material access agreements with CCTV and provided CCTV and other Chinese broadcasters with their services, the emerging trend of distributing unedited
video from partners has several implications for the global news
business. First, subscribers gain access to a broader range of news
frames than would be the case were they to rely solely on third-party
materials vetted through the agency editorial process, the traditional
way of dealing with third-party material. Second, because China
restricts the number of journalists' visas it issues, the agencies' news
pools were deepened by partnering with CCTV. Third, CCTV gained
access to the agencies' clients and global distribution networks which
are a vital component of the global television news system. Fourth,
the agencies have started to abandon editorial authority and the
related ability to generate coherent narratives about the world, that is
"make sense" of reality, in favour of pluralism in the news. This dis-
junctural development indicates an emerging shift from a modern to
a postmodern news paradigm, the latter characterized by competing
claims to truth grounded in different news logics.

In this chapter, I examine the history, actuality and implications of
the CCTV Reuters relationship, using content analysis to ground the
argument. Since CCTV paid Reuters and AP to distribute the same
material gratis to clients, I focussed on Reuters since I am more familiar
with the history of its dealings with CCTV than I am with AP's.[3] Given
the focus of this book, the literature review also addressed the history
of Reuters' coverage of India, since the analysis of the CCTV–Reuters
deal is relevant in understanding where and how the national and
global news systems intersect, and India's media development could
offer insight into possible future trajectories for China's media reform.

Reuters in India and China

Although Reuters opened its first office in India in 1866 (in Bombay)
and in China in 1871 (in Shanghai), neither country has been an easy
beat for the agency.[4,5] For different reasons, India and China provided
obstacles to coverage.

After the communists came to power in China in 1949, news acquired a political value that over-determined its commodity value or value as a public service. News served power directly rather than indirectly through mediation by the market and editorial agency, which determined what Reuters would or would not recognize as news. China's communist leadership takes a Leninist perspective on news media, seeing them as part of the political system, the "mouth-piece" of the Party and State.[6] CCTV's former president, Hu Zhanfan, reaffirmed that role in January 2011. Speaking in his capacity then as editor-in-chief of the *Guangming Daily*, a newspaper linked to the Central Publicity Department (CPD), ideological watchdog of China's news media, Hu said, "Some news workers don't see themselves as party propagandists, but rather as news professionals. This is a funda-mental error."[7]

Leninism was one development within the Marxian news para-digm, which emphasizes the ideological character of news and the manner in which economic, political and cultural contexts of news production shape stories. The Marxian and post-Marxian news para-digms are fundamentally at odds with the objective (professional) news paradigm, to which Reuters is party and which treats social real-ity as non-ideological, a realm separable from the position of the observer who accurately records the facts of an event or process, with-out in any way being either influenced by or influencing the event or process under observation. Despite these differences, the Marxian, post-Marxian and professional news paradigms share a commitment to fact-based reporting that has allowed Reuters and China's main-stream media to find a modus vivendi. CCTV's forerunner, Beijing TV, signed in 1963 its first material exchange and purchase agreement with Visnews, forerunner to Reuters Television.[8] The relationship was suspended during the early part of the Cultural Revolution (1966–1976), but revived in 1971.[9] In 1980, CCTV began taking Visnews' daily satellite feeds.[10] The basic form of the relationship would then remain unchanged until the News Content deal in January 2011. Each side provided the other with material, which each side reserved the right to re-edit should it so choose. The new element in the News Content deal was the decision to distribute CCTV material without filtering it through the Reuters editorial process.

In the case of India, prior to independence, Reuters attempted to balance its close association with the colonial British government with business pragmatics.[11] However, India's political and business elites who were agitating for independence considered that under political pressure from London and British government representatives in Delhi, Reuters was toning down its reports on the strength of anti-British sentiment on the sub-continent.[12] Meanwhile, India by the mid-1930s had emerged as Reuters' largest source of foreign revenue.[13] To protect that revenue, Reuters' general manager in India in 1937 suggested a change in tone: "British control in India is being relaxed... We are not in favour of unduly emphasizing British or Empire news at a time when Indian nationalists are taking an increasing share in the government of this country."[14]

However, Reuters' attempts to retain control of its operations in India were at odds with the drive to political independence, which was paralleled by a demand for press independence. In the climate of rising nationalism and aware of the role that the British-oriented press played in India, the local owners, editors and journalists called for a national news agency: "The desire to shake off the imperial domination in the field of news supply was at the heart of this evolving thought," said Ramnath Goenka, the chairman of the Press Trust of India (PTI), which subsequently was established in 1947.[15] Under threat of losing its license to transmit news from India after independence, and under pressure in London from a newly elected Labour government seeking accommodation with the emergent nation, Reuters in 1947 reluctantly transferred control of its India operations to PTI.[16] The following year, PTI began supplying Reuters with news from the newly independent sub-continent.[17] However, the relationship only lasted four years. For Reuters, the PTI service was relatively unprofitable, while PTI accused the agency of breaking the terms of the agreement by deploying journalists in areas reserved for its own correspondents. PTI pulled out of the partnership in 1952, leaving Reuters at the time with two correspondents and several stringers to cover the country.[18]

A decade later, one of those working for Reuters in India was Prem Prakash, who was also working for Visnews since 1957, when the British Broadcasting Corporation (BBC), Rank Organization, Australian Broadcasting Corporation (ABC) and Canadian Broadcasting Corporation (CBC) founded the British Commonwealth International Newsfilm Agency (BCINA) to counter the US dominance of the emerging medium.[19] Reuters in 1960 bought into BCINA, which in 1962 was renamed Visnews.[20] In 1985, Reuters upped its stake to a controlling share of Visnews (55 per cent), then, in 1992, acquired the agency outright, renaming it Reuters Television.[21] Meanwhile Prakash in 1975 had founded Asian News International (ANI), which developed as a de-facto monopoly supplier of news from India for Reuters Television. ANI in 2011 provided 99 per cent of Reuters' coverage from India.[22]

Ahead of the deal with News Content, the conundrum facing Reuters was understandable. Effectively, the agency was locked out of providing more than a minimum of its own cover from the world's two most populous nations, and two increasingly powerful political economies, which see television as a state and public service. China established television in 1958. Today, the Communist Party (CPC) remains committed to the state control of news, bolstered by its successful switch to commercial funding of media beginning with the launch of advertising in early 1979. India established television a year later than China. As in China, terrestrial broadcasting was structured as a state-owned monopoly. Launched in 1959, Doordarshan functioned as a de-facto "mouthpiece of the government of the day."[23]

Although China and India have begun to commercialize their television systems, and India to liberalize its system, a second problem for the agency is insurmountable in both countries. The size of India and China—geographically, economically and population-wise—would prevent more than token coverage by Reuters' journalists. This problem is not new and not restricted to big developing countries. Reuters has traditionally relied on third parties for much of its coverage, including from the United States, Great Britain and Japan. Partnerships such as those with ANI and CCTV have been the norm throughout the agency's history. In 2011, for example, Reuters was a source of only 55 per cent of the material it distributed in its core package of feeds to all broadcast clients.[24] The other 45 per cent was bought from or exchanged with broadcasters and video suppliers worldwide.[25] Recent modelling of the global news "ecology" by Esperidião[26] and Paterson[27] generated a complex picture of the agency–client relationship, which emphasized the inter-dependency of agencies (wholesalers) and broadcasters (retailers) and the multi-directional flow of news in local, national, regional and global contexts. However, they also reiterated the pivotal role the agencies play in the overall system because of their well-documented agenda-setting function, which gives AP and Reuters leverage far in excess of their actual size.[28] As a British television news editor noted in 1986, "The role of the agencies is the crucial thing ... the major force deciding what ends up on television screens from abroad."[29] Recent research by Paterson[30] suggested that dependency continues unmitigated today.

Key, then, is the question of who sets the agencies' agendas? The answer according to Esperidião[31] is that "the news transmitted by these companies is, in its great majority, determined by the political and economic interests of their biggest clients."[32] Historically, these clients were based in the United States, Britain and Western Europe.[33] As Esperidião[34] noted, 30 years after the MacBride Report (1980),[35] there was "still a great asymmetry in the international news in which countries, regions and subject matters are neglected and excluded."

Nevertheless, the global news system is dynamic, not static and reflects as well as contributes to the shifting ebb and flow of power within the global political economy. As the relative power of major players in the system changes, this change will eventually alter the hierarchy of clients influencing the agencies' agendas. Given the current realignment of the global political and cultural economy towards an increasingly multipolar world, the increasing visibility of the traditional periphery is to be expected. Significantly Esperidião,[36] found in recent years that the agencies' coverage of Asia has been improving. The decision by Reuters (and AP) to distribute material from CCTV was indicative of this shifting power of different players within the global news system and a pivotal moment that reflected the emerging influence of China's news media.

China's Soft Power and Media Reform

The News Content deal is part of China's "going out" project, which then CPD deputy head Xu Guangchun launched in 2001 as a soft power exercise to take China's voice to the world.[37] The government's 2007 White Paper on Foreign Affairs emphasized soft power and then President Hu Jintao's report to the 17th CPC Congress urged the PRC "to enhance culture as part of the soft power of our country to better guarantee the people's basic cultural rights and interests."[38] According to news reports, the government in early 2009 earmarked 45 billion Yuan (USD 6.6 billion) for overseas expansion of the PRC's central media. Major recipients included CCTV,[39] which has since aggressively expanded, opening broadcast centres in Washington DC and Nairobi, Kenya in 2012, with a European hub planned for London. In mid-2014, CCTV broadcast in Arabic, Chinese, English, French, Russian and Spanish. Online programmes were also available in Kazakh, Korean, Mongolian, Tibetan and Uighur (see www.cctv. com). Its global English-language operation is called CCTV News, which evolved out of CCTV's English-language news service, which began life in the late 1980s as an English-learning programme called "Follow Me."[40] Today, CCTV News is directly targeting domination of the global English-language news discourse exercised by the likes of Al Jazeera, the BBC and CNN. News Content drew most of its material from the Chinese and English news services at CCTV.

Whether the agencies have become an instrument of soft power and conduit of propaganda for the CPC and Chinese government might seem an obvious question. However, such a question would do justice neither to the historical evidence which suggests that the agencies have always served power, nor to the complexity of China's evolving news system. Analytic paradigms compete. On one hand, they focus on the structural and institutional subordination of all Chinese news media to the CPD,[41] assuming a top-down flow of directives out of this institutional black box that tell media what to and what not to report. On the other hand, they emphasize negotiated news narratives that reflect a struggle for editorial control, the result of the ever-shifting conjuncture of forces associated with state ownership of media, their commercial funding, and the agency of journalists and editors.[42]

Seminal in recognizing what I shall call the "middle-out" (as opposed to top-down or bottom-up) character of media reform in China has been the work of Pan Zhongdang and Lu Ye,[43] which emphasized its gradualist and negotiated character.[44] Pan and Lu drew on the work of Michel de Certeau[45] to analyze the tactics journalists deployed against the strategies of controlling institutions such as the CPD. In Foucauldean terms, which de Certeau critiqued, the CPD operates a panopticon which oversees media discipline and punishment. However, de Certeau[46] confronted a theoretical blind spot in Foucault's[47] analysis of the panopticon, pointing to the tactical refashioning of strategic initiatives to serve local interests. De Certeau's understanding of the manner in which the weaker party negotiates with the stronger provided insight into the middle-out and improvised character of much media reform in China. In similar vein, Sun[48] drew on the later works of Foucault[49] to show how television managers "rework the institutional implements emanating from the power centre in accordance with their own needs and interests."[50] What these analysts have identified is the corrosive effect editorial and journalistic agency has on the ability of organs such as the CPD to translate control over the newsroom to control within the newsroom.

The middle-out character of media reform emphasizes media agency. Increasingly in China, including at CCTV, editors and journalists have turned the Party's news discourse on professionalism against the CPD's control of news by arguing that as good communists they were falling short as professionals by relating only those facts supportive of the Party's side of the story.[51] Ironically, the space opening up for more balanced journalism was created by the Party itself, as an unintended consequence of the shift to commercial funding of media. As Pan[52] noted, media reform was never a carefully planned project with a clear aim, beyond the need to grapple with a lack of funding. Advertising started out as a non-routine experiment by media managers in Shanghai in the late 1970s in an attempt to finance radio in the wake of the Cultural Revolution after Deng Xiaoping returned to power and launched his reform and opening policy in 1978.[53] Deng's reforms were characterized as "crossing the river by groping for stones." In effect, Deng made local initiative key to the dynamics of communist control in China. Reform comes from the middle. What works rises to the top, is institutionalized, and then flows back down as policy.

The impetus for the News Content deal with Reuters came from the CCTV management.[54] Should the experiment prove successful, it could open up the possibility for CCTV of similar deals with major retailers such as the BBC, CNN and Al Jazeera, or provide a conduit for municipal and provincial broadcasters such as Shanghai TV to expand their services.

Method

To answer the questions of what News Content supplied to Reuters, and how the former's content related to Reuters' overall output, I analyzed a representative sample of material from 2011, covering seven weeks from June 23 to August 10. Every eighth day was sampled, which showed constructed an efficient and representative sample.[55] The method was a variation of that used in the 1985 UNESCO report.[56] The unit of analysis was the television script (including its shot list). The coding scheme was adapted from Sreberny-Mohammadi et al.[57] Coded variables identified where news happened, what was reported, who were the actors and what types of news predominated.[58] Variables coded were duration, dateline (where the story happened), places mentioned in stories, topic, type, speakers and language. Topic was assigned two values (double-coded), following recognition in the UNESCO study that few stories are only about one event, process, person or issue.[59] For the sake of comparison, News Content and Reuters' content were separately coded with the same variables. The seven-day sample totalled 1,303 stories, on average 186 stories per day.[60] News Content contributed 76 stories (11 per day), accounting for 6 per cent of Reuters' output and 12 per cent of material provided exclusively by third parties.

CCTV News Content

The average News Content story was two minutes and five seconds in length. Fifty-five per cent of stories had a domestic focus, including Tibet (4 per cent) and Taiwan (1 per cent). Twenty-nine per cent had a foreign policy focus, defined as any story including sport that involved China and at least one other country or international institution such as the United Nations or the International Monetary Fund. Sixteen per cent had a foreign focus, defined as any story that had no reference to China.

Measuring regions in the news by mentions of countries in stories produced the emphases shown in Figure 12.1. For the sake of comparison, China is included.

Figure 12.1:
Regions in the news on News Content

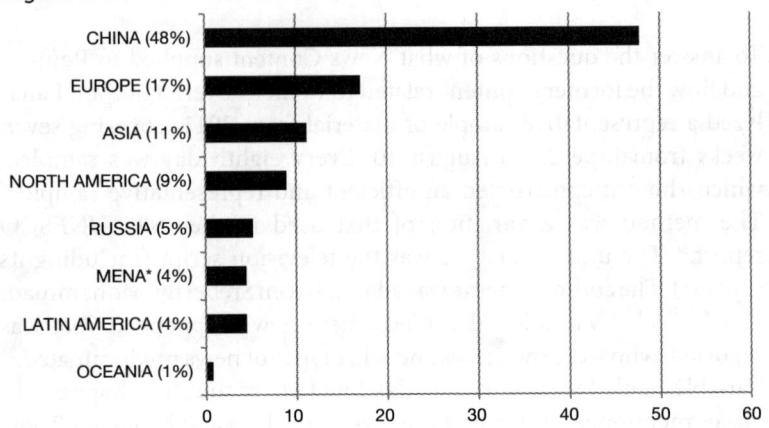

Source: Calculated from author's sample survey, 23 June to 10 August 2011.
Note: *MENA (Middle East and North Africa).

Figure 12.2 breaks the bigger picture into constituent parts. The focus is on Western Europe (9 per cent) and North America (9 per cent), overwhelmingly the United States. China's close neighbours were a secondary focus: Southeast Asia (5 per cent); Russia (5 per cent); East Asia (4 per cent). China's giant Western neighbour, India (South Asia), was practically absent from the news. African countries other than several involved in recent political upheavals in the Arab world (the "Arab Spring") were invisible in the news.[61]

Looking at individual countries and treating the European Union (EU) as a country for the sake of comparison (Figure 12.3), the sub-regional emphasis on Western Europe and North America was again obvious. Only 15 countries were mentioned in the news more than once, with 23 countries mentioned once.

Within China, at the provincial and municipal level, Beijing (18 per cent), Zhejiang (14 per cent) and Shanghai (11 per cent) dominated datelines. Guangdong, Inner Mongolia and Tibet each provided 5 per cent of datelines. Chongqing (municipality) and five provinces each provided two datelines (4 per cent) and Tianjin (municipality) and 11 provinces provided one dateline (2 per cent). Comparison of urban and rural datelines indicated that 68 per cent of news was urban (municipalities and cities), the other 32 per cent was at county,

Figure 12.2:
Sub-regions in the news on News Content

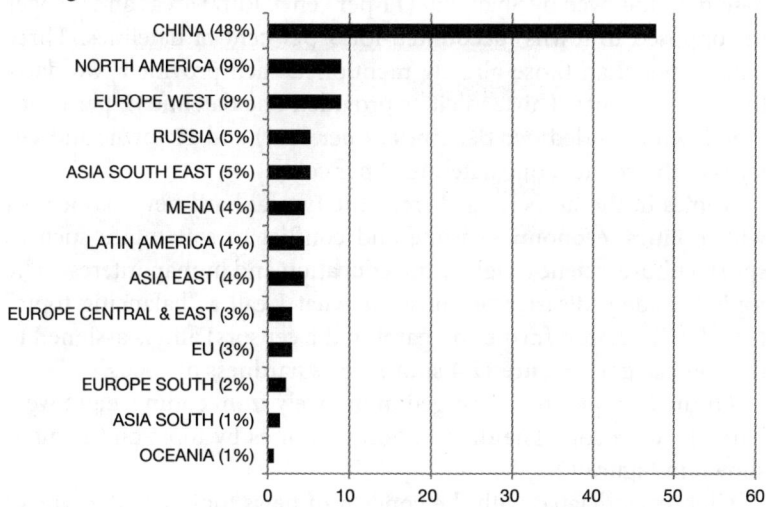

Source: Calculated from author's sample survey, 23 June to 10 August 2011.

Figure 12.3:
Countries in the news on News Content

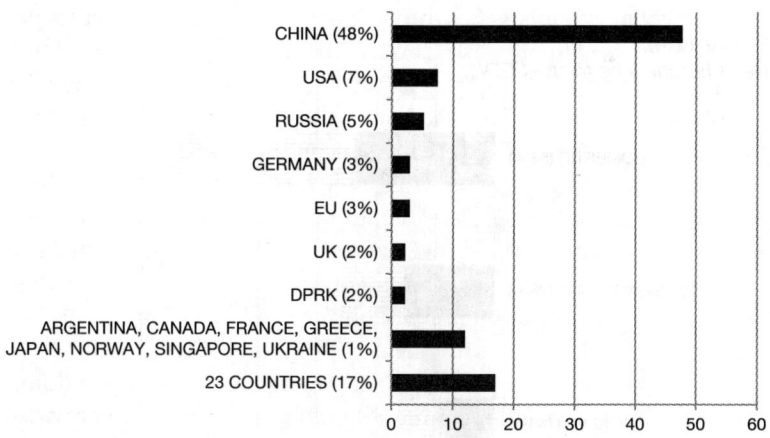

Source: Calculated from author's sample survey, 23 June to 10 August 2011.

township and village level. Beijing (18 per cent) dominated all datelines, followed by Shanghai (11 per cent). Rural areas and villages (as opposed to towns) accounted for 9 per cent of datelines. Three cities other than those already mentioned each provided two datelines (4 per cent). Thirteen cities provided one dateline (2 per cent). One town provided two datelines (4 per cent) and 11 towns and villages each provided one dateline (2 per cent).

Topics in the news ranged from the typical hard news associated with politics, economics, crime and conflict to soft topics such as sport, culture, science, rights, aid, education and human interest. The topic "accident/disaster response" is what I call a "balancing topic" (see the discussion further on gaming the censors) and is assigned to the soft category. Figure 12.4 shows news hardness by focus.

Of the 22 topics that emerged inductively from coding, eight were hard, 14 were soft. The distribution of stories by topic and focus is shown in Figure 12.5.

Closely associated with the concept of news topic was the type of news: event or process (Type 1); disruptive or non-disruptive (Type 2); and routine or non-routine (Type 3). Table 12.1 shows the breakdown of news by type.

Figure 12.4:
News hardness by focus—CCTV

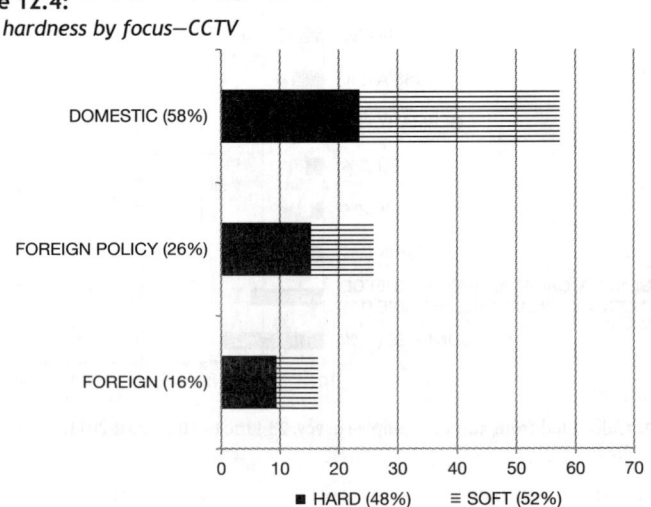

Source: Calculated from author's sample survey, 23 June to 10 August 2011.

Figure 12.5:
News topics on News Content[62]

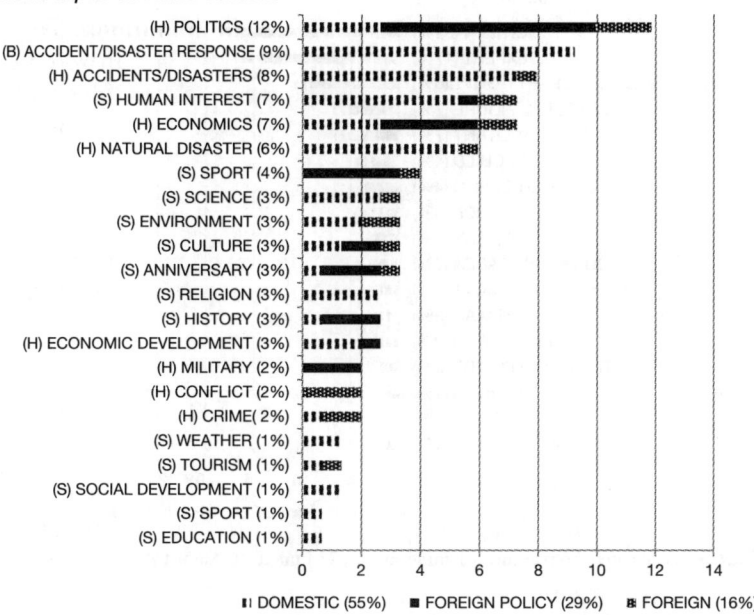

Source: Calculated from author's sample survey, 23 June to 10 August 2011.

Table 12.1:
News type by focus on News Content (percentage)

	News Type 1		News Type 2		News Type 3	
	Event	Process	Disruptive	Non-disruptive	Non-routine	Routine
Domestic	73	27	36	64	61	39
Foreign Policy	100	0	4	96	82	18
Foreign	100	0	18	82	53	47

Source: Calculated from author's sample survey, 23 June to 10 August 2011.

In terms of sound on the news, 97 per cent of stories had a natural soundtrack. Seventy-nine per cent of stories also had at least one sound bite (person speaking). Chinese (68 per cent) dominated sound bites. English was second with 16 per cent of sound bites. Spanish provided 4 per cent of sound bites. Arabic, Japanese, Russian and Turkish each provided 2 per cent of sound bites. Chinese nationals

Figure 12.6:
Speakers by role and focus

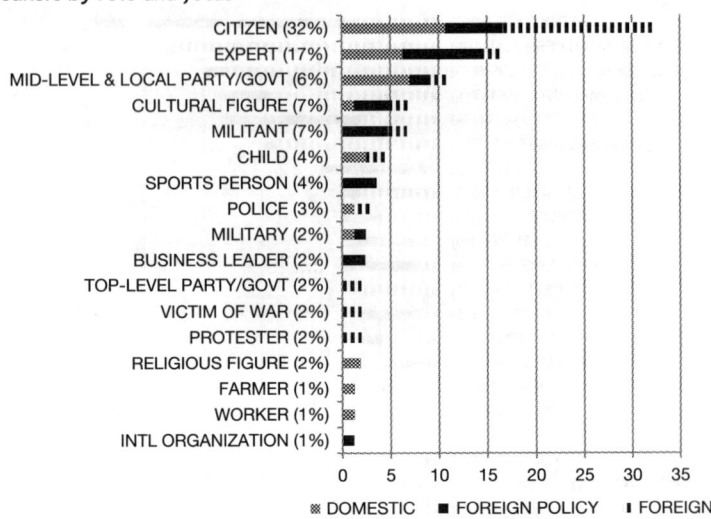

Source: Calculated from author's sample survey, 23 June to 10 August 2011.

and Taiwanese (two instances) provided 72 per cent of sound bites. The US nationals were second with 4 per cent. Sixteen countries shared the remaining 26 per cent of speaking roles. The roles of different persons who spoke are shown in Figure 12.6.

Reuters' Stories about China

In the period analyzed, Reuters did 30 stories about China, just over 4 per cent of its output. Reuters was the exclusive source of 23 stories (77 per cent), the joint source with CCTV of three stories (10 per cent) and the joint source with a source other than CCTV on two stories (7 per cent). CCTV was the exclusive source on two stories (7 per cent). Fifty per cent of the Reuters' stories had a domestic focus; 50 per cent a foreign policy focus. The stories averaged 2 minutes and 30 seconds in length. All stories had a natural sound track. Twenty-five stories (83 per cent) had sound bites. The languages were Mandarin (14 stories; 56 per cent); English (7 stories; 28 per cent),

Figure 12.7:
News hardness by focus—Reuters

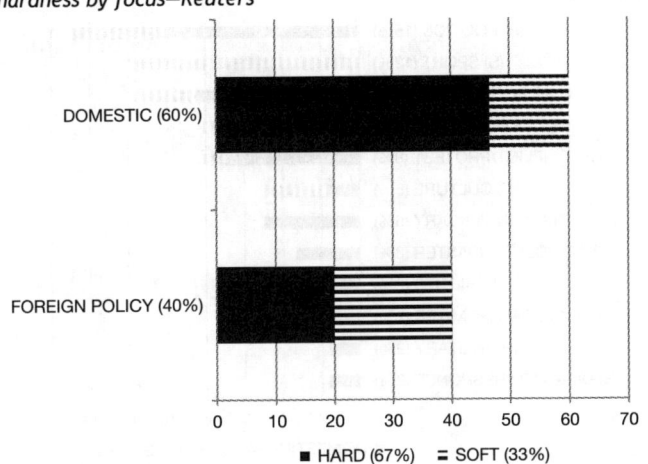

Source: Calculated from author's sample survey, 23 June to 10 August 2011.

Cantonese (two stories; 8 per cent) and Spanish and Italian (one story each; 8 per cent total). The distribution of hard and soft news by focus is shown in Figure 12.7.

The hardness of the news was reflected in the distribution of topics, shown in Figure 12.8. Politics (15 per cent) was the top story. Sport (12 per cent), a soft story, followed, but then hard topics (economics, courts/crime and conflict/protest) were highly visible and well ahead of soft topics like culture (5 per cent) and anniversary stories (5 per cent).

Reuters' stories were primarily event-oriented, non-disruptive and non-routine (Table 12.2).

Datelines associated with Reuters-sourced stories (as opposed to stories that CCTV provided Reuters) are shown in Figure 12.9. The political and economic centres of Beijing, Hong Kong and Shanghai dominated, providing 76 per cent of the news. One relatively developed province, Zhejiang, provided three datelines (10 per cent), while four provinces provided one dateline each (14 per cent).

Of those who spoke on the news, 77 per cent were Chinese nationals, including 21 per cent from Hong Kong. The nationality of 13 per cent of speakers was unclear. The US nationals were the group next most heard from at 6 per cent of sound bites. The roles of persons who spoke in the news are shown in Figure 12.10, distributed by focus.

Figure 12.8:
Topics by focus

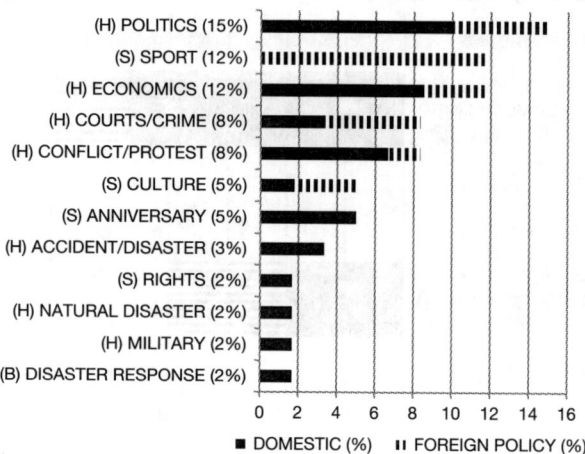

Source: Calculated from author's sample survey, 23 June to 10 August 2011.

Table 12.2:
Type of news by focus on News Content (percentage)

	News Type 1		News Type 2		News Type 3	
	Event	*Process*	*Disruptive*	*Non-disruptive*	*Non-routine*	*Routine*
Domestic	87	13	33	67	80	20
Foreign Policy	93	7	7	93	87	13

Source: Calculated from author's sample survey, 23 June to 10 August 2011.

Discussion

Overall, News Content balanced hard news (48 per cent) with soft news (52 per cent). However, 59 per cent of the domestic news was soft, whereas foreign policy and foreign stories were predominantly hard. Domestic and foreign policy stories provided 45 per cent of soft news, and 39 per cent of hard news, suggesting that News Content was softer on domestic and foreign policy stories than it was on foreign stories.

Politics at 12 per cent of news was the top story, but not for domestic news, in which accident and disaster response stories (9 per cent) were the priority. The accident and disaster stories to which the former were responding were the next biggest contributor to domestic stories

Figure 12.9:
Datelines in Reuters' stories (percentage)

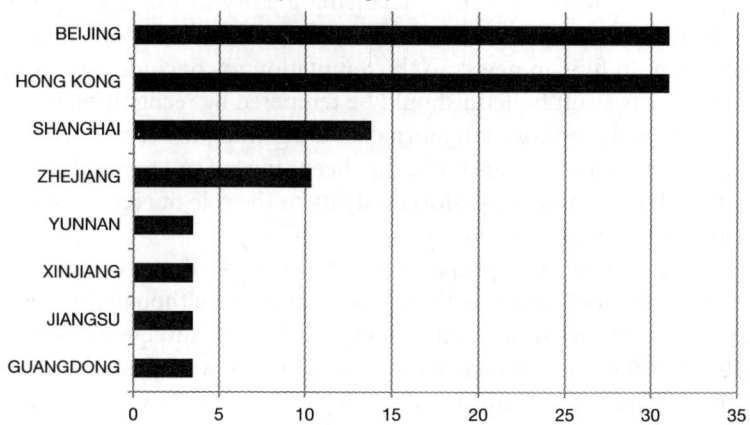

Source: Calculated from author's sample survey, 23 June to 10 August 2011.

Figure 12.10:
Speaker by role and focus

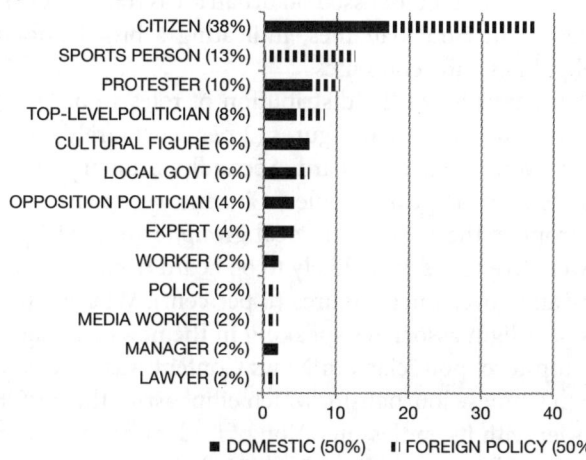

Source: Calculated from author's sample survey, 23 June to 10 August 2011.

on News Content at 8 per cent of the news. In terms of de Certeau's analysis of tactics that the weaker party deploys in its struggle with the more powerful party, the literature has long recognized that one way China's news editors get negative hard news past the CPD's surveillance system is to add a soft element.[63] A typical example of this has been recognized as disaster stories that emphasize the government response and rescue efforts.[64] Balancing a story in this fashion was evident in the domestic and foreign policy news on News Content, but absent in foreign news. So the temptation to conclude that News Content was a soft bulletin should be tempered by recognition of the degree to which editors and journalists are gaming the censors by softening hard stories. Against this, the sheer range of soft topics did suggest a soft emphasis and editorial fidelity to the role of News Content as an instrument of soft power.

Domestic news was primarily event-oriented (40 per cent). Most domestic stories (64 per cent) were not disruptive, although they were also non-routine (61 per cent). Foreign policy and foreign news were 100 per cent event-oriented, although again both were primarily non-disruptive and non-routine. The range of datelines was relatively restricted, with a focus on the political and economic power centres Beijing (18 per cent) and Shanghai (11 per cent), respectively. The province of Zhejiang was in the news in the period sampled primarily because of a high-speed rail crash that generated multiple stories. Although News Content focussed on urban areas (68 per cent), 32 per cent of news had rural datelines, indicating a broader focus than high-level politics and economics.

Two characteristics of the distribution of roles stood out. Firstly, central Party and government figures (2 per cent) rarely spoke in the news. They were seen, not heard. Secondly, ordinary citizens (32 per cent) dominated speaking roles. Citizens were twice as likely to be heard from as the next most vocal group, experts (17 per cent). Citizens were five times more likely to be heard from than even mid-level Party and government figures (6 per cent). Whereas the objective news paradigm associates speaking in the news with agency, the silence of top-level politicians in News Content was in keeping with mainstream Chinese journalism, which emphasizes the performative role of power with its endless iteration of leaders' meetings, attention to visits with ordinary people and solicitude for the victims of man-made and natural disasters. Foucault noted something similar with France's Louis XIV, whose power was exercised in his visibility (1977). Nevertheless, in keeping with the tactics journalists deploy in their struggle with the strategies of the CPD, by giving ordinary people voice in the news the power of central authorities was undermined without being directly confronted. By allowing ordinary people to speak, the gulf separating the silent central authorities from the audience was emphasized. Viewers saw their own voices on television and were reminded that their leaders were aloof and inaccessible, despite pretensions to the contrary.

To sum up, News Content provided Reuters with event-oriented stories that emphasized non-routine, non-disruptive news. Although politics, accidents and disasters were a priority, they were handled in a way that balanced negative impact with a government or institutional response, resulting in predominantly soft news. The result was in keeping with the soft power role of CCTV News. Nevertheless, the emphasis on accidents and disasters and the silence of central authorities perhaps undermined trust in the central leadership, even as the manifest content of the news was affirming it. When I asked a Reuters manager in 2011 how hard he expected News Content to be, he replied, "CCTV isn't going to cover the hard stories. They never do. It's still a government mouthpiece service."

By contrast, the Reuters' story about China was primarily hard. Sixty-seven per cent of stories overall were hard and 60 per cent of domestic news was hard. Like News Content, politics (15 per cent) was the top story. But unlike News Content, the focus of hard politics was primarily domestic. In keeping with the hardness of Reuters' stories, the political and economic centres Beijing, Shanghai and Hong Kong predominated. In contrast to their silence in News Content, top-level politicians were relatively vocal, providing 8 per cent of sound bites. In addition, several categories of persons invisible in News Content were visible and vocal in Reuters' stories. Protesters provided 10 per cent of sound bites, including 12 per cent of sound bites in domestic stories. Opposition politicians in domestic stories datelined Hong Kong provided 4 per cent of sound bites. The only soft story that ranked high in Reuters' editorial priorities was sport (12 per cent), the second most visible topic. Like News Content, Reuters' stories were primarily event-oriented, non-disruptive and non-routine.

One conclusion obvious from the comparison of News Content and Reuters stories was that News Content was a relatively soft bulletin. In line with the literature, it served soft power, projecting China's image as a relatively benign partner in the global political economy. Does this mean though that Reuters has become an agent of China's soft power and a propaganda instrument of the CPC and Chinese government? The answer is "yes" only if one accepts at face value the objective news paradigm, and that Reuters' stories accurately reflected reality. An alternative conclusion would be to see the addition of News Content to Reuters' overall output as a corrective to the imbalance in news flow and emphasis on negative news that was identified by MacBride[65] in the call for a New World Information and Communication Order (NWICO). That criticism has been a conclusion of every analysis of agency-output from the original work associated with the MacBride[66] report through to the very latest work. Given China's status as a developing country, making News Content available to Reuters' clients could be read as a step towards righting an historical problem of the global news system.

Perhaps undermining its own historical antipathy to NWICO was an unintended consequence of Reuters' addition of News Content to its file. When the MacBride[67] report was published, Reuters' managing director Gerald Long slammed it as an attempt by UNESCO to get the West "to put up the money and provide the technical, human and operational resources to spread throughout the world that very view of information that is most repugnant to us."[68] Therefore, it would be ironic were analysts to focus on the soft power function of News Content as propaganda and the attendant loss of editorial authority for Reuters. Instead, it would be more fair to recognize that Reuters' embrace of News Content was overdue acknowledgement that China's state-controlled media have a legitimate role to play in providing the world a more balanced picture of a country as important as China than traditionally was made available by the agencies. Regardless of whether Reuters understood this, given the agenda-setting function of the agencies for foreign news worldwide and given the historical portrayal of the developing world primarily in terms of political dysfunction, coups, earthquakes and disasters, the very softness of News Content and emphasis on accident and disaster response was part of that corrective. To wit, the distribution of News Content has strengthened the Reuters file by introducing to clients a broader and more comprehensive range of news topics and datelines than traditionally has been available to the agency's subscribers.

Conclusion

Given that News Content was only available from early 2011, it was too early to tell where the experiment was headed. Both sides benefited from the relationship. Reuters (and AP) got better access to the China story and strengthened its relationship with CCTV. CCTV gained access to Reuters' global distribution system and benefited from the association of its name with the Reuters' brand, regardless of Reuters' disavowal of any editorial responsibility for News Content.

In the struggle for editorial control internal to China's media reform, News Content can be seen as a tactical move by CCTV's managers, editors and journalists to displace the meaning of professionalism from the Leninist to the objective news paradigm. If the strategy of the Party and government is to deploy News Content as an agent of soft power, CCTV can argue that its best chance of success is to mimic the Reuters' file by adopting the editorial values associated with the professional news paradigm. In the very process of realizing the Party's and government's ambition, the authority of the CPD is undermined. However, at risk in embracing the objective news paradigm is the loss of understanding that Marxian and post-Marxian analysis bring to the analysis of ideology. Also at risk is the corrective that News Content in its current form brings to the partial character of the Reuters file. Whether News Content can find a balance of objective professionalism and Party professionalism remains to be seen.

A risk for Reuters in its relationship with CCTV is the latter's ambition to become a global player in its own right and compete with the agencies as a news wholesaler. CCTV has stated that News Content aims "to improve and expand our services for broadcasters worldwide."[69] The opening of broadcast centres in the Americas and Africa is part of that service. Undoubtedly those centres have already contributed to changes in the News Content file that were not evident in the sample analyzed here. However, the global expansion of CCTV is also a problem for News Content. In agreeing to the distribution deal, Reuters saw News Content primarily as a source of news from China. Whether the world needs another global news wholesaler is debatable, especially one that would mimic those already at work. What is not debatable though is the need for CCTV News and News Content to develop an alternative and more comprehensive picture of China than was historically made available by the agencies. Given the "middle out" character of media reform in China, perhaps CCTV is testing whether greater editorial autonomy for its services outside China can eventually translate into greater editorial autonomy on the domestic and foreign policy story. That remains to be seen. Meanwhile, CCTV risks repeating the past and the mistakes that led to the call for a NWICO, if its global expansion was to make it indistinguishable from Reuters and AP.

What currently distinguishes News Content is its commitment to news that balances a historically one-sided representation of China. At the same time, the weakness of the service is its subjection to CPD oversight. Here, the experience of India is instructive. Although the state-owned broadcaster Doordarshan does not have editorial independence, the public sphere is alive in the Indian press and television sector. How public discourse develops in India's increasingly diverse media could provide pointers for the further development of broadcasting in China. Given the almost complete absence of India from News Content, perhaps CCTV is looking in the wrong direction.

Notes

1. I use Reuters throughout, rather than Thomson Reuters, following the agency's sale to Thomson in 2008, as Reuters continues to assert its own identity within the larger company. See the Reuters website at http://reuters.com

2. Reuters, *Press Release: Reuters Delivers China's News to the World: CCTV content strengthens Reuters broadcast news file,* 18 January 2011, thomsonreuters.com (accessed 3 December 2012) from http://thomsonreuters.com/content/press_room/media/2011_01_18_reuters_delivers_china_news

3. The author was a television news producer with Reuters from 1992–1999. He worked at CCTV as a foreign expert from 1999–2000 and then again from 2003–2005.

4. K. M. Shrivastava, *News Agencies from Pigeon to Internet* (New Delhi: New Dawn Press, 2007), from books.google.com (accessed 13 January 2013); Thomson Reuters, *Emerging Markets Expertise – China.* http://thomsonreuters.com/content/financial/pdf/cross_asset/EM_China.pdf (accessed 13 January 2013).

5. Ambassador Liu Xiaoming Visits Thomson Reuters, 10 May 2010, chinese-embassy.org.uk (accessed 13 January 2013), http://www.chinese-embassy.org.uk/eng/sghd/t693515.htm

6. A.-M. Brady, "Guiding Hand: The Role of the CCP Central Propaganda Department in the Current Era," *Westminster Papers in Communication and Culture*, 3(1):58–77, 2006; A. Esarey, "Cornering the Market: State Strategies for Controlling China's Commercial Media," *Asian Perspective*, 29, no. 4 (2005): 37–83; Z. Pan (26–30 May 2005). *Media Change through Bounded Innovations: Journalism in China's Media Reforms*. Paper presented at the International Communication Association, New York, USA. http://www.lib.utexas.edu:2048/login?url=http://search.ebscohost.com/login.aspx?direct=true&db=ufh&AN=18655460&site=ehost-live (accessed 18 October 2006).

7. D. Bandurski, "Goebbels in China? China Media Project—The University of Hong Kong," 5 December 2011. http://cmp.hku.hk/2011/12/05/17324/ (accessed 2 January 2013); *Hu Zhanfan couplet*. (18 January 2012). China Digital Times. http://chinadigitaltimes.net/space/Hu_Zhanfan_couplet (accessed 2 January 2013).

8. Huang Yu, "Chinese Television in Mao's Era (1958–1976): A Historical Survey," *Guangbo yu dianshi*, 2, no. 3 (1985): 143–170.

9. X. Li, "The Chinese Television System and Television News," *China Quarterly*, 126 (1991): 340–355.

10. Li, "The Chinese Television System."

11. A. Parthasarathy, "Second Coming" for Reuters. *Frontline*, 21, no. 22 (23 October 2004 to 5 November). http://www.frontlineonnet.com/fl2122/stories/20041105003909800.htm (accessed 4 January 2013).

12. R. Chaudhuri, "The Story of the Indian Press," *The Economic Weekly*, 8, no. 11 (12 March 1955): 347–349. http://www.epw.in/system/files/pdf/1955_7/11/the_story_of_the_indian_press.pdf (accessed 4 January 2013).

13. Parthasarathy, "Second Coming," 2004.

14. Ibid., para 6.

15. Shrivastava, *News Agencies*, 2007, p. 45.

16. Ibid., pp. 45–46.

17. Shrivastava, *News Agencies*, 2007.

18. Parthasarathy, "Second Coming," 2004; Shrivastava, *News Agencies*, 2007, pp. 46–47.

19. L. McKernan, "Newsreels: Form and Function," In R. Howells and R.W. Matson eds., *Using Visual Evidence* (New York: Open University Press, 2009), pp. 95–106, 13 January 2013, from books.google.com; *Media of the masses*, 2006. ZoomInfo. http://www.zoominfo.com/CachedPage/?archive_id=0& page_id=1975248277&page_url=//www.eamedia.org/history/2006/report/media&page_last_updated=2011-12-02T23:53:08&firstName=Prem&lastName=Prakash (accessed 14 January 2013); M. Nelson, *Castro and Stockmaster: A Life in Reuters* (Leicester: Troubador Publishing Ltd, 2011). http://books.google.com/books?id=rr0labVTgxIC&q=visnews#v=snippet&q=visnews&f=false (accessed 13 January 2013); J. Tebbutt, News from Asia. *Media History*, 17, no. 3: 289–303.

20. ITN. (n.d.). *Visnews*. ITN Source. http://www.itnsource.com/en/partners/visnews/ (accessed 13 January 2013).

21. Nelson, *Castro*, 2011, pp. 112–113.

22. J. Jirik, "The World According to (Thomson) Reuters," *Sur Le Journalisme*, 2013, http://surlejournalisme.com/rev/index.php/slj/article/view/65 (accessed 24 April 2013).

23. D.K. Thussu, "The 'Murdochization' of news? The case of Star TV in India," *Media, Culture and Society*, 29, no. 4 (2007): 593–611. http://mcs.sagepub.com/content/29/4/593 (accessed 20 January 2013).

24. Jirik, "The World," 2013.

25. Ibid.

26. M. Esperidião, "Invisible Giants in Broadcast Journalism: News Agencies and the Global News Ecosystem," *Brazilian Journalism Research*, 7, no. 1 (2011b): 104–127.

27. C. Paterson, *The International Television News Agencies: The World from London*. (New York: Peter Lang, 2011).

28. E. Bielsa, "The Pivotal Role of News Agencies in the Context of Globalization: A Historical Approach," *Global Networks*, 8, no. 3 (2008): 347–366.

29. P. Harrison and R. Palmer, *News Out of Africa: Biafra to Band Aid* (London: Hilary Shipman, 1986); C. Paterson, "Global Television News Services." In A. Sreberny-Mohammadi, D. Winseck, J. McKenna and O. Boyd-Barrett eds., *Media in Global Context: A Reader* (London: Arnold, 1997), pp. 145–161.

30. Paterson, *International Television News Agencies*, 2011.

31. M. Esperidião, *Gigantes do telejornalismo mundial: Mutações editoriais e tecnológicas das agências internacionais de notícias*, 2011a, Ph.D. Dissertation, Universidade Metodista de São Paulo (UMESP), São Paulo.

32. M. Esperidião, *Gigantes*, 2011a.

33. C. Paterson, "International News on the Internet: Why More is Less," *Ethical Space: The International Journal of Communication Ethics*, no. 41/2 (2007): 57–66; Paterson, 2011; T. Rantanen, "The Globalization of Electronic News in the 19th Century," *Media, Culture and Society*, 19 (1997): 605–620; Boyd-Barett, O. 1980. Boyd-Barrett, *The International News Agencies* (Beverly Hills, CA: Sage; Esperidião, 2011b).

34. Esperidião, *Gigantes*, 2011a, abstract.

35. S. MacBride, [MacBride Report]. *Communication and Society Today and Tomorrow, Many Voices One World, Towards a new more just and more efficient world information and communication order* (London: Kogan Page, 1980; New York: Uniput; Paris: UNESCO).

36. Esperidião, "Invisible Giants," 2011b.

37. J.S. Nye, *Soft Power: The Means to Success in World Politics* (New York: Public Affairs, 2004); Y. Wang, "Public Diplomacy and the Rise of Chinese Soft Power," *The ANNALS of the American Academy of Political and Social Science*, 616 (2008):257–273. http://ann.sagepub.com/cgi/content/abstract/

616/1/257 (accessed 23 September 2009); G. Xu, 'Speech Given at the National Meeting of the Chiefs of Broadcasting and Film Bureaus.' In *The Important Documents of Broadcasting and Film Work 2001* (pp. 523–543), 2002. Beijing: SARFT; G. Liu, *From China to the World: The Development of CCTV International in the Age of Media Globalization.* Master's Thesis (London: University of Westminster, 2006).

38. Wang, "Public Diplomacy," 2008, p. 258.
39. V. Wu and A. Chen, "Beijing in 45b Yuan Global Media Drive: State Giants to Lead Image Campaign," *South China Morning Post,* pp. 1, 13 January 2009. www.lexisnexis.com (accessed 13 January 2009).
40. Liu, "From China to the World," 2006.
41. A. -M. Brady, "Regimenting the Public Mind: The Modernisation of Propaganda in the PRC," *International Journal,* 57, no. 4 (2002): 563–578; Brady, 2006.
42. Chan, A. "From Propaganda to Hegemony: Jiaodian Fangtan and China's Media Policy," *Journal of Contemporary China,* 11, no. 30 (2002): 35–51. http://www.lib.utexas.edu:2048/login?url=http://search.ebscohost.com/login.aspx?direct=true&db=aph&AN=5596091&site=ehost-live; S. H. Donald, "The Uses of Media in the People's Republic of China," *Continuum: Journal of Media and Cultural Studies,* 17, no. 3 (2003): 229–231. http://www.lib.utexas.edu:2048/login?url=http://search.ebscohost.com/login.aspx?direct=true&db=ufh&AN=10573496&site=ehost-live (accessed 18 October 2006); S. G. Dong and A. Shi, "Chinese News in Transition: Facing the Challenge of Global Competition." In D. K. Thussu ed., *Media on the Move: Global Flow and Contra-flow* (London: Routledge, 2007), pp. 182–197; A. Esarey, *From Propaganda to News: the Transformation of Print and Television Media Operations in the People's Republic of China 1979–2004.* Paper presented at the Conference on Voice and Citizenship: Rethinking Theory and Practice in Political Communication (University of Washington, 23–24 April 2004); A. Esarey and X. Qiang, "Political Expression in the Chinese Blogosphere: Below the Radar," *Asian Survey,* 48, no. 5 (2008): 752–772. Research Library database (Document ID: 1597668651, accessed 31 January 2009); J. Jirik *Making News in the People's Republic of China: The Case of CCTV-9,* Ph.D. dissertation (Austin, TX: The University of Texas at Austin, 2008). http://hdl.handle.net/2152/3907 (accessed 7 February 2009); Chin-Chuan Lee, Chinese Communication: Prisms, Trajectories, and Modes of Understanding. In Chin-Chuan Lee ed., *Power, Money, and Media: Communication Patterns and Bureaucratic Control in Cultural China* (pp. 3–44). Evanston, Il: Northwestern University Press; Pan, 2005; W. Sun, "A Small Chinese Town Television Station's Struggle for Survival: How a New Institutional Arrangement Came into Being," *Westminster Papers in Communication and Culture,* 3, no. 1 (2006): 42–57. www.westminster.ac.uk/__data/assets/pdf_file/0011/20153/4-Sun-interim.pdf (accessed 5 March 2012); Y. Zhao, *Media, Market, and Democracy in China: Between the Party Line and the Bottom Line* (Urbana, IL: University of Illinois Press, 1998); Y. Zhou (Zhao), "Watchdogs on Party Leashes? Contexts

and Implications of Investigative Journalism in Post-Deng China," *Journalism Studies*, 1, no. 2 (2000): 577–597.

43. Z. Pan and Y. Lu, "Localizing Professionalism: Discursive Practices in China's Media Reforms," 2003. In Chin-Chuan Lee ed., *Chinese Media, Global Contexts* (pp. 215–236). London: Routledge Curzon.

44. Pan and Lu, "Localizing Professionalism," 2003.

45. M. de Certeau, *The Practice of Everyday Life* (S. Rendall, Trans.) (Berkeley, CA: University of California Press, 1984).

46. de Certeau, "The Practice," 1984.

47. M. Foucault, *Discipline and Punish: The Birth of the Prison* (A. Sheridan, Trans.). (New York: Pantheon, 1977). (Original work published (1975) Surveiller et punir. Naissance de la prison).

48. Sun, "A Small Chinese Town," 2006.

49. Foucault (1977); Foucault, M. The Subject and Power. In H. Dreyfus ed., *Michel Foucault: Beyond Structuralism and Hermeneutics* (Chicago: University of Chicago Press, 1982), pp. 208–226; M. Foucault, *Histoire de la Sexualitié (Chinese translation)* (Shanghai: Century Publishing Group, 2002); M. Foucault, *Society must be defended: lectures at the Collège de France, 1975–76* (D. Macey, Trans.). (New York: Picador, 2003). (Original work published Original publication. Il faut défendre la société (edited by Mauro Bertani and Alessandro Fontana; general editors, François Ewald and Alessandro Fontana) (Paris: Editions de Seuil/Gallimard, 1997). I have cited where possible the English rather than Chinese translations on which Sun drew.

50. Sun, "A Small Chinese Town," 2006, p. 43.

51. My sense in 2014 was that the balance of force in media had shifted under President Xi Jinping away from journalistic agency to institutional control, a tactical retreat in de Certeau's sense warranting further research.

52. Pan, "Media Change Through Bounded Innovations," 2005, p. 7.

53. Z. Gao, "Advertising with Chinese Characteristics: The Development of Advertising in China, 1979–1999," In W. Jia, X. Lu and D.R. Heisey eds., *Chinese Communication Theory and Research: Reflections, New Frontiers, and New Directions* (Westport, CT: Ablex Publishing, 2002), pp. 195–206; X. Li, *Significant Changes in the Chinese Television Industry and Their Impact in the PRC: An Insider's Perspective*. The Brookings Institution, Center for Northeast Asian Policy Studies, August 2001. www.brook.edu/fp/cnaps/papers/li_01.htm (accessed 4 March 2002); Pan, 2005.

54. Personal communication from a CCTV manager.

55. D. Riffe, C.F. Aust, and S.R. Lacy, "The Effectiveness of Random, Consecutive Day and Constructed Week Sampling in Newspaper Content Analysis," *Journalism Quarterly*, 70, no. 1 (1993): 133–139; D. Riffe, S. Lacy, J. Nagovan and L. Burkum, "The Effectiveness of Simple and Stratified Random Sampling in Broadcast News Content Analysis," *Journalism and Mass Communication Quarterly*, 73, no. 1 (1996): 159–168.

56. A. Sreberny-Mohammadi, K. Nordenstreng, R. Stevenson and F. Ugboajah, *Foreign News in the Media: International reporting in 29 Countries* (Paris: United Nations Educational Scientific and Cultural Organization, 1985). unesdoc.unesco.org/images/0006/000652/065257eo.pdf (accessed 27 April 2012).

57. A. Sreberny-Mohammadi, K. Nordenstreng, R. Stevenson and F. Ugboajah, 1985; A. Sreberny and R. Stevenson. 1995. *Global News-Flow.* Ibiblio.org. http://www.ibiblio.org/newsflow/ (accessed 9 May 2012) http://www.ibiblio.org/newsflow/results/Newsmap.htm

58. Inter-coder reliability was assumed from an earlier test done on a related dataset that was generated in an identical fashion to the data analyzed here (Jirik, 2013). The test generated reliable values for Scotti's Pi, set at a minimum of 0.75 (based on R.D. Wimmer and J.R. Dominick, *Mass Media Research: An Introduction*, 8th edition (Boston: Cengage Learning, Wadsworth, 2006).

59. Sreberny-Mohammadi et al., "Foreign News," 1985, p. 15.

60. This figure counted each story once. It excluded stories that were repeated on different feeds, whether identical to their first run, or re-edited, including voiced packages. It also excluded a set of feeds that Reuters produced exclusively for German-language subscribers.

61. The dataset preceded the opening of CCTV's broadcast centre in Kenya, which undoubtedly changed the mix of news on News Content. Likewise with the opening of the broadcast centre in Washington D.C.

62. The topics add up to 86%, not 100% of the news because a dummy variable was required to double code certain topics, which were single topic stories. A dummy variable was used for the same reason in Figure 12.8, which shows topics in Reuters stories about China.

63. Li, "Chinese Television System," 1991; Pan and Lu, "Localizing Professionalism," 2003.

64. Jirik, "The World," 2008.

65. MacBride, *Communication and Society*, 1980.

66. Ibid.

67. Ibid.

68. K. Nordenstreng, *The NWICO Debate.* Leicester: Leicester University Centre for Mass Communication Research (CMCR), 1995.

69. http://newscontent.cctv.com/public/about.jsp; B. Zhao, "Mouthpiece or Money-spinner? The Double life of Chinese Television in the Late 1990s." *International Journal of Cultural Studies*, 2, no. 3 (1999): 291–305.

13

Covering Commerce: How Indian Newspapers Treat Business, Economics and the China Story

Subhomoy Bhattacharjee

Subhomoy Bhattacharjee heads the business coverage of the Express Group of newspapers. His column on finance and economy appears in the *Indian Express*. He started out as a civil servant in the early 1990s working in villages of Odisha, one of India's most backward states. Later, he joined as a reporter with *Business Standard* in Delhi and then the *Economic Times* covering finance and regulatory issues. His book on special economic zones (SEZs) in India, co-authored with Amitendu Palit, tracks the country's aborted manufacturing revival plan. In this chapter he examines how Indian media have handled business news from China in war and peace.

The level of sophistication within the Indian media to explore and analyze business themes grew in step with the economic liberalization after 1991. Previously, Indian media concentrated on politics and even major economic developments in the 1960s (bank nationalization and the beginning of industrial licensing) got only nodding acknowledgments. Two strands emerged as the economy shed this isolationist position. There was a sharp rise of interest in international events such as the General Agreement on Tariffs and Trade (GATT) and later the Southeast Asian crisis of 1997. Both impacted India. The other strand was a growing depth of coverage of domestic business themes as the share markets attracted more retail investors. Interest in international economic news receded from front pages as the media developed the ability to expose dubious domestic corporate practices and crony capitalism within the government. Correspondents even ventured into the emerging sectors like climate change and social equity. The emergence of a stable bipolar polity—either the Congress Party or the Bharatiya Janata Party (BJP) formed the core of national governments after 1998—encouraged the media's insular attitude.

By 2013, three events again jerked the Indian business media out of its groove: the global meltdown of 2008, the subsequent foray by Indian business overseas and the explosion of social networking sites. China's emergence as a key player even in supposedly non-tradable sectors like Indian small and medium enterprises (SME) also shocked Indian business media into keener interest in global economic developments. Even more than the English media, Indian-language media responded with alacrity to the increasing role of major neighbours like China as trading and investment partners. But even then compared with the rapidly urbanizing Indian mainstream, media still lag in connecting news on inflation, corruption and competition to events beyond the national boundaries.

Introduction

On 7 December 2012, the Maldives took back the management of its airport in Male from an Indian infrastructure company GMR Infra, citing problems in the contract the company had signed with the island nation. The coverage of the story prior to the cancellation and after could have remained a bilateral India–Maldivian issue but a number of reports linked the cancellation to a possible Chinese interest in the project and in the island in general. The connection was plausible, but the lack of background information from China ensured that none of the reports could establish the connection with certainty.

A fortnight before this event, India and China became the members of the Regional Comprehensive Economic Partnership, a sizable group that also included South Korea, Japan, Australia and New Zealand along with the Association of Southeast Asian Nations (ASEAN). It sprang from an ambitious plan to stitch the bilateral free trade agreements among these nations into a wider canvas and even more important to rival the Trans-Pacific Partnership (TPP), of which India and China are not members. Although the potential for future conflict and cooperation between these two blocs had immense implications, the attention to these developments in the Indian media was thin.

Speaking with the *Indian Express*, the Australian high commissioner, Peter Varghese, contextualized India–China economic relations:

> The interesting thing about Asia at the moment is that for the first time in a very long time, you've got several Asian economies becoming strong at the same time. You've got China rising, India rising, you've got Japan, notwithstanding its economic problems, you've got Korea, Vietnam, Indonesia—all moving much faster than the global average on economic growth. All of us in the region want to ensure that economic growth does not spill over into strategic instability and therefore, we need to find ways to ensure that countries are part of a system and not standing outside of the system and that applies to China as much as it applies to anyone else.

This ability to report on Asia, and especially on China, was still evolving in the Indian newsroom in 2013. The effort was hamstrung by the lack of first-hand information about China and the fact that Indian media organizations posted few correspondents in Asia as a whole, never mind China.

Indian Business Media since Independence

Exhaustive coverage of business news by Indian media is fairly recent. The coverage expanded with the economic liberalization since 1991.

This contrasts with the sophisticated coverage of political developments from the time of independence and before. Newspapers, especially those in Indian languages, were suffused with nationalist values since many of them were founded by well-known freedom fighters. They did not shy from critical reportage even if the tone was at times less than dispassionate, but this was absent from the coverage of economic news[1] in the post-independence era. Partly this was because attention of the media focussed on the compelling political narrative of a nation confronting combustible circumstances. The capacity and the motivation to dissect economic news took time to build.

This is visible in any sample of news selections from major newspapers. The first Indian business newspaper arrived in 1961. It was the decade that provided several exciting economic themes. These included nationalization of banks and insurance companies, the beginning of a strict industrial licensing policy that crippled enterprise for several decades, decisions to abandon aid from the US, devastating droughts and the first battle with inflation and shortages. There were three long-term results: issues of corruption, black money and scepticism about the role of the private sector became features of public discussion, and there were two wars, including the one with China.

The war with China in 1962 did little to encourage the analysis of the Chinese economy, even by the infant Indian business press. If the latter reported on foreign economics and business at all, the focus was on the UK and the US. Only in the late 1970s, after the death of Mao Zedong and the opening of the Chinese economy, did occasional stories begin to appear on the business pages of Indian newspapers.

Questions about the role of the government and its relationship with specific companies became significant topics for newspapers only in the late 1980s, after the death of Indira Gandhi. Of the two news stories which defined this decade, one involved allegations of corruption in defence armament purchases, while the other related to accusations of over-zealous support from the government for Dhirubhai Ambani's rapidly expanding Reliance Industries Ltd. The coverage of these two issues set the tone for business reporting which grew in the 1990s after the liberalization of the Indian economy began in 1991.

The Economic Context of Business Reportage in India

The business press inherited the economic narrative adopted by India after independence. The primary theme was an autarkic model of development, which was only slowly abandoned after 1991. Consequently, the Indian press fell into the trap of analyzing economic policies independent of what was happening in global markets or economic policy-making.

Even after the crisis of 1991 led to convulsive changes in the Indian economy and a consequent expansion of business journalism, editorial positions often harked back to the days and the virtues of an isolationist economy. An early example of this strand of thought was the debate over the GATT rules.[2] The reportage of the debate, even within segments of the English press, was insular. On issues like opening up the industrial sector to global competition, this line predominated.

A further break with the past came with the so-called "Harshad Mehta scam" in the Indian stock market in 1992–1993. The scale of the rigging in what was then the Bombay stock market shook pre-existing beliefs in the business press. As the government moved to establish a new stock exchange conducted under rules derived from global best practice, the business press became avid followers of the rule-based, globalized market economy.

But even here, as the business press began an informed debate about facets of globalization, rarely did it discuss China. Reports about the Chinese model of development tended to be impressionistic travelogues.

The first systemic reportage on China was triggered by the East Asian crisis of 1997. As the crisis unfolded, the effects disrupted India too, though not nearly as profoundly as countries of East and Southeast Asia. The media became aware of developments in the Chinese economy in the context of the reports about the East Asian tiger economies, and terms like the "SEZ" and "infrastructure-led development" gained currency. Journalists also began to contextualize the rapid but already decelerating rate of growth of the Indian GDP compared to the Asian economies. The Indian government had presented in 1997–1998 a "dream budget," but as two central governments fell in the same period and the growth rate plummeted, the media learnt to connect the crisis in Asian markets to the economic uncertainties at home. An editorial in December 1997 in the *Financial Express*, "Dream budget raised hopes, but only just," exemplified the connections that were now being made.

These developments spurred the rapid spread of news television. By 2001, the GDP from radio and television had reached ₹980 crore ($200 million), 16 times that of 1990–1991.[3] Since foreign direct investment was first permitted in electronic media before spreading to print, the connection with global developments was more easily established there. Print media too reaped benefits. Analysts expected the sector to grow in the years to 2016 at a compound annual growth rate of 9.1 per cent, down from 14.5 per cent expected before the global meltdown.[4]

How Indian Media Discovered China[5]

Three themes dominated the reportage and commentary about China that took off in the new century. These were the SEZ episode, the impact of Chinese manufacturing on Indian SME, and the globalization of Indian industrial groups. The most dramatic of these were the events surrounding the SEZs. In 2000, India's commerce minister Murasoli Maran visited SEZs in China. The experience led him to champion the development of similar zones in India. His government was swept up in the excitement, and a decade-long bittersweet affair with these zones started. The story has been told elsewhere, and the Indian media began to report on China with reference to these zones. Since the development of Indian SEZs coincided with Chinese entry into the World Trade Organization (WTO), interest grew significantly. The media reportage on the SEZs emphasized that these were the fulcrum of the rapid and persistently high growth rate China had achieved for more than two decades prior to 2001. As Indian rules for the establishment of SEZs were framed, comparisons with China became more acute. A weakness, however, was that few reports were constructed on the basis of personal experience in China. Reports were mostly sourced from international news agencies and carried all the bias that such reports are prone to.

Media dissected the SEZ model to try to discover what made SEZs so resilient in the face of population pressure. The zones also seemed to flourish regardless of fluctuating central and state government support and they seemed to promote stunning growth in manufacturing.

The reportage at this stage was almost uniformly complimentary, attempting to find ways in which India could build on the learning from these zones. In terms of the Indian media's "discovery" of China, this was the "China impresses" phase.

By 2005–2006, India's policy towards SEZs had lost direction with the government ministries fighting among themselves over whether to extend tax concessions. There was also indecision and rumour of legislation relating to land acquisitions and charges of improprieties in the case of earlier acquisitions. With so much domestic furore, Indian business media became more insular.

SEZs affected urban India because they brought factory-style jobs, and they affected some areas of rural India because they acquired land and sometimes provided work for people who previously worked mostly on the land. But the rapid incursion of Chinese manufacturing as a competitor for the Indian small-scale sector impacted the populations in between—people living in small cities and towns.

Cheap imports from China began to affect domestic small-scale industry from about 2003–2004 when growth revived in the Indian economy. As the Indian market fell under the charm of cheap supplies of Chinese manufactures, the media only discovered the implications sporadically. A fear about China's economic influence began to grow, particularly in sections of the electronic media. The discovery of the scale and effects of the inroads of Chinese goods were first made by the Indian-language media and came into the English press much later. This was the beginning of the second phase—"China depresses."

Central government ministries helped to propel this second phase by launching anti-dumping cases against China. Often it appeared there were sufficient grounds, but the government usually failed to win court cases.

The third phase arrived when Indian companies, especially in the manufacturing sector, began venturing abroad from about 2005. The ventures had two components—either scouting for raw materials or planning to buy companies. Examples of the latter included Tata Steel's acquisition of Corus Steel, UK in 2007. Major foreign investment into India included the Vodafone buy-out of Hutchison-Essar in the telecom sector. By 2012, all the top 20 Indian companies by market capitalization had a significant foreign presence. This also included state-owned enterprises like the Oil and Natural Gas Corporation (ONGC), the National Thermal Power Corporation (NTPC) and to a lesser extent the State Bank of India (SBI). This globalization of Indian business gave depth to the pattern of reportage for the Indian business media too.

As Indian companies went abroad, however, they encountered stiff competition from Chinese companies, especially in the acquisition of raw materials in Asia and Africa. In 2005, the China National Petroleum Corporation bought Petrokazakhstan, the largest oil company of the former Soviet Union, and in the same year China concluded a US $2 billion oil-for-loan deal in Angola.

These encounters with Chinese capital in Asia and Africa drew the attention of Indian policy-makers. The Working Group on Coal, which prepared background papers for the government of India's 12th Five Year Plan, noted:

> In the face of a government-backed Chinese merger and acquisition model, it would become difficult for Indian companies to acquire coal assets, or any other mining assets for that matter, in emerging economies like Mozambique, Indonesia and South Africa.

India business, economic departments of government and media woke up to the scale of Beijing's presence in everything from energy to the financial sector.

As company after company came upon an apparently homogenous set of competitors from China, and this fact was recognized by the Government of India, Indian media initially responded with predictable jingoism. As business journalism gained experience, this picture changed. In the case of the GMR (Grandhi Mallikarjuna Rao), investment in the Maldives airport in 2012 or the dispute of the steel company, JSPL (Jindal Steel and Power Ltd), with the Bolivian government, Indian media were more diverse in their approach and did not take an unvaried, nationalistic position.

Foreign Investment

Investment abroad and foreign investment into India gradually trained the business press from the early 1990s in reporting on the economy and its implications. An early debate in the 1990s involved the media themselves: should foreign direct investment in Indian media be allowed? The trigger was the application by the English-language business newspaper *Business Standard* to the central government to allow the *Financial Times*, London, to become a partner. Debate over the larger question of foreign direct investment polarized over where the respective media groups' investment plans stood.[6] If they were seeking foreign investment, they were for it; if they were not, they were against.

More independent and analytical discussion of FDI fairly quickly entered the larger publications in the English and Indian-language press. But there remained in much of the smaller newspapers, a discomfort with foreign investment, equating it as an intrusion into the economy. The narrative about China often got trapped in the same way. The coverage pattern changed noticeably in 2012, however, with coverage of the debates over whether to open multi-brand retail to foreign players.

Two stand-out events are the reportage of the discovery at two oil fields abroad where India confronted Chinese interests. These are in Sakhalin III and in the South China Sea. In the case of Sakhalin, coverage began in a fairly neutral way,[7] but became shrill soon after.[8] The standoff on the South China Sea remained unresolved in 2013.

Such India–China encounters are inevitable. Both countries have embarked on a rapid path of growth that will require enormous quantities of minerals to feed their energy-industrial complexes. Resources on that scale are available neither in China nor India, and so the contest will be one of the most significant of the twenty first century. The sense of achievement or despondency—winning or losing—as perceived by the media in India (and presumably in China too) will colour the way in which business news is presented to mass readerships.

By the year 2000, the Indian business press had acquired considerable ability in evaluating government and corporate developments. This was on display in the analysis of the complicated standoffs between government and business, such as the 2G telecom case. The media, especially the print media, dissected how a government minister had misinterpreted a cabinet decision to favour real estate companies (mostly) to obtain licences to use radio frequency spectrum for mobile communications at low prices. The same media capacity was on display in questioning the profit-share formula adopted by the government for oil and gas discoveries made through public–private partnerships, and reports on the off-balance-sheet activities of companies like Satyam, a case that eventually led to an exposure of a $1.2 billion fraud.

These skills often fell short in discerning trends in the activities of Indian businesses abroad. The media tended to rely on the government or on companies for information. This made it easy for the India government to claim innocence, and in some cases to lay the blame for faulty policies on foreign governments. Coal India Videsh was a messy amalgam of the business interests of five state-owned companies straddling three ministries. The aim was to secure coal-mining blocks abroad. Though the company managed to secure not a single mine, it was rarely dragged over the coals for this failure (A better arrangement would have been to pool the funds and allow one company to anchor the venture.).

Similarly, the business press tends to take its lead from government when "threats" from Chinese investment, either in the form of money or men, arise. A case study illustrates this. In the telecom sector, the India government struggled to break the encryption code of devices like Blackberry Messenger. That in itself was a reflection on the inadequate level of investment in the security infrastructure of the country. But the Home Ministry, responsible for internal security including cyberspace, came up with a facile solution. It asked Research in Motion (RIM), makers of Blackberry, to share its security apparatus. It cited unconfirmed reports from China that the company had complied similarly there. Even though Research in Motion repeatedly stated that it had no means to break the encryption in India or elsewhere because it does not possess a master code, it made no difference to the Home Ministry. The incident dragged on in an unsatisfactory standoff.

When the Indian government accused RIM of adopting double standards, India's business press tended to accept the contention. The government subsequently extended the argument to demand decryption facilities from social media companies Google and Facebook and then extended the demand to Yahoo! and Microsoft.

The Home Ministry used the security argument again when it claimed there were security concerns stemming from the presence of large numbers of Chinese workers at power project sites. It also discussed the possibility of remote sensing devices being planted in imported Chinese electronic equipment. The business media broadly accepted the government line without demur.

In short, the Indian business press largely depended on the government for its approach to foreign countries and the relationship of their economic activities to India. It was shrill when the government was shrill, adopted a more conciliatory stance when the government did so and even adopted a subdued tone when the government did likewise with respect to China.[9]

We then begin to observe a split in the reportage pattern between the coverage of business and the coverage of politics. In spite of a commitment to offer unbiased reporting, the business press takes its cue from government in its coverage of events abroad.

Since there is a strong popular interest in China, this usually has meant that sensational events get precedence over the mundane and lack of expertise about China, including a paucity of Mandarin-speaking Indians, creates a bias in favour of secondary news sources, such as the global wire agencies. In the midst of such circumstances, China became India's largest trading partner, and it is a little known fact that some of the key processes adopted in the Shanghai stock exchange were borrowed from India's largest stock exchange, the National Stock Exchange (NSE).

Sections of the Indian business press became less one-dimensional in the twenty-first century. This was illustrated in the reporting on the India government's plans to allow foreign direct investment in multi-brand retail. Newspapers reported in detail on the likely consequences if the plan went through. The *Financial Express*, for example, ran a week-long series from domestic and foreign commentators on the ramifications of the proposal, including analysts who had reservations about the opening up of the sector. The media also tracked the Chinese experience with the retail revolution.

The Way Ahead

The GDP of China and India is about 12 per cent of the world GDP (2011 figures). But for Indian or Chinese media, the best commentators on the economies of each other's countries come from outsiders. There is a dearth of specialists in India on the Chinese economy and it appears vice versa. The situation is acute when one looks for the analysis of detailed issues like government budgets, policies on sectors such as finance and power, demographics or socio-political indicators. In 2013, there was not even the colloquial "handful of commentators."

The gap will take time to fill. Lack of knowledge of each other's languages is a reason but that can be overcome. What was not happening in Indian newsrooms was a sense of urgency to improve knowledge and coverage of China.[10] It would, I suspect, take one major corporate acquisition (it does not matter from which side) to make that urgency happen. There were suggestions of this in 2010, when one of India's largest industrial groups, the Anil Dhirubhai Ambani Group (ADAG), took out a $3 billion loan from the China Development Bank, and when the market for renminbi bonds opened up. In the absence of such blockbusters, India–China business news (rather than economic news, like trade statistics) remain listless and under-researched. Relatedly, the restrictions on the employment of the other country's citizens persisted, partly because there was no debate in the media about the debilitating impact of these restrictions on business relations.

Negative and superficial portrayals of China in Indian business media were not unique. Xenophobia had surfaced in reports about Australia, coloured by racial issues in the case of Indian students, but of more salience were the coal-exploration stories involving Indian companies.[11] Similarly reports about Russia and oil exploration have often been controversial.

For media in India and China, it is vital to cultivate a knowledge bank about each other's economy. Even without that knowledge, the engagement of the two countries will rise. But without improved knowledge, such increases in economic connections risk disruption from the two isolated media systems. If Indian and Chinese media operate in their own national vacuums, poorly researched "bad news" will often get prominence, as demonstrated in the South China Sea episode. Because India is a democracy, there will always be voices that ask for cutbacks of trade and investment relations with China.

There is a need for independent think tanks to study key annual economic events in the two economies and report on them. Media in both countries would be likely to use such reports. There will continue to be discordant noises. The dominant theme in the business coverage of China and India is bound to be the race for minerals. This story will be played out in a number of regions across the globe. Since it will be portrayed as a competition, there will be occasions when the coverage in both countries will be biased and nationalistic. The trick is for the media to recognize which stories are merely politicians at play and which involve solid economic issues that need to be explained to the citizens of each country.

Notes

1. In this chapter the terms economic news and business news will be used interchangeably.
2. Arthur Dunkel, the chief of GATT, became a highly well-known name even in suburban India as an epitome of the evils of globalization. http://www.cuts-citee.org/pdf/MONOGRAPH02-01.pdf
3. "Foreign Direct Investment for Media," in *New Oxford Companion to Economics in India*, p. 261.
4. The Indian M&E industry grew from ₹652 billion in 2010 to ₹728 billion in 2011, registering an overall growth of 12 per cent. The sector was projected to grow at a healthy CAGR of 14.9 per cent to reach ₹1,457 billion by 2016. English print was expected to grow 6.3 per cent, according to the FICCI–KPMG report of 2012.
5. In much of what follows, despite evidence that Chinese media too must have gone through a phase of growing up, for the purpose of this chapter, I have restricted the comments to Indian media.
6. http://www.cscsarchive.org:8081/MediaArchive/clippings.nsf/(docid)/875B43E0B716FE85E5256C5D0005835A
7. *Business Standard*, 3 May 2008, http://www.rediff.com/money/2008/may/03russ.htm
8. http://www.thehindu.com/news/international/article19495.ece
9. http://blogs.reuters.com/india/2011/01/11/does-the-indian-media-over-play-indo-chinese-tension/
10. In March 2012, both India and China presented their annual budget. Indian media reported the Chinese budget only in the context of its defence plans, if at all. The finalization of the 12th Five Year Plan was never on the front page of any business newspaper. The compliment was returned by the major Chinese newspapers.
11. http://www.smh.com.au/business/political-indecision-strangles-indias-coal-industry-20120507-1y95y.html

Notes

PART IV
Dissections

14

Media Control as Stability Maintenance: The Case of the Sichuan Earthquake

Ming Xia

Ming Xia, who started his career in political science three decades ago in Shanghai, is a professor at the City University of New York at the Graduate Center and the College of Staten Island. He has published three books on political governance and transition in China, co-edited books on the Falun Gong and Nobel Prize laureate Liu Xiaobo, and written more than a hundred articles. His involvement in making the Oscar-nominated documentary, *China's Unnatural Disaster: The Tears of Sichuan Province*, led him (a Sichuan native) to write this chapter on the relationship between the state and media in China.

Having emerged as a unique twentieth-century phenomenon, totalitarianism (both fascist and communist) separates itself from all previous autocracies by its cross-the-board incorporation of modern technology into technique and mechanism of political control. Entering the twenty-first century, which was foremost defined by globalization, the Chinese state has become more aggressive but more sophisticated in relying on new technologies for improving its efficiency in political control. Technology's dubious application in human society is clearly demonstrated in the role of media technology for the existing Chinese regime.[1] As political scientists already realized decades ago, "there is a peculiarly intimate relationship between the political process and the communications process" and "the state of politics is a function of the communications process."[2] It is important to take mass communication as an access point to examine the negotiation between the Chinese state and the citizens over the nature of political governance and political life. This approach provides a way to understand how under the communist rule for more than 60 years, the Chinese state has been transforming itself from a draconian totalitarian system to a resilient authoritarianism.[3]

"TINA" (There Is No Alternative) politics has been the signature of Chinese communist rule. Starting with an infallible and irreplaceable "wise and great leader" Mao Zedong, its content has shifted to an emphasis upon the unchallengeable ruling Party, and as a part of the package, the indisputable development vision and sometimes policies impervious to deliberation and contestation. However, in terms of the style, there has been a smooth glide from an Orwellian "Big Brother" state to a Huxleyan "Brave New World," wherein the former people were denied choice under the terror of poverty and deprivation and in the latter, people are programmed or intoxicated to embrace false consciousness under "comfortable unfreedom."[4] During the 10 years of Hu (Jintao) and Wen (Jiabao) partnership (2003–2013, the two stepped down in March 2013), the "Beijing consensus" and "China model" were constructed with an ambition to challenge the dominant liberal democracy. Now, as the Chinese Party-state has tried to convince its people that "socialism with Chinese characteristics" is the "sole correct pathway," to manufacture, promote and sustain this idea has become a huge enterprise. A comprehensive and ambitious media campaign has been carried out on domestic and global fronts. Such projects include "The Great Fire Wall" to control the internet; the closing down of Google search service in the Mainland; the promotion of Chinese soft power by establishing Confucius Institutes to reach a target of 500; and the "Great Foreign Propaganda Campaign" that in 2009 was allocated 45 billion Yuan (more than US$7 billion)[5] to take over or support Chinese media overseas, infiltrate the foreign news market, attack websites maintained by Chinese political dissidents and fabricate positive "foreign news coverage" for internal consumption. The Chinese and the people all over the world have been witnessing the most expensive and sophisticated "propaganda campaign" since the fall of Nazi fascism and the Soviet empire.

In this chapter, I focus on the episode of Sichuan earthquake in 2008 to illustrate the state-media relationship in China. The Chinese media, which still hold an image of a semi-bureaucratic establishment despite their embracing marketization and commercialization, are often caught in the conflict between the Party (CPC) and its people.[6] Under a static structural and bureaucratic model, multi-layered control mechanisms have been imposed upon the media to keep them closer to the Party line than the Mass line. After the 2008 earthquake in Sichuan, the Party mobilized the mass media to create a well-coordinated campaign for presenting a positive image and accomplishment of the state triumvirate—the Party, the state and the Army—in order to shore up the legitimacy of the regime by means of education of patriotism and nationalism.[7] But to the surprise of a Party-state unprepared for the uncertainties that lay ahead, the grievances of parents whose children were killed in the collapsed school buildings prompted them to organize protests and appeal to the mass media for support. In response, a meticulously controlled mass media tried to intercept them in between the bureaucracy and protesters, some discovered and asserted their existential subjectivity in counterbalancing the instrumentality imposed by the Party.

Based upon a field trip to the Sichuan Earthquake zone in 2008, I present a dynamic model to illustrate a complex competition between the protestors and the government. The former wanted to recruit the mass media to witness and record their efforts to redress their grievances. The latter wanted to enforce an exclusion of the media from the massive demonstrations. This chapter examines how the presence of media helped socialize the scope of conflict against the wish of the government to keep it private and how it radically transformed the context of conflict. On the one hand, it curtailed the arbitrary use of power by the government and boosted the weak and marginalized protestors; on the other hand, it empowered the protesters and created a strong potential to encourage bystanders to become participants. This chapter discusses under what circumstances the media could quickly switch from being the traditional helpmate of the government into an ally of protestors against the interest of the government in an unexpected crisis.

The Background: The Year 2008 and the Wenchuan Earthquake

For China, the year 2008 was destined to become "a year of great significance."[8] The *People's Daily* New Year's editorial, which was entitled, "Greeting the Great Year of 2008 with Joy," anticipated: "The year 2008 will be an important chapter in the annals of achieving the great renaissance of the Chinese nation." This heightened anticipation was due to the coming Beijing Olympiad in the summer and the 30th anniversary of China's "reform and opening up era."

Not to miss a golden opportunity to showcase China's great achievements and to reintroduce itself as a great power onto the world stage, the Chinese Party-state formulated a clear political agenda to promote patriotism and nationalism among the people, and carefully stage a series of extravagant activities to shore up its own legitimacy. The Party-state lessened its control over mass media, and the foreign media especially were granted more freedom to conduct interviews. Building upon the momentum of increasing transparency and accountability in the government since 2004 after the SARS crisis, a series of state regulations and laws were passed to provide standards for how to respond to unexpected public crises, to require speedy release of information with more accuracy and to promise people the right to know, in particular with regard to disaster-related information that used to be concealed under the excuse of maintaining state secrets and social stability. For example, in 2007, "The Emergency State Law" (突发事件应对法) was passed and implemented. Meanwhile, "The Open Government Information Regulations" (政府信息公开条例) were passed and set to take effect on 1 May 2008. Specifically serving the needs of the Beijing Olympiad, the central government passed *The Regulations for the Interview by Foreign Media during the Olympic Games* (有关奥运期间国外媒体采访的规定), which stipulated that from 1 July 2007 to October 2008 when the Beijing Olympiad concluded, foreign media were granted more access and freedom to conduct interviews in China. One concession was that foreign media could interview people without the pre-approval from the government.[9]

Although the lessening of control over the foreign media was intended for a specific period and exclusively for interview and reporting to serve the needs of the Olympiad, the two-front liberalization in both the management of information and control of media created an environment for more aggressive and creative coverage of China in terms of scope and depth. It was like *déjà vu* of 1989 when Western media swarmed to Beijing to cover the historic visit of Mr Gorbachev intended to turn a new page in Sino-Soviet relationship.

Then, unexpectedly, the Western media were on the ground for the massive protests and the massacre at the Tiananmen Square.[10] Before the opening ceremony of the Beijing Olympiad, two big events were more newsworthy because of their surprising eruption at the time of the stage-managed Olympic extravaganza. The two events were the political riots by Tibetans in March and the earthquakes in May.

The fact that protest movements can exert an amplified impact often results from two factors. First, intense repression releases an explosion of resistance. Second, the resistant force has found and exploited a convenient stage, created by the powerful, on which to vent its counter-hegemonic grievances. As for the first, the weak and the marginalized in China were conveniently sacrificed under the name of order and security. As for the second, the state-sponsored Olympic torch relays worldwide were turned into a battleground by human rights activists and Tibetan supporters, especially in the major cities of the West, such as London, Paris and Los Angeles, to expose the widespread abuses of human rights in China. The Lhasa riots in Tibet on 14 March 2008 were not covered in an open and fair way in the official media. The international and unofficial Chinese media (such as microblogging and Twitter) revealed information that proved costly for the Chinese government's public relations and public image in the world.

On 12 May 2008, a massive earthquake at the Richter scale of 8 hit Sichuan province. According to the official statistics released weeks after the quake, 69,195 people were killed, 18,403 remained missing and among the dead, 5,335 were school children. About 14,000 schools were damaged and 7,000 of them collapsed.[11] The official death tolls for students were contested by people. For example, artist Ai Weiwei organized his volunteers to collect and list the names of killed students. Within one year, his list reached 5,205. Ai believed that since his team had not visited some known schools that suffered serious damage, this number could easily go beyond 6,000.[12] Another research report written by Dr Feng Congde, the former student leader of the Tiananmen hunger strike and a native from the Sichuan quake zone, estimated the death toll for students and teachers ranged from 13,000 to 19,000. Feng's high-end estimate was corroborated by Wei Hong, Vice Governor of Sichuan, in a news conference (later the government retracted the revelation as "a slip of the tongue") in November 2008, who gave the number as 19,065.[13] Understandably, the massive collapse of school buildings and the accurate number of killed students became the lightning-rod that attracted attention and questioning from all directions.

The Wenchuan Earthquake was sandwiched between the Tibetan riots and the Beijing Olympiad. Thus, the activism of the news media and the state's crisis management during the quake were conditioned by a unique transitional period from a more relaxed and open atmosphere to a suppressive one. The central government sent out new instructions for the coverage of the quake by the media, and the News Office of the Sichuan provincial government replaced interview permits with new ones specific to foreign media in the quake zone. Meanwhile, President Hu Jintao urged China's domestic media to "maintain strict propaganda discipline," "properly guard the gate" and "manage the extent [of reporting] on major, sensitive and hot topics."[14] Later, Hu would confront more challenges, including the controversy over the Olympic Games, the Melamine-tainted milk crisis and the global financial crisis. The year drew to a close with the release of the CD "Chinese Democracy" by the *Guns N'Roses* band and the arrest of political activist Dr Liu Xiaobo for initiating *The Charter 08 Movement* to demand freedom and democracy for China; he won the Nobel Prize in Peace in 2010.

The Protest Movements and the Tensions between Mass Media and the State

On 22 May 2008, 10 days after the earthquake, I arrived at the quake zone with a team of filmmakers (Directors/Producers Jon Alpert and Matthew O'Neil, and Peter Kwong, professor of sociology at the City University of New York), which was financed by HBO Documentary for making a documentary film on the disaster. The invitation to include me into the team was probably due to the three factors: I am a native of Sichuan; I have done most of my research on local governance in China; and I had travelled to the region just one year before the earthquake. My observation is based upon my field trip to the earthquake zone from 22 May to 1 June 2008. On the first day, our team was divided into two groups and visited two cities separately.

Although we visited two most devastated townships (Hanwang in Mianzhu and Xiang'e in Dujiangyan), went to collapsed school sites and saw a heavy presence of police, the military police and army soldiers, we did not encounter any trouble from the authorities.

In the aftermath of Wenchuan Earthquake, a "tectonic change" happened to news reporting and coverage. The Chinese official media launched the "most intense," "most open" and "longest news bombing" in Chinese history.[15] This phenomenon was a result of several converging factors. First, "The Open Government Information Regulations" took effect on 1 May and created a liberalizing atmosphere for the new media. Most likely under the slogan of "taking people-oriented approach" from the leadership and a belief that the earthquake was a "typically natural disaster," the government held a more open attitude toward the press; this was the first litmus test of its sincerity to abide by its own law. The press was encouraged and emboldened to be more responsive to the disaster, more aggressive in reporting and more open about the traditionally forbidden topics. Second, Premier Wen Jiaobao was a skilful media spinner who carefully exploited the event to project him as a "People's Premier" and to create an amicable image of "Grandpa Wen."[16] He brought reporters from the central news agencies with him and held his first news conference on the airplane as he was flying to Sichuan two hours. On 24 May, when the chilling effect of retraction already was felt by reporters on the ground, Mr Wen held another unique news conference on the ruins in the epicentre to reaffirm that "this rescue work has adopted openness as the guideline," and he reiterated his support and welcome to foreign reporters.[17] Furthermore, facing the enthusiastic participation of citizens with cameras in their mobile phones and microblogs and Twitter as their outlets, the mainstream media were pressed even harder to not let unofficial channels scoop the news. This rare opportunity released the "professional instinct" of reporters based upon their professional trainings.[18] A *laissez faire* and even an anarchic situation characterized the state-media relationship before the bureaucracy fully recovered and formulated a coherent response strategy.

But it was immature to predict the birth of a new "open and transparent China" out of the quake.[19] On 18 May, the State Council announced 19 May as the "National Mourning Day" for the dead; the entire country would observe mourning for three days. On 22 May, the government and official media started to steer the entire country from the rescue mode to the recovery mode. Saving life gave way to restoring order. One commentator called on the Chinese: "Wipe out the tears, start a new march with the nation-state."[20] The Chinese Party-state quickly resumed its upper hand over the press and mass media.

My field trip started in parallel with this transition. During this period, the parents created memorials on many school sites and gathered there to mourn their lost loved ones. In the Fuxin Primary School where our team shot most of the footage, the parents carefully lined up more than one hundred school bags in different colours next to the uncollected sneakers and surreal rubble. As the parents decorated the memorial with framed colour pictures and banners, other visitors brought more wreathes and flowers. The site quickly turned into a forum for the parents to tell visitors and the media about how the school was not properly built and how their rescue was not helped quickly enough by either the army or local authority. To add insult to injury, the local officials stayed away from the site and underreported the death toll by half to the higher authority.

Interestingly, the Chinese government decided on the "National Mourning Day" by referring to a tradition that the seventh day after an event is an important time for observation. The parents who lost their children chose the second seventh day (i.e. 14 days after the event) as a crucial day for their protest. Local people believe that after two weeks, the soul of the dead leaves this world to the other world. After the National Mourning period, the parents shifted to their active mode to demand official explanations for what had happened to the schools and their children and moved their "forum" or "arena" to the streets where they protested in a march. This turn obviously ran against official signals.

On Sunday, 25 May 2008, our team was searching for stories as the hired Chinese driver carried us in an SUV. By asking around, I got a clue from a local farmer that a primary school named Fuxin lost 128 students and that day the grieving parents were marching out of their school site. They planned to go 100 miles to the provincial capital to petition the higher authority for an investigation into the shoddily built schools. Our team with two video cameras and two regular cameras was one of the few media crews present at the very beginning of the march. Although *New York Times* photographer Shiho Fukada was probably the earliest Western reporter, since she is Japanese, she was not so eye-catching compared to the two white men with video cameras in our team. A photographer in a black T-shirt with the "Police" sign was active in taking pictures, in particular zooming in on our team.

Jiang Guohua, the municipal Party Secretary and the Chairman of the municipal people's congress in Mianzhu, was running with the marching parents, trying to persuade them to stop and to talk to him. Despite being frustrated and humiliated, Jiang was responsive and self-restrained to the media. Chen Zhengquan, the deputy mayor and police chief of Deyang City (which is one level higher than Mianzhu in the administrative hierarchy) also rushed to meet the parents who had already walked 20 kilometres and appealed to them to have a talk with the Deyang authority, instead of going to the higher level of authority, the provincial capital. Surrounded by cameras and foreign media, Chen showed his annoyance towards us on his face but did not order his officers to interfere with us.

The local authority realized that the public protest and the march could ruin the political careers and fortunes of many officials and cause a snowballing effect: the march had attracted more bystanders and encouraged some to bring in their grievances. Some brawls broke out among the crowd. Party Secretary Jiang told an interviewer later that "A fuse could easily lead [to] an explosion of complex conflicts, if the march had been exploited by the people with ultra-motives, [and] the consequence could be beyond imagination." He was told by his assistant that another group of angry parents were also gathering in another school at Hanwang only 1 km away. Fearful of a riot in the making, he could not restrain himself from kneeling down in front of the angry parents four times.[21] One government official kept reminding the agitated bystanders that they should control themselves and present a good image for the Chinese nation in front of "foreign friends." Very soon, Deputy Mayor Chen brought in two big buses to transport the marchers to a government official compound, offering promises to listen to their grievances and to find solutions as soon as possible. The parents, in particular the leaders of the march, discussed among themselves the trade-off about whether to go with the Mayor or to continue the march. They decided that they would go with the buses only if the media were allowed to accompany them. The government officials allowed the media to travel with the parents.

In the bus, the parents were concerned about the possibility that the government would treat them roughly behind closed doors, so they insisted on getting off the bus outside of the compound gate and persisted with the government officials for a guarantee that they would be treated fairly and have the freedom to come out. As they were escorted into an auditorium where lunch and medical supplies were prepared with medical personnel on site, the parents were further afraid of being isolated from the media. A female deputy mayor of Deyang, Ms Song Yuhua who was in charge of education and health affairs, used her charm to convince the parents that "On the territory of the People's Republic of China, citizens are guaranteed the freedom of movement." One mother complained that "We have been cheated to have only fears left. We have no trust in officials." The parents insisted on inviting the media to accompany them into the auditorium. But the government officials (many from the Party propaganda department) and police officers tried to separate the parents from the media by arguing that the parents needed rest, relaxation and counseling and not being bothered. Some local TV station crews (some from other provinces, such as Yunnan) were more cooperative. One female reporter from the official Xinhua News Agency tried to enter the auditorium and was stopped. After she protested the refusal to allow reporters in, a male official from the propaganda department pushed her out rudely. The surrounding local officials even started inspecting her credentials and pointed out that one more red stamp was needed for a full validation. Even when the Xinhua reporter threatened to publicize what was happening on the next day's Xinhua News Net, which represents the highest authority in Chinese official news bureaucracy, the local officials did not budge.[22]

Our team was treated with less physical aggression because we had four strong men and could manoeuvre around to find opportunity. In order to calm us down and get rid of us as soon as they could, the officials later allowed two of us with one camera to shoot some snapshots in the stadium as the parents were eating their lunch. Then all the media personnel were kept out of the stadium as they were carrying on the dialogue and the executive deputy mayor of Deyang, Zhang Jinming, made a speech. Our team was also approached by three police officers who identified themselves as the "police officers for foreign affairs" from the municipality of Deyang. They attempted to check our passports, press credentials and visa types. Since we did not show them, we were warned to stop our activities. Unexpectedly at 4:21 PM, an aftershock at the Richter scale 6.4 hit the region and the

buildings shook and tiles fell. The parents had to be evacuated out-
doors to a basketball court. This made it more difficult for the officials to keep the media off limits. With our begging and schmoozing,
the city director for foreign affairs on the site allowed our cameras to
come close to the crowd for some shots. The mayors (both Zhang and
Song) gave the parents three promises: (a) They would inspect the
school site the next day. (b) They had already created an investigation
team led by senior engineers from the provincial capital to start the
investigation about the quality of school buildings. (c) The investigation would be finished within a month and a final investigation report
would be released to determine whether there were wrongdoings and
who should take the responsibilities. Finally, the parents agreed to be
sent back to their villages by the government-provided buses.

In the following two days, to avoid any confrontation with the
police, we decided to interview parents at home or in the field. On 27
May, as we were returning to the Fuxin Township, we stumbled into
another protest. About 100 parents from Hanwang Township were
blocking the highway and demanding the government investigate the
collapse of their children's school. As we started shooting, we met
deputy mayor and police chief Chen of Deyang again. Very soon the
three police officers we met three days ago came to us. There was a
video photographer from the Police Department busy shooting our
images. This time the police officers threatened to arrest us if we did
not leave or if we returned to his territory again.

In the coming three days, we travelled to other cities in guerrilla-
war style for our investigations. We met police officers and special
commando officers; some took pictures of us with suspicious and
hateful stares, but did not go further. On two occasions, the police
officers either blocked our camera lens or drove us off the school
ground. Then on 1 June, International Children's Day, we were
informed by the parents who were in touch with us that they would
have a memorial service on the site of Fuxin Primary School. In the
early morning, our two SUVs approached the township and we saw
dozens of police officers were positioning themselves to surround the
school and to block the entry ways. Being aware of the arrest warning,
our team decided to give up our shooting plan and left the site. A local
reporter with press credentials was working with our Chinese co-
producer. From their footage, I saw the three officers we met were on
the site and a police photographer was filming as thoroughly as

possible. In the late afternoon, as the Chinese reporter and our co-producer were returning to the provincial capital, the local police chased them all the way to our hotel. That evening as our team was shopping in a supermarket to prepare for our departure the next day, we were surrounded by more than a dozen of police cars from both the Deyang Police Bureau as well as the Sichuan Provincial Police Bureau for Entry and Exit of Foreigners. All of us, including our Chinese co-producer, were taken to the Headquarters of the Provincial Police Bureau for questioning. After eight hours of questioning, we were all warned to leave China immediately, except that I was allowed to have some extra days to spend with my mother in the city.

My friends and classmates working for the government revealed to me that before 1 June, a new directive had been issued from the central government to tighten control over the media, especially the foreign press. The major factor prompting this quick change could be attributed to the changing tone of the mass media from sympathetic and cooperative to inquisitive, reflective and muckraking. On the one hand, the parents of killed students started their petitions and protests in local government sites or had gone to Beijing. Starting from 20 May, hundreds of parents protested in front of their municipal governments or court houses in Beichuan, Dujiangyan and Mianzhu and dozens of them successfully broke through the bans from the local government and reached Beijing to petition for an investigation of collapsed school buildings, an adequate insurance and compensation for the parents and punishments for corrupt officials and contractors who were responsible for unsafe school buildings.[23]

On the other hand, the domestic media started discussing the state failures in building and maintaining schools, in rescuing in a timely manner and in responding to people's petitions. On 19 May at a "Dedication of Love Evening" (爱的奉献晚会), broadcast live, Tie Ning, chairwoman of China's Writers' Association, emphasized that the enormous rescue work symbolized the important growth of and contribution from the "civil society." The attending propaganda czar of the Party, Li Changchun, reportedly dismayed and dismissed these remarks as wrong-placed compliments because they eclipsed the omnipotent role of the Party and the state.[24]

The liberal newspaper *Southern Weekend* based in Guangzhou published sharp and critical commentaries in their special issues (22 and 29 May, respectively) on some problems exposed by the quake, especially raising the question about the quality of school houses.[25] In Sichuan, there were four valiant musketeers, Huang Qi, Tan Zuoren, Liao Yiwu and Ran Yunfei, who used pen as sword in this crusade. Outside Sichuan, artist Ai Weiwei in Beijing and Ai Xiaoming, a professor in Guangzhou, organized volunteers to start their investigations and used video cameras to record and expose horrifying findings. Some writers and commentators criticized the incompetence of people's deputies in legislatures, proposed to erect a "wailing wall" for the victims, urged the government to establish a "management system for disasters," called for future construction to meet quality standards and called on a spiritual reconstruction out of moral failures, etc.[26]

The government had noticed that some foreign media (the official media targeted the German weekly *Spiegel* and the overseas Falun Gong media) had increasingly questioned the Chinese government for turning the disaster into a PR blitz as well as concealing some problems.[27] Just a week before, the Chinese government had been happy to see that "China has won respect and praise from the entire world"; now, however, it saw a growing conspiracy to provoke the Chinese against their government, damage the image of the Party and destabilize China. It has become a pattern that positive coverage of China from the international media is shown to the domestic audience as confirmation and admiration of the Chinese government's great achievements, while any negative or critical coverage is quickly labelled as an "evil-spirited conspiracy" against China. The Central Party Propaganda Department sent directives to local governments to restrict reports on the widespread collapse of school buildings.[28] The authorities at all levels started to harass foreign reporters, drive them out of the school sites, smash their equipment, close down dissenting internet sites and arrest dissidents (such as Huang Qi who was sentenced to five-year jail term).[29] The local governments also warned the parents not to do interviews with foreign media and threatened to arrest them if they did so.

The propaganda departments from the centre to the localities actively promoted the *leitmotif* of patriotism, nationalism, positive images of the leaders, great sacrifices of the military and admirable achievements by the governments at all levels. Overall, the media had to serve the call from Premier Wen: "Much distress helps regenerate a nation" ("Trials help resurrect a nation—*duonan xingbang*").

On 5 June, Yu Qiuyu, a noted writer based in Shanghai, published on his blog, "A Tearful Appeal to the Petitioning Victims in Earthquake," in which he mentioned the interrogation of our team by the police ("five reporters from foreign country") and warned the parents: "Some people with malicious intention against China are wishfully waiting for something to go wrong." He further said: "Several internationally renowned seismologists have said that theoretically speaking all houses would collapse in a quake with the Richter scale 7.8 and above." He also said:

> A Buddhist master has told me, with the blessings from more than one billion people all the past survivors would have become bodhisattvas, who would give further blessings to China. If your children have souls in the heaven, they must have been in peace now.[30]

On 6 June, Wang Zhaoshan, Vice Chairman of Shandong Writers Association, published a poem, entitled "Personal Statement from Beneath the Ruins," which read:

> Natural Disaster is inevitable
> Death does not deserve too much talk
> Hearing calls from the president, cries from the premier
> Being grieved by the Party, loved by the state,
> Having one billion people shed tears in group,
> Even though I have become a ghost,
> What happiness I have!
> Silver airplanes and armored vehicles rushed to save us youngsters,
> Being assisted by Uncle Soldier at the left and Auntie Police Officer at the right,
> With the grand love of a nation, I find it satisfactory to experience death.
> I would hold only one wish in my heart: a TV set in front of my grave,
> To watch the Olympiad and join in the celebration![31]

The temporary "thawing" in media control ultimately ended up falling into a trite formula, namely a "ten-step flow chart of disaster management with Chinese characteristics" as summarized by a news weekly based in Hong Kong: (a) order to ban reports on incidents or disasters; (b) focus on positive and encouraging aspects; (c) clean up the site in a mysterious and speedy way; (d) entice victims to sign compensation agreements as soon as possible; (e) report highly affirmative reactions from the masses; (f) hold rally to celebrate great achievements; (g) commend heroes and model workers/peasants/soldiers; (h) shift responsibility to the lowest level or the least important person; (i) hire writers to give lavish praise; (j) organize reporters to revisit the disaster zone and report about achievements in recovery during the first Spring Festival after the disaster.[32]

In March 2009 at the National People's Congress gathering in Beijing, the vice-governor Wei Hong on behalf of the Sichuan provincial government categorically denied that the school collapses were both natural and man-made and insisted that considering the level of destruction in the quake, school buildings were destroyed by the sole factor of natural force. For that reason, no further investigation was warranted and no legal procedure was allowed for petitioners.[33] However, this conclusion was impossible for the parents to accept. In the winter of 2010–2011, I conducted a telephone questionnaire survey among the parents who lost their children. 272 answered the phone call and 239 responded to the questions. I asked them the following question: "With regard to the death of your child in the collapsed school building, what caused it?" 215 parents gave valid answers; 23 did not answer the question. 15 chose the answer (a) that "It's a pure natural disaster," 97 chose (b) that "It's partially a natural disaster, partially caused by human failure (factor)." 101 chose (c) that "The corrupt local officials and contractors are to blame." One respondent chose both (b) and (c). One chose (d) "I have no idea." In another question: "Some parents have complained and some media have reported that the collapsed school buildings were shoddy 'Tofu projects'. Do you agree?" 26 did not give an answer. 213 gave a valid answer. Among 213, 37 (17.37%) chose (a) "Basically agree," 153 (71.83%) chose (b) "Completely agree," 22 (10.33%) chose (c) "Not agree." Understandably, given the huge discrepancy between the official verdict and the opinions of parents, tensions and conflicts between the government and parents are inevitable.

Consequently, a widespread crackdown was implemented upon the parents and the dissenting voices from the outside. For example, Tan Zuoren was arrested in the same month after the National People's Congresses meeting and later sentenced to five years in jail; Ai Weiwei's blog was closed down one year after the Sichuan Earthquake and later he was beaten up and detained while he was in Sichuan to show his support to Tan. Huang Qi was sentenced to three years in jail later in the year. Several documentaries, including *Our Children* by

Ai Xiaoming, *No Disturbance* by Ai Weiwei, *Who Killed Our Children?* by Pan Jianlin, and *1428* by Du Haibin were either all banned (the first three) or shown within a controlled circle in China.[34] *China's Unnatural Disaster: The Tears of Sichuan Province,* the movie resulting from our film-making trip, was invited for the screening at the Beijing Independent Movie Festival in 2009, but the two directors/photographers were denied visas. Later, this movie was nominated for the 2010 Academy Award in the Short Documentary category. The CCTV (China Central TV) suspended the live relaying of the announcements of the short documentary awards, and the published news did not include our movie title in the list of Oscar nominees.[35]

Analytical and Concluding Remarks

What is the essence of my one-week experience in the Sichuan earthquake zone? How will my observation help us understand an exceptional, short-lived outburst of Chinese media which was characterized by unprecedented activism and candidness? Why did the Chinese Party-state abruptly change its view of the media as a helpmate to one of trouble maker with regard to the Sichuan earthquake? My explanations to these questions are built upon one crucial variable: the oscillating role of the media in an asymmetric power relationship between the Party-state, the local governments and ordinary Chinese people.

Chen Jibing, an editorial writer for a Shanghai newspaper, offered this observation:

"News media are the mouthpiece of the Party and the people." This principle is the keystone for both the theory and practice of Chinese socialist journalism. But in the hands of some wicked officials, it degenerates first to read as "News media are the mouthpiece of the Party committee and government at one specific level" and finally "News media are the mouthpiece of the leader first in command." It is not the worst that some local officials regard news media as a tool for glorifying their own achievements and flattering themselves. Worse than turning news media into "trumpeter and drummer" for advertising themselves, some local officials turn them into "smoke bomb" to attack people with dissenting voices, confuse people and twist facts, mislead people under their jurisdiction and the superior officials.

This author believes, in today's China with pluralistic interests, the Center and the ordinary people have their interests most compatible, for both take the stable governance in the long run as their core concern. But in this sociopolitical matrix, the Center stays atop, the populace the lowest bottom, in between lie many levels of local and industrial powers. News media are the nexus between the Center and the populace and turn the two into a unity to counterbalance the interest groups in the middle. Excessive control over mass media not only impairs the Center from hearing the populace, but also weakens the central authority at local levels.[36]

In this three-tier game of power, a pluralist media that consist of the central, local and foreign could align with or alienate the actors in this asymmetric power structure. Under normal circumstances, the Party and government at all levels can be congealed into the state, and the state-populace relationship is that between a controller and an obedient population. The media tend to have less freedom and serve as the mouthpiece of the Party-state for political control. But under the circumstances of calamity, the antagonism between the Party-state and populace gives way to an "organized dependency,"[37] and a patron–client relationship emerges, in which the Party-state behaves as savior of a people who are in distress and desperation. The Chinese phrase that characterized the 2008 earthquake is "combating the earthquake and going in for relief work," which denotes that natural calamity confronts all human beings and is like an invading army. A common enemy unifies the people with the Party-state, especially the Centre that controls disproportionately more resources than the local governments, and this compatibility provides a rare opportunity for the mass media to report disasters more aggressively. The 2008 Sichuan Earthquake is a case in point, just as any dispute with a foreign country can generate this unifying patriotism and nationalism.[38]

With regard to the Sichuan earthquake, the Chinese government and its media control cartel (especially the propaganda departments and the police) diverged from their classic script at the very beginning as the media was converging with the state at the fundamental level of saving life. But as soon as the rescue and relief are over, news media often turn to issues of "summing up experiences and learning lessons." Responsibility has to be located somewhere, blame placed on somebody. The state quickly relapsed into its traditional mode to reassert its grip upon the media once the latter started to dig out deep-seated problems. These included the collapse of school buildings that pointed to the pervasive corruption and negligence of government officials. Media also began to question the motives of the official propaganda campaign to raise a holy trinity of the Party-State-Army out of the ruins. At this moment, local new media often retreat to the traditional role of "trumpeter and drummer."

If the final responsibility for calamity can be localized, the Centre would lend support to the news media to work as a helpmate to supervise the local authorities. This explains why the central media were very aggressive in reporting the confrontations between the local government officials and the protesters in the quake and why the local governments wanted to keep the central media away. However, more and more evidence was exposed to point at a pervasive pattern of school collapses: official corruption, insufficient funding or misallocation of funds for school, and failure to abide by the building laws and regulations. Then, the attention paid to jerry-built schools ultimately amounted to an indictment of the entire state and its policy. The Centre realized that news media had to be reined in and the discussion on school collapse to be stopped. At this juncture, the only media that would keep muckraking were from foreign countries. Thus, the angry and frustrated parents turned to foreign media for help.

As political scientist E. E. Schattschneider points out, "[T] he outcome of every conflict is determined by the *extent* to which the audience becomes involved in it" and "the outcome of all conflict is determined by the *scope* of its contagion" (Italic original). The "audience" or the "spectators" are an integral part of conflict. Often, "it is the loser who calls in outside help." As the weak party has incentive to socialize the conflict to involve more spectators and participants, the strong often try to resort to privatization to control the scope of conflict.[39]

From the very beginning, the parents held their grudge against the school authority and local officials at the township or county level. However, the scope of crisis and its high-profiled publicity made it impossible for the local officials to find resources and courage to solve the conflicts at the local level. The parents were aware of the presence of the top leaders and mass media in the quake zone, so they had strong incentive to appeal to the higher authority and the media to put pressure upon the local officials. The parents we interviewed organized their protests and road-blockades because they had information that either the Premier or a Politburo Standing Committee member would inspect the area. By creating newsworthy events, the parents further opened up a new arena to contest the official discourse over the school collapse. In addition, news media were not a mere "arena." In Chinese political conflicts, often shrouded in an opaque decision-making process that gives the authorities unrestricted discretion in exercising power and coercion, the presence of new media introduces the possibility for multifaceted roles: a bystander, a recorder, a witness and even an important participant and an active player. The "neutrality" of such media is an antidote to the asymmetric power relationship that privileges the officials. As William A. Gamson points out, "A mass media-directed framing strategy provides the central mechanism for affecting scope. A full-fledged symbolic strategy aims not only at increasing the mobilizing potential among bystanders but also at increasing the readiness of one's primary constituency to act collectively and thereby neutralizing the framing efforts of one's adversaries."[40] In our case, the protesters' "adversaries" are often the state or its surrogates.

But by creating the "contagion of conflict," the parents ran a high risk of alienating the central leadership once they believed the protests could spill over to other issues and regions and destabilize the entire regime. The parents attempted many times to go to the provincial capital and Beijing to petition, and they were either intercepted at the train stations or caught and forced back home by the local police officers who chased after them to Beijing. The court system was instructed by the Centre not to accept any lawsuit concerning school collapse. After all channels for their grievances were blocked, the unofficial media and foreign media became the only available allies and continued the coverage. In the winter of 2010–2011, I conducted the telephone survey among the parents who lost their children that I referred to earlier. I asked: "Do you want the outside world (including the foreign countries) to continue to pay attention to the investigation and punishment of those implicated in the collapsed school buildings?" One hundred and eighty-seven

(78%) answered "yes," 18 "no," 8 "does not matter" and 26 did not give an answer. Clearly the absolute majority of earthquake victims viewed the foreign media as a positive presence and still expected help from the outside world.

In conclusion, for a period of less than 20 days, the state–media relationship in the Sichuan Earthquake case experienced three distinctive stages (see Table 14.1). Under Stage I from 12 May to 19 May, the National Mourning Day, a natural calamity acted as a great unifier to guide the Party-state and the people to fight in solidarity against the disaster. The media did not have to choose a side between the Party line and the people line and could act with least constraint in a professional and spontaneous role. During Stage II from 20 May to 31 May, as the parents became active in raising questions over the causes of school collapse and the deaths of their children, local governments took the brunt of this contestation and the Centre was not implicated yet. Often, the protestors followed the "rightful resistance" pattern, namely they often framed their demands in the spirit of the documents, public statements and official rhetoric from the central Party-state and top leaders (Wen Jiabao and his words were often referred to).[41] The central media still had space to manoeuvre in order to act as a helpmate between the Centre and the people against some local interests. However, entering Stage III from 1 June, the news media lost support and even tolerance from the Party-state if they tried to cover controversial issues that the Party had designated as taboos. If they persisted, the reporters and editors risked being purged from the state-owned media or being clamped down on as political dissidents. Clearly, the litmus test of the freedom of press and media does not come from a scenario that the state, the populace and the media happen to align along the same line. It has to come from the "bipolar moment" when the state and the people have conflicts. Viewed from this test, even the most applauded Sichuan Earthquake case fails to substantiate the claim that the state–media relationship in China had achieved a qualitative breakthrough. No autonomous and free mass media are allowed to speak truth to power within China.

Table 14.1:
Interest, actors, political alignment and the role of media: The case of Sichuan earthquake

State–Media Relationship	Official Media (Central)	Official Media (Local)	Unofficial Media	Foreign Media
Stage I: Unanimous Moment (12–19 May, The primary interests of the Centre, local state and the people coincide)	Active, spontaneous participant with more professional autonomy.	Active, spontaneous participant with more professional autonomy.	Active, spontaneous participant with fear and critical edge.	Aggressive coverage with some scepticism but less harsh criticisms. Access is granted.
Stage II: Triangular Moment (20–31 May, local government and the people diverge on key interests, the Centre does not take a clear stand and reserves the leeway to intervene more as a final arbitrator)	Seek an active helpmate role to the Centre and at the same time try to assume more the role of social conscience on behalf of the ordinary people.	Tend to exercise self-censorship and keep low-profile in reporting. They become bolder only when they report on other local governments beyond their home region.	As the participants would dwindle as some take precaution, the remaining (mainly on the internet) would become more critical and with increasing intensity.	Aggressive coverage with heightened scepticism and sharper criticism of government officials. The sympathy given to the weak increases. Access is restricted.
Stage III: Bipolar Moment (1 June and thereafter, The Centre and local state join together to defend their converged interest, emerges a dichotomy of the state vs people)	Exercise self-censorship or completely disappear from the controversial issue.	Keep silent and treat the contentious issues as taboo.	Only a few dissidents would continue their crusade against the state on behalf of the victims.	Energized zeal and interest to create a muckraking campaign and focus more on exposé with some kind of news sensationalism. Access is denied.

Source: Graph made by the author.

Notes

1. He Qinglian, *The Fog of Censorship: Media Control in China* (New York, NY: Human Rights in China, 2008).
2. Pye in Lucian W. Pye, ed., *Communications and Political Development* (Princeton University Press, 1963), p. 6, 8.
3. Andrew Nathan, "Authoritarian Resilience," *Journal of Democracy*, 14, no. 1 (2003): 6–19; Xiaoling Zhang, *The Transformation of Political Communication in China: From Propaganda to Hegemony* (Singapore: World Scientific, 2011).
4. Herbert Marcuse, *One-Dimensional Man* (Boston, MA: Beacon Press, 1991), p. 1.
5. He Qinglian, "Unveil the Mysterious 'Grand Foreign Propaganda' Plan" (何清涟，"揭开神秘的"大外宣"计划之面纱，"原载：《看》 双周刊), from: *China in Perspective*, Sunday, 29 November 2009, http://www.chinainperspective.com/ArtShow.aspx?AID=3822 (accessed 22 November).
6. Zhang, He Qinglian, 2009.
7. Liang Xiaotao, ed., Shock Trilogy: Notes in the Field, Reflections by the Media, and TV Files, all from Beijing: Zhongguo Minzhu he Fazhi chubanshe, 2008 (梁晓涛 著，震撼：战地手记：5·12汶川大地震备忘, 北京：中国民主与法制出 版 社; 震撼：媒体回想5·12汶川大地震备忘; 震撼：电视档案5·12汶川大地震备忘).
8. Kate Merkel-Hess, Kenneth L. Pomeranz and Jeffrey N. Wasserstrom, *China in 2008: A Year of Great Significance* (Lanham, MD: Rowman and Littlefield, 2009).
9. http://politics.people.com.cn/GB/1026/5113799.html
10. Mike Chinoy, *China Live: People Power and the Television Revolution* (Lanham: Rowan and Littlefield, 1999).
11. Sha Yongzhong, et al.: *The Annual Report on Chinese Politics,* 2008 (沙勇忠、刘亚军、徐刚，《2008中国政治年报》, 兰州：兰州大学出版社, 2009), p. 47; *The Global Times* (环球时报), 8 May 2009, http://china.huanqiu.com/eyes_on_china/politics/2009-05/455272.html (accessed 12 August 2012).
12. Ai Weiwei, Interview with the Voice of Germany, 11 May 2009, http://www.bullogger.com/blogs/aimomo/archives/294186.aspx (accessed 12 September 2012).
13. Feng Congde, 封从德：汶川地震师生遇难人数估算报告(5.20版), 观察, 23 May 2008, http://ncchinesenews.com/Article/gd/200805/20080523004018_8.html (accessed 6 July 2008); Tan Zuoren et al., An Investigative Report of Student Death Tolls in the Sichuan Earthquake (谭作人等：四川地震死难学生调查报告), 25 April 2009, http://transgressionism.blogspot.com/2009/04/blog-post_25.html. Vice Governor Wei Hong's number was reported by the Xinhua News Agency on 21 November 2008, available at:

http://news.xinhuanet.com/local/2008-11/21/content_10391561.htm (accessed on 12 October 2010). Video recording is also available at: http://v.ku6.com/show/DTQrVYFl043OcXUu.html?nv=1 (accessed on 12 October 2012).

14. Human Rights Watch report, "China's Forbidden Zones: Shutting the Media out of Tibet and Other 'Sensitive' Stories" (中国的禁域: 封锁媒体, 不得进入西藏, 不得报道 "敏感" 话题), pp. 7–10, 6 July 2008, http://www.hrw.org/reports/2008/china0708/(accessed 12 August 2012).

15. Li Hongbing, "The Earthquake Shook out the Openness of News" (李泓冰, "震"出来的新闻公开, 新闻记者), *The Journalist Monthly*, no.305 (July 2008) http://xwjz.eastday.com/eastday/xwjz/node271090/node271092/ula3694635.html (accessed on 21 September 2012).

16. Jiang Wenze, ed., *The Premier's Five Days: 2008.5.12-2008.5.16* (姜文泽编著,《总理五日: 2008.5.12–2008.5.16》, 北京: 中国华侨出版社, 2008).

17. Chen Wenjiang, et al., *The Annual Report on Chinese Society* (陈文江、商艳光、赵秉前,《2008中国社会年报》, 兰州: 兰州大学出版社, 2009), 2008, pp. 115.

18. Shi Ying, Weekly News Focus: A Short-lived Openness of Press in the Earthquake (施 英: 一周新闻聚焦: 大地震中昙花一现的新闻开放), Independent Chinese PEN Center, 16 June 2008, http://www.chinesepen.org/Article/hyxz/200806/Article_20080616010917.shtml (accessed on 12 October 2012).

19. Chen and Shi Ying, p. 115.

20. Wu Xingren, ed., *Sublimation upon the Ruins: Collection of Commentaries on Wenchuan Earthquake* (吴兴人主编,《废墟上的升华: 汶川大地震新闻时评选》: 四川出版集团和四川人民出版社, 2008), p. 161.

21. Huang Yuhao, "Jiang Guohua, the Kneeling Party Secretary, Reflects after the Quake" (黄玉浩,"下跪书记"蒋国华的震后神情), New Capital Gazette (新京报), 11 May 2009, http://news.163.com/09/0511/09/5917IETM00011SM9.html (accessed 12 October 2012).

22. Ming Xia, *Political Venus: From Nothing under My Name to Chinese Democracy* (夏明,《政治维纳斯: 从一无所有到中国民主》; Hong Kong: Morning Bell Publishing House, 2012) p. 166; Wan Yizhong, Special Report: One Year after the Sichuan Earthquake: Making a Documentary and Reflection (万毅忠, 多维专访: 川震一周年, 纪录片拍摄与思考), Duowei News, 6 May 2009, http://politics.dwnews.com/news/2009-05-06/4896084.html (accessed 12 October 2012).

23. Shen Hua, "The Victims of Sichuan May 12th Earthquake Intensify Petitions" (申华, 四川5·12地震灾民密集请愿), VOA News, 22 May 2008, http://www.voachinese.com/content/article-20120222-sichuan-quake-victim-families-139958963/810684.html (accessed 12 October 2012).

24. This was relayed to me by a well-informed friend in China and Li's unhappiness was corroborated by the deletion of Tie Ning's remarks in the later issued DVD by CCTV and China International TV Corporation in 2008.

25. Hao Hong, "What Kind of Reports Do We Need for Disasters?" (郝洪, 我们需要什么样的灾难报道: 从《南方周末》震灾报道引发的争议谈起, 新闻记者), *The Journalist Monthly*, No. 305, July 2008, http://xwjz.eastday.com/eastday/xwjz/node271090/node271091/ula3694701.html (accessed 21 September 2012); Ran Yunfei, "List of News Reports and Commentaries on the Collapses of School Buildings and Deaths of students in the Earthquake" (冉云飞: 地震校舍倒塌、学生死难报道和评论一览), *New Century* (新世纪), 11 June 2008, http://news.boxun.com/news/gb/pubvp/2008/06/200806112120.shtml (accessed 12 October 2012).

26. Wu Xingren, pp. 183–209.

27. Ibid., pp. 210–219.

28. "Beijing Orders the Media to Restrict Reports on the Collapses of School Buildings" ("北京要求媒体控制报道校舍倒塌"), in *FT Chinese*, June 2, 2008, http://www.ftchinese.com/story/001019748 (accessed 12 October 2012).

29. The editorial committee, Reports on the Wenchuan Earthquake in Sichuan: We are together (四川日报报业集团和四川出版集团, 编著,《四川汶川大地震纪实: 我们在一起》, 成都: 四川出版集团和四川文艺出版社), 2008, pp. 51–53; Shi Ying, Weekly News Focus: A Short-lived Openness of Press in the Earthquake (施 英: 一周新闻聚焦: 大地震中昙花一现的新闻开放), *Independent Chinese PEN Center*, 16 June 2008, http://www.chinesepen.org/Article/hyxz/200806/Article_20080616010917.shtml (accessed 12 October 2012).

30. Yu Qiuyu, "A Tearful Appeal to the Petitioning Victims in Earthquake" (余秋雨, 含泪劝告请愿灾民, 5 June 2008, http://yuqiuyu.blog.sohu.com/89351261.html (accessed 12 October 2012).

31. http://blog.ifeng.com/article/1518205.html (accessed 12 October 2012).

32. "Disaster Management with Chinese Characteristics" (中国特色的灾难处理) "in *iSun Times* (阳光时务), 9 August 2012, http://www.isunaffairs.com/?p=10240 (accessed 12 October 2012).

33. See official report http://www.china.com.cn/2009lianghui/2009-03/08/content_17401306.htm (accessed 12 October 2012).

34. XinYu, 心语, 三部四川地震纪录片均受打压封杀, 24 September 2009, Radio Free Asia, available at: http://www.boxun.com/news/gb/china/2009/09/200909240022.shtml (accessed 13 December 2012); 汶川地震纪录片"谁杀了我们的孩子"在釜山参展, 多维新闻 (Duowei News), 10 October 2008, http://life.dwnews.com/news/2008-10-10/4404465.html; http://life.dwnews.com/news/2008-10-10/4404465.html (accessed 13 December 2012); Li Tiecheng, "A Contrastive Study of 'Our Children' and '1428,'" *Journal of Guizhou University, Art Edition*, 25(4):6–12, December 2011.

35. To find out more detailed about how the Chinese government orchestrated a campaign to scuttle our efforts to win an Oscar, see: Ming Xia, pp. 114–131.

36. Chen Jibing, "It should be institutionalized for long term" (陈季冰, "要形成制度长期坚持", 新闻记者, 2008年八月, 第306期), *The Journalist Monthly*, August 2008, No.306, http://xwjz.eastday.com/eastday/xwjz/node275238/node275239/ula3771985.html (accessed 21 September 2012).

37. Andrew G. Walder, *Communist Neo-Traditionalism: Work and Authority in Chinese Industry* (Berkeley, CA: University of California Press, 1986).

38. Peter Hayes Gries, *China's New Nationalism: Pride Politics and Diplomacy* (Berkeley, CA: University of California Press, 2004); Zheng Wang, *Never Forget National Humiliation: Historical Memory in Chinese Politics and Foreign Relations* (New York, NY: Columbia University Press, 2012).

39. E. E. Schattschneider, *The Semi-Sovereign People: A Realist View of Democracy in America* (New York: Holt, Rinehart and Winston, 1960), pp. 2, 16–18.

40. William A. Gamson, "Bystanders, Public Opinion, and the Media," in David A. Snow, Sarah A. Soule and Hanspeter Kriesi, ed., *The Blackwell Companion to Social Movements* (Malden, MA: Blackwell, 2004 and 2007), p. 259.

41. Kevin J. O'Brien and Lianjiang Li, *Rightful Resistance in Rural China* (New York, NY: Cambridge University Press, 2006).

15

When Officials and Media Failed: The Response to the Uttarakhand Floods, 2013

Anup Kumar

Anup Kumar is associate professor of communication in the School of Communication, Cleveland State University. He started as an environmental scientist and then made a transition into journalism. He was a practicing journalist for many years, after which he made a second career transition into academia. He is the author of *The Making of a Small State: Populist Social Mobilisation and the Hindi Press in the Uttarakhand Movement* (2011) and research articles on the interaction between the news media and politics.

At the peak of the summer pilgrim–tourist season from 15–17 June 2013, more than 1.5 million people in the three mountain districts of Uttarakhand state in the northwestern Indian Himalayas were traumatized by the destruction caused by a series of cloudbursts, landslides and flash floods in all the tributaries of the mighty Ganga. The entire region received very heavy rain, but the worst affected districts in loss of life and property were Pauri, Rudraprayag, Chamoli, Uttarakashi and Pithoragarh (see Figure 15.1).[1] The centre of the disaster in terms of fatalities and missing persons was the temple town of Kedarnath, situated at a height of 3,969 metres, and the way-stations along the Mandakini River on the pilgrimage route to the shrine.[2] In the deluge, which the news media later framed as the "Himalayan Tsunami,"[3] about 5,700 people were assumed to have died.[4] Most bodies of the missing were never recovered from remote ridges and

Figure 15.1:
Uttarakhand state and places affected by floods and landslides, 2013

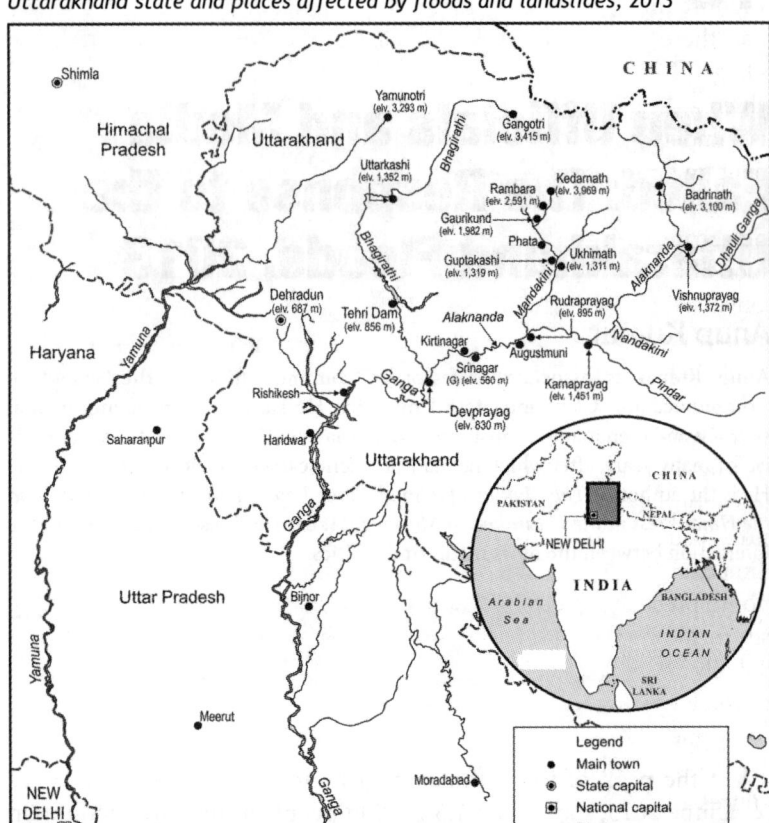

Source: Drawn by Lee Li Kheng, Geography, National University of Singapore, for the Institute of South Asian Studies.
Note: This figure is not to scale. It does not represent any authentic national or international boundaries and is used for illustrative purposes only.

mountain hollows.[5] Tens of thousands of Uttarakhandis also lost their homes and livelihood. A large number of the dead perished in the cold without food or clothing while trying to find their way back to the towns downstream.

In his influential work, *Everything in its Path: Destruction of Community in the Buffalo Creek Flood*, sociologist Kai Erikson,[6] explaining the effects of unregulated mining and delayed official response in the flash flood in the Appalachian Mountains, concluded that "there are at least two sound reasons" to study disasters—the first is to get the story straight, and the second is to understand the ways in which a discrete moment, in a series of disasters, helps social scientists understand the "anatomy of disasters."[7] Following Erikson's argument, my purpose in this chapter is twofold. The first is to show how the news media and the authorities did not get the story straight; and the second is to understand the anatomy of the Uttarakhand flash floods of 2013 (a) by engaging with the information collected from conversations with journalists, activists and experts in July 2013 and again a year later, and (b) by analyzing published reports by government agencies and the NGOs.[8]

The volume of rain in the three-day period broke an 88-year record in the state capital.[9] In June, the local moisture generated by summer heat in the valleys in this part of India causes some rain, but massive downpours are rare. The rising monsoon winds from the plains of India usually arrive in the mountain ranges of Uttarakhand and Himachal Pradesh in the first week of July, which is why June, the month preceding the rains, is the peak season for pilgrimage and tourism in the mountains. However, with the changing weather patterns globally and in the sub-continent, a massive downpour in June, though unusual, was not unlikely.[10]

I argue that the scale of the calamity requires an explanation that also takes into account the compounding effects of official negligence, failures of news media and a public discourse held hostage by a hegemonic developmentist paradigm that overlooks the geomorphology and ecology of the young mountains. The very high number of deaths seemingly resulted from failures of local and state authorities to quickly acknowledge the unprecedented scale of the disaster and launch appropriate rescue and relief operations. Such operations were not started until 19 June when the Indian military took control of the situation and launched operation Rahat and Surya Hope. According to the official accounts, about 100,000 people, many of whom were children and the elderly, had to be rescued all across the Badri–Kedar[11] region from the open on mountain ridges that became freezing as night fell.

Most disaster experts point out that unrestricted flow of information and quick response saves lives. In a disaster, the first responders are the local citizenry and news media. Media maintain a flow of information that reduces anxiety and fosters a more orderly rescue and relief.[12] The significance of media coverage in a natural disaster was also exemplified in a report on the Uttarakhand floods by the All India Disaster Mitigation Institute.[13] I hope to show that rather than improvising a rescue and recovery plan using whatever resources were available, the first reaction of the state authorities was to place restrictions on the flow of information and encourage the local news media to practice self-censorship, especially when it came to reporting on the number of people who had died in the disaster.

Media in Uttarakhand

There was a failure in obtaining and disseminating information quickly in the first 36 hours after the disaster, which was one of the factors that delayed the organizing of a rescue and relief operation, thereby increasing the number of fatalities. The failure of communication was not because Uttarakhand is a largely mountainous and remote region with poor communication systems. The state has a relatively well-developed information network, both in the fields of the news media and telecommunication infrastructure, when compared with other remote parts of India.

News Media in Uttarakhand

Newspaper circulation in Uttarakhand has been steadily growing, as it has elsewhere in India and in other emerging economies such as China and Brazil.[14]

About 80 per cent of Uttarakhand's 10.2 million people are literate, even though nearly half live in the rugged mountain districts. Newspaper circulation in 2013 was also quite high with audited daily circulation of all newspapers of 550,000 or about 55 dailies for every 1,000 people.[15] Much of the growth in circulation and revenue has been in Indian-languages media. Until recently, despite large circulations Indian-language newspapers lagged in advertising revenues. Big-budget advertisers opted for English. However, this is changing in all states including Uttarakhand. The advertising revenues of Hindi-language newspapers are catching up with the English-language newspapers.[16]

Outside the metropolitan cities, Hindi and other Indian-language newspapers, and news channels dominate the field, and we see similar trends in Uttarakhand. The top newspapers in Uttarakhand both in terms of paid circulation and readership[17] are *Amar Ujala* (Hindi), closely followed by *Dainik Jagran* (Hindi), *Hindustan* (Hindi) and *The Times of India* (English). Seeing the potential for growth in Hindi-language newspapers, owners of national English-language dailies such as Bennett and Coleman Company Ltd (BCCL), publisher of *The Times of India* and the HT Media group which publishes *Hindustan Times* (English), started investing in their Hindi-language subsidiaries such as *Navbharat Times* and *Hindustan*, respectively. *Hindustan* has grown significantly in circulation in Uttarakhand since the founding of the state in 2000. In addition to these major newspapers, there are about 20 other local dailies that are not included in the circulation figures reported by the audit agencies, but they serve small communities in the state.[18]

The three leading Hindi-language newspapers—*Amar Ujala, Dainik Jagran* and *Hindustan*—are not only important because of their circulation and readership, but unlike the other national newspapers that focus on national news, these newspapers in their Uttarakhand editions focus on local and regional reporting. To provide a daily account of news and events from all over the state, they have staff reporters in all the major cities and rely heavily on stringers in all the towns in the state. It would be fair to suggest that these newspapers have eyes and ears on the ground in every part of the state including the pilgrim towns in the high Himalayas that were affected by the flash floods in 2013. In a way, *Amar Ujala* and *Dainik Jagran* are viewed in the state as the two megaphones when it comes to media influence. Some local English-language newspapers, such as *Garhwal Post* and *Pioneer,* published from Dehradun, have also emerged as influential sources because of their circulation among the state officials and the elites in the capital city.

Uttarakhand also has a few regional news TV channels that run on the cable network and Direct to Home (DTH) via satellite. This is in addition to a daily regional news broadcast on Doordarshan, the public-owned terrestrial TV. Some of the popular regional channels are *TV 100*-Uttarakhand, Aapna Uttarakhand on *Eenadu TV*, *Sahara Samay*-Uttarakhand, *ANI* and *News Nation*-Uttarakhand (launched in 2014 after the floods). Again like the regional newspapers, these news channels are viewed as important sources of regional news, in comparison to the major national news channels, because they have reporters on the ground in the mountain districts. Other popular Hindi-language national news channels that have frequently reported on the region are *Zee News* (Hindi), *Aaj Tak* (Hindi), *India TV* (Hindi), *NDTV-India* (Hindi), *IBN7* (Hindi) and *Sahara Samay* (Hindi). There are no reliable ratings available for the regional channels, and my informants said that when it comes to getting hyper-local news, channels such as TV 100 and Aapna Uttarakhand (ETV) are often the only sources on TV.

There are 21 FM/MW public-owned All India Radio (AIR) stations in Uttarakhand. The radio stations are spread across the state, including three stations in the areas worst affected by the flash floods of 2013—Ukhimath, Chamoli and Uttarkashi. These radio stations broadcast regular news bulletins. In addition to AIR stations, there are three community radio stations, but by law community radio stations are not permitted to report news. Radio is not the first thing that people in the region or pilgrim–tourists go to for news and updates.

Telecommunication and Internet

India, along with China, accounted for about 40 per cent of all new mobile phone connections in 2012. Although penetration of mobile phones in India was still low (roughly 70 per cent) compared to China (90 per cent) and other emerging economies, it has grown fast.[19] Most people living in the remotest part of Uttarakhand rely on cell phones to remain connected with family members, often men who migrate to work in the plains. Before the cell-phone transformation, the region was provided with a relatively high density of post offices to serve the families back in the mountain villages.

Uttarakhand is part of the western Uttar Pradesh telecom circle and is classified in the B category from the perspective of telecom density. Telecom density is about 61 per cent overall with 32 per cent in rural areas and 161 per cent in urban areas. In 2012, all-India telecom density was estimated at about 73 per cent, with 40 per cent rural and about 149 per cent urban. The state was covered by 3G service offered by all providers including BSNL, the government-owned telecom company.[20]

With the ubiquity of mobile phones, SMS and social media emerged as the fastest growing source of news and information. In a study reported to the Indo-German E-Governance Forum, it was found that SMS over the phone is the most efficient way to communicate weather information to small farmers in the hills.[21] Because of high pilgrim–tourism traffic in the Badri–Kedar region, all major mobile phone companies had their operations in the mountains of Uttarakhand, but the operators with the most widely available network were BSNL, Idea and Airtel. Other providers such as Reliance, Tata and Vodaphone also operated in the state. BSNL had over 800 mobile phone towers in the state out of which 272 towers were damaged during the floods.[22] Most private operators relied on towers built and managed by one of India's major tower companies. In 2013, this company had 668 towers in Uttarakhand, which were contracted to serve multiple mobile operators in the region. The company reported that during the floods, 400 of their towers were damaged. Most of the affected towers were in Rudraprayag and Uttarakashi and were put back in service by 21 June.[23]

The government-owned BSNL offered internet connection with all its landline connections in the region, and all mobile service providers offered 3G internet data connection to subscribers. Accessibility did not mean that everyone who had a landline phone or a mobile was using the Internet. A study of the digital divide in Uttarakhand found that about 62 per cent of those with Internet connection access used the web at least once a week.[24] Internet accessibility meant that many citizen journalists in the region were active on social media where they set up virtual information kiosks for disseminating information and news. Some of the popular online sources of information were Pahari Forum, Uttarakhand News, Uttara Live, Joshimath Daily, Pahari Roots, etc. Internet connectivity was also reflected in the readership surveys[25] that reported the growing popularity of Hindi newspaper websites including the e-papers of *Amar Ujala*, *Dainik Jagran* and *Hindustan*. There seems to be a heightened perception of the impact of the online sources. Though the audience amounted to only a few thousands and was far lower than the circulation and readership of printed newspapers, anecdotal evidence suggested that social media had emerged as an important link in the information chain. The traditional news media, such as regional newspapers and TV, were, however, still on top and wielded tremendous power to influence the authorities, which is why their performance during the flood disaster must not be overlooked.

Flash Floods of 16–17 June 2013

Most lives were lost in the town of Kedarnath and the way-stations on the path through the Mandakini Valley. The two flash floods, first in the evening of 16 June and second in the early morning of 17 June, crashed through the entire town of Kedarnath leaving only the eighth century AD temple standing. The way-stations downstream along the Mandakini River—Rambara, Gaurikund, Phata, and Chanderpuri—were washed away. The settlements built close to the river banks in the townships of Uttarkashi, Augustmuni, Gobindghat, Karnaprayag, Rudraprayag and Srinagar—in the valleys of other tributaries of the Ganga—were also washed away.

On 16 June, because of the unrelenting downpour most pilgrims were in Kedarnath, and had taken shelter in hotels and lodges. Others, walking the 14-kilometre path from Gaurikund to the shrine, were either rushing to reach the shrine or had taken shelter in a few lodges in Rambara, the halfway house. Many were waiting in Gaurikund for the rain to slow down. Still others had taken shelter in Phata where the helipad was located for helicopters that carry pilgrims who have the means to pay. The operators, however, had suspended the helicopter service for the previous few days due to protests by the providers of hiking and lodging services. They saw the helicopters as cutting into their income from high-paying pilgrims. This also meant that when the weather deteriorated most helicopters operated by the tour companies were not close by. They were either in Gauchar, a town further downstream, or in Dehradun, the state capital.[26]

In the evening of 16 June about 7 PM, massive cloudbursts took place over the mountain ridges behind Kedarnath shrine. The deafening sounds were heard all over the Mandakini Valley, and within minutes a wall of water carrying boulders and debris from landslides crashed down from the mountain slopes on the temple town. Seeing the wall of water in the distance, many people rushed to higher ground, climbed onto the top of the buildings and took shelter inside the temple, which stands on a 635-square-metre plinth few feet above from the ground.[27]

It is known from the stories of survivors that on 16 June when the first flash flood came crashing down the Mandakini, only about 40 or 50 people were swept away in Kedarnath. Most people in Kedarnath had a miraculous escape: they ran to higher ground, climbed rooftops and took shelter inside the *sabha griha* (assembly hall) of the temple. However, the first flash flood destroyed a significant portion of the upper part of the town. As the wall of water rushed down the gorge, the torrents destroyed the two main way-stations, Rambara and Gaurikund, on the path to Kedarnath. Further downstream, major portions of Phata, where the pilgrim helipad was located, and Chanderpuri, further down before Augustmuni, were flooded. The police post by the river bank in Phata was also destroyed by the first day's torrent.

At Rambara, where thousands had taken shelter on 16 June, about 300 pilgrims who had taken shelter in a multi-storey dharamsala (pilgrim hotel), drowned in the rushing flood waters.[28] The entire seven-storey building resting on land reclaimed from the river was washed away as the pillars could not take the force of the torrent. It was said that the victims had no escape as the caretaker had locked the main door on the ground floor. Other people in and around the shrine and elsewhere were oblivious of what had happened downstream in Rambara. There was a total communication breakdown on the night of 16 June because of power failure and damage to the towers of the mobile-phone networks. Communicating with anyone outside the Mandakini Valley became impossible for the victims in the Kedar hollows.

As night fell in the Kedar hollows, the survivors, who were in tens of thousands, huddled together in whatever shelter they could find. As dawn broke, survivors from the previous evening's deluge heaved a sigh of relief and ventured outside looking for signs of rescue helicopters. Some had already started contemplating a way out from the hollow using local guides and alternate routes, as the footpath had already vanished. But before most survivors could do that, at about 7 AM on 17 June, they were again caught by another round of flash floods. This time the wall of water was much bigger and came down from the side of the Chorabari Glacier, the source of Mandakini, four kilometres behind the temple. The second deluge was caused by a breach in the Gandhi Sarovar[29]—a moraine lake that had formed many years ago at one of the two snouts of the Chorabari Glacier because of a dam formed by debris from earlier landslides. According to scientists the massive downpour from the cloud burst in the previous evening had filled the lake to capacity and had started melting the moraine ice causing a breach in the dam releasing millions of tonnes of water to crash down on Kedarnath town.[30]

This second torrent was many times bigger, and the entire town of Kedarnath was drowning under water. Thousands were washed away in the 17 June floods. Most fatalities, running into thousands, occurred in the way-stations, before Augustmuni on the route to Kedarnath and in the temple town itself. Most of those who survived had climbed to higher ground. However, an even bigger tragedy was that many of those who had survived the two flash floods were lost in the wilderness and were never found by the rescue teams. They probably died of hunger and exposure.

On 16–17 June, multiple cloudbursts were reported from other parts of the Badri–Kedar region. The other tributaries of the Ganges such as the Alaknanda and Bhagirathi were also carrying huge torrents of water. According to the locals, the flash floods in some areas were compounded by the sudden opening of the gates on the barrages built to divert water for hydroelectric projects. On the Vishnu Ganga, one of the tributaries of Alaknanda near Badrinath, water was released from the barrage without warning to prevent the diversion tunnels from clogging with boulders and collapsing under the tremendous pressure. As the gates were opened, water rushed down with huge force destroying the settlements of Pandukeshwar and Gobindghat. Many pilgrims from Hemkund Sahib, the Sikh shrine east of Badrinath, were caught in the deluge. Hundreds are reported to have perished in Gobindghat. As the torrents in the Alaknanda merged with the Mandakini at Rudraprayag, they rushed towards Srinagar, where there was another barrage on the river. Here too the gates had to be opened to save the barrage and diversion tunnels. Many of the low-lying settlements of Srinagar were flooded. By now, however, the force of the river had fallen. It started depositing debris and silt as the valley opened up before bending and again entering into a gorge at Kirtinagar. The river at Srinagar had risen more than 100 feet. The residents of Srinagar could hear the river smashing against the city on the nights of 16 and 17 June.[31] Srinagar took the final brunt before the torrents calmed down.

On 25 June, the Uttarakhand Government and the Government of India filed an Action Taken Report in the Supreme Court.[32] The court had instructed the two governments to speed up rescue operations. The two governments claimed that the rescue operation would be completed by the Indian military within 72 hours and that the focus now was relief. Indeed, the military had airlifted all the stranded victims from Badri–Kedar by 27 June. However, thousands still remained unaccounted for, and had to be categorized as missing, mostly because of the initial delay. Where were media and officials during these agonizing days?

Official and Journalistic Response

The flash floods struck on a weekend when many district level officials were on a break in Dehradun, the state capital. The first responders were the people living in the surrounding villages and the soldiers of the Indo-Tibetan Border Police. They did whatever they could to rescue people and provide food and shelter. At first, the small helicopters operated by tour operators were put into service to rescue stranded pilgrims on 18 June, more than 24 hours after the second flash flood in Kedarnath. It took almost 36 hours for the state authorities in the capital to respond. A proper rescue and relief operation only began on 19 June when the Indian military and the National Disaster Response Force (NDRF) took control of the rescue and relief from the state government and the local district administration.

The regional news media failed in their primary duty of reporting the facts from the ground. Natural disasters rank at the top of the pecking order of news values for the gatekeepers of daily news coverage. Journalists rush to get stories of disasters, and news organizations deploy all resources at the command of their journalists to access a disaster site. Media coverage of natural disasters is not only about witnessing, but also about ensuring that the authorities do the right thing to help the victims. Unfortunately, we also see that for governments and local authorities, the management of media coverage often takes precedence over the organization of rescue and relief operations. In the initial days social media—YouTube, Facebook and Twitter—played an important role in getting out news about the scale of the damage, especially when the state government had succeeded in getting the regional news media to practice self-censorship and underplay the scale of the disaster and the number of deaths.

A few official statements in the local news media show that either the authorities were totally unaware of the scale of disaster or were stunned and did not know how to proceed. Because of the breakdown of wireless communication, even journalists who had sources in Kedar hollow were unable to get eyewitness accounts until June 18. However, in a state that has hundreds of hydrological engineers working on various hydroelectric projects, it should not have been difficult to make scientific estimations of what must have happened upstream, especially looking at the torrents in Rudraprayag, Srinagar and Rishikesh. Moreover, the government also had access to satellite imagery from the Indian Space Research Organization and its own metrological offices. The official silence during the crucial first 36 hours became a puzzle. Many activists in the state later filed Right to Information (RTI) requests to try to learn what the authorities knew and when they came to know it.

Weather Warnings, Alerts and Advisories Ignored

A few days before the weekend that the flash floods struck, Uttarakhand regional newspapers reported that the national and state authorities had forecast that the monsoon may arrive a couple of weeks early. The meteorological authorities sent out alerts and advance warnings on 13 June to the state government and district officials. The alert forecast a very high probability of very heavy rains for 72 hours starting on June 15. On 14 June, the Garhwal editions of the regional newspapers carried the story on page 1, and the regional cable news channels, such as TV 100, reported the forecast, though in a tone that was not alarming.[33]

As predicted by the meteorological office, the downpour was very heavy all over the north-western Himalayas, especially in Uttarakhand. On 15 June all the rivers were flowing above the flood-mark. By late evening in the towns downstream such as Uttarkashi and Srinagar, the Bhagirathi and Alaknanda rivers had breached their embankments and washed away settlements along their banks. Reports were coming to Dehradun of numerous landslides all over the state. Stalled pilgrim–tourist traffic at multiple places had led to gridlocks on all the major roads to pilgrim destinations.

We now know that neither the authorities nor the pilgrims heeded the alerts and the warnings. The professionals in the weather office had advised the state government, including the district administrations, to suspend the pilgrimage and stop the pilgrim–tourists from proceeding ahead to the sacred sites in Badri–Kedar region. However, the alert by the meteorological professionals, and the advisories to stop the movement of pilgrim–tourists and ensure the safety of pilgrims already in the Himalayan region, did not come up for discussion at any level in the government. It was not even on the agenda of the meeting of the state cabinet held on 15 June. Ironically, the meeting did discuss the trip in the next week of the chief minister and a few senior officials to Switzerland, a country known for its sound mountain-tourism practices.[34]

On 15 June, the day after the weather alert was published in the local papers, a news item, tucked away in the inside pages of *Amar Ujala* and *Dainik Jagran,* national Hindi-language dailies that covered the region, talked about how ill-prepared was the state's disaster-mitigation office, and how most of the activities of the centre were only on paper. It was reported that an official audit had found that the centre *had not formulated any rules, regulations, policies and guidelines to mitigate a natural disaster in the state.* The state-level centre, created in 2007, had no plans or trained manpower, either at the level of district administrations or the state government, to deal with a major natural disaster in the mountains. A similar centre at the national level in Delhi also did not have plans to handle a natural disaster in the Himalayas. When the disaster struck, the authorities decided to stick their heads under their desks, perhaps hoping like ostriches that they would be able to ride out the crisis.

Delayed Official Response

Initially local people, tour operators, government authorities as well as journalists viewed the rising rivers and landslides as disruptive, but routine for the mountain region. The coverage in the newspapers and regional news channels, on 15 June, had stories on the overflowing rivers, landslides and blocked roads, but the tone of the reporting was not alarming. There were no screaming headlines. However, on June 16 when reports started pouring in from all over the state that at numerous places mountain roads were blocked due to landslides, some seriousness could be seen in the tone of the news reports. On 17 June, the first reports of death and destruction in low-lying settlements started coming. However, from the newspapers of 17 June and the news channels, there was no way to learn that a major calamity had struck the entire Mandakini Valley and upper reaches of the Alaknanda Valley. Perhaps this was because the first series of cloudbursts in Badri–Kedar region struck in the evening of 16 June and missed the news cycle. Thereafter, the flash floods and heavy rain severed all communication networks between the Mandakini Valley and towns downstream. The flow of traffic to and from the valley came to a standstill on 16 June as the main road connecting the towns in the Kedar hollows with Rudraprayag was totally washed away near Augustmuni.

By the evening of 17 June, though the rivers were still flowing above the flood marks, the flow had calmed down relative to the torrents of previous night. By the afternoon of that day, the state authorities were aware of the scale of the disaster in Kedarnath. The officials in the state capital instructed a tour company that ferried pilgrims to Kedarnath to conduct a reconnaissance. The helicopter pilot reported that the settlements of Rambara, Gaurikund, Phata and Chandrapuri were washed away and only water could be seen everywhere: "Rambara has been completely wiped out."[35] However, even after an eyewitness account confirming that a major calamity had struck the state, there was little to show what officials and their political masters in the state capital were doing to organize rescue and relief operations. On the evening of 18 June, some decided to call on the Indian military for help. Although the Garhwal region has numerous army and paramilitary camps, no request was made to them to come to the assistance of the civilian administration.[36]

Not surprisingly, at first the unprecedented fury of nature must have paralyzed the administrative machinery of the state, especially in the affected districts. However, my conversations with officials and people from Rudraprayag, the worst affected district, suggest that because the floods struck on a weekend, the lower level state functionaries were leaderless and without authority to act. Many senior officials at the district levels and in the state capital were not immediately available to take command of the situation. Reporters who tried to reach out to the state authorities to confirm the scale of the disaster and ask about rescue plans were surprised that there was a total silence from the state government from 17 June, which was a Monday, until late afternoon on 18 June.[37] The only press statement came from the district magistrate of Rudraprayag district. He told the reporters that he had ordered the helicopters operated by tour operators to start rescuing victims stranded on the ridges in Kedarnath areas.[38] However, the small helicopters operated by the travel companies were not suited for a large rescue operation. The leadership of the state including the chief minister was not seen or heard until late on 18 June. Full-scale rescue and relief operations did not start until the morning of 19 June the Indian Air Force and Army launched Operation Rahat and Operation Surya Hope respectively.[39]

Self-censorship by Uttarakhand News Media

With all the roads having been washed away in the floods, local people were the only ones who had the knowledge of alternative hiking routes to Kedarnath. They could have been a major asset, but instead of using them, the Rudraprayag district authorities stopped villagers who were searching for family members from going beyond Augustmuni on 17 June. Large numbers of men and adolescent boys from the villages in the Mandakini Valley worked on the Kedarnath route in hotels, lodges and other support services for the pilgrims and tourists. A large number of those killed or trapped in the Kedar hollow were from local villages. In many families only women, children and elderly were left to fend for themselves.

The Rudraprayag and Chamoli district administrations had placed prohibitory orders on the movement of civilians, including locals who were searching for their family members, beyond Augustmuni and

Joshimath, respectively. Many locals felt that the prohibitory orders were intended to keep a lid on the scale of tragedy and the large numbers of people who had died.[40] It is unfortunate, but often the first official act of most governments is an attempt to check the flow of information from a disaster zone. However, in this age of social media and intense media competition, attempts to regulate the flow of information often end up being counterproductive. Citizens with mobile phones and access to the Internet are walking-talking news outlets.

By the afternoon of 17 June as news of the scale of destruction started coming from other towns downstream, in the Mandakini and Alaknanda valleys, people started fearing the worst. Those living in the towns and settlements downstream were able to gauge from the massive wall of flood water rushing towards them that a major calamity must have taken place upstream. On 18 June, local news channels and newspapers carried stories from all over the state on the large-scale destruction caused by the flash floods in all the tributaries of Ganges, but the death counts in the stories were not yet alarming. There were stories on the destruction of Gaurikund, Chandrapuri, Augustmuni and Gobindghat, but there was no news from Kedarnath or Rambara, the last way-station, in the regional news media.[41]

When on 18 June, a few survivors—mostly locals who could find their way back from Kedar hollow—trickled into Guptakashi and Ukhimath, mobile phones started ringing all over Uttarakhand and across the country.[42] The eyewitness accounts spoke of thousands dead, with bodies lying everywhere in the valley, and tens of thousands stranded on ridges all along the trek route from Gaurikund to Kedarnath. As mentioned earlier, on 18 June, the district administration in Rudraprayag had started organizing some rescues using the helicopters operated by tour companies. But the helicopters returned empty as it was not safe to land or to try to select who to rescue from among the thousands of victims cramped on small ridges crying out for help. These initial attempts to rescue the survivors enabled some local journalists to hop on the helicopters to witness for themselves the destruction in Kedarnath.[43] By evening, all major news channels were reporting that a major calamity had struck the Badri–Kedar region and the entire town of Kedarnath had been destroyed. This sent alarm bells ringing in New Delhi and other state capitals.

On 19 June, the front pages of all regional newspapers in Uttarakhand had pictures of the washed-out temple town of Kedarnath with headlines screaming "Everything destroyed in Kedarnath" and stories announcing that thousands of pilgrims, tourists and locals were missing. Additionally there were stories and pictures from Uttarkashi in the Bhagirathi Valley, Gobindghat near Vishnu Prayag and Srinagar that further confirmed the worst. Some resourceful news channels had also made a trip to Kedarnath and captured the destruction on camera. Others who could not make it were recycling the mobile phone video footage that was being uploaded by citizen journalists. The local papers were still not reporting on the front pages that thousands had died; but in the inside pages there were eye-witness accounts that talked of dead bodies lying everywhere in the Kedar hollows. After the big breaking story about the disaster on 19 June, a follower of any of the local newspapers or news channels would on 20 June have thought the rescue operations were being carried out smoothly. According to reporters I interviewed, it seemed that the management of the regional newspapers had come to some sort of agreement with the state government not to report the unprecedented scale of the tragedy, especially the large numbers of dead, until the government had come up with a rescue and relief plan. A few reporters on the ground in the affected districts were sending stories detailing the tragedy, but they were not seeing them in the newspapers or broadcast on the local channels.

It appears that the editors of local newspapers and news channels realized how stupid they must have looked, especially when multiple survivor accounts reporting thousands of dead had started flooding social media platforms such as You Tube, Facebook and Twitter.[44] Moreover, by then reporters from national and international news media had also started arriving, and they were reporting that a large number of pilgrim–tourists and locals had died and tens of thousands were stranded on the open ridges in and around pilgrim destinations in Badri–Kedar region. As most of the victims were pilgrims from other parts of the country, reporters from their states were also building pressure on the government to act fast. Some states even started organizing their own relief and rescue plans to save their citizens from the harrowing conditions in which they were stranded.

With each passing hour, more eyewitness accounts of the calamity of 16–17 June started surfacing in the news media and social media. On 21 June, the media narrative moved from the "biggest tragedy" to the hopeful stories of the "biggest rescue" operation that the region had seen in recent recorded history. The news media narrative and social media posts and pictures were now mostly about the valiant efforts made by the soldiers of the Indian Army and NDRF in rescuing more than 100,000 victims.[45] There were stories on how local villagers helped the victims with whatever food, water and clothing they had. There were a few stories about stealing from the dead. To rescue the stranded victims from remote areas, large military helicopters flying from airbases in north India were put into service. The army set up its own relief camps with food and medical facilities. Social media once again played an important role in providing a continuous flow of information that reassured the victims, their families and the people in general.

The local administration and the state government watched from the sidelines as the Indian military conducted Operations Rahat and Surya Hope to rescue victims and provide relief. The Uttarakhand government was left to count the dead, arrange for appropriate funerals and work on the policy implications of the flash floods of 2013. The most important question was—did authorities in the state learn the policy implications of their shortcomings and take corrective actions?

Conclusion

Pilgrimage to the sacred destinations in the Himalayas was always associated with *kathinayee* (physical and emotional difficulties), and folk memory in the region abounds with stories of natural disasters and pilgrim tragedies. But despite the known dangers, the faithful have continued to undertake the arduous trip to sacred sites in Badri–Kedar. Scientists view periodic disasters as endemic to the geomorphology and ecology of the young mountains of the Himalayas. However, over the centuries, the *paharis* developed a mountain ethos and ecological consciousness that had taught them to minimize the effects of natural disasters such as landslides, cloudbursts and regular rumblings inside the earth. The unpredictable power of nature had also taught them humility and respect for the mountains. In order to not compound the effects of a natural disaster they had evolved an intricate set of norms and rituals, including a reverence for the uninterrupted flow of the river, that on the surface seemed superstitions, but in the past regulated settlements along the river. Centuries of experience had given them the wisdom to choose the safe slopes and higher ground in the hollows in river valleys to build their homes and cut terraced fields. Even the flow of pilgrims to destinations in higher sacred grounds of Badri–Kedar Himalayas was regulated by an intricate set of norms and values. In the past, locals and pilgrims knew the dangers and took precautions. They saw pilgrimage to Badri–Kedar as an end-of-life act of faith, whereas today, because of a network of mountain roads that leads to the doorstep of most sacred shrines, entire families including old and very young children undertake the pilgrimages.

However, much of that wisdom was laid aside following the encroachment into the *pahari* life world of the apparatuses of the modern nation state. The latter claimed to be equipped with scientific and engineering knowledge that could master the vagaries of nature and unleash the economic potential of the network of rivers in the region. Despite all the knowledge and resources at the command of the modern state, we are witnessing more loss of life and property in natural disasters. Equipped with scientific knowledge and engineering technology, the modern state with total disregard for sustainable ecology has blasted its way through the river valleys building a network of roads to facilitate tourism and hydroelectric projects to harness the potential energy stored in the river systems.

Ironically, there seems to be a foolhardy invincibility associated with the hegemonic discourse of technology and development. It is not surprising that to access the transportation facilities and economic opportunities associated with pilgrim–tourism and hydroelectric projects, people living in villages built on higher ground and stable bedrock, moved closer to the roads built along the river banks. As more and more people relocated, the scarcity of flat land by the roadside encouraged the authorities to permit encroachment on the flood zone of the rivers in the small towns at the *prayags* (river confluences). The old pilgrim way-stations were small *kasbas* (settlements), where pilgrims stopped for the night. These developed into bustling towns with flourishing commerce, and a series of hydroelectric projects on the Ganga River system further increased urbanization close to the river banks.

When we compare the 2013 floods with the previous natural disasters including the earthquakes, landslides and flash floods of 1894 and 1970 in the Alaknanda Valley, we find that the loss of life and property was the highest in 2013. Previously, there was a sense of awe at nature's fury, and precautionary efforts were put in place.

When in 1970 a cloudburst led to a breach in the Gohna Tal (lake) that emptied the reservoir, massive flash floods brought with them uprooted trees that in turn precipitated an ecological movement. The destruction in 1970 was compounded because of soil erosion due to rampant tree felling that had weakened the slopes. The 1970 floods precipitated the formation of the now famous Chipko Movement that culminated in a ban on commercial logging in the Himalayas. Many scholars have argued that the demand for creation of Uttarakhand state, which was created in 2000, was a logical culmination of the eco-logical consciousness associated with the *pahari* ethos articulated in the Chipko Movement and other social-ecological protests in the region.[46] The demand for a separate state of Uttarakhand was expressed in terms of local autonomy and the need for sustainable management of mountain ecology—*jal, jungal* and *zameen* (water, forest and land). In the movement for the creation of Uttarakhand, activists often cited the absence of mountain-specific policy on devel-opment and the failures of a distant government in Lucknow to organize rescue and relief operations after the earthquakes of Uttarkashi (1991) and Chamoli (1999), and the landslides of Malpa and Ukhimath (1998). Will the destruction of 2013, like the floods of 1970, change anything?

My purpose has been to understand the "anatomy of a disaster" and to explain the official and journalist response. There was a sym-biotic relationship between official response and journalistic response. The official failure to react with alacrity and organize rescue and relief in the first 36 hours fed the failure of the news media to report the facts from the ground. Not surprisingly, many reporters working for the regional news media, including *Amar Ujala* and *Dainik Jagran*, who were seen as practising activist journalism during the statehood movement in Uttarakhand before 2000, confessed that it seemed that the news media engaged in self-censorship when it came to question-ing the state government's policies, especially about urban settlement and hydroelectric dams.

Will the flash floods of 2013 bring a shift in the hegemonic developmentalism that has had an iron grip over public policy in Uttarakhand since its founding as a separate state in 2000? If we go by the official reports produced by the government agencies on the events of 2013, the answer is likely, "No". After the floods in 2013, a group of citizens approached India's Supreme Court. The court ordered the government to constitute a committee to undertake an impact assessment. The report titled "Assessment of Environmental Degradation and Impact of Hydroelectric Projects During the June 2013 Disaster in Uttarakhand"[47] was submitted to the government in April 2014. The committee recommended drastically scaling down the hydroelectric projects in the region. On the first anniversary of the great Himalayan tsunami, the state government still did not have a policy response to disasters.[48] Future decisions will depend to a large extent on how the Kedarnath tragedy informs public discourse in news media and social media and how public opinion forms on the issues of sustainable development and the mountain ethos.

Notes

1. R. N. Misra, S. C. Agarwal and A. Sharma, "Disaster in Uttarakhand—its Causes, Impact on Infrastructural Development and Mitigation Measures," *Water and Energy International*, 57b, no. 2 (2014): 46–52.
2. V. Varshney, "Kedarnath temple in Uttarakhand survives glacier, floods," *Down To Earth*, June 2013.
3. See http://www.ndtv.com/article/india/uttarakhand-the-making-of-the-himalayan-tsunami-393901
4. See the official government list on the dead and missing here, http://dmmc.uk.gov.in/pages/view/87-death-certificate-issued-state-wise and http://dmmc.uk.gov.in/pages/view/77-missing-person-from-uttarakhand-state
5. Mountain hollow, often chosen for building settlements, is a small valley between mountain slopes.
6. K. T. Erikson, *Everything in its Path: Destruction of a Community in the Buffalo Creek Flood* (New York: Simon & Schuster, 1976).
7. Erikson, *Everything in its Path*, 1976, p. 247.
8. I credit Dr Sunil Kainthola and Himanshu Ahuja for enlightening me about the man-made aspects of an otherwise natural disaster. They, with the volunteers of the Mountain Shepherd's Initiative, a community-based organization, like many other NGOs, had rushed to help in the relief work.

9. See "Record Rainfall in Doon, Normal Life Affected," *The Daily Pioneer*, 17 June 2013, http://www.dailypioneer.com/state-editions/dehradun/record-rainfall-in-doon-normal-life-affected.html

10. See chapter on South Asia and the extremes of water scarcity and excess and the impact of changing regional climate patterns in World Bank, *Turn Down the Heat: Climate Extremes and Regional Impacts and the Case for Resilience*. Washington D.C.: International Bank of Reconstruction and Development, pp. 105–138, 2013.

11. The high Himalayan region where the Hindu shrines of Yamunotri, Gangotri, Kedarnath, Badrinath and the Sikh Gurudwara of Hemkund Sahib are located is locally known as Badri–Kedar or Chardham.

12. See chapter by Ming Xia, "Media Control as Stability Maintenance: The Case of the Sichuan Earthquake" in this book. Also see discussion of media's role in social control during the Katrina disaster in K. Tienery, C. Bevec and E. Kuligowski, "Metaphors matter: Disaster Myths, Media Frames and Their Consequences in Hurricane Katrina," *The Annals of the American Academy* 604 (2006): 57–81.

13. All India Disaster Mitigation Institute, "Disasters attract media, and media attracts politicians," p. 6, 2014.

14. See http://www.pewresearch.org/fact-tank/2013/06/07/chart-of-the-week-newspaper-circulation-around-the-world/

15. See Audit Bureau of Circulation figures for June 2013.

16. See special report on print media, *afaqs! Reporter*, August 2013, http://www.afaqs.com/all/news/misc/38475_Print_Special.pdf

17. See Report of Indian Readership Survey Q3, 2013, by Media Research Users Council (http://www.mruc.net/). The readership findings have been disputed by some media houses, http://www.thehinduhub.com/pdf/irs-2013-news-coverage-in-th_bl.pdf

18. See Annual Report of the Registrar of Newspapers India.

19. See Annual Report of Cellular Operators of India, http://www.coai.com/search?ArticleKeyword=COAI

20. Telecom Regulatory Authority of India report on performance indicators, http://www.dot.gov.in/sites/default/files/Telecom%20Annual%20Report-2012-13%20(English)%20_For%20web%20(1).pdf

21. http://www.giz.de/en/downloads/giz2014-en-indo-german-e-governance-forum-2013.pdf

22. See http://www.thehindubusinessline.com/industry-and-economy/info-tech/bsnl-to-fix-mobile-towers-at-crucial-spot-uttarakhand-in-3-days/article4837652.ece

23. See http://gadgets.ndtv.com/telecom/news/most-mobile-towers-in-uttarakhand-restored-indus-towers-382684

24. A. Kaushal and D. Pant, "Bridging Digital Divide Challenges in Uttarakhand," *International Journal of Advance Research in Computer Science and Software Engineering*, 3, no. 7 (2013):1425–1428.

25. See Report of Indian Readership Survey, 2013.
26. Interviews with local people, and also see "Protests Kept Out Helicopters, Trapped Many Before Disaster," *The Indian Express*, 23 June 2013.
27. The reconstruction of the events of 16–17 June has been done from a series of conversations with the victims.
28. See an eyewitness account of the destruction of the pilgrim hotel in H. Joshi, *Tum Chup Kyon Rahe Kedar: Himalaya Ki Sabsi badi Trasdi Se Uthe Sawal* (Why did you remain silent Kedar: Questions arising from the biggest tragedy in Himalaya). New Delhi: Aalekh Prakashan, 2014.
29. The glacial lake was named as Gandhi Sarovar (Tal) after the immersion of Mahatma Gandhi's ashes in its water.
30. K. H. V. Durga Rao, V. V. Rao, V. K. Dadhwal and P. G. Diwakar, "Kedarnath Floods: A Hydrological and Hydraulic Simulation Study," *Current Science*, 106, no. 4 (2014): 598–603; D. P. Dobhal, A. K. Gupta, M. Mehta and D. D. Khandelwal, "Kedarnath Disaster: Facts and Plausible Causes," *Current Science*, 105, no. 2 (2013): 171–174; N. Rana, S. Singh, Y. P. Sundriyal and N. Juyal "Recent and Past Floods in the Alaknanda Valley: Causes and Consequences," *Current Science*, 105, no. 9 (2013): 1209–1212.
31. Interviews with the local victims from Joshimath and Srinagar.
32. See news item by J. Venkatesan, "Speed up Rescue: Court tells Centre and Uttarakhand," *Hindu*, 26 June 2013.
33. See *Amar Ujala* and *Dainik Jagran*, Garhwal editions, 14 June 2013.
34. My source was a government official who must remain anonymous. Also see story by Bhavana Vij-Aurora and Amarnath K. Menon, "Lessons Still Unlearned," *India Today*, 28 June 2013.
35. See a compelling account of the first aerial survey carried out at the behest of the state government on June 17 in M. Bhatt, M. Pandya and H. C. Goh, (2013). "Floods in Uttarakhand: A New Deal of Relief," *Experience Learning Series 60*. Ahmedabad: All Indian Disaster Mitigation Institute, pp. 17–22.
36. Interviews with low-level district officials in the region.
37. Interviews with journalists working in the region.
38. See *Amar Ujala* and *Dainik Jagran*, 18 June 2013.
39. A. K. Chordia, "Airlift During Disasters: The Uttarakhand Experience," *Centre for Air Power Studies*, 11 July 2013.
40. Interviews with victims from Rudraprayag and Srinagar.
41. See *Amar Ujala* and *Dainik Jagran*, Garhwal editions, 18 June 2013.
42. One of the first series of videos of the flash floods in Kedarnath were put out by Raghubeer Bisht, were reposted by the American Geophysical Union on its website and seen by many across the world, http://blogs.agu.org/land-slideblog/2013/07/06/videos-of-kedarnath-on-the-day-of-the-disaster-and-in-the-aftermath/
43. M. Bhatt, M. Pandya and H. C. Goh, *Floods in Uttarakhand: A New Deal of Relief* (*Experience Learning Series 60*) (Ahmedabad: All Indian Disaster Mitigation Institute).

44. Some of the popular Twitter handles were #Uttarakhand and #kedarnath. Many Facebook pages had cropped up such as Uttarakhand Disaster: Khoya, Paya (Lost, Found); Uttarakhand Floods Damage; Uttarakhand disaster 2013: information, help and relief, etc.

45. One of the most popular Twitter handles was #SaluteIndianArmy.

46. R. Guha, *The Unquiet Woods: Ecological Change and Peasant Resistance in the Himalaya* (Berkeley: University of California, 2000); A. Kumar, *The Making of a Small State* (Hyderabad and New Delhi: Orient Black Swan, 2011); S. Ishizaka, "Re-evaluating the Chipko (forest protection) Movement: The Emergence of the Vernacular Public Arena in the Uttarakhand" in Taberez A. Niazi, Akio Tanabe and Shinya Ishizaka, eds. *Democratic Transformation and the Vernacular Public Arena in India* (New Delhi: Routledge, 2014), pp. 123–138.

47. The expert committee submitted to the Ministry of Environment and Forests, Government of India, http://www.indiaenvironmentportal.org.in/files/file/environmental%20degradation%20&%20hydroelectric%20projects.pdf

48. See news story by Prashant Shishir, "A Year After Uttarakhand Floods: No Disaster Mgt Policy to Combat Nature's Fury," *Business Standard*, 17 June 2014.

16

Social Media: China and India Compared

Jonathan Benney and Nimmi Rangaswamy

Jonathan Benney teaches at Monash University, Melbourne. A graduate of the University of Melbourne, he has been a lecturer at Macquarie University and a fellow at the University of Oklahoma, the Asia Research Institute at the National University of Singapore and the Goethe University in Frankfurt. His research explores activism, political communication and new media in contemporary China. He trained as a lawyer, but realized that his passions for China and for new media deserved a more suitable outlet. He has worked as a teacher of Chinese language and politics, as a sub-titler for Taiwanese television, and in 2007, he represented Australia in the world Chinese-language debating competition.

Nimmi Rangaswamy is a social anthropologist who started out studying Dravidian identity politics in South India and moved on to researching the digital behaviours and practices of urban youth in Indian slums. She is Area Manager, Human Interactions, at Xerox Research Lab India, adjunct professor in the Department of Liberal Arts, Indian Institute of Technology, Hyderabad, and was previously a researcher with Microsoft Research India.

The narrative of media growth, particularly in the developing world, is characterized by a transition from traditional media to new media—and from then, perhaps, to social media. But the diversity and size of China and India is such that social media are complex to define. For the purposes of this chapter and to facilitate an effective comparison between China and India, we examine those technologies of new media which are primarily designed to facilitate communication between individuals as individuals, rather than as representatives of larger organizations.

We thus consider—in terms of the internet—online social networking services (SNSs), instant messaging sites, blogs and media-sharing sites, and—in terms of purely mobile communication—SMS-based communication technologies. The differing states of technological development in China and India mean that in China, our emphasis will be on internet-equipped devices, and in India, on mobile phones. Consequently, we explore two corresponding case studies—the micro blog service *weibo* in China, and the SMS-based social network SMSGupShup in India. Our methodological approach is necessarily different for these two cases. In considering China, we are able to draw on a substantial secondary literature. This literature is lacking in the Indian case, and therefore we rely more on recent field research.[1] Hence, we devote relatively more time to characterizing the background of Chinese social media and to examining the Indian case study in depth.

In the academic and journalistic world, two burning questions surrounding social media in China and India have become obvious: in China, whether social media can function as a means of democratization; and in India, whether it can act as a tool for development. In exploring these issues, this chapter demonstrates that the notions of social media and information and communication technology for development (ICTD) cannot merely be integrated: expanded social media does not imply expanded development. But, at higher levels of society, especially in the middle class, our research demonstrates high levels of social media integration into the existing social practices, particularly in relationship formation and entrepreneurship. Therefore, we suggest that it is advance in social media, rather than development alone, which increase the possibility of social and political participation. Furthermore, our comparison illustrates the importance of the prevailing culture and, in particular, the influence of the state (which are often interlinked) and demonstrates that set developmental pathways often cannot be applied to countries so large and complicated as China and India. Finally, our research confirms the applicability in China and India of a worldwide literature of creative uses (so-called "hacks") of the existing forms of social media.

China

The Development of the Internet in China

As compared to other large countries, China's internet has two distinctive characteristics. First is that it is, in general, written in the Chinese language. This is not a trivial observation. Chinese is the only major language which does not rely, whether in whole or in part, on an alphabet or syllabary, and so the dynamics of communication, both in terms of the ways in which people can express themselves and in the ways in which language is encoded and sent over the internet, are measurably different in China.

Second, China's internet experiences greater state control than any other country of comparable size. The history of online communications in China—in which academic intranets were merged and gradually granted access to the World Wide Web, thus creating a "Chinese internet" to which first commercial organizations, then private citizens, were admitted—is a history in which any form of access to online material is inherently approved and monitored by the state, which acts as gatekeeper,[2] and in which any perceived free transfer of information should really be regarded as having been granted by the state.

These two areas of difference provide substantial challenges to the development of an interpersonal or social internet in China (as opposed to a commercial internet, or networks focussed solely on the transfer of data). Nonetheless, the sheer number of potential internet users in China and the level of their engagement with the internet have altered, to a large extent, the ways in which information is communicated in China, and, furthermore, the degree to which the public is able to engage critically with information. It would be extremely optimistic to suggest that the internet and social media are changing the political or democratic structure of China, or that the existence of new forms of media works as a "mobility multiplier."[3] However, the aesthetics and language of the internet are, for the majority of citizens, now an integral part of Chinese society, and internet trends and "events" now make a substantial contribution to the formation of Chinese citizens' world views.

Growth and Diversity

A high level of state control over the internet—when combined with a booming economy, a growing middle class and a large human and technical resource base—has made the development of the Chinese internet especially rapid. The regular statistical reports produced by the China Internet Network Information Center (CNNIC), a non-profit organization operated by the Ministry of Industry and Information Technology, demonstrate the size and scope of the growth of the Chinese internet since the first email was sent in 1987.[4]

Despite China's large size, its social and geographic diversity, and in particular its hundreds of millions of rural poor, it now has more internet users than any other country. From the early 1990s onwards, the state has developed an advanced engineering infrastructure, capable of carrying data across the country.[5] Its internet penetration rate reached 39.9 per cent in 2012,[6] higher than the world average and substantially higher than the average for Asia (25.2%) and India's penetration rate (11.4%) (Internet World Stats, 2012). Among those with a junior college education or higher, China's penetration rate is 96.1 per cent, comparable to any developed country. Rural penetration, however, may have reached a plateau: without substantial efforts from the state to facilitate rural internet use, it appeared to have stabilized at a rate of approximately 27 per cent.[7]

The behaviour of Chinese internet users is unsurprisingly diverse, with only one especially noticeable overall trend: compared to other countries, it has been observed that users are more likely in China than in other countries to use the internet for "entertainment."[8] "Entertainment" is a vague label, but, in the terms used by the CNNIC surveys, it is defined in opposition to commerce, study and personal communication.[9]

Online entertainment media in China have taken various forms over time. The earliest days of the Chinese internet were characterized by an emphasis on BBSs (bulletin board systems), often localized to a particular geographic area or academic institution,[10] and not necessarily using the World Wide Web.[11] By the early 2000s, these BBSs mostly took the form of web forums (*luntan*).[12] In parallel with these forums, which were largely confined to particular local or niche groups, the early 2000s saw an explosion of novel social media: online role-playing games;[13] online simulations, such as "virtual marriages";[14] and, most noticeably, the new popularity of blogs.[15] Certain aspects of the Chinese entertainment internet, such as the popularity of online novels, are distinctly absent from the English-speaking internet.

As Fengshu Liu points out, by the mid-2000s, Chinese internet users' "online social production" was heavily oriented towards "personal life, lifestyles, and consumerism."[16] Internet cafes, now supervised closely by the state, initially provided a physical social space for internet use which paralleled the creation of virtual social spaces. The use of blogs helped to reinforce a social sphere in which personal expression was paramount and in which online celebrity became important:[17] cultures of discussion relating to fashion, music, television and personalities eventuated. But blogs and BBSs also allowed for political communication and social critique, resulting in the re-emergence of a *minjian* (unofficial) online culture of criticism of government.[18]

From the late 1990s onwards, at the same time as the rise of the internet, the use of mobile telecommunications has also become an integral part of Chinese culture, and one which, unlike computer-based networking, has been able to reach the rural and working-class population, a group which has been termed the "information have-less."[19] Given the growth of entrepreneurship across all of China, and massive trends towards rural–urban migration, the mobile telephone has played an enormous role in commerce and interpersonal communication. Its role as a tool for social mobilization was first demonstrated in southern China in the early 2000s, where the opposition to government decisions and unofficial sources of information often spread through SMS messaging.

Mobile phones are now so commonplace in China, and— particularly as many of them are now "smartphones," with the capacity to access the internet, take photos and videos, read long documents, and so on—mobile communication now tends to merge seamlessly with internet communication and indeed with the physical world, such that distinctions between online and offline life are increasingly meaningless. The recent research of Wallis[20] and Oreglia[21] demonstrates that, even in the working classes, individuals treasure their mobile phones and use them constantly, for diverse purposes, and in a technically adept way. But class, rather than geographic location, gender or ethnicity, remains the largest barrier to participation in sophisticated forms of telecommunication. The use of a mobile phone for social communication, even when other forms of social media may in theory be available, is a "necessary convergence" of information services for the poor.[22]

All of these factors—infrastructure, availability, and culture—have meant that China has jumped on the Web 2.0 bandwagon with vigour. The popular social media sites in China—which include Sina Weibo, the QQ messaging service, the social networking site Renren, and Douban, a social network and forum site concentrating on music and art—attract both large numbers of users and high levels of participation from these users. For the generation born after 1980, social media services like QQ are so important to their everyday lives that they are described as being like "air" or "water" to them.[23] The migratory nature of Chinese families has led to a trickle-up effect, where children have encouraged their parents to learn to use the internet or mobile phones so that they can communicate with each other.[24]

Getting Things Done on Social Media in China

For the "information rich"—the middle class, those with access to sophisticated internet devices and high-bandwidth connections—the world of social media is very diverse. Individuals with computers and smartphones may access instant messaging, social networking sites, video sites and blogs. Often these services are integrated seamlessly or accessed simultaneously so that the user is immersed in a virtual world of audio-visual and social data. Modern phenomena in Chinese media, such as the wave of *egao* or satirical videos, are intrinsically linked to the communication mechanisms of social media.[25]

But as the research by Hjorth and Arnold cited above demonstrates, communication and networking—the reinforcement of existing social networks, in particular—remains the chief use of social media in China. Such online social networks generally consist of family, fellow students, co-workers, and so on. Wallis, for example, describes cases of young female migrants to cities who use mobile messaging as a means of constantly keeping up to date with relatives and friends, sending substantive personal updates, very brief "hello" messages, and forwarded material such as jokes. The aim is not merely to transmit information, but also what is termed "communication as ritual":[26] reinforcing individuals' "realities," and their relationships with the self and others, through the development of a relationship with the fetishized object, the mobile phone.

The latest social media trend in China—the internet-based short messaging service WeChat (*Weixin* in Chinese)—is an even more obvious manifestation of this trend.[27] It demonstrates that post-Web 2.0 social media developments in China are more likely to focus on communication within small groups (in so-called social-local-mobile or SoLoMo networks) than on the formation of large or diverse online communities.

The networking potential of social media can of course also be used to develop relationships with people whom the user does not already know. Traditionally, BBSs, such as those organized by university students, allowed users to expand their social circles by making contact with those sharing similar interests. This tendency is particularly clear on the internet services such as Douban, on which groups are formed based on interest in music groups, film makers, types of literature and so on—even WeChat has a "shake" function designed to connect users randomly with other users.

Such services offer obvious potential for individuals with specific interests to communicate with others—a process which can entertain, educate and indeed improve individuals' psychological wellbeing and self-actualization. While fans of obscure bands may congregate freely on Douban, and while the Chinese internet provides a novel type of safe space for sexual minorities and sex workers (among others),[28] the party-state monitors such communities closely. Even an entertainment-focussed site such as Douban has experienced censorship—a process which necessitates close and constant contact between the state and the operator.[29] Nominally private and interpersonal networks like WeChat, Skype and QQ have also experienced considerable state censorship.[30]

The potential of the internet and social media for political and social mobilization has consequently been limited in China. While the Chinese internet infrastructure, and its number of users, is certainly capable of sustaining large-scale "slacktivist" events such as the Kony phenomenon of 2012, such centrally organized events generally do not occur, largely because of the state censorship apparatus. For marginalized groups such as the gay community, an online presence has not led to changes in acceptance in the wider community.[31]

Between State and Citizen

As the evidence given earlier suggests, the Chinese internet has developed under the close supervision and management of the Party-state. State planning of internet infrastructure, censorship and close links between internet companies and the state have shaped the Chinese internet in the image desired by the state. Commerce, entertainment and personal communication have been prioritized; group discussion and politics have been minimized.

By blocking most of the Western social media services (such as Facebook, Twitter, Tumblr and YouTube) and facilitating the development of approximate Chinese-language replacements (Renren, Weibo, Diandian and Youku, respectively), the state has made censorship easier. The companies which run these services, the most prominent of which are the Sina Corporation and Tencent Holdings, have generally enjoyed a clientelist relationship with the state, characterized by close personal relationships between management and the Party-state and stringent supervision of officials and their work.[32] Most censorship is done by the service providers themselves (for example, the deletion of posts which contain politically or socially "sensitive words," such as the names of leaders or controversial events). The police and the state apparatus frequently detain or arrest those who make use of the internet to spread information critical of the state. The design of social media services is also aesthetically targeted towards entertainment and away from political debate.[33]

However, despite these factors, the internet has been a crucial source of information and networks for resistance against the state. Yang[34] has argued that Chinese internet users are now highly accustomed to creating what he has termed "digital hidden transcripts": circumventing the supervision and violence of the state by technical and linguistic means. Circumvention devices allow users to gain access to censored sites, but more relevant to social media is the multitude of aesthetic and linguistic strategies, intended to subvert both the discourse of the state and its programme of censorship, developed by communities of users.

The case of the Grass Mud Horse, the subject of a "viral" internet video, spread on social media, illustrates this. The point of the video is to make various crude puns ("Grass Mud Horse" is *caonima* in

Chinese, pronounced similarly to the phrase for "fuck your mother") which satirize the state discourse of harmony and the anodyne style of the state media.[35] One could point to many similar examples: the case of the artist Ai Weiwei, who has become a focal point for Chinese activists and malcontents,[36] is another striking one.

The relationship between citizen and state is thus constantly fluid and negotiative. The speed, spread and diversity of data on the Chinese internet is such that the party-state cannot effectively control all of it. It therefore makes use of a palette of strategies—based on aesthetic manipulation, personal coercion, and the control of information—in order to bias the available information in its favour. But most of these strategies are transparent to the users of Chinese social media, and therefore can be circumvented or subverted. While the vast majority of political power remains in the hands of the state, the rise of social media has made power over discourse and communication more democratic.

ICT in Society

Academic debate about the internet in India[37] has prioritized notions of "ICT for development" (ICTD), mounting arguments about ways in which information technology might accelerate or aid the process of poverty reduction and economic modernization, particularly in rural areas. With a few exceptions,[38,39] the analysis of the Chinese internet has not made use of the ICTD framework. Rather, it has followed the line of analysis we describe above: characterizing the internet as a potential means for the representation and communication of the Chinese people as a whole: ICT for *social* and *political* development, rather than development in the conventional sense.

This is commensurate with the suggestion made by the CNNIC statistics cited earlier, namely that the Chinese Party-state has little interest in facilitating the use of ICT by the rural poor. ICTD projects have been isolated and poorly funded; so-called "working class ICTs", such as the *Xiaolingtong* mobile phone system, have received little state funding or support.[40] Even if the Party-state can be characterized as taking a positive or facilitative approach to ICTD, rather than neglecting or deliberately preventing it, state progress in this area can only be described as half-hearted and fragmented.

However, in the middle class and the manufacturing sector, the state and the corporate sector have long collaborated to integrate ICT into every aspect of society. This is so in part because of the necessity of information literacy and ICT for commercial purposes and in part because the state sees ICT, particularly entertainment services and social media, as a useful "safety valve" for middle-class discontent, especially political discontent.[41]

India

The Development of Social Media in India

In extremely generalized terms, the new Chinese media narrative around growth, increasing sophistication and support from government also prevails in India. But as we have suggested earlier, levels of internet use are much lower in India than in China, and, as we suggest below, mobile phone usage has also developed differently. We can attribute these differences first to the empirical fact that India's economic development currently lags behind China, and second to the very different landscape of political ideology in nation building and governance. Linked to these are differences in the regulatory climate and market innovations and devolutions preceding the beginning of the second millennium. Limited investment in infrastructure delayed serious reforms in broadband installation. At the same time, telecom policy and market liberation have allowed mobile telephony in India to gather huge momentum. The loose and unformed body of regulation governing internet use and dissemination has benefited the user base as a whole, propelling both legitimate and pirated uses of internet and computing technologies.

As mobile telephony infrastructures and market innovations rapidly make inroads into even the hinterlands of India, individuals are leapfrogging directly to the mobile age without any prior experience in computer use. More than a decade ago, the uptake of mobile telephony began at the higher income segments and devolved gradually to economically challenged consumers. Nasscom's 2012 annual report mentions only 44 million smartphone subscribers in a 900 million strong mobile market, but the report also states that the 88 million internet users were added in the country over the last half decade (2008–2012) constitute the second largest such addition during this period after China. With 137 million internet users, and a 26 per cent growth year-on-year, the internet penetration rate for India is currently 11 per cent. The emergence of the mobile phone in India meant that "Indians of every status were able to speak to each other as never before."[42]

This means that the mobile phone can now undermine deeply embedded structural and socio-economic hierarchies by providing opportunities to historically excluded social groups. In the period from 2002 to 2012, a majority of Indians gained the ability to communicate independently and access information, and India soon developed the cheapest mobile call rates and the cheapest data consumption rates in the world through pre-pay micro subscriptions, possibly the most complex in the world.[43] The mobile internet, now widely accessible, gave rise to new practices of articulating and being visible in new media productions that gave voice to different experiences of living in today's India.

About 17 per cent of the Indian population is between 15 and 24 years old; sometimes, members of this group are the first person in their family to hold any telephone in their hands. Youth and new media practices in India, having received little scholarly attention, are usually understood under one of the two representations: either as savvy techno-elites, or as poverty-stricken subjects in need of philanthropy to bridge the digital divide.[44] The new media practices of these young Indians are the focus of the section on SMSGupShup, the largest microblogging platform in India. But Indian youth is by no means a homogenous category: their various socio-economic segments greatly affect how they engage with new media technologies.

The rise of India's IT industry was facilitated by the government's deregulation of the telecom industry from the mid-1990s. Mobile phones arrived in India in 1995: by 2012 for a population of 1.22 billion, there were more than 900 million mobile phone subscriptions. The teledensity is almost 80 per cent in any given coverage area, four to seven companies provide mobile phone services and dozens of tariff plans and pre-paid cards are available and affordable across socio-economic segments.[45] While the personal computer market is not a particularly dynamic one in India, mobile phones and the mobile internet are available to increasingly larger parts of the Indian population revolutionizing the availability and access to entertainment content, which is the main driver for the adoption of the mobile internet among the BOP[46] consumer segment.

The growth of the mobile telecommunications industry in India from 1990 to 2005 represents a particularly useful demonstration of the co-evolution of organizational strategies, technologies and regulations.[47] According to these authors, the telecom industry evolution was marked by three critical periods which they call "phases of evolution": 1990 to 1997, 1997 to 2002 and 2002 to 2005. The first phase was triggered by the introduction of mobile technology and entry of privately owned organizations. The second phase was governed by conflict of interest among the government, the policy maker and the service provider characterized by the establishment of an independent regulator that introduced tariff regulations and also resolved disputes among service providers. The third phase resulted in regulatory changes to accommodate technologies in the Universal Access Licensing System. The intense interplay among the three elements produced greater stability in the overall telecom policy and service climate. Samarajiva[48] has explained this phenomenon, from a supply-side angle, as a "budget telecom model" where service providers under hostile external conditions, low purchasing power and pressure from disruptive competitors have implemented innovative processes—technical, marketing, acquisition and customer service—to exploit long-tail markets.

These policy and market transformations have brought about revolutionary adoption patterns at the lowest level of consumption. There will be more and more people at these levels emerging in India and joining the information society by adopting Web 2.0 services, not necessarily because they see "developmental" benefits in them but more to be in touch with friends and family, occupy their leisure time with Bollywood trailers, and join Facebook to expand global community networks.[49] Given that the mobile phone is rapidly becoming the most-wanted device, how is this technology mediating user experiences among the bottom of the consumer pyramid in India? Scholarship around the use of Web 2.0 technologies in emerging and low-income segments of India is especially needed, not only to describe the interplay of policy and economic strategies, but also the phenomenon of high socio-cultural valency.

Arguably, and among other things, the mobile phone has been characterized as a masculine cultural technology.[50] Such a description speaks to the social divides existing in India in adopting new media and demands a more fine-grained understanding of how gender plays out in the IT soaked environment of urban India. Caste-based communities on social media (especially Orkut), ordered along the spectrum of caste hierarchies with Brahmin and Dalit communities at either end, also reflect the offline divisions in Indian society and highlight the varying access to technological and other resources resulting from them.[51] These findings seem to suggest a fairly uncomplicated correspondence of class and caste biases in the real and virtual societies and that social inequalities can be further exacerbated through the medium of the internet. But in our opinion claims such as these do not necessarily contribute to a nuanced understanding of market innovations and the participation of hitherto under-represented groups in the world of Web 2.0. The same holds true for political divisions, especially the BJP political party and the Hindu Nationalist movement, who deploy the internet to promote their political interests.[52] During the 2009 national election, called India's "first digital election,"[53] blogs, social networking communities and Twitter were actively deployed to reach young, urban, technology-savvy first-time voters. On the other hand, Dalits and other low castes are also using the internet as a means of organizing communities.[54] In the first "mass mobile phone election" in 2007 in Uttar Pradesh, mobile phones became a mass device and created conditions to elect a Dalit-based party and with a Dalit woman as Chief Minister. The mobile phone was compared to a "box of matches" that can ignite nascent political trends, rather than a "magic wand" performing miracles on the political stage.[55] It is unclear how much sway social media platforms will have as a stage for political combat or the power to swing socio-political currents in the IT-empowered India. But there is no denying that the ICT revolution will have a huge bearing on electoral politics in the largest democracy in the world.

If politics in the Indian youth context is still a work in progress, the use of new media technologies has gained momentum in the social networking terrain. Dovetailing traditional and modern forms of social networking, in which dating and marriage sites dominate, sites like shaadi.com have skilfully aligned traditional cultures of arranged marriage to online cultures of searching and browsing for marital partners. The phenomenal success of the site suggests the penetration and deepening of internet technologies in specific ways to specific cultural contexts in India.

Case Studies

Weibo: The Potential and the Risk of Social Networks

We now turn to the case studies. *Weibo*, or microblogs, have now become so popular in China that they are often regarded as a discrete medium of their own. All the *weibo* services in China are at root derived from the English-language service Twitter, which was founded in the mid-2000s, essentially as a means for individuals to provide brief updates to a list of followers on what they were doing at a particular moment. The length of Twitter and Weibo posts, 140 characters, is roughly derived from the maximum length of an SMS message, whereas the idea of broadcasting to a series of followers is closer to more elaborate social networking services like Facebook. The *weibo* medium, therefore, functions as an intermediate stage between short-length messaging services such as SMS and QQ and sophisticated social networking services that combine various forms of media.

Chinese *weibo* services, the most popular of which are Sina Weibo, operated by the Sina Corporation, and Tencent Weibo, operated by Tencent Holdings, attracted more users in China in 2013 than Twitter did worldwide.[56] Most of these *weibo* users were of course individuals, but the most popular users fell into several categories: celebrities (actors, sportspeople, well-known bloggers); media outlets (newspapers, television channels and so on); corporate representatives (of brands); sources of general entertainment (jokes, horoscopes, cartoons and cute pictures); and, increasingly, representatives of government, in particular local government.[57] These *weibo* services could be used on a computer or smartphone, with limited SMS integration. The *weibo* services were particularly useful case studies for our purposes, as they demonstrate many of the defining characteristics of Chinese social media, illustrating the tensions between interpersonal networking and social mobilization, and between state control and individual expression.

The *weibo* services used in China in 2013 were the result of a wave of censorship which took place in 2009. Twitter had become increasingly popular in China, particularly because it gave its users easy access to uncensored news and political comment: for example, through the CNN and *New York Times*, and through the Twitter feeds of famous activists like Ai Weiwei.[58] After a purge of all existing microblog services in 2009, involving the censorship of Twitter and various other Chinese-language microblogs,[59] Sina Weibo, and later Tencent Weibo became the chief microblogs available to the Chinese public.

As compared to microblogs worldwide, *weibo* in China are biased towards entertainment and consumption, a tendency presumably engineered by the state. For example, first-time users of Sina Weibo are forced to follow particular sets of popular accounts, which include sports, celebrities, cars, food and so on; even in the "media" set, most of the accounts are based around entertainment (fashion, cooking and celebrity) rather than political news. The design of *weibo* sites is relatively more complicated than Twitter, and also emphasizes entertainment; it incorporates pictures and videos into the flow of posts and incorporates features of gaming.[60]

However, the speed and ease of access of microblogs, combined with their very large user base, have made them difficult to censor. *Weibo* "events"—explosions of posts and reposts stimulated by a particular public occurrence—are now extremely common. The first of these microblog explosions that came to the public eye concerned accidents and crises, such as the 2011 train crash in Wenzhou;[61] however, *weibo* responses to news have become so widespread and so frequent over the past two years that it is difficult to distinguish one "event" from another. Complaints on *weibo* are gradually moving from criticism of the state or other bodies for their mishandling of particular current events, such as crises and natural disasters, to conceptual criticism of the state, for instance by restricting freedom of speech.[62]

Even though it is curtailed by the state, the discursive potential of *weibo* is enhanced by technical and cultural factors. The strategies of social networking are crucial to the rapid spread of information on microblogs: first, the networks formed by microblog users tend to mix interpersonal networks (with friends and acquaintances, in the style of QQ or WeChat) and networks which connect local individuals with sources of authority (the media and celebrities)—thus bridging the gap in social networking and transcending the state's preference for interpersonal internet communication. Second, on microblogs the mix of serious and entertaining, and personal and public, creates incentives for users: both to use the service frequently, to see what people are doing and to pass on messages of interest to themselves, both to communicate ideas to their followers and to reiterate that they are on the service. Personal and conceptual incentives thus combine to send pieces of information around China with great speed and vigour.

Furthermore, as compared to non-character-based languages, one can say more in a single Chinese *weibo* post than in an English Twitter post, even though both are restricted to 140 characters. As Chinese characters convey more information than English letters, while taking up the same amount of "space" in Twitter's character count, roughly four times more content can be conveyed per post.[63] This allows for discussions and contributions from various contributors to be nested in a single post, and for short essays to be written.[64] Hence, although many *weibo* "events" consist of the constant reposting of various individual short posts, it is possible for relatively elaborate debate to take place. In an attempt to stifle discussion of matters where the state might be criticized, *weibo* administrators censor posts and search results which contain words deemed to be "sensitive", but in response to this, internet users have manipulated language to create new terms, both as a means of censorship and as a way of asserting their identity as a community and their autonomy from the state.[65]

The Chinese Party-state is now in a curious position with respect to microblogs. Despite the broad scope of the network, the state's capacity is such that it can censor *weibo* services at will and even shut them down. It is strengthening its role as internet gatekeeper by gradually enforcing the use of real names by *weibo* users.[66] Since 2010 at least, it has used microblog posts as a basis for detaining citizens who criticise the government.[67] But, at the same time, the size and scale of the *weibo* network makes censorship challenging, and the level of integration of microblogs into citizens' lives means that the power of the state may be at risk if people's social "air" or "water" is compromised or taken away. Furthermore, since—apart from its aesthetic manipulation of the medium—the state's control strategies are transparent to users, excessive state control of *weibo* risks inflaming users rather than controlling risks. Since a considerable proportion of the population uses *weibo* services, management of the *weibo* system, which the state has always closely monitored, presents China with a substantial new challenge. From the state's point of view, one mitigating factor is that *weibo* are becoming gradually less engaging to users; from 2013 onwards, reports have suggested that—while *weibo* are still extremely popular— fewer users are signing up to weibo or actively using them.[68] A corollary of this, however, is that users are increasingly opting to use intra-personal networks like WeChat. When coupled with our discussion of SMSGupShup in India, this may in fact suggest an increased level of online convergence between China and India, albeit achieved through very different pathways.

The Rise of SMSGupShup in India

The way India has consumed entertainment material has changed over the years. Nationalized television channels, once the only source for video content, have been replaced by cable networks, on-demand channels, mobile content, and malls and multiplexes, among other avenues. Slowly and steadily, not just at the apex of the consumer pyramid, but also at the bottom of it, a significant proportion of youth in low income and slum communities in the metropolitan cities of India are turning to the mobile internet, cashing in on some of the lowest mobile data tariffs in the world.[69] It is in this context of market and servicing innovations that we locate one of the world's largest mobile micro-message phenomena, which demonstrates unique characteristics specific to an emerging social media user market.

SMSGupShup ("gupshup" is Hindi for "chitchat") is a predominantly user-driven SMS-centric social networking technology, functioning as the only low-cost, ubiquitous and informal broadcasting channel in the emerging markets for social media in India. With nearly a billion mobile phones, India has birthed a market replete with deals, plans and services from multiple mobile network operators. Talk time and mobile internet can be had for less than 1 cent per SMS and a day's worth of internet. Plunging subscription charges, dual SIM cards and a plethora of micro pre-pay recharge offers are services available from the mobile service provider markets and mobile stores everywhere in urban India.

Friendship, instant connection and sharing via an affordable *one click* SMS channel and competitive pricing are ostensibly why users flocked to SMSGupShup. Amidst these varied uses and aims, however, the platform was particularly notable as a hot bed of non-elite and resource-constrained young men who use this low-cost platform to connect with broader geographies. Pioneering new techniques for information exchanges, leisure behaviours and skill transfer in a developing market, GupShup gave rise to new mobile communication practices and enhanced computer literacy among users. However, possibly due to the specific demographic of users, GupShup was viewed as a "resource" for the creation of economic benefits. Users employed innovative ways to enlist, connect and promote behaviours leading to the formation of a large mobile community for specific personal and economic benefits. This, in turn, drove many of the behaviours we describe in this chapter.

Close on the heels of the global launch of Twitter in July 2006, SMSGupShup began as a group text-messaging service provider and racked up 15 million users within just a year of inception. The initial agenda was to develop an offline web browser for laptops and mobile devices. The company soon realized that social media, as they existed in developed markets, are basically an internet and web-centric phenomenon; but in India and other emerging markets, they are predominantly mobile-centric. The company quickly developed the idea of providing a complete social networking experience on mobile phones with little need to connect seamlessly to the internet. Hence, GupShup began as a free, social, short messaging service that allowed users to communicate and connect with family, friends and followers using ordinary mobile handsets.

The product, launched in April 2007, was an immediate hit. But the company had to pay operators for every message sent through their platform, a substantial amount given 300–400 million messages per month. Though GupShup had millions of users, it did not make profits, and needed quickly to build an advertising base, guaranteeing clients not just branding but an effective profit-making strategy. The next few years saw GupShup position its platform as a product that offered client companies opportunities to gauge and measure product impact as opposed to simple product branding. In 2012, GupShup had supposedly enlisted nearly 60 million users in India and served the marketing needs of over 500 large brands and 25,000 small businesses. The company had 200 employees and aimed to continue growing a social community and innovating on platform applications that would target more upwardly mobile smartphone users but still work well for all mobile users and phones.

Motivations and Reasons for Indian Citizens to Use Social Media

Gupshup is described as a "social messaging service to share and connect with friends and fans," allowing users to create, manage and broadcast messages to mobile communities or groups. It soon expanded its business to include a range of services such as "mobile marketing solutions to help businesses acquire and engage customers." Unlike Twitter or Weibo, GupShup evolved specific social networking services and uses in India. The platform adopted a twin approach, combining personal and business social-networking by offering both the free group messaging service (in the style of WeChat) and several paid business networking services, which are peculiar to GupShup. We will emphasize and delineate two of its main features: (a) the entwined and informal nature of social and business networking of users on the platform's free services; and (b) the lack of conversations among mobile communities and the "borrowed" nature of content in messages/posts from secondary sources.

In order to set up a free SMS group, a person only needed an email address or a mobile number. Such groups could be private or public and one user could create up to five. The owners of free groups could invite up to 25 users beyond which membership increased when people "opt-in" and sent a "Join Group Name" message to the group owner. Most importantly, group owners could send messages no longer than 140 characters. By contrast, the users of the enterprise edition, a paid service offered by GupShup, could send messages with up to 700 characters or use Flash. Most subscribers to this plan were businessmen and entrepreneurs interested in advertising their products or building a new consumer base. This aspect of the service did not really take off for two reasons: first, from the company's perspective, there was still reservation about the impact of branding products on a low-cost SMS channel; and second, as our research demonstrates, there was overwhelming evidence that users gained monetarily from the free social messaging service by virtue of owning a large group membership.

As a social media platform, GupShup had an all-India character, catalyzing social and geographic reach for nascent mobile communities. These included towns and villages having little else other than a mobile phone for communicating over long distances. GupShup was the only platform enabling users to post from a basic mobile phone to a group consisting of hundreds of thousands of people for the price of a single SMS.

Analyzing GupShup

The analysis of the 79 most-joined groups on the GupShup website in April 2010 allowed us to categorize the nature and content of messaging: posts, replies and re-posts. We mined group pages to identify the behaviours of forwarding a reply with something akin to "retweeting." Groups are defined by the kinds of messages they choose to post and broadly fall into three categories: fun, news and tricks. There are other distinctions one could make (the GupShup website mentions 20 group categories), but these three most popular and prominent categories mentioned above capture some of the most interesting behaviours. The "fun" category includes popular Hindustani romantic poetry, recycled jokes or inspirational quotes for the day; the "news" category consisted of breaking and headline news (political/sports); and the "tricks" category offered tips and advice on how to use internet and mobile technologies. Some of the largest groups on GupShup, with membership numbers greater than 100,000, post a combination of such messages. In our analysis of the 79 most-joined groups, 49 (62 per cent) belonged to the category of "fun". A group named "Sartaj" had a base of over 200,000 members, one of the largest groups on GupShup, with a majority of posts consisting of jokes, inspirational quotations and poetry (some of them in Hindi transliterated into English), and almost all of the content drawn from secondary sources with unclear copyright status. Almost all the groups in the "fun" category broadcast popular jokes, poetry and quotes taken from the internet, or borrowed from oral popular culture and "two-penny" pamphlets or used material taken from posts of other GupShup groups. Thus, "fun" messages were broadcast to an audience that consumed but did not reply. The news groups are equally large and consisted of 16 (20 percent) out of the 79 most-joined groups. Groups provide news that can be national breaking news in English or regional news in English transliterations of Indian regional languages.[70]

A group named "Vignesh" began under the category "education and campus news" and gathered a membership of over 90,000, mostly across northern India. It broadcasts education and employment news alerts. Group Vignesh had specific content to share; such content was easy to procure, usually from local newspapers and word of mouth from a network of teachers, college students and government employees. The "tricks" category belongs to a set of groups that specialize in posting tricks or hacking tips either to increase talk time on a mobile phone or access free mobile internet by inputting various codes via the keypad. Content for this group was usually found by mining the internet and by scavenging posts from other "tricks" groups on GupShup. These tricks reportedly had intermittent success rates but by and large enjoyed the faith of broadcasters and their followers. Apart from hacking tips, the groups also posted basic skills to operate windows, shortcut keys and a range of useful information about websites. We see a growing trend in this category on GupShup.

The GupShup Demographic

Though we base our research hypotheses on a small sample, the results point to broader trends about GupShup user profiles. We note that users circulate information on the GupShup platform through multiple channels like the web and the mobile phone. A majority of GupShup users are male, under 30, college students or teenagers, and spread across not only metropolitan areas but also small towns and villages in India. Most subjects depend financially on their parents and are cautious about expending internet and talk time. While effectively using platform features for social networking, they take care to their keep user expenses as low as possible. These concerns of users drive a set of practices that are keen to exploit the commercial potential of the GupShup platform.

Much information sharing happened through the SMS channel and most followers or members of the group accessed messages and experience the platform solely through the SMS medium. The latter was mainly driven by affordable pricing of receiving and accessing messages on the mobile phone as opposed to the internet. Equally important was the lack of internet or PC infrastructure in the localities and residences of users. The SMS was the predominant broadcasting channel for a group owner to reach an optimum number of members. It was also the primary channel to advertise and grow one's GupShup group. The overwhelming presence of requests to promote one's group on GupShup was the reciprocal behaviour by two or more groups to advertise their respective groups. One of our participants had joined 500 groups in a bid to grow his own by requesting all 500 group owners to advertise his group! Likewise, group owners, through their broadcasting privileges, were mindful of their influence over a large mobile group of members.

Networking on GupShup

A group's popularity and membership strength is nurtured through two key behaviours, namely the types of posts or content the owner chooses to broadcast to his group and the strategies adopted by the owner to promote and expand group membership. GupShup is not only for "egocentric" users, who are active broadcasters of messages (posts), but also for individuals who consume but never post messages. The latter are members of the groups on GupShup and never form or own a group of their own and are never allowed by the platform to publish or broadcast posts. Active publishers are group owners posting 1 to 12 messages per day depending on the number of groups they own. Much of this falls into two main categories: first, posts related to the main content of the group. The most popular formats are short poetry, jokes, inspirational messages and a variety of regional and national news, borrowed from secondary unattributed sources. The second category of posts are replies to groups that are mainly promotional messages inviting them to join one's own group (only a small number of replies are conversational, informational or a response to a specific post from another group owner or member).

The stand-out features of the platforms are:

(i) the unabashed promotion of one's own group;
(ii) the covert advertisements for products and services that GupShup explicitly bans from free messaging services;
(iii) the dominance of borrowed or secondary content in the posts; and consequentially and
(iv) the lack of conversational dialogue between owners and their audience.

Group owners do not initiate dialogue among and between members of the group's network. Rather they perform the function of keeping their audience engaged and entertained. This also links with the premise that GupShup behaviours are optimized to populate a network with people (not friends) and to engage the network with jokes, news or tricks to ensure and retain membership.

Networking on GupShup commonly takes the form of following a number of groups and inviting group owners to follow one's own group. The more activity there is (e.g., more messages and reply posts per day), the more it helps to maintain and attract members to a group. The flurry of reciprocal behaviour activity—"please join my group and I will join yours"—seems to be a default expansion strategy. This behaviour attains viral proportions with new groups employing similar strategies to expand their numbers. The reply function on the platform is another route to expand GupShup groups. Groups of all sizes receive a flood of replies from smaller groups to promote their specific groups. Indeed, it appeared that group owners on GupShup joined many groups explicitly to promote and advertise their own group.

Owners of large groups spend a good part of their time (4 to 8 hours a week) searching for appropriate content and circulating information. This happens in two ways: on the internet and by GupShup users scanning posts in other groups. Group owners actively browsing the internet are able to circulate that many more tips and tricks through the platform impelling a second tier of circulation through SMS of the same messages among the mobile-centric platform users. As Abhishek, a group owner with more than 10,000 followers said: "I browse and fetch content from the big world of the internet … I also feel much of my audience do not have this kind of access and benefit a lot … I get a lot of responses on my phone from followers … Maybe this motivates me more than anything else." Large group owners can "sell" their group to other group owners who are desperate to grow their groups.

The Future of GupShup

We have seen that Indians took enthusiastically to GupShup, with millions joining every month. While this study begins to explore how they were using it, several questions remain. For instance, this inquiry focussed on group owners who publish regularly and struggle to increase their audience. But what of the vast majority of users who are passive consumers of content? What motivates them to join groups and how are they consumed? Another important question: Are the behaviours we observe due to the particular architecture of posting on SMS GupShup (e.g., the asymmetrical relationship between posts and replies)? Is it due to the dominance of SMS as the interaction medium? Or are we seeing something uniquely related to the culture of middle-class India? Clearly a great deal of research remains as usage evolves on GupShup. Although it is often called India's answer to Twitter, SMS GupShup is unique in many ways. Indeed, GupShup may require us to broaden our view of how we think about social networking services. Rather than connecting friends or building community, GupShup mainly acts as an informal medium for publishers to build an audience. "Friends" in GupShup are not really friends in any conventional sense, but are akin to members/associates on the list of a group owner. While group owners are captivated by the idea of transcending geography and connecting with people all over India, the primary motivation is not conversation or building common interests, but rather the potential for commercial gain associated with a large audience. This, in turn, drives many of the unique behaviours we describe in this paper.

SMS GupShup represents a fascinating hybrid of communication technologies firmly anchored to SMS, a low cost and ubiquitous channel in the developing world. As mobile internet technologies move beyond urban areas and the upper class which can afford them, it will be fascinating to see how the use of GupShup transforms. Will it remain an informal broadcast channel or will millions of Indians "join the conversation"?

Conclusion

The case studies we consider in this chapter suggest that localized social media reflect the organization of societies and economies in China and India more than they do the cultures or languages of these countries. In India, the predominantly "grey" economy has led to a "grey" form of social media, where SMSGupShup has been overwhelmingly appropriated by an emerging down market, eager for geographic reach and political freedom. In China, however, the state's higher level of control, both over the economy and over the media, has led to a situation where social media, despite being very popular, have closer links with the corporate and the state sphere. The advent of WeChat in China demonstrates that there is an inherent market for SoLoMo services in both countries, but the enormous flexibility of use of SMSGupShup compared to Weibo suggests that one key motivation for innovation in social media is the desire for financial and social gain.

While both cases illustrate the potential for social media to spread throughout diverse social spheres, they also demonstrate the limits of this potential. India, for example requires a microblogging service that can cross-over consumer segments without compromising freedom of expression or dismantling the pay-as-you-go model; unless there is vertical integration of richer platform affordability and functionality, GupShup will eventually plateau out. In China, state intervention – from the apparatus of censorship to the state's influence on the design of social media—restricts the potential for social media to provide a substantial new communicative facility.

To return to the big questions we posed at the beginning of this chapter, it is true to suggest that India's social media interact with

India's key priority of economic development, just as China's social media are influencing, and being influenced by, the popular demand for political change. However, social media in and of themselves are not enough to make any substantial difference in these areas. Their role is negotiative: it influences public discourse and governance, often subtly and indirectly, at the same time as it is constrained by those very factors.

Notes

1. Nimmi Rangaswamy and Edward Cutrell, "Re-Sourceful Networks: Notes from a Mobile Social Networking Platform in India," *Pacific Affairs*, 85 (2012): 587–606.

2. David Kurt Herold, "Noise, Spectacle, Politics: Carnival in Chinese Cyberspace," In David Kurt Herold and Peter Marolt ed., *Online Society in China: Creating, Celebrating and Instrumentalising the Online Carnival* (Oxford, UK: Routledge, 2011), pp. 1–21.

3. Carolyn Cartier, Manuel Castells and Jack Linchuan Qiu, "The Information Have-Less: Inequality, Mobility, and Translocal Networks in Chinese Cities," *Studies in Comparative International Development*, 40 (2005): 9–34.

4. Jack Linchuan Qiu. "The Internet in China: Data and Issues" (12 January 2013), p. 1. http://www.usc.edu/schools/annenberg/events/normanlearcenter/icbak/Papers/JQ_China_and_Internet.pdf.

5. Zixiang Tan, William Foster and Seymour Goodman, "China's State-coordinated Internet Infrastructure," *Communications of the ACM*, 42 (1999): 44–52.

6. China Internet Network Information Center (CNNIC). *The 29th Statistical Report on Internet Development in China*. China Internet Network Information Center, 2013, p. 4. http://www1.cnnic.cn/IDR/ReportDownloads/201209/P020120904421720687608.pdf.

7. CNNIC, 2013, pp. 18, 24.

8. Fengshu Liu, "Wired for Fun: Narratives by Members of China's E-generation," *Young*, 19 (2011): 69–89; Yongchi Liang, Shaonan Li, Wenhui Luo, Dengyu Xiong and Tingjun Wu. *Hulianwang Zai Zhongguo Shehui Zhi Jueqi: Si Da Chengshi de Bijiao Yanjiu* (Hong Kong: Hong Kong Institute of Asia-Pacific Studies, Chinese University of Hong Kong, 2009); Liang Guo, *Surveying Internet Usage and Its Impact in Seven Chinese Cities* (Beijing: Center for Social Development, Chinese Academy of Social Sciences, 2007).

9. CNNIC, 2013, p. 33.

10. Min Pu, Hui Ling and Chaoyang Yu, "Guoneiwai BBS Luntan Fazhan Ji Guanli Bijiao Yanjiu," *Sixiang Lilun Jiaoyu Daokan (Journal of Ideological*

and *Theoretical Education*), 68–72, 2007; Jack Linchuan Qiu. *Working-Class Network Society: Communication Technology and the Information Have-Less in Urban China* (Cambridge, MA: The MIT Press, 2009).

11. Similar BBS systems, run through the Telnet protocol rather than the web, have remained extremely popular in Taiwan (as described by Huang, Daphne Li-jun. "Language Use in Asynchronous Computer-mediated Communication in Taiwan." *Australian Review of Applied Linguistics*, 32 (2009): 12.1–12.22.

12. CNNIC. *Zhongguo Hulian Wangluo Nianjian*. Beijing: China Internet Network Information Center, 2002.

13. Yong Cao and John D.H. Downing, "The Realities of Virtual Play: Video Games and Their Industry in China." *Media, Culture & Society*, 30 (2008): 515–529.

14. Anne E. McLaren, "Online Intimacy in a Chinese Setting," *Asian Studies Review*, 31 (2007): 409–422.

15. Liu, Fengshu, *Urban Youth in China: Modernity, the Internet, and the Self* (London and New York: Routledge, 2010).

16. Liu, *Urban Youth*, 2010, p. 49.

17. Louise Edwards and Elaine Jeffreys, *Celebrity in China* (Hong Kong: Hong Kong University Press, 2010).

18. Yongming Zhou. "Living on the Cyber Border: Minjian Political Writers in Chinese Cyberspace." *Current Anthropology* 46 (2005): 779–803.

19. Cartier et al., "The Information," 2005.

20. Cara Wallis, *Technomobility in China: Young Migrant Women and Mobile Phones* (New York: NYU Press, 2013).

21. Elisa Oreglia, "5 Facts, 3 Lessons, and 2 Rules," 2012.

22. Wallis, 2013, pp. 7–8.

23. Larissa Hjorth and Michael Arnold, "Home and Away: A Case Study of Students and Social Media in Shanghai," In *New Connectivities in China: Virtual, Actual and Local Interactions*, edited by Pui-lam Law (Heidelberg, London, New York: Springer, 2012), 171–184.

24. Hjorth and Arnold, 2012, pp. 180–181.

25. Haomin Gong and Xin Yang, "Digitized Parody: The Politics of Egao in Contemporary China." *China Information*, 24 (2010): 3–26.

26. Wallis, 2013, p. 5.

27. Xixian Peng, Zhao Yuxiang and Zhu Qinghua, "Understanding Post Adoption Switching Behavior For Mobile Instant Messaging Application In China: Based On Migration Theory," (2014). *PACIS 2014 Proceedings*. http://aisel.aisnet.org/pacis2014/239; Negro, Gianluigi. "Dal Web 2.0 al SOLOMO (da Sina Weibo a Weixin)." In Paolo Paderni ed., *Atti del XIV Convegno: Procida, 19–21 Settembre 2013* (Napoli: Il Torcoliere, 2014).

28. Jonathan Benney, "How to Avoid the Centre: The Strategies of a Small Feminist Workshop in Rural China," *International Journal of China Studies*, 3 (2012): 383–410; Day Wong. "Hybridization and the Emergence of 'Gay' Identities in Hong Kong and in China." *Visual Anthropology* 24 (2010): 152–170.

29. Gary King, Jennifer Pan and Margaret E. Roberts, "How Censorship in China Allows Government Criticism but Silences Collective Expression," *American Political Science Review,* 1–18, May 2013.
30. Jedidiah R. Crandall, Masashi Crete-Nishihata, Jeffrey Knockel, Sarah McKune, Adam Senft, Diana Tseng and Greg Wiseman, "Chat Program Censorship and Surveillance in China: Tracking TOM-Skype and Sina UC," *First Monday,* 18, no. 7 (2013), http://firstmonday.org/ojs/index.php/fm/issue/view/397
31. Thomas Chase, "Problems of Publicity: Online Activism and Discussion of Same-Sex Sexuality in South Korea and China," *Asian Studies Review,* 36 (2012): 151–170.
32. Josh Chin and Loretta Chao, "Beijing Communist Party Chief Issues Veiled Warning to Chinese Web Portal," *Wall Street Journal,* 2 November 2012, http://online.wsj.com/article/SB10001424053111904279004576526293276595886.html; Scott Kennedy, "The Stone Group: State Client or Market Pathbreaker?" *The China Quarterly,* 152 (1997): 746–777; Xin Hu, "The Surfer-in-Chief and the Would-be Kings of Content: A Short Study of Sina.com and Netease.com," In Stephanie Hemelryk Donald, Michael Keane and Hong Yin eds, *Media in China: Consumption, Content and Crisis* (London: RoutledgeCurzon, 2002), pp. 192–199.
33. Jonathan Benney, "The Aesthetics of Chinese Microblogging: State and Market Control of Weibo." *Asiascape: Digital Asia* 1, no. 3 (2014): 169–200.
34. Yang, Guobin. *The Power of the Internet in China: Citizen Activism Online.* New York, NY: Columbia University Press, 2009.
35. Lijun Tang and Peidong Yang, "Symbolic Power and the Internet: The Power of a 'Horse'." *Media, Culture and Society,* 33 (2011): 675–691.
36. Yuntao Zhang and John Tomlinson, "Three Constituencies of Online Dissent in China," *Chinese Journal of Communication,* 5 (2012): 55–60.
37. T. T. Sreekumar, *ICTs and Development in India: Perspectives on the Rural Network Society* (London and New York: Anthem Press, 2011).
38. Jinqiu Zhao, "ICTD: Internet Adoption and Usage Amongst Rural Users in China," In *New Connectivities in China: Virtual, Actual and Local Interactions,* edited by Pui-lam Law, (Heidelberg, London, New York: Springer, 2012), pp. 215–227.
39. Qiu, 2009.
40. Jack Linchuan Qiu, "Mobile Phones, the Bottom of the Pyramid and Working-class Information Society in China," *The Electronic Journal on Information Systems in Developing Countries,* 44 (2010): 1–14.
41. Jonathan Hassid, "Safety Valve or Pressure Cooker? Blogs in Chinese Political Life," *Journal of Communication,* 62 (2012): 212–230.
42. Assa Doron and Robin Jeffrey, *The Great Indian Phone Book: How the Cheap Cell Phone Changes Business, Politics, and Daily Life* (Cambridge, MA: Harvard University Press, 2013).
43. Doron and Jeffrey, 2013, p. 7.

44. Rangaswamy and Cutrell, 2013, "Anthropology, Development and ICTs: Slums, Youth and the Mobile Internet in Urban India," Special Issue, Reflections at the Nexus of Theory and Practice, *Information Technology and International Development* 9(2): 2012, 51–63.

45. Doron and Jeffrey, 2013.

46. Prahalad, C. K. *The Fortune at the Bottom of the Pyramid.* Philadelphia, PA: Wharton School Publishing, 2004, argued that multinational companies not only can make money selling to the world's poorest, but also that such efforts are necessary to close the growing gap between rich and poor countries. Key to his argument for targeting the world's poorest is the sheer size of that market: an estimated four billion people. Prahalad's book demonstrates a fundamental shift in the behaviour of companies towards what we now call emerging markets.

47. Sharma and Ojha, 2011.

48. Rohan Samarajiva, "Leveraging the Budget Telecom Network Business Model to Bring Broadband to the People," *Information Technologies & International Development*, 6, no. SE (2010): 93–97.

49. Nimmi Rangaswamy and Payal Arora, "The Mobile Internet in the Wild and Every Day: Digital Leisure in the Slums of Urban India," *International Journal of Cultural Studies*, pp. 1–16 (online prepublication, 1 April 2015), http://ics.sagepub.com/content/early/2015/03/31/1367877915576538. abstract).

50. Anandam Kavoori and Kalyani Chadha, "The Cell Phone as a Cultural Technology: Lessons from the Indian Case," In Anandam Kavoori and Noah Arceneaux eds, *The Cell Phone Reader: Essays in Social Transformation* (New York, Bern, Berlin, Bruxelles, Frankfurt am Main, Oxford, Wien: Peter Lang Publishing, 2006).

51. Gaurav Mishra, "Caste-Based Communities on Orkut Mirror India's Splintered Society," *Gauravonomics*, 9 June 2009, available at: http://global-voicesonline.org/2009/06/09/caste-based-communities-on-orkut/

52. Rohit Chopra, *Technology and Nationalism in India: Cultural Negotiations from Colonialism to Cyberspace* (Amherst, NY: Cambria Press, 2008).

53. Robin Jeffrey and Assa Doron, "Mobile-izing: Democracy, Organization and India's First 'Mass Mobile Phone' Elections," *Journal of Asian Studies*, 71, no. 1 (2012): 63–80.

54. P. Thirumal, "Situating the New Media: Reformulating the Dalit Question," In *South Asian Technospaces*, edited by Radhika Gajjala and Venkataramana Gajjala, 36: 97–122. Digital Formations. New York, Bern, Berlin, Bruxelles, Frankfurt am Main, Oxford, Wien: Peter Lang Publishing, 2008; Rohit Chopra, "Global Primordialities: Virtual Identity Politics in Online Hindutva and Online Dalit Discourse," *New Media and Society* 8, no. 2 (2006): 187–206.

55. Jeffrey and Doron, 2012.

56. In late 2012, Twitter claims over 500 million registered users (O'Carroll, Lisa. "Twitter Active Users Pass 200 Million." *The Guardian*, 2012), while

Sina Weibo claims over 400 million (Ong, 2012). Collectively, in 2011, the Sina and Tencent Weibo services claimed over 550 million (Russell, 2011).

57. It has recently been claimed that an examination for candidates for work in a county government in Zhejiang province required the candidates to write microblog-length posts promoting particular initiatives (Yu, Jincui. "Weibo Skills Essential for Officials to Interact with Public." *Global Times,* 1 November 2012. http://www.globaltimes.cn/content/723345.shtml).

58. Louis Yu, Sitaram Asur and Bernardo A. Huberman, "What Trends in Chinese Social Media," *Association for Computing Machinery,* 2011, http://arxiv.org/pdf/1107.3522.pdf.

59. Steven Millward, "Sina's Twitter-esque Microblogging Site: A Closer Look," (31 October 2012), http://asia.cnet.com/blogs/sinas-twitter-esque-micro-blogging-site-a-closer-look-62115894.htm.

60. Benney, 2014.

61. Jiuchang Wei, Bing Bu and Liang Liang, "Estimating the Diffusion Models of Crisis Information in Micro Blog," *Journal of Informetrics,* 6 (2012): 600–610.

62. Edward Wong, "In China, Widening Discontent Among the Communist Party Faithful," *New York Times,* 19 January 2013, available at: http://www.nytimes.com/2013/01/20/world/asia/in-china-discontent-among-the-normally-faithful.html

63. The modern social network, in which languages using many different scripts, be they Roman, Cyrillic, Chinese, South Asian or others, can co-exist owes its existence to the general adoption of a Unicode standard for encoding and displaying characters online (see Klensin, J. and M. Padlipsky. "Unicode Format for Network Interchange," 2008. https://www.ietf.org/rfc/rfc5198.txt). Rajesh Chandrakar, "Unicode as a Multilingual Standard with Reference to Indian Languages." *The Electronic Library* 22, no. 5 (2004): 422–424, discusses the benefits of this to the Indian Internet.

64. Jonathan Benney, "Twitter and Legal Activism in China." *Communication, Politics and Culture,* 44 (2011): 5–20.

65. Perry Link and Xiao Qiang, "From 'Fart People' to Citizens," *Journal of Democracy* 24 (2013): 79–85.

66. Johan Lagerkvist, "Principal-Agent Dilemma in China's Social Media Sector? The Party-State and Industry Real-Name Registration Waltz," *International Journal of Communication* 6 (2012): 2628–2646.

67. Aliyah Shahid, "Chinese Woman, Cheng Jianping, Sentenced to a Year in Labor Camp over Twitter Post," *Daily News,* 18 November 2010, http://www.nydailynews.com/news/world/chinese-woman-cheng-jianping-sentenced-year-labor-camp-twitter-post-article-1.454253

68. Patrick Boehler, "Is Anti-Rumour Crackdown Silencing Voices of Online Dissent at Weibo?" *South China Morning Post* (13 September 2013). http://www.scmp.com/news/china/article/1308860/anti-rumour-crackdown-silencing-voices-online-dissent-weibo (accessed on 24 May 2014).

69. Rangaswamy and Cutrell, 2012.
70. The use of language online presents different challenges for Indian users and Chinese users. Whereas people literate in Chinese, even speakers of various dialects, use basically the same set of characters, Indian languages involve many different phonetic scripts. Although the Unicode standard hypothetically allows all these scripts to be viewed simultaneously on the web or on smartphones, users of mobile phones with fewer features, both in India and China, must sometimes rely on transliteration into Roman characters; Prasenjit Majumder, Mandar Mitra, and Kalyan Datta. "Multilingual Information Access: An Indian Language Perspective." 22–27. Seattle, WA: ACM-SIGIR, 2006. http://research.microsoft.com/en-us/um/people/cyl/download/papers/mlia2006/book.pdf?q=proceedings-of-the-workshop-on-multilingual-language#page=32 (pp. 25–26) discuss some of the issues relating to South Asian languages online.

17

Shooting the Messengers

Simon Long

Simon Long is a messenger who studied Mandarin and has worked in the land of the Mughals as well as in China as a journalist. As a student, he was in Beijing when Mao died. In 10 years with the BBC, he had stints in both Beijing—from just before the killings in 1989—and Hong Kong. He joined *The Economist* in 1995, served in Delhi from 2002 to 2006, and in 2005 wrote a supplement comparing India and China. He writes a weekly column ("Banyan") that covers all of Asia.

This chapter will examine three common preconceptions about the role of the media in India–China relations:

(a) that the Chinese press acts as an arm of government policy;
(b) that the Indian media, in contrast, are uncontrolled, uncontrollable and guilty of a systemic anti-China bias and
(c) that third-country, Western, media play a pernicious role in perpetuating a narrative of Sino-Indian "rivalry" as opposed to "partnership."

It will challenge each preconception.

At a two-day workshop in Singapore in May 2012 organized by the Institute of South Asian Studies at the National University of Singapore, from which some of the chapters in this book sprang, there was a striking contrast in the descriptions Chinese and Indian journalists gave of their jobs. Chinese journalists said that, in writing about relations with India, they had a duty to help foster them. Indian journalists felt their role in bilateral relations was simply to report them.

In fact, taken as a whole, neither group is fulfilling its intended mission very successfully. Far from promoting smooth relations, the Chinese media are in fact often a source of views and reports that worsen Indian suspicions of China. And the Indian media are sometimes guilty of inaccuracy, alarmism and partiality. They fall short of the journalists' avowed aim of objective reporting and analysis.

The Chinese Media

Even if the Chinese government did want the press to devote its India coverage purely to the diplomatic task of improving bilateral relations, it would find it difficult. The Chinese press is no longer monolithic and does not offer a coherent or consistent interpretation of India or Sino-Indian relations. The "official line" is now hard to discern. In particular, the *Global Times*, a newspaper produced out of the Communist Party's *People's Daily* stable, takes a strongly nationalist and, hence, sometimes anti-Indian line—even when this seems at odds with the policy pursued by the Ministry of Foreign Affairs.

Take, for example, its coverage of India's launch in April 2012 of an Agni-V missile, with a range of over 5,000 km and, hence, capable of reaching Chinese cities. India, as is usual for countries that test missiles, insisted its purpose was "not country specific."[1] China's official reaction, in the form of a statement from a foreign-ministry spokesman, was exemplary in its imprecision:

> As major developing countries and emerging economies, China and India are cooperative partners rather than competitive rivals. The two sides should cherish the hard-won sound relations, join hands to adhere to China-India friendship, deepen strategic cooperation and promote common development, in a bid to contribute to peace and stability of the region and the world as a whole.[2]

Global Times, however, took the opportunity to lecture India on the dangers of joining an arms race with China, implicitly accusing it, in effect, of engaging in an American-concocted plot to contain it:

> India should not overestimate its strength. Even if it has missiles that could reach most parts of China that does not mean it will gain anything from

being arrogant during disputes with China. India should be clear that China's nuclear power is stronger and more reliable. For the foreseeable future, India would stand no chance in an overall arms race with China.

India should also not overstate the value of its Western allies and the profits it could gain from participating in a containment of China. If it equates long range strategic missiles with deterrence of China, and stirs up further hostility, it could be sorely mistaken. [3]

There are two ways of interpreting this. The first is that *Global Times* is performing a useful service for the government, expressing its real thinking in forceful terms that diplomatic norms forbid its officials from using themselves. The bland tenor of its diplomatic exchanges with India remains unaffected, yet the warning has been given. The second is that the *Global Times* writer is expressing his or the paper's own view. The difficulty is in knowing which of these two interpretations is right. Many in India would continue to take the former view—understandably believing that a party paper is expressing the party view. Yet there are times when *Global Times* (and other "official" newspapers) take positions which it would certainly not be in the government's interests to have taken as the "official line". It is a confusing way of communicating.

The confusion is compounded by the proliferation of online media. Here, at least, there is no doubt in one respect: these cannot be confused with "official" outlets. However, it is hard to dismiss "unofficial" views, especially those expressed in the blogosphere, as irrelevant. Cyberspace remains heavily policed in China. So, the dividing lines between "outrageous-but-tolerated," "officially sanctioned" and "official policy" are very blurred.

This has an impact on views of bilateral relations. A study of online opinion of India and Indians published in 2011 in the *China Quarterly*, an academic journal, by Simon found netizens "more nationalistic, xenophobic and chauvinistic" than official policy.[4] Yet the views expressed were self-evidently not so far out of line with government policy as to be worth censoring.

To take one example of the confusion this can sow: in 2009 a Chinese website, calling itself the official-sounding "China International Institute for Strategic Studies" posted an article arguing that "if China takes a little action, the so-called Great Indian Federation can be broken up into 30 pieces." The Indian press duly reported this as a threat,[5] emanating from an "authoritative" site. In fact the website has no official status whatsoever. It is certainly not China's policy to advocate the dismemberment of India.

The Indian Media

It is conventional to portray the Indian media as fiercely independent of the government. On China, however, one can argue that it in fact mirrors the Chinese media on India: taking a consistently harder line than the government itself does. In China, the media may, under official direction or with official connivance, perform a useful service for the government by appearing to reflect popular nationalism, and hence putting pressure on the government not to be "soft" on India. In India, the press provides exactly the same service, apparently without the direction or the connivance. Yet, that the press tends to take a harder, more suspicious line on bilateral relations than the government itself does leads to accusations that it is highlighting difficulties, ignoring good news and harming bilateral relations.

An especially embarrassing example was a television report on the Times Now rolling-news channel in April 2012.[6] To the backing of an insistent, threatening drumbeat, it set out a history of more than 50 years of "systematic" Chinese build-up on India's borders. It recalled how roads have been extended to India's "very door-step". Glaciers have been tampered with, affecting India's water supply. And now, in the latest "provocation," China was planning an astronomical observatory in the Aksai Chin, a remote area, neighbouring Indian Ladakh, and claimed by India. Japan and South Korea had been asked to help on the project. So, China was not just "muscle-flexing"; it was "internationalizing" its claim to disputed territory. The basis of the report was false.[7] If the observatory—the point of the story, slotted into this narrative of consistent Chinese malevolence—is built at all, it will not be in the Aksai Chin.

Such blunders are grist to the mill of the many Indian and Chinese officials, including a former Chinese prime minister, Wen Jiabao,[8] who have accused the Indian press of sensationalizing disputes and so worsening the perennial tensions in India–Chinese relations. One Indian newspaper, reporting Mr Wen's remarks (in 2010), defended the press by concluding its report: "where there is smoke there is fire,"[9] hardly a reasoned justification.

The press's critics point out that it is 50 years since China humiliated India in the 1962 war over their territorial disputes, including the Aksai Chin, and 25 years since they agreed to put the disputes "to one side" while they got on with other stuff. And get on they have. China is now India's biggest trading partner. And the two countries cooperate on a range of issues, such as climate change, both bilaterally and in forums such as the "BRICS," with Brazil, Russia and South Africa. Both governments insist they want good relations.

So it does not seem fanciful to accuse the Indian press of a systematic anti-China bias. This can be so subtle as to be almost imperceptible. In August 2010, for example, the Indian media made quite a fuss when an Indian general was refused a visa to China, apparently because of his work in Kashmir.[10] This was taken as evidence of a strengthening of Chinese support for Pakistan's side of that bitter dispute. Yet, at the time, some of the foreign media reported a simple tit-for-tat retaliation for India's unexplained refusal to allow a Chinese diplomat to fulfil a speaking engagement in a troubled north-eastern state, Manipur.[11] The Indian press mostly ignored this.

It is simplistic, however, to blame Indian journalists for an inherent bias. They are reporting what their sources tell them. Far too few Indian reporters are based in China (just four in 2013). That was fewer than even one Chinese news agency, Xinhua, has in India, though there are a total of only a dozen or so Chinese journalists in India. In reporting about China, Indian journalists based in New Delhi rely too often on the view from Ministry of External Affairs, or on the opinions of a small band of commentators. Likewise, "independent" commentary on China tends to be monopolized by government spin and a few loquacious and alarmist hawks, including retired members of the security and intelligence establishment. One, for example, on 1 May 2012, warned that China "may wish to try a limited border war sooner than later."[12] That was not a hysterical journalist, working up a story on a slow news day. It was the former head of India's external intelligence service.

This author attended panels on India–China relations at academic conferences in Gurgaon, in September 2012,[13] and Seoul in December 2012.[14] At both events, the Indian commentators spent much of their presentations describing the strategic distrust between the two countries. One frequently cited example of suspicious Chinese activity directed at India is the development of Gwadar port in the Pakistani province of Baluchistan. This is sometimes portrayed as the one of a "string of pearls" with which the People's Liberation Army Navy intends to strangle India's maritime ambitions. As yet, however, there is no naval element to China's involvement, and, as C. Raja Mohan has pointed out,[15] it can also be interpreted as part of China's "look West" policy, of developing its poorer inland provinces (in this case the Xinjiang Autonomous Region). Securing their access to the sea would constitute a huge benefit.

Nor are Indian journalists likely to present a rosier picture of bilateral ties if they trouble themselves to talk to Chinese scholars of the relationship. At the Seoul forum, Chinese participants were equally alarmist about India. Li Tao, a scholar based in Sichuan province, accused India of using "the Tibetan issue as a card to contain China."[16] India, she elaborated used "Dalai Lama groups as a tool to pressure China and turn Tibet into a buffer state." In India, this sounds like paranoid nonsense.

The Role of the Western Media

As for the third preconception, analysts in both countries can agree in accusing the Western press of playing up tensions and frictions between China and India, and thereby influencing perceptions in both countries. There may be an element of truth in this: the foreign press, with more of its own correspondents based in the two countries, may have a disproportionate role in forming opinions. And it is probably also true that the Western press has probably written more about strategic rivalry between India and China than about the astonishing growth of bilateral trade. In August 2010, for example, *The Economist* ran a cover story about the relationship, called "Contest of the Century: China v. India."[17]

Its analysis seemed uncontentious to many in the West and indeed in India:

A tradition of strategic mistrust of China is deeply ingrained [in India]. India sees China as working to undermine it at every level: by pre-empting it in securing supplies of the energy both must import; through manoeuvres to block a permanent seat for India on the United Nations Security Council; and, above all, through friendships with its smaller South Asian neighbours, notably Pakistan. India also notes that China, after decades of setting their border quarrels to one side in the interests of the broader relationship, has in recent years hardened its position on the disputes in Tibet and Kashmir that in 1962 led to war. This unease has pushed India strategically closer to America—most notably in a controversial deal on nuclear co-operation.

To more paranoid Chinese readers, however, such analysis would seem ill-intentioned: designed to perpetuate the very suspicions it purports to report. At the Singapore workshop, the reporting of the Agni-V missile launch, noted earlier,[18] was cited by a Chinese journalist as another example of this Western prejudice. In his view, the mention in virtually every report of the fact that these missiles could reach most Chinese cities was subjective, alarmist and malicious, when India had made clear that they were not aimed at any country.

He was wrong on two counts. First, the notion that Indian journalists and opinion would be formed on an issue such as this by what was written in Western outlets is simply preposterous. Second, Western journalists, like their Indian counterparts, would have been remiss in their duty to the truth had they omitted the important context of the missiles' role in the calculus of deterrence between India and China. As we have seen, *Global Times* took a similar view. The media are not making it up that the focus of India's nuclear posture is China. Though China was not explicitly mentioned, there could be no doubt about which country was alluded to when Atal Behari Vajpayee, India's prime minister at the time, wrote to President Bill Clinton to justify India's nuclear test in May 1998.[19]

> We have an overt nuclear weapon state on our borders, a state which committed armed aggression against India in 1962. Although our relations with that country have improved in the last decade or so, an atmosphere of distrust persists mainly due to the unresolved border problem.

Similar Chinese attacks on the Western media have been routine since 2008 and the preparations for the Beijing Olympics. In March 2008, the Tibetan capital, Lhasa, erupted in anti-Chinese rioting. Some foreign coverage of the unrest played down the violence committed by ethnic Tibetans, but reported the story as one of the continued Chinese repression. Then, the global Olympic-torch relay was disrupted in Paris and elsewhere by protests against the Chinese government, with Tibet the most prominent issue. Many Chinese saw this as a concerted campaign to spoil China's hosting of the games, a moment of great national pride. A website set up then to police the foreign media's reporting on China, anti-CNN.com, has changed its name to April Media and keeps up the battle.

So it is not surprising that the West's reporting of the strains in China–India relations finds itself subject to such scrutiny in China. But that does not mean that the Western media are inventing the strains; nor that the Indian media need Western encouragement to report on them in sometimes sensationalist terms.

All three sets of press outlets—Chinese, Indian and Western—are guilty of mistakes, inaccuracy and sometimes one-sided reporting; but not of concocting an artificial narrative of rivalry to supplant a less juicy story of burgeoning partnership. In creating tension and mutual distrust, the two countries' governments and academic communities do not need the press' help.

Notes

1. http://www.asiantribune.com/news/2012/04/22/indian-strategic-move-agni-missile-%E2%80%93v-tes
2. http://www.fmprc.gov.cn/eng/xwfw/s2510/t925291.html
3. http://www.globaltimes.cn/NEWS/tabid/99/ID/705627/India-being-swept-up-by-missile-delusion.aspx
4. "Exploring the Neglected Constraints on Chindia: Analysing the online Chinese Perception of India and its Interaction with China's India Policy," *China Quarterly*, 207 (September 2011): 541.
5. http://www.rediff.com/news/2009/aug/10china-should-break-up-india-suggests-chinese-strategist.htm
6. http://www.timesnow.tv/Chinas-dangerous-diplomatic-game/video-show/4400201.cms
7. http://www.deccanchronicle.com/channels/nation/north/scientist-dis-misses-china-observatory-site-795
8. http://www.indiaeveryday.in/news-wen-blames-media-for-exaggerating-border-dispute-oneindia-1001-2093491.htm
9. http://www.economist.com/node/21556236

10. http://www.economist.com/blogs/banyan/2010/08/china_and_kashmir
11. Ibid.
12. http://soodvikram.blogspot.com/2012/05/tawang-chinas-fixation.html
13. *Trilateral Forum*, organized by the German Marshall Fund of the US and the Swedish Foreign Ministry.
14. *China Forum*, organised by the Asian Institute.
15. C. Raja Mohan, *Samudra Manthan: Sino-Indian rivalry in the Indo-Pacific* (New York: Carnegie Endowment for International Peace, 2012).
16. http://www.asanchinaforum.org/
17. http://www.economist.com/node/16846256
18. See, for example, http://www.economist.com/node/21553475
19. http://www.nytimes.com/1998/05/13/world/nuclear-anxiety-indian-s-letter-to-clinton-on-the-nuclear-testing.html

Glossary

Adivasi	Name applied to so-called "tribal people"; the official term is Scheduled Tribe
caonima	Literally, Grass Mud Horse, but the term is used cheekily and ironically by Chinese netizens
choli	A blouse
Dalit	Term applied to people once referred to as "untouchable"
Doordarshan	India's government-run television broadcaster
fenqing	Angry youth
garba wali	A woman who performs in a Gujarati folk dance
gurbani	Hymns; spiritual songs of Sikhs
Huawei	China's biggest manufacturer of telecom equipment
jal	Water
jungal	Forest
Lǎoshī	Senior Chinese editors; gatekeepers; censors; "teacher"
luntan	Web forums
minjian	Unofficial
pahari	A person from the Himalayan hill country of India
Parsis, Parsees	Members of a small, prosperous religious community of western India, descended from Zoroastrian migrants from Iran
Scheduled Caste	The official term for Dalits, used especially in relation to affirmative action by government
Scheduled Tribe	The official term for "tribal people" in India, used especially in relation to affirmative action by government. See *Adivasi*, above
SoLoMo	Social-local-mobile
weibo	Microblogs
Xiaolingtong	Low-tech, low-cost system providing mobile phone capacity
Xinhua	Chinese news agency
zameen	Land
Zhan Lue	Strategist

About the Editors

Robin Jeffrey taught in a school in India from 1967 to 2009 and completed D.Phil. in Indian history at Sussex University in 1973. He taught for 25 years in the Politics programme at La Trobe University in Melbourne, worked twice at the Australian National University (ANU) in Canberra and has lived for 6 years in India between 1967 and 2015. He is a Visiting Research Professor at the Institute of South Asian Studies, National University of Singapore. His most recent book, co-authored with Assa Doron of ANU, is *The Great Indian Phone Book* (2013), published in India as *Cell Phone Nation*. His current research is on garbage in India. He is the author of *The Decline of Nair Dominance* (1976), *What's Happening to India?* (1986), *Politics Women and Well-being* (1992) and *India's Newspaper Revolution* (2000).

Ronojoy Sen has worked for over a decade (1997–2010) in leading Indian newspapers. He was last with the *Times of India,* New Delhi, where he was a Senior Assistant Editor for the editorial page.

Dr Sen has done PhD in political science from the University of Chicago and BA in history from Presidency College, Kolkata. He has been a Visiting Fellow at the National Endowment for Democracy, Washington, D.C., and the East-West Center, Washington, and Fellow of the International Olympic Museum, Lausanne, Switzerland.

Dr Sen is the author of *Articles of Faith: Religion, Secularism, and the Indian Supreme Court* (2010). He is the co-editor of *More Than Maoism: Politics, Policies and Insurgencies in South Asia* (2012) and *Being Muslim in South Asia: Diversity and Daily Life* (2014). He has contributed to edited volumes and published in several leading journals, including the *Journal of Asian Studies, Pacific Affairs, South Asia: Journal of South Asian Studies, Journal of Democracy* and *Sport and Society*. He also writes regularly for newspapers.

Index*

---

* "f" denotes figure; "t" denotes table.